PLANT
SUPERVISOR'S
COMPLETE
DESK BOOK

W.H. WEISS

PRENTICE HALL
Englewood Cliffs, New Jersey 07632

Library of Congress Cataloging-in-Publication Data

Weiss, W.H. [date]
   Plant supervisor's complete desk book / W.H. Weiss
     p. cm.
   Includes index.
   ISBN 0-13-678954-4
   1. Factory management. I. Title.
TS155.W448 1992
  658.5—dc20
                                  92–23924
                                      CIP

Prentice-Hall International (UK) Limited, *London*
Prentice-Hall of Australia Pty. Limited, *Sydney*
Prentice-Hall Canada, Inc., *Toronto*
Prentice-Hall Hispanoamericana, S.A., *Mexico*
Prentice-Hall of India Private Limited, *New Delhi*
Prentice-Hall of Japan, Inc., *Tokyo*
Simon & Schuster Asia Pte. Ltd., *Singapore*
Editora Prentice-Hall do Brasil, Ltda., *Rio de Janeiro*

© 1992 by Prentice-Hall, Inc.
Englewood Cliffs, New Jersey 07632
A Division of Simon & Schuster

10 9 8 7 6 5 4 3 2 1
Printed in the United States of America

ISBN 0-13-678954-4

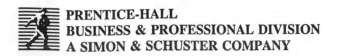

PRENTICE-HALL
BUSINESS & PROFESSIONAL DIVISION
A SIMON & SCHUSTER COMPANY

ABOUT THE AUTHOR

W.H. Weiss has 42 years' experience in various management positions in the Technical, Production, and Engineering Departments of The Goodyear Tire & Rubber Company. Once a contributing editor for *Supervision* magazine and Editor-Midwest for *Plant Services* magazine, he now writes for Dartnell. Mr. Weiss has written more than 900 articles on management, human relations, engineering, and maintenance for a wide range of journals and trade magazines. He also has written several books including: *Supervisor's Standard Reference Handbook* and *Manager's Script Book*, both published by Prentice Hall, and *The Art and Skill of Managing People*, *The Supervisor's Problem Solver*, and *Decision Making for First-Time Managers*.

Over a 25-year period, Mr. Weiss has become well known as a speaker and chairman at National Plant Engineering and Maintenance Conferences. A Registered Professional Engineer in Ohio, he holds a B.S. in Chemical Engineering from the University of Illinois and an M.B.A. from Kent State University.

How This Book Can Help You Be An Effective and Efficient Plant Supervisor

Whether you have little experience as a supervisor or have been on the job for some time, undoubtedly there have been occasions when you wished you had better answers to the many and varied problems you've faced. And even though you may feel you know how to handle your major problems, if you are like most plant supervisors, you're continually looking for ways to improve your techniques and your style of managing.

Plant Supervisor's Complete Desk Book is written to aid you with these objectives and to answer all your questions on the subject of supervising in a plant. Since it covers the full range of the plant supervisor's responsibilities and provides practical solutions to everyday plant problems, you should have it handy to refer to daily.

This book was written also because of the widespread need of supervisors to know how to get along with the union and how to meet the many regulations of governmental agencies. Although a plant supervisor's prime task is to get the work done, the job is much simpler and easier if you understand plant operations, production, and maintenance functions, and the many tools used in the plant to achieve the company's objectives.

The *Plant Supervisor's Complete Desk Book* deals with these subjects in a clear, descriptive, and comprehensive fashion. The book is divided into 16 chapters, each one dealing with an important and critical function in today's plants. All the chapters are organized around the types of problems you face in your day-to-day work. I show how successful supervisors have effectively dealt with them in solving plant problems and getting jobs done.

The information and how-to-do-it are presented in as concise a manner as possible. In covering practically all plant problems, the material confirms the premise that skill and knowledge of plant procedures and equipment operation are a must if you want to be an effective and efficient supervisor.

Plant Supervisor's Complete Desk Book is intended to be kept on your desk, ready for use. The information and data are therefore arranged so that you can locate it quickly. Thus, the material is given not only in the usual manner by subject and section, but also by subtitle sections. With a very expansive index that is extensively cross-referenced, you can easily find information and data you're looking for.

Much effort has been made to fill this book with the latest successful supervisory procedures covering most of the troublesome situations or problems a plant supervisor encounters. Here are just a few of the wide range of subjects included:

- Guidelines on planning and scheduling
- Overcoming objections to wearing protective clothing
- Solving refusals to perform dangerous work
- Contending with shortages of parts and materials
- What to do to prevent union organizing
- Techniques for effective training and instructing
- Ways to take the pain out of change
- How to work with contractors and service organizations

With information and subject coverage like this, *Plant Supervisor's Complete Desk Book* will prove to be a big help to you in your plant supervisory job and will enable you to get ahead in your company.

W.H. Weiss

Contents

1

How to Be an Effective Leader, *1*

UNDERSTANDING THE ORGANIZATIONAL STRUCTURE OF
THE PLANT, *1*
    The Supervisory and Managerial Structure, *2*
    Writing Job Descriptions, *4*
    Assigning Employee Responsibilities, *5*
UNDERSTANDING WHAT YOUR SUPERVISORY AUTHORITY
DEPENDS ON, *5*
GUIDELINES FOR PROMOTING GOOD HUMAN RELATIONS IN
THE PLANT, *7*
HOW TO BE A LEADER RATHER THAN A DRIVER, *8*
    Tips on Giving Orders, *9*
HOW TO PERSONALLY GET ORGANIZED, *9*
ENFORCING PLANT RULES AND REGULATIONS, *10*
HOW TO GET OTHER SUPERVISORS TO COOPERATE, *11*
    Promoting Cooperation in the Plant, *13*
HOW TO EFFECTIVELY DELEGATE, *14*

STEPS TO FOLLOW IN SELECTING A PLAN OF
ACTION, *15*
>   Diagnosing the Problem, *16*
>   Looking for Alternative Solutions, *16*
>   Analyzing and Comparing Alternatives, *17*
>   Selecting the Best Alternative, *17*

HOW TO MAKE A DECISION UNDER PRESSURE, *18*

WAYS TO MAKE PARTICIPATIVE MANAGEMENT WORK, *20*

GUIDELINES FOR EFFECTIVE TEAMWORK, *21*

TIPS ON HOW TO AVOID COMPLACENCY, *22*

UNDERSTANDING WHY LOYALTY IS IMPORTANT, *23*

TIPS ON THE ART OF NEGOTIATING, *23*

PROVEN BENEFITS OF PERFORMANCE APPRAISALS, *25*

HOW TO GAIN PLANT WORKERS' SUPPORT, *26*
>   Tips on Running a Productive Meeting, *28*

HOW TO PREVENT SMALL PROBLEMS FROM BECOMING
BIG, *29*

GUIDELINES FOR MANAGING BY OBJECTIVES, *30*

HOW TO HANDLE COMPLAINTS IN THE PLANT, *32*

TIPS ON COMBATTING ABSENTEEISM, *33*

GUIDELINES FOR HANDLING EMPLOYEES ON PROBATION, *34*

CONTENDING WITH THE SOCIALIZING PROBLEM, *35*

UNDERSTANDING CLIQUES, *36*

WHEN AND HOW TO DISCIPLINE PLANT WORKERS, *37*
>   Guidelines for Using Positive Discipline, *38*

HOW TO HANDLE TEMPORARY AND PART-TIME PLANT
EMPLOYEES, *40*

ADOPTING FLEXIBLE WORK HOURS AND JOB SHARING, *42*

HOW TO AVOID CHARGES OF DISCRIMINATION, *42*

HOW TO GET ALONG WITH THE PLANT'S STAFF
PERSONNEL, *43*

UNDERSTANDING YOUNG PLANT EMPLOYEES, *44*

GUIDELINES ON SUPERVISING YOUNG EMPLOYEES, *45*

HOW TO HANDLE THE EMPLOYEE WHO PREFERS TO WORK
ALONE, *45*

2

Conveying Company Policy and Plant Procedures to Workers, *46*

UNDERSTANDING COMPANY POLICY, *46*
>   Guidelines for Critical Company Policy, *47*
>   Evaluating and Promoting Company Policy, *48*

HOW TO EXPLAIN COMPANY POLICY TO PLANT WORKERS, *49*

HOW TO SELL CHANGE EASILY TO PLANT WORKERS, *49*

MAKING CHANGES EFFICIENTLY, *50*

GUIDELINES ON INTRODUCING NEW PROCEDURES, *51*

TECHNIQUES FOR IMPROVING COMMUNICATIONS, *52*
    Communicating with Your Staff, *53*
    How to Promote Upward Communication from Your Staff, *53*

GUIDELINES FOR SELLING SUGGESTION SYSTEMS IN THE PLANT, *54*

HOW TO MAKE SURE YOU'RE UNDERSTOOD, *55*
    How to Write Memos, *56*
    Developing Your Communication Style, *57*
    How to Effectively Communicate with Plant Workers, *58*
    Tips on Using Nonverbal Communication Techniques, *58*

HOW TO ISSUE PLANT OPERATING SPECIFICATIONS AND GET WORKERS TO IMPLEMENT THEM, *60*

OVERCOMING BARRIERS TO EFFECTIVE COMMUNICATIONS IN THE PLANT, *60*

3

Techniques for Effective Training and Instructing Manufacturing Plant Workers, *63*

HOW TO DETERMINE EMPLOYEE TRAINING NEEDS, *63*

ESTIMATING THE COST OF UNTRAINED WORKERS, *64*

WAYS TO GET PLANT WORKERS TO WANT TO LEARN, *65*
    How to Sell Plant Workers on Training, *65*

HOW TO DEVELOP PLANT TRAINING PROGRAMS, *66*
    Meeting Three Objectives in Training Plant Workers, *66*
    Four Ways to Evaluate Plant Training Programs, *67*

EFFECTIVE TRAINING METHODS AND HOW TO USE THEM IN THE PLANT, *67*

GUIDELINES ON USING VIDEOS TO TRAIN PLANT WORKERS, *69*
    Determining How Much You Should Teach Plant Workers at One Time, *69*

POSITIVE WAYS TO TRAIN THE SLOW LEARNER, *70*

HOW TO SUPERVISE INEXPERIENCED PLANT WORKERS, *70*

HOW TO MAKE SOUND WORK ASSIGNMENTS, *71*

TIPS ON TRAINING MACHINE OPERATORS, *72*

WAYS TO TRAIN MAINTENANCE WORKERS, *73*

HOW TO DEAL WITH OBSOLESCENCE OF PLANT MAINTENANCE WORKERS, *74*

RETRAINING PLANT PRODUCTION WORKERS TO OPERATE
NEW MACHINES AND EQUIPMENT, *75*
　　How to Sell Plant Workers on Retraining, *75*
　　Following Up, *76*
PITFALLS TO AVOID IN TRAINING PLANT WORKERS, *76*

4

How to Raise Productivity of Plant Workers, *78*

UNDERSTANDING PRODUCTIVITY, *78*
BARRIERS TO ACHIEVING PRODUCTIVITY IMPROVEMENT IN
PLANTS, *79*
HOW GOOD COMMUNICATION WITH PLANT WORKERS
INCREASES THEIR PRODUCTIVITY, *80*
　　Alternative Methods of Improving Productivity, *81*
THREE EFFECTIVE WAYS OF MOTIVATING PLANT
WORKERS, *82*
　　How Technology Raises the Productivity of Plant Workers, *82*
POSITIVE WAYS TO MAINTAIN HIGH PRODUCTIVITY, *83*
SATISFYING EMPLOYEES' NEEDS: A WAY TO MOTIVATE
THEM, *84*
HOW TO EFFECTIVELY DELEGATE JOBS TO PLANT
WORKERS, *84*
　　Tips on Talking to Plant Workers about Their Jobs, *85*
HOW TO PROMOTE COOPERATION AND TEAM EFFORT, *86*
USING WORK SAMPLING TO RAISE PRODUCTIVITY, *86*
　　Procedures for Making a Study, *88*
　　Reliability of Work Sampling Results, *89*
POSITIVE WAYS TO DEAL WITH UNPRODUCTIVE
EMPLOYEES, *90*
EFFECTIVE WAYS TO USE PLANT EMPLOYEES' IDLE TIME, *90*
HOW COMPUTERIZED SYSTEMS IMPROVE PRODUCTIVITY, *91*
　　How to Convince Plant Workers that Computerized Maintenance
　　Improves Productivity, *91*
HOW BETTER PRODUCTIVITY RESULTS FROM GOOD
HOUSEKEEPING, *92*
TECHNIQUES FOR REDUCING MACHINES AND EQUIPMENT
DOWNTIME IN A PLANT, *93*
HOW TO TRAIN EMPLOYEES TO AVOID PRODUCTION
DISRUPTIONS, *95*
OPTIMIZING PRODUCTIVITY OF THE MAINTENANCE WORK
FORCE, *96*
　　Benefits from Planning and Scheduling Plant Maintenance, *96*
DEALING WITH PLANT EMPLOYEES' MISTAKES AND
CARELESSNESS, *97*

HOW TO HANDLE PLANT EMPLOYEES WHO WASTE TIME, *98*

UNDERSTANDING PLANT OPERATING COSTS, *99*

    How to Cut Labor Costs, *101*

    How to Control Material Costs, *101*

    How to Hold Down Machine and Equipment Costs, *102*

    How to Minimize Utility Costs, *102*

HOW TO PREVENT LITTLE COSTS FROM BECOMING BIG, *103*

HOW TO DETERMINE PLANT OPERATING COSTS, *103*

SETTING UP AN EFFECTIVE ENERGY CONSERVATION
PROGRAM, *104*

TECHNIQUES FOR SAVING ENERGY IN PLANT
OPERATIONS, *106*

    Ways to Save Energy in Plant Design, *107*

HOW TO SELL CONSERVATION OF ENERGY TO PLANT
WORKERS, *108*

5

How to Maintain Quality and Improve Employees' Work Performance, *109*

GUIDELINES ON PROCESS CONTROL, *109*

HOW TO PERFORM STATISTICAL PROCESS CONTROL, *110*

    Tips on Training Employees in Quality Control Using Statistical
    Techniques, *112*

    Explaining to Plant Workers the Importance of Quality Inputs, *112*

POSITIVE WAYS TO GET EMPLOYEES TO HELP IN
PREVENTING MACHINE DOWNTIME, *113*

HOW TO SET AND IMPLEMENT QUALITY STANDARDS FOR
EMPLOYEE OUTPUT, *114*

    Answers to the Relationship Between Quality and Worker
    Productivity, *115*

HOW TO CONVINCE EMPLOYEES THAT HIGH QUALITY KEEPS
COSTS DOWN, *115*

HOW TO PREVENT WORKER STRESS FROM AFFECTING
QUALITY, *116*

TIPS ON PREVENTING WORKER ATTITUDE FROM AFFECTING
QUALITY, *117*

HOW TO GET HELP FROM EMPLOYEES ON PRODUCTION
QUALITY PROBLEMS, *118*

HOW TO SET UP A QUALITY CIRCLE (QC) PROGRAM, *119*

    How Plant Management Participates in Quality Circle Programs, *119*

    Functions of Quality Circle Meetings, *120*

    Maintaining Commitment to Quality Circles, *120*

    Benefits and Advantages of Quality Circles, *121*

HELPING PLANT EMPLOYEES TO MINIMIZE REWORK OF POOR QUALITY PRODUCTS, *121*

HOW TO ENFORCE EMPLOYEES' ADHERENCE TO PRODUCT INSPECTION PROCEDURES FOR QUALITY, *122*

8 WAYS TO IMPROVE EMPLOYEES' WORK PERFORMANCE, *122*

PITFALLS TO AVOID TO GET COOPERATION BETWEEN PRODUCTION SHIFTS, *123*

    How to Get Along Better with Other Supervisors, *124*

6

How to Ensure Employees Use Computers for Operations and Control, *125*

PLANT USE OF COMPUTERS, *125*

    The Computer's Communication Capabilities, *125*

INSTRUCTING EMPLOYEES ON THE USE, TYPES, AND CAPABILITIES OF PLANT COMPUTERS, *126*

ENSURING DOCUMENTATION TO HELP WORKERS USE THE COMPUTER, *127*

HOW TO GET BUDGET APPROVAL FOR A COMPUTER, *128*

    Collecting and Determining Current Costs, *128*

    Showing How Computer Reports Help to Achieve Goals, *129*

    Describing Your Implementation Plan, *129*

    Calculating the Payback, *129*

    Making the Budget Request to Management, *130*

7 PITFALLS TO AVOID WHEN IMPLEMENTING THE COMPUTER, *130*

COMPUTER PORTABILITY: A PLUS TO AUTOMATION, *132*

HOW TO GET PLANT WORKERS TO CONQUER COMPUTER ANXIETY, *132*

SELLING PLANT WORKERS ON USING THE COMPUTER, *133*

    How to Promote Computer Use, *134*

TECHNIQUES FOR USING THE COMPUTER TO RAISE WORKER PRODUCTIVITY, *134*

    Material Handling and Inventory Control, *135*

    Manufacturing Operations, *135*

    Process Control, *137*

OVERCOMING COMPUTER OPERATOR FEARS, *138*

    How to Sell the Use of Personal Computers, *139*

    Tips on Making Employees Computer Literate, *139*

HOW TO TRAIN PLANT WORKERS ON USING THE COMPUTER, *140*

7

Proven Techniques for Handling Plant Workers' Safety Problems, *141*

HOW TO CREATE EMPLOYEE INTEREST IN PLANT SAFETY, *141*
 Communicating About Plant Safety, *142*
 Training for Plant Safety, *142*
 How to Indoctrinate Workers in Plant Safety, *143*
 How to Personalize Safety Training, *144*

HOW TO IMPROVE YOUR EMPLOYEES' AWARENESS OF PLANT HAZARDS, *146*
 8 Ways to Help Your Employees to Think and Work Defensively, *146*

PROTECTING WORKERS FROM MACHINE HAZARDS, *148*
 Barriers, *148*
 Pull-backs, *149*
 Presence Sensors, *149*
 Brakes, *150*
 Clamps, *150*

PROVIDING EMPLOYEES WITH INFORMATION ON SAFETY DEVICES AND EQUIPMENT IN WORK AREAS, *150*
 How to Ensure that Plant Workers Use Protective Devices, *151*

HOW TO DEAL WITH UNSAFE ACTS OF EMPLOYEES, *152*
 What to Do When an Unsafe Act Occurs, *153*
 Preventing Slips, Trips and Falls, *153*

HOW GOOD HOUSEKEEPING PROMOTES SAFETY, *154*
 Identifying Hazards by Color Coding Equipment, *155*

GUIDELINES FOR SETTING UP A FIRST AID PROGRAM, *156*

HOW TO LIFT AND CARRY LOADS SAFELY, *157*

TECHNIQUES FOR USING ERGONOMICS TO IMPROVE PLANT SAFETY, *159*
 Layout and Design, *160*
 Procedures and Tools, *160*
 Computer Operations, *161*

PROMOTING THE USE OF PROTECTIVE CLOTHING AND EQUIPMENT, *161*
 Adopting a Hand Protection Program, *161*
 Selecting Appropriate Protective Gloves, *162*
 Protecting Against Eye and Face Injuries, *163*
 Safety Shoes: The Answer to Foot Protection, *165*
 Providing Adequate Head Protection, *166*
 Guidelines on Avoiding Work Clothes That Are Dangerous, *168*
 Tips on Selecting Protective Clothing, *168*
 Overcoming Workers' Objections to Wearing Protective Clothing, *169*

WHERE TO GET SAFETY DATA AND INFORMATION, *169*

TIPS ON CONDUCTING SAFETY INSPECTIONS, *171*

HOW TO GET PLANT WORKERS TO SHARE SAFETY
RESPONSIBILITY, *172*

ANSWERS TO PLANT ACCIDENTS THAT KEEP REPEATING, *173*

SUPERVISING PLANT EMPLOYEES WHO DO DANGEROUS
WORK, *173*

HOW TO HELP PLANT WORKERS AVOID PITFALLS, *174*

HOW TO INVESTIGATE ACCIDENTS, *175*
    What an Accident Investigation Involves, *175*
    When to Investigate an Accident, *176*
    How to Investigate an Accident, *176*
    How to Talk to a Witness, *177*
    Writing the Accident Report, *177*
    The Value of Accident Investigations, *178*

UNDERSTANDING THE FREQUENCY AND SEVERITY OF
PLANT ACCIDENTS, *178*

HOW TO MAKE A SAFETY "NEAR MISS" REPORT, *179*

WAYS TO PROMOTE ELECTRICAL SAFETY, *182*
    Protecting Plant Workers Against Electrical Shock, *182*
    Grounding Equipment to Prevent Electrical Shocks, *183*
    Using Ground Fault Interrupters to Prevent Electrical Shocks, *183*

HOW TO ENSURE THE SAFETY OF PLANT WORKERS FROM
ELECTRICAL HAZARDS, *186*
    10 Safe Practices When Working with Electricity in the Plant, *186*
    Precautions on Supervising Employees Who Work with Electrical
    Systems, *187*

TIPS ON WORKING SAFELY ON VERTICAL STRUCTURES, *188*
    Establishing a System to Prevent Falls, *188*

WAYS TO ASSURE THE SAFETY OF PLANT WELDERS, *189*
    Protecting the Safety and Health of Welders, *190*
    Helping Plant Welders to Work Safely, *192*

DEALING WITH THE HAZARDS OF WORKING IN CONFINED
SPACES, *192*
    Following Specific Entry Procedures, *194*

HOW TO IMPROVE PLANT WORKERS' SAFETY AT LOADING
DOCKS, *195*

HELPING THE WAREHOUSE AND DOCK EMPLOYEE TO WORK
SAFELY, *196*

GUIDELINES TO SAFE OPERATION OF ROBOTS, *197*
    How to Ensure the Safety of Workers Using Robots, *198*

8

Ensuring Plant Workers' Compliance with OSHA and EPA Regulations, *199*

DEALING WITH PLANT EMPLOYEES' ADHERENCE TO THE OCCUPATIONAL SAFETY AND HEALTH ACT (OSHA), *199*
    Achievements and Influences of OSHA, *200*

HOW THE NATIONAL INSTITUTE FOR OCCUPATIONAL SAFETY AND HEALTH (NIOSH) FUNCTIONS, *200*

WHAT PROMPTS AN OSHA INSPECTION, *201*

HOW OSHA INSPECTIONS ARE MADE, *202*

GUIDELINES ON OSHA'S VIOLATIONS AND PENALTIES, *203*

10 WAYS TO WORK WITH PLANT EMPLOYEES TO AVOID AN OSHA INSPECTION, *204*

RECOGNIZING PLANT EMPLOYEES' RIGHTS UNDER OSHA, *205*

POSTING AND RECORD KEEPING REQUIRED BY OSHA, *206*

HOW TO ENSURE THAT EMPLOYEES CARRY OUT THEIR OSHA RESPONSIBILITIES, *213*

REPORTING SAFETY STATISTICS BY THE OSHA METHOD, *214*

HOW OSHA PROMOTES PROPER HOUSEKEEPING, *214*

HOW TO PROMOTE A WELLNESS PROGRAM FOR PLANT EMPLOYEES, *215*

INCENTIVES FOR PLANT EMPLOYEES' COMPLIANCE WITH OSHA REGULATIONS, *216*

WAYS TO ENFORCE PLANT EMPLOYEES' COMPLIANCE WITH OSHA AND NIOSH REGULATIONS, *216*

CONTENDING WITH EMPLOYEES' REFUSAL TO WORK BECAUSE OF "UNSAFE" CONDITIONS, *217*
    How to Handle the Problem, *218*

KEEPING UP WITH CHANGES IN OSHA, *219*

WAYS THAT ENVIRONMENTAL LAWS AFFECT MANUFACTURING PLANTS, *219*
    Common Features of Most Environmental Laws, *220*

HOW THE EPA IS ORGANIZED, *221*

GUIDELINES FOR DEALING WITH WATER POLLUTION, *221*
    Types of Pollutants, *222*
    Regulations on Effluents, *222*

HOW TO ENSURE THAT WORKERS CONTROL PLANT EFFLUENTS, *223*

GETTING PLANT WORKERS TO FOLLOW YOUR INSTRUCTIONS, *223*

OBTAINING AND USING DISCHARGE PERMITS, *224*

RECOMMENDED WAYS TO CONTROL WATER POLLUTION, *225*
    Treatment Systems and Equipment, *226*

HOW TO HANDLE SAMPLING OF PLANT EFFLUENTS, 227
   Methods of Sampling Effluents, 228
   Implementing a Sampling Program, 229
GUIDELINES FOR CONTROLLING AIR POLLUTION, 230
   Air Quality Standards, 230
   Maintaining the Standards, 232
   Standards for New Sources, 232
   Other Regulatory Techniques: Bubbles, Banking, Offsets and
   Netting, 234
EQUIPMENT USED TO CONTROL AIR POLLUTION, 234
MEASURING AND MONITORING AIR POLLUTANTS, 235
   Sampling Instrumentation and Analytical Devices, 236
POSITIVE WAYS TO HANDLE PLANT EMPLOYEES'
COMPLIANCE WITH EPA REGULATIONS, 236
COMPLIANCE WITH THE EPA: A PRECAUTION, 237

9

Ways to Help Plant Employees Deal with Hazardous Materials and Toxic Substances, 238

HOW THE EPA PROTECTS THE ENVIRONMENT, 238
   Tips on Disposing of Solid Wastes, 239
   Tips on Disposing of Liquid Wastes, 239
   Contracting for Waste Disposal, 240
TECHNIQUES FOR DEALING WITH HAZARDOUS WASTE, 241
   Waste Treatment Methods, 242
GUIDELINES ON DEALING WITH TOXIC SUBSTANCES, 242
RELIEVING EMPLOYEES' FEARS OF WORKING WITH
HAZARDOUS MATERIALS, 243
CONTENDING WITH SPILLS OF HAZARDOUS MATERIALS, 243
   Why Spills in Plants Are Serious Matters, 244
PREVENTING AND CONTROLLING IN-PLANT SPILLS, 244
   How to Prepare a Plan for Spill Prevention Control and
   Countermeasures, 245
   What the Plan Should Contain, 245
   Putting the Plan in Effect, 246
   Training Employees in Spill Prevention and Control, 247
HOW TO HELP EMPLOYEES TO AVOID SPILLS, 248
MONITORING WORKERS WHO HANDLE HAZARDOUS
MATERIALS, 248
PROVIDING EMPLOYEES WITH INSTRUCTIONS ON HANDLING
SPILLS, 249
HOW TO DETECT HAZARDOUS GAS AND WARN OF ITS
PRESENCE, 250

GUIDELINES FOR HANDLING HAZARDOUS GASES, *251*
How to Assuage Employees' Fears Through Controls, *251*
The Need for a Monitoring System, *252*
Training Plant Employees in Dealing with Hazardous Gases, *252*

HOW TO REDUCE EXPLOSION HAZARDS IN THE PLANT, *252*

PROTECTING PLANT WORKERS FROM RESPIRATORY HAZARDS, *253*
Using Proper Equipment for Protection, *254*

TRAINING EMPLOYEES TO USE RESPIRATORY DEVICES, *255*
Training Employees in the Care of Respiratory Protective Devices, *256*

DEALING WITH MATERIAL SAFETY DATA SHEETS AND LABELS, *257*

PROVIDING WORKERS WITH INFORMATION ON MATERIAL SAFETY DATA SHEETS, *258*

EDUCATING PLANT EMPLOYEES ABOUT HAZARDOUS MATERIALS, *259*

WHAT RIGHT-TO-KNOW LAWS ARE ALL ABOUT, *259*
How Plants Are Affected by the Law, *260*

10 STEPS TO ENSURE EMPLOYEES' COMPLIANCE WITH RIGHT-TO-KNOW LAWS, *261*

HOW TO MOTIVATE WORKERS TO FOLLOW RULES WHEN HANDLING HAZARDOUS MATERIALS, *262*

TRAINING EMPLOYEES TO USE HAZARDOUS MATERIALS SAFELY, *262*
Why Responsibility for Training Employees Is a Serious Matter, *263*

DEALING WITH ASBESTOS AS A HAZARD, *264*
Adopting an Asbestos Management Program, *265*
Training and Communicating with Workers, *266*

TIPS ON AVOIDING SKIN DISEASE IN THE PLANT, *267*

HOW TO DEAL WITH PCB WASTE, *268*
Notification, Identification, and Disposal, *269*

HANDLING SPILLS OF PCB MATERIALS, *269*

ENSURING WORKERS' COMPLIANCE WITH REGULATIONS ON HAZARDOUS MATERIALS, *270*

GUIDELINES FOR FIRE PREVENTION, *271*
How to Avoid Accumulations of Combustible Materials, *271*
Controlling Oxygen, *272*
Techniques for Eliminating Sources of Ignition, *272*

GUIDELINES FOR FIRE PROTECTION, *273*
Establishing and Maintaining an In-plant Fire Brigade, *273*

TRAINING EMPLOYEES TO USE FIRE EXTINGUISHERS, *275*

WHAT TO DO ABOUT RADON, *277*
Reducing High Radon Levels, *278*

10

Guidelines for Planning and Scheduling Work for Plant Employees, *279*

HOW PLANNING HELPS ORGANIZATIONS, *279*

TECHNIQUES FOR RECOGNIZING PEOPLE WHEN PLANNING, *280*

WAYS THAT PLANNING AND SCHEDULING PAY OFF, *280*

HOW PLANNING CAN HELP YOU CUT MATERIAL HANDLING COSTS, *282*

HOW TO OPERATE YOUR DEPARTMENT EFFICIENTLY AND AVOID WASTE, *283*

    Increase Productivity of Employees by Keeping Them Fully Occupied, *284*

HOW PLANS AND SCHEDULES IMPROVE PLANT EMPLOYEES' ATTITUDES AND MORALE, *284*

GUIDELINES FOR EFFECTIVELY MAKING WORK ASSIGNMENTS, *285*

HOW PLANNING HELPS YOUR PERSONAL DEVELOPMENT, *286*

TECHNIQUES FOR ESTABLISHING AND REVISING PRODUCTION STANDARDS FOR PLANT EMPLOYEES, *287*

    How to Handle Employees' Complaints on Standards, *287*

GUIDELINES FOR SHORT-INTERVAL SCHEDULING PLANT WORKERS' JOB ASSIGNMENTS, *288*

TECHNIQUES FOR PLANNING, SCHEDULING, AND PROJECT MANAGEMENT, *289*

    Organization of Operations Management, *289*

PROJECT ORGANIZATION AND MANAGEMENT, *290*

    Tips on Project Scheduling, *290*

    Guidelines for Scheduling, *290*

HOW TO MAKE AND USE A GANTT CHART, *291*

PLANNING WITH THE PROGRAM EVALUATION AND REVIEW TECHNIQUE, *293*

USING THE COMPUTER IN NETWORK MANAGEMENT SYSTEMS, *295*

    Advantages of the Computer in Project Management, *295*

GUIDELINES FOR EFFECTIVE PROJECT MANAGEMENT, *296*

FIVE KEY ELEMENTS OF AN ACTION PLAN, *297*

TECHNIQUES FOR COORDINATING WITH PRODUCTION CONTROL, *297*

REASONS FOR PUTTING PLANT WORKERS ON SHIFTS, *299*

GUIDELINES FOR ESTABLISHING AND CONDUCTING SHIFT
OPERATIONS, *299*

CONTENDING WITH PROBLEMS ARISING FROM MORE THAN
ONE SHIFT, *300*

11

Guidelines to Plant Design and Material Flow to Improve Plant Workers' Efficiency, *302*

WAYS TO MAKE CHANGES IN PLANT LAYOUT, *302*

HOW TO GET EMPLOYEES INVOLVED IN PLANT LAYOUT AND
DESIGN, *303*

UNDERSTANDING MATERIAL HANDLING AND MATERIAL
FLOW, *304*

HANDLING THE PROBLEM OF FLOOR SPACE
UTILIZATION, *305*

    Coping with Complaints of Not Enough Working Space for
    Employees, *306*

MATERIAL-HANDLING FUNCTIONS AND OPERATIONS, *306*

HOW TO PROMOTE EMPLOYEES' UNDERSTANDING OF
EFFICIENT MATERIALS FLOW, *307*

    The Importance of the Right Place, *308*

HOW ERGONOMICS IMPROVES PLANT WORKERS'
EFFICIENCY, *308*

    Why You Should Apply Ergonomics to Plant Workers' Jobs, *309*

IMPROVING THE SAFETY OF PLANT WORKERS WHO HANDLE
MATERIALS, *310*

BENEFITS AND ADVANTAGES OF EFFICIENT MATERIAL
HANDLING, *310*

HOW TO SELECT A LIFT TRUCK, *311*

TECHNIQUES FOR PROPER AND SAFE LIFT TRUCK HANDLING
BY PLANT EMPLOYEES, *312*

MAKING SURE LIFT TRUCK OPERATORS RECEIVE
TRAINING, *313*

HOW ROBOTS AID IN MATERIAL HANDLING, *314*

INSTRUCTING PLANT EMPLOYEES WHO WORK WITH
ROBOTS, *314*

AUTOMATIC GUIDED VEHICLE SYSTEMS: INTELLIGENT
MATERIAL HANDLERS, *315*

    Advantages and Disadvantages of Automatic Guided Vehicle
    Systems, *316*

PROMOTING EMPLOYEE INGENUITY TO SOLVE MATERIAL
HANDLING PROBLEMS, *317*

12

How to Handle Plant Inventories and Promote Just-in-Time Operations, *319*

THE IMPORTANCE AND NECESSITY OF INVENTORY CONTROL, *319*
 How to Improve Inventory Accuracy, *320*
GUIDELINES ON AUTOMATED STORAGE AND MATERIAL HANDLING SYSTEMS, *321*
 The Role of the Computer, *322*
INDUSTRIAL BAR CODING: AID TO MANAGING INVENTORIES, *322*
 Bar Code Scanner Applications in the Plant, *323*
 Understanding Bar Code Label Standards, *324*
HOW TO GET PLANT EMPLOYEES' SUPPORT FOR INVENTORY MANAGEMENT, *324*
CONVINCING PLANT EMPLOYEES THAT COMPUTERIZED INVENTORY CONTROL SAVES MONEY, *325*
HOW TO CONTROL INVENTORIES OF STORES MATERIALS, *326*
 Understanding the Terminology of Inventory Control, *327*
 Calculating an Economic Order Quantity, *330*
 Solving a Purchasing Problem, *332*
 How to Handle Lead Time Problems, *333*
HOW TO ADD AN ITEM TO STORES, *334*
 How to Handle Insurance Items, *335*
TRAINING PLANT EMPLOYEES IN THE USE OF INVENTORY MANAGEMENT TOOLS, *335*
THE RELATIONSHIP OF INVENTORY TO JUST-IN-TIME PRODUCTION, *336*
 Techniques Involved in the Toyota System, *337*
 How Layouts in Just-In-Time Plants Differ from Conventional Layouts, *338*
 How to Avoid Pitfalls of Kanban, *339*
 How Just-In-Time and Quality Control Go Together, *340*
HOW TO SET UP AN EFFECTIVE HI-USE STORES SYSTEM, *340*
 Giving Workers Instructions on the Use of Double Bin Systems, *342*
HOW TO CONTEND WITH EQUIPMENT SHORTAGES, *343*
HOW TO GET PLANT WORKERS' INPUT ON JUST-IN-TIME OPERATIONS AND INVENTORY CONTROL, *344*

13

Getting Plant Workers to Adopt Japanese Management Techniques, *345*

UNDERSTANDING THE TOYOTA MANUFACTURING SYSTEM, *345*
 Worker Involvement: Key to the Toyota System, *346*
 Techniques Involved with the Toyota System, *347*
UNDERSTANDING TOTAL PRODUCTIVE MAINTENANCE, *348*
 How to Implement a Total Productive Maintenance Program in the Plant, *349*

HOW JAPANESE MANAGEMENT METHODS ARE DIFFERENT FROM AMERICAN METHODS, *350*

HOW THE JAPANESE HANDLE THE MAINTENANCE FUNCTION, *351*

HOW TO EXPLAIN JAPANESE BUSINESS SUCCESS TO PLANT WORKERS, *352*

PLANNING AND CONSENSUS: JAPANESE STRENGTHS, *354*

HOW TO TAP THE CREATIVE CAPABILITIES OF YOUR WORK TEAM, *354*

PROBLEMS WITH ADAPTING EMPLOYEES TO JAPANESE MANUFACTURING METHODS, *355*

14

Techniques for Supervising Plant Maintenance Workers, *358*

MAINTENANCE: A MAJOR FUNCTION IN MANUFACTURING PLANTS, *358*

UNDERSTANDING THE TYPES OF MAINTENANCE USED IN PLANTS, *359*

HELPING PLANT EMPLOYEES UNDERSTAND PREVENTIVE MAINTENANCE, *359*

GETTING EMPLOYEES INVOLVED IN PREVENTIVE MAINTENANCE, *360*

    Preventive Maintenance of Critical Machine Parts, *362*

EXPLAINING PREDICTIVE MAINTENANCE, *362*

HOW TO SELL PREDICTIVE MAINTENANCE TO PLANT EMPLOYEES, *363*

HOW PREDICTIVE MAINTENANCE TECHNIQUES WORK, *364*

    Vibration Analysis, *364*
    Ultrasonic Monitoring, *365*
    Oil Analysis, *365*
    Infrared Imaging (Thermography), *370*

HOW TO HELP WORKERS PREVENT BEARING FAILURES, *370*

HOW TO CONTROL THE QUALITY OF PLANT MAINTENANCE, *371*

    Purchasing, *372*
    Work Performance, *372*
    Variances of Quality, *372*
    Motivation of Maintenance Workers, *373*
    Planning and Scheduling, *373*
    Reliability and Verification, *374*

SELLING PLANNING AND SCHEDULING TO MAINTENANCE WORKERS, *375*

THE ROLE OF THE MAINTENANCE PLANNER, *375*

HOW COMPUTERIZED CONTROL IMPROVES MAINTENANCE OPERATIONS, *376*

How a Computerized System Works, *377*
Work Orders, *377*
Analyzing by the Computer, *378*
PROVIDING WORKERS WITH KNOWLEDGE OF MAINTENANCE
COMPUTER SYSTEMS, *379*
PITFALLS TO AVOID WHEN INSTALLING A COMPUTERIZED
MAINTENANCE SYSTEM, *380*
TIPS ON CUTTING MAINTENANCE DOWNTIME OF MACHINES
AND EQUIPMENT, *380*
COORDINATING MAINTENANCE WORKERS' JOB
ASSIGNMENTS WITH PRODUCTION OPERATIONS, *381*
COORDINATING PRODUCTION OPERATIONS WITH
MAINTENANCE ACTIVITIES, *382*
HOW TO USE CHECKLISTS TO REDUCE EQUIPMENT
DOWNTIME, *383*
HOW TO TRAIN MAINTENANCE WORKERS, *384*
Elements of Typical Courses, *384*
Providing a Qualified Trainer, *385*
TRAINING MAINTENANCE WORKERS FOR PLANT
AUTOMATION, *386*
HOW TO ENSURE THAT MAINTENANCE EMPLOYEES WORK
SAFELY, *387*

15

Guaranteed Methods for Dealing with Union Matters, *388*

HOW TO PREVENT UNIONIZATION OF THE PLANT, *388*
Disadvantages of Having the Plant Unionized, *389*
Answers to Why Employees Join a Union, *390*
UNDERSTANDING THE UNION/MANAGEMENT CONTRACT, *390*
How Management Prepares for Contract Negotiations, *391*
How to Help the Company During Contract Negotiations, *392*
COLLECTIVE BARGAINING: WHAT IT IS AND HOW IT
WORKS, *392*
Contending with Claims of Unfair Labor Practices, *393*
Understanding Bargaining in Good Faith, *395*
How to Lawfully Restrict Union Activity, *395*
TIPS ON PROMOTING GOOD UNION/MANAGEMENT
RELATIONS, *396*
WHY KNOWING THE CONTRACT IS A "MUST," *397*
HOW TO GET ALONG WITH UNION STEWARDS, *398*
DEALING WITH EMPLOYEES' RIGHT TO UNION
REPRESENTATION, *398*
ARBITRATORS: HOW THEY ARE SELECTED AND THEIR
RESPONSIBILITIES, *399*
Dealing with Employees' Claims of Past Practice (Precedents), *400*

HOW TO HANDLE SENIORITY/ABILITY PROBLEMS WHEN
PROMOTING, *400*

DISCIPLINING EMPLOYEES FOR CAUSE OR JUST CAUSE, *401*

3 REQUISITES FOR IMPOSING DISCIPLINE IN A UNIONIZED
PLANT, *401*

GUIDELINES ON WORKING WITH THE GRIEVANCE
PROCEDURE, *402*

EMPLOYEE OFFENSES THAT ARE RESOLVED BY THE
GRIEVANCE PROCEDURE, *403*
    Determining When a Grievance Goes to Arbitration, *404*

HOW TO CONTEND WITH A STRIKE, *405*
    What to Do When the Strike Is Over, *405*

DEALING WITH COMPLAINTS OF SUPERVISORS DOING UNION
EMPLOYEES' WORK, *406*
    The Extent of De Minimis, *407*
    How to Handle Training Situations, *407*
    The Effect of Supervisors Doing Nonsupervisory Work, *408*

16

Working with Contractors and Service Organizations, *410*

DECIDING WHEN TO USE CONTRACTORS IN THE PLANT, *410*

HOW TO SELECT CONTRACTORS, *411*
    The Selection Procedure, *412*

MAINTAINING GOOD PLANT EMPLOYEE RELATIONS WHEN
CONTRACTING, *412*

HOW TO ASSURE SUCCESSFUL USE OF CONTRACTORS, *413*

GUIDELINES ON HANDLING CONTRACTOR PROBLEMS, *415*

HOW TO ENSURE THAT CONTRACTORS WORK SAFELY, *416*

COMPARING IN-PLANT WITH CONTRACT MAINTENANCE
COSTS, *417*

HOW SERVICE CONTRACTS HELP PROTECT PLANT
EQUIPMENT, *418*

UNDERSTANDING TYPES OF AGREEMENTS AVAILABLE FROM
SERVICE COMPANIES, *419*
    Guidelines on Evaluating the Options in Service Contracts, *420*

DEALING WITH SERVICE ORGANIZATIONS WORKING IN THE
PLANT, *421*

GUIDELINES ON USING A REPAIR SERVICE VS BUYING NEW
EQUIPMENT, *422*

HOW TO SET UP IN-HOUSE REPAIR OF MACHINE AND
EQUIPMENT COMPONENTS, *423*
    Benefits and Advantages of the Program, *424*

Index, *425*

How to Be an Effective Leader

UNDERSTANDING THE ORGANIZATIONAL STRUCTURE OF THE PLANT

Products aren't created by themselves. You need able workers in the plant, good leadership from middle and upper management, and efficient departments other than your own to assist in the plant operations.

The objective of organization is to set up a system of relationships in which employees can obtain the best results from their combined efforts. This is to be accomplished while minimizing the negative factors of conflict and confusion. The better the structure of the organization, the smoother running and more efficient the plant will operate.

Since the organizational structure is based on what the plant is to accomplish in the quantity, quality, and cost of its output, there must be specific goals in the mind when it is established. Means must be provided for the organization to:

- *Assure the safety and health of employees.* The continuing safety and good health of employees are major responsibilities of all plant organizations. Although long a cliché, "people are our greatest asset" remains a truism for management, who must see that all employees are protected and provided clean and healthy workplaces.

- *Perform production operations.* This means supplying sufficient numbers of trained people to operate machines and equipment, control processes, and carry out productive procedures. In addition, support personnel must be provided to move materials, control quality, service and repair machines, and supervise all operations.

- *Minimize cost.* With a good organizational structure, labor waste is avoided just as an efficient production process avoids wasting material. Every job in the plant should be assigned to the lowest hourly or salary level at which it can be performed competently. But while the organization is supplying sufficient numbers of people to do the work, it should not do this in excess.

- *Specify lines of authority and responsibility.* All employees in the organization must understand what their jobs consist of and where their authority begins and ends. Without this, individual performance will be hampered by confusion and internal friction, chain of command will be jeopardized, and general inefficiencies will result.

- *Be inherently flexible.* All plants experience varying production levels and changes in machines, processes, and the kinds of products manufactured. Similarly, individuals leave the organization and new ones take their place. The organizational structure must be designed to meet these changing conditions and situations without losing the ability to continue production and without incurring excessive cost.

- *Offer advancement opportunity.* Some employees may leave an organization if they see no chance to advance to a better job and earn more. When an organization is built to encourage employees to broaden their knowledge and skills, and to reward those who do, it achieves greater flexibility and gains employee loyalty.

The Supervisory and Managerial Structure

Performance of the managerial group often makes the difference between a profitable plant operation and one that barely makes ends meet. Figure 1-1 shows a typical organization chart for a small manufacturing plant. This plant operates 24 hours a day, 7 days a week, and with 3 shifts. The horizontal line across the chart separates hourly from salaried employment levels.

The management structure becomes more complex as the organization expands and the scope of the various managers' jobs increases. However, the point at which the structure needs to be changed because of the growth of the plant cannot be determined by a set of rules; it must be determined by the circumstances of the plant. As an illustration, a small

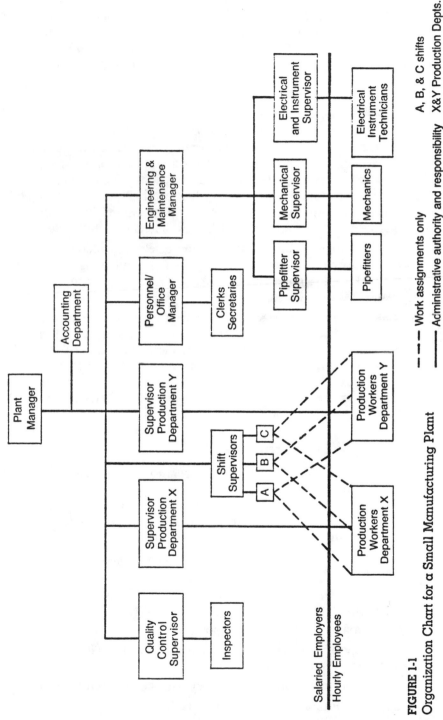

FIGURE 1-1
Organization Chart for a Small Manufacturing Plant

- - - Work assignments only　　　A, B, & C shifts
—— Administrative authority and responsibility　X&Y Production Depts.

plant might need a technical superintendent and a staff of electronic specialists if it is engaged in high technology processes or is manufacturing computers. Regardless of the size of the plant or the extent of its development, management must adopt and implement the following principles when building the managerial structure:

- *Establish a chain of command.* Every individual in the plant reports to and takes orders from one superior only. In Figure 1-1, the production workers are hired, trained, promoted, and receive their primary work instructions from the department supervisors. When on shift, however, they accept assignments and take instructions from the shift supervisors regarding certain work situations. The chart shows this by dotted lines. When dotted-line situations exist, the point where the authority of one management ends and another begins should be defined clearly.

- *Minimize management numbers.* If more help is needed later, it is easier to add people than to face the problem of eliminating some if there is no work to do. Innocent people should not be made to suffer because of a management error.

- *Agree on span of control.* Management experts say that the optimum number of people one manager can supervise is 8 to 12, but this number is more appropriately determined by the conditions of the job. When workers are spread out over a large area, or are performing complex operations, a smaller number may be better. When they are all in the same room, or doing relatively simple jobs, a supervisor may be able to handle 30 people or more.

Writing Job Descriptions

Job descriptions are critical to the operation of the plant because they cover the areas of responsibilities for each member of management and staff. The best job descriptions are simple and to the point. They should not be written to impress job candidates, and it should not take a lawyer to decipher them. Job descriptions should include:

- Job title
- Minimum requirements for eligibility, including education, skills, and work experience
- Short summary describing the position
- List of specific duties and responsibilities, starting with the most important elements of the job
- Duties and responsibilities that may later be assigned to the position
- Extent of authority that goes with the job

- Job location in the chain of command
- Personal qualifications.

Many plants review their job descriptions every year or so. Jobs change, and in some industries change is frequent. Therefore, if you want to review a job description, note the date it was written. Don't rely on information recorded several years ago because the description may be out of date.

Assigning Employee Responsibilities

While major job responsibilities are easily defined, minor ones sometimes can be a problem. Plants should never rely on verbal assignments on matters of this importance; they are too confusing, may be easily misinterpreted, and sometimes overlap. The most complete and reliable document for determining the responsibilities of individuals is a Plant Operations Manual or a compilation of Standard Practice sheets. Usually consisting of printed forms and notices, and distributed in a looseleaf binder, a manual contains all the responsibilities of both plant departments and individuals. It often also includes the procedures to be followed in the plant.

You should revise and update responsibilities as personnel are reassigned and as process methods, equipment, and operational procedures change. The reassignments should be as clear and formal as the original assignments, and made prior to or at the same time as the changes requiring them.

UNDERSTANDING WHAT YOUR SUPERVISORY
AUTHORITY DEPENDS ON[1]

Before you exercise authority in the plant, you should understand how it is obtained. Some supervisors mistakenly believe that it comes with the job, but there are many other sources.

Authority is the right to command, use resources, and influence behavior. You'll find that certain managers in a plant wield much more authority than others, although they are all at the same job level. In addition, there are supervisors who make decisions and provide input on a variety of high-level issues. In some cases, they have more clout than other managers.

These varying degrees of authority can be best explained by examining the sources. To a large extent, the amount of authority depends on function, responsibilities, performance, expertise, behavior, and trust.

---

[1]Jean Guarino, "Authority: It Just Doesn't Come with the Job," *Successful Supervisor*, May 28, 1990, Dartnell, Chicago, IL 60640.

- *Function.* Some functions in an organization gradually take on more importance than others; supervisors of those functions come to have more inherent authority. For example, in recent years, quality assurance groups and R&D departments have become more important.

    These shifts in organizational authority by function will continue to occur, and supervisors involved in those functions will have more authority than others since they will have the ability to influence others significantly.

- *Responsibilities.* Much of your authority is based on your job responsibilities—the only legal authority you possess. It represents the decision-making limits inherent in the job and the control that you exercise over the employee who reports to you.

- *Performance.* Supervisors have authority based on their individual performance. Top performers command respect and are able to influence others. They have the ability to get things done and make things happen. Others respect their opinion even though these supervisors are not in the legitimate chain of command.

    Other supervisors, even managers in the plant, will seek their guidance and direction. They may call on them to solve organizational problems that may be outside their normal scope of responsibilities. This type of authority is developed over time through consistently high levels of performance.

- *Expertise.* Some supervisors have authority based on their expertise, which is a function of their skills, knowledge, and ability. Supervisors with high levels of competence are valuable to the plant, particularly if they share their knowledge and skills with others. They are very knowledgeable about their work unit, technical processes, or organizational goals and objectives. They are usually labeled technical experts and may have such credentials as advanced degrees or professional certifications. They have a consistent pattern of knowing what to do at a given time.

    As a result, they exert much influence over others. Some of these supervisors bring this authority with them at the time of production. In other cases, it is developed on the job through years of repeated successes.

- *Behavior.* Supervisors also have authority based on their personal behavior or actions toward others in the plant. They look, feel, believe, think, act, and react to events and other employees in a positive manner and consequently attract others and influence their behavior.

- *Trust.* Authority based on trust refers to the quality of relationships with other supervisors and those others with whom they have regular contact. Supervisors with high degrees of this kind of authority work with people in an open and honest way. They have no ulterior motives or hidden agendas.

Other individuals know where they stand and will trust these supervisors and their actions because they have the best interests of others in mind, as well as those of the plant. Once this trust is lost, however, it is difficult to regain. Some supervisors never fully develop an adequate level of trust to get others to do what needs to be done.

GUIDELINES FOR PROMOTING GOOD HUMAN RELATIONS IN THE PLANT

There's a lot more to the job of a supervisor than just assigning work—that is, if you expect cooperation, good workmanship, and high productivity from your workers. To get such behavior, you need to be skilled in communicating with them and understand them. You must be honest, fair, unprejudiced, and you must set a good example by the way you act.

Think about how you get along with your boss and your peers. Recognize that you need to be on good terms with your boss for direction and guidance. Peers share their experiences and work with you on mutual problems; so it pays to have rapport with your fellow supervisors. You'll find that maintaining such relations will make your job a lot easier.

When you consider all these matters, it's very easy to justify adopting the generally accepted rules for getting along with people and treating them as you'd like to be treated. Of course, there are many ways of being considerate of others. Here are a few of the common ones.

- *Be punctual.* Show respect for other people's time by being on time for appointments and meetings. Punctuality includes getting your work done on or ahead of schedule.
- *Look ahead.* Anticipate problems and plant employees' reactions to various situations. If you plan and schedule your work and that of your workers, you'll be taking preventive steps to minimize stress on them and yourself. Avoid muddling your way through each day attending primarily to emergencies. Get a reputation for always being in control and on top of a job.
- *Keep promises.* Be careful in making promises—this will cut down on the number you make. Be quick to keep your word, and you will become known for being reliable and trustworthy.
- *Spread the word.* Greet people with a smile. Keep your workers up to date on matters that affect them, and tell them why something has to be done. Explain changes before you make them. Give credit when it is due, and be liberal with praise. Above all, thank people when they do something for you.
- *Be consistent.* Your workers want to believe that you'll think and act today as you did yesterday. Avoid procrastinating; it indicates a lack of

self-confidence among other things, and it isn't good for your reputation. Be decisive; you'll move forward, and people will more readily follow you. Make steadiness and dependability your watchwords.

- *Do it now*. Handle each little job in the plant when you learn of it, and it will never have a chance to turn into a big one. Watch for opportunities to do something for someone. Show what you're made of by keeping up with your job even when you don't feel like working.

- *Be truthful*. Honesty always pays off. People like to deal with those they can trust. One of the ways to gain this is to never betray confidences. Always admit your mistakes, and never pass the buck.

- *Make yourself available*. Workers will be more willing to talk to you and accept your advice if you offer to help them without being asked. Join in when your workers are working on tough problems. Please your boss by volunteering to do unpleasant or distasteful jobs.

HOW TO BE A LEADER RATHER THAN A DRIVER[2]

How well do you get along with the workers you supervise? Do they respect and admire you? If there is a question in your mind about this relationship, maybe you are more a driver than a leader. A driver demands things be done rather than requesting something in a normal way. A driver doesn't really look for respect or cooperation, relying mostly on authority to move subordinates.

If you are a driver, you are probably weak in handling the human relations aspect of your job as well. Nevertheless, you should be aware that pressure tactics simply don't pay off in dealing with workers in the plant. Here are some of the most common taboos, when it comes to treating workers, along with why they are considered poor supervisory techniques.

- *Don't set impossible goals*. If you allow workers to plan their own work and set their own goals, you avoid setting impossible goals for them. Few activities provide as much potential for increasing one's motivation as the determining of one's own schedule. When you demand increased productivity, you gain only stressed and frustrated workers.

- *Don't find fault*. Avoid finding fault with the work or performance of workers. Everyone needs to feel that they're doing a good job, even though you may occasionally point out where they can make improvements. Since most jobs are done well rather than poorly, show that you are as skilled at recognizing good work as you are at recognizing bad.

[2] T. R. Weiss, "Pressure Tactics Don't Pay Off," *Foremanship*, October 21, 1985, Dartnell, Chicago, IL 60640.

- *Don't instill fear.* Realize that you can't get more work or better performance out of workers by threatening them. Punishment has only a minimal, if any, effect on productivity. What you most likely get from threats are poor morale, high absenteeism, and dissatisfied workers.

- *Don't oversupervise.* When you assign workers jobs, move out of their way and let them do the work. Show confidence in their abilities by not oversupervising them. If you furnish too much direction or stand over them constantly, you deprive them of being creative; they will not be permitted to learn.

- *Don't argue.* There is never a need for you to argue with any of your workers; they know that you are in charge. If a worker does poor work, or is wrong in his or her thinking, say so. But if you make an argumentive remark, you are in for trouble. Although you may win an argument, you lose something much more valuable—the cooperation and respect that you need to be a successful supervisor.

- *Don't overrule.* Always have a very good reason to reverse or overturn one of your worker's decisions. Never blame someone for a bad decision. Instead, take the opportunity to improve your communications with the individual and commend initiative. If you don't have a face-saving reason for overruling a worker, look for one. You don't want to destroy a person's ego and self-confidence.

Tips on Giving Orders

To give an order is a comparatively easy thing to do. But to give an order and get results is something different. The results you get usually are directly proportional to how much thought and planning you did before giving the order. By analyzing what you want done and then giving the order clearly and completely, you have a much better chance of getting good results.

Recognize that orders given too briefly may not be carried out properly. Consider all the information required, and then state each item in as few words as possible. With this procedure, you are not likely to confuse the person receiving the order.

HOW TO PERSONALLY GET ORGANIZED

If your work piles up periodically to the point where you become frustrated and you worry about which job to do first, you probably are disorganized. Don't despair. There's a simple and quick way to become organized. It's in widespread use by supervisory personnel in plants large and small, and you can make it work for you. Here's how to go about it:

- Make two lists, one that covers all the jobs and tasks you'd like to do, and one that covers everything you must do today. Add to your to-do list as you think of more things to do. Each evening, list what you must do the next day.

- Get a file that contains 31 sections, tabbed for each day of the month. If you want to be reminded of something at a later date such as a deadline for a report you make, write a note to that effect and put it in the appropriate section.

- Carry a note pad in your pocket at all times. If you think of something while away from your desk that you should add to you lists or date file, make a note of it. Refer to your note pad occasionally during the day so that you can transfer the item to the proper place.

- Begin each day on the job by first looking in your date file and acting accordingly. Then start working on your list of jobs and matters to be handled that day.

- When the mail comes in, go through it immediately and handle the urgent items. Those requiring some time should be added to your to-do list and placed in a drawer or "hold" box. Whatever you do, don't let the work pile up on your desk. Either do it now, or add it to your to-do list and put it out of the way.

- As you work on each item from the list of what you must do today, keep only the materials pertaining to that project on your desk. This will avoid the clutter that spells disorganization. It will also prevent or minimize being reminded of all the work you have to do.

- When you complete all the jobs you must do today, begin working on your to-do list. You will experience a sense of satisfaction whenever you reach this point, so you should always be aiming for it during your work day.

- Keep your to-do list reasonably short—no more than you can expect to complete within a week. If the list begins to get too long, transfer some of the items to the date file. You will feel less pressure.

The greatest benefit you get from this procedure is that it enables you to get your work done without frustration. You can't possibly forget something you have to do, and you will get things done in the order of their importance. Best of all, you will be more efficient because you're organized.

ENFORCING PLANT RULES AND REGULATIONS

One of your responsibilities is to enforce the plant's rules and regulations. But if you are practical and knowledgeable about human nature, you know that you can't continually enforce *all* the rules to the letter. There are too many factors to consider.

This means that you must give your workers some leeway before you take action on a rule violation. Here are some guidelines on how to handle these problems:

- Treat a safety violation as a more serious matter than a production matter involving quantity or quality.
- Handle a new employee, who may be unfamiliar with the rules, differently from a worker who has been on the job for some time.
- Give a flat-out, deliberate violation your special attention immediately.
- Agree that the breaking of a well publicized rule deserves different discipline than the breaking of a rule that is not as well-known.
- Try to learn how long the violation has been taking place before you act on it.
- Recognize that a violation of a rule for the first time is a factor to be considered.
- Know how many workers are involved in a first-time infraction before you take action.

HOW TO GET OTHER SUPERVISORS TO COOPERATE[3]

If everybody did their job as you do, there would be no problems. But if you work in a plant having several departments, you know that not all of your fellow employees are responsible and cooperative. When a plant sets up its operations so that someone else's output is your input, you have to depend on other employees' willingness to do their jobs in order for you to do yours. In many companies, there can be many such in the production process.

When getting your job done on time means waiting for an output from another supervisor, your problem is getting the other supervisor to cooperate. Don't expect that talking to the supervisor will always suffice. What you would like to say is, "Get your job done so I can do mine." But since you and the supervisor may be on equal rungs on the hierarchy ladder, you have to be more diplomatic, even subtle, in getting that message across. This is where you need to come up with a plan.

1. Start by setting up and keeping careful records. A calendar or punch file is of great help in noting the date-specific information or material

[3] W. H. Weiss, "The Problem of Getting Other Supervisors to Cooperate," *Successful Supervisor*, April 23, 1984, Dartnell, Chicago, IL 60640.

that is requested, the person from whom it is requested, and the deadline either that you set or that was expected.

2. When you anticipate you might have a problem in meeting a responsibility, see the supervisor whose output you need to set a deadline that both of you agree is reasonable. Set the deadline a few days before you really need the information or material, and put it in writing. Send the supervisor a copy and keep a copy on file.

3. Call the supervisor a day or two before the deadline is reached as a reminder of your need. While you're talking to the person, ask if there's any way you can help, such as stopping by to pick up what you need. If the supervisor tells you it is not ready, you might offer to extend the due date to the day when you really need it. But be sure to ask why it is not ready. Also, let the supervisor know you are extending a favor.

4. Call again a day before the second deadline. If the supervisor again says the information or material is not ready, it's time to take more drastic action.

5. Write a memo to your boss stating the problem and what has happened. Mention the deadlines you set and give the other supervisor's reasons for missing them. Conclude by telling the boss that, as a result, you are not able to carry out this part of your job. Since your boss may decide to show your memo to the other supervisor or the supervisor's boss, avoid being accusatory. Simply state the facts. Make sure your boss realizes that you are a conscientious person and that it bothers you when you are unable to get your work done.

6. Your boss probably will mention the matter to someone in authority over the other supervisor and your problem will be handled. But if it isn't, your last hope of getting the supervisor to cooperate is to threaten him or her with bypassing. If the supervisor is preventing you from doing a job, tell your boss you'd like to know where the supervisor gets the information or material. Ask whether your boss can arrange for you to get it directly. Since most people tend to be protective of the work they control, the threat of being bypassed may spur the supervisor to be more cooperative.

You can greatly increase the cooperation you get from other supervisors if you acknowledge their help when preparing a report on a completed assignment. Everyone likes to know his or her work isn't going unnoticed. If you can call it to the attention of the higher-ups, so much the better.

The opposite is true too. If you "hog" all the credit for yourself, you might find that you're not getting the cooperation you need lately. If that has been your habit, be sure to change it.

Sharing the credit, when it is justified, is a good way to make your job easier. Giving credit to those below you who have helped out is a wise move too. It shows top management that you are aware no one person can do everything alone and that teamwork is required.

Promoting Cooperation in the Plant[4]

Lack of cooperation in a plant invites frustration, causes loss of enthusiasm, wastes time, and lowers the quality of the service provided by employees. On the other hand, an abundance of cooperation among employees creates a positive work atmosphere, facilitates solving problems, and upgrades the treatment of everyone.

While most employees may give lip service to cooperation, there often isn't enough of it in today's plants. Apparently few know the secret of getting cooperation from others. Those who seem to get the most cooperation may not be able to explain how they get it. However, if you observe them closely, you'll see they have learned how to treat persons courteously and with respect—the way successful service workers treat customers. For example:

- They talk to *everyone* as though that person is a close friend.
- They make no distinction on the basis of a person's status, whether it be within the company or outside it.

These individuals usually have also learned how to get along with those who exhibit difficult behaviors. The more complicated the human aspects of their work, the more interpersonal skills they put in play to get what they want or need.

By treating plant employees well, you can often save time. Consider, for example, members of the staff who help you on the job, such as those in the Safety Department and the Personnel Department who supply you with information and data you use on the job. If you treat them as special individuals, they'll do their best to return the favor and to not keep you waiting for something you need.

Conversely, if you treat someone disrespectfully, you can expect that, sooner or later, the person will find a way to get even. That should not surprise you, human nature being what it is.

Showing respect, of course, doesn't always result in favors being done for you in return. Nothing in life *always* works the way we want it to. Occasionally, you must take a different approach. Getting some plant employees to cooperate may require that you try another technique—one, for example, that makes them feel important. Here's how to do it:

[4] W. H. Weiss, "Rally Cooperation from Coworkers," *Working Together*, October 8, 1990, Dartnell, Chicago, IL 60640.

- Ask for their advice or opinion to show that you're aware of their expertise in a given field.
- Compliment them for other jobs they've done well.
- Explain why you currently need their help.
- Show appreciation for their efforts after the fact.

HOW TO EFFECTIVELY DELEGATE

Your effectiveness and success as a supervisor depend greatly on your ability to delegate responsibility and authority to others, and to hold those delegated accountable for results. The following principles of delegation explain how you should go about it:

- The best way to expand your personal authority is to delegate as much responsibility as you can. Hoarding authority serves to diminish your own status and importance.
- Understand that delegation of responsibility does not mean that you give up responsibility. As the head of your work group, you are ultimately responsible for every job performed by it.
- Take into consideration that some risk is inherent when responsibility is delegated, and that some degree of error and misjudgment is usually inevitable.
- When you delegate responsibility, always be sure to delegate the authority that goes with it.
- In delegating responsibility, clearly draw the lines of, and limits to, authority with regard to decisions and actions.
- Prior to delegating assignments, pave the way with the training and guidance required to equip individuals with the skill and understanding they need to do a good job.
- When delegating, set high but realistic work standards. Spell them out clearly, and make the results you expect known.
- Avoid confusion and conflict in delegating by making sure the person receives instructions from a single source only.
- After delegating, give people a fair chance to prove their ability without interference and interruption.
- After delegating, back up your subordinates when their authority is questioned.
- Follow up on each delegated responsibility to make sure the desired results are achieved.

By far the most common reason supervisors give for not delegating is the fear that, once delegated, a job will not be done right. This is usually the case where technical or highly complex jobs are involved in which the supervisors are experts. Many such supervisors believe that performing the jobs themselves will maintain and increase their job security and recognition. This is especially the case if they were promoted from the rank of workers.

To delegate effectively, you should establish and follow well-defined plans and procedures. You must show subordinates how to complete assignments successfully and, having done that, restrain yourself from interfering with them, even though everything is not being done the way you would do it.

Instead, adopt the viewpoint that results are the final measure, and that there are different solutions to any problem.

STEPS TO FOLLOW IN SELECTING A PLAN OF ACTION

You and other supervisors are more than decision makers in operating your department in the plant. You also organize, initiate, and control. But none of these activities are more important than making wise decisions. Decisions about actions to be taken in your departments are crucial.

Although there are alternative ways of selecting a plan—intuition, precedent, divine guidance, and others—a rational decision is usually best in business situations. Nevertheless, many supervisors do not follow the basic steps of rational decision making. Instead, they rely on other methods in making their plans.

Rational decision making is not easy; knowledge, skill, and time are required in its use. Consequently, as a practical matter, most supervisors use the rational procedure for only the more important decisions they make. Fundamentally, rational decision making is quite forward and simple. The four essential steps are:

1. Diagnosing the problem

2. Looking for alternative solutions

3. Analyzing and comparing these alternatives

4. Selecting the best alternative as a plan of action[5]

---

[5]Parts of the following sections include ideas and concepts from the book W. H. Weiss, *Decision Making for First-Time Managers* (New York: ANACOM, 1985).

Diagnosing the Problem

Your decision can be no better than the information it's based on. How much information you go after and collect depends on the complexity of the problem and how much time you have to spend on it. You may make a poor decision if you know too little about a problem but you seldom err because you know too much.

In trying to define a problem, consider how it originated and why it exists. Look at its scope. More than likely, the problem consists of several subproblems that can be worked on separately. To gain a basic understanding of the problem, you must be able to answer a series of questions about it—such questions as:

- What is the real problem? Is it based on opinion or fact? Is the information you have on the problem truthful? Are bias and prejudice factors to be considered?
- Could the problem be only a symptom? Would you attack it differently if that were the case? Has the problem been defined too narrowly?
- How did the problem originate? Has it existed for some time? Is the problem common or unique? What are the chances of it solving itself if you do nothing?
- Is the problem critical? How quickly must an answer be found? Should only part of the problem be tackled now?
- What will be achieved by solving the problem? Is there a goal, objective, or purpose? Are the company's plans or goals involved?

Looking for Alternative Solutions

When you have a clear objective and must make a decision to reach that objective, your next step is to consider the alternatives. Seldom do you find that you have no alternatives. In fact, if it appears that you have only one course to follow, there's a good chance that it's wrong. In such a case, you probably have not forced yourself to consider other ways. This is necessary if your decision is to be the best one possible under the circumstances.

The ability to develop and consider alternatives is often as important as choosing the best one. Yet ingenuity, research, and innovation may uncover so many choices that you can't properly evaluate every one. Your best bet in this situation is to limit your search for alternatives to those that answer or satisfy a requisite of your decision.

A *requisite* is a condition that your decision must meet if the decision is to accomplish your objective. The common definition of a requisite is that which is essential or necessary. If you clearly recognize a requisite, you should confine your search for alternatives to those that will meet it.

The better you are able to do this, the better job you will do in selecting the best course to follow.

Looking for and recognizing requisites in planning never ends. For one project at one time, a certain requisite may be critical to the decision; but at a later date and for a similar decision, the requisite may be something else.

Analyzing and Comparing Alternatives

Once you have recognized the alternatives, the next step is to evaluate them and select the one that will best enable you to reach your objective. While you may be inclined to favor the alternatives that are *quantitative* (the consequences of their adoption can be measured), you risk making a bad decision if you ignore those that are *qualitative* (intangible in nature). In numerous cases in industry, management's quantitative plans were voided by an unexpected sitdown or strike, or a new equipment installation didn't solve a problem because of a government agency regulation. Give equal attention to quantitative and qualitative factors in the comparison of alternatives.

An easy way to evaluate alternatives is to try them to see what happens. Of course, often it is not possible to do this, particularly when a decision involves a commitment and cannot readily be reversed. But in many situations the only way a supervisor can make sure a plan is right is to try the alternatives to see which is best.

Research is a very effective technique for selecting alternatives, especially when major decisions are involved. The procedure requires that a problem be completely understood in order that the relationships between the factors, variables, and premises may be determined. The technique is well suited for the use of the computer to provide guidance in selecting the best alternative.

Selecting the Best Alternative

Experience serves a decision maker well, although it may not deserve the high rating it is often given. Experienced supervisors generally feel that what they have accomplished and what they have learned from the mistakes they made on the job furnish them an almost error-proof guide to future decision making. This feeling is likely to become stronger as the manager gains experience.

After you've made decisions for some time, you'll learn that your best decisions are those that are most objective—ones made without personal and emotional considerations. Consequently, you'll try to make more and more decisions that way. Of course, this is easier said than done. A way to go about it is to eliminate all arguments unsupported by facts so that your prejudices aren't in control.

If you are relatively inexperienced in making decisions, your boss will know, even more surely than you, that you will make mistakes. When you do, it's better to admit them freely. You may be nervous, but tell your boss calmly why you made the mistake, what you've learned from it, and what you've done to prevent it from happening again. Since few people are willing to admit their errors, your boss will probably be sympathetic and understanding. Very few supervisors are fired today for an error honestly made and forthrightly admitted.

You shouldn't worry about making bad decisions—that is, provided you don't make too many and you also learn from them. There are sometimes penalties for making right decisions as well as for making wrong ones. Reprimands may be received for doing nothing or for doing too much. The decision maker who is successful makes decisions objectively and decisively, choosing the right decision calmly from the best alternatives available.

HOW TO MAKE A DECISION UNDER PRESSURE

Although many of your problems in the plant that seem to require an immediate decision will not turn out that way, quite a few will. Periodically, you will have to make a decision without being able to calmly consider it. Here are some of the skills and abilities you'll need on those occasions.

Quick Thinking

While good decision makers are never rash and impetuous in resolving issues, neither are they procrastinators. Their most obvious characteristics are the spontaneity and quickness with which they make decisions once they've analyzed all the factors. If you are competent, know the principles of management and human relations, and understand the company business, there is seldom a need for excessive delay in reaching a decision.

One indication of the ability to think quickly is being able to perform mental calculations rapidly. But whereas persons with this ability will have an advantage in making quick decisions, their decision will not necessarily be good. For one thing, such persons are often not adept at handling the human relations aspects of a problem. Thus, the advantage given them by a quick mental process may be overridden by a lack of understanding as to what a good decision entails.

Most supervisors must face the reality that they will never be quick thinkers. But that doesn't mean that they are doomed to mediocrity. In place of quick thinking, they can substitute reflective action. For example, you may simply listen carefully to what others say, and occasionally interject statements that are merely repetitions of statements already made, rather than suggest something new. When a decision is required, you may search for insights into the problem in the remarks made by others. By riding on the ideas of others and offering a suggestion or two, you may come up with a solution. But the solution doesn't arrive by way of a quick decision, it is the result of mutual discussion.

You can facilitate quick thinking by setting up procedures for handling problems similar to the ones that you have tackled in the past, on the expectation that they will probably come up again. Such planning gets around the need to think about a problem from scratch at the time it arises. A common example of this is a fire drill. The advantage of such training is that the actual incident is handled routinely when it occurs, increasing both the effectiveness and the efficiency of the action taken.

Rapid Recall

By selectively committing specific information to memory, you can prepare for the times when you need to come up with a quick decision. When you have such a backlog of pertinent information, not only will you be able to handle matters with authority and confidence, you will also boost your reputation for widely ranging intelligence and knowledge, thus gaining the respect of both your subordinates and superiors.

A sharp supervisor is able to answer specific questions without hesitation. Such instant response is a valuable ability. If you have it, you can withstand the greatest tests provided by the pressure of time. To do well in such situations requires not only a good memory, but also an at-ease nature, an ability to think quickly, and a confidence that prevents you from becoming easily rattled.

If you can concentrate well and learn easily, you will likely have a good memory. But anyone with an average mental capacity and a strong desire to learn can improve his or her memory capability. Persons remember best the things they have tried the hardest to remember.

Discretion and Judgment

You must not take decisions lightly if you want them to hold up. This means that some degree of effort and thought should be put into every decision, including those you make quickly. One sign of an inept decision maker is the making of snap decisions when they aren't necessary. Even though your batting average might be good, it could be even better if the first answer or solution to a problem that comes to mind isn't the one that is adopted.

Recognize that even good decisions should be rejected if they are proposed at the wrong time or with such aggressiveness that they generate resistance. Everyone resists change to some degree. Except when what is proposed is exactly what is hoped for, a person tends to look for reasons to oppose or reject it. Discretion is the mark of a good decision maker.

WAYS TO MAKE PARTICIPATIVE MANAGEMENT WORK

Many supervisors today believe that they should ask workers to help them in making decisions about the work and how the plant procedures are carried out. They think that such participation results in greater productivity and improved morale in the plant. Participation by workers is good, in their opinion, and they welcome it.

Other managers and supervisors do not agree. They have found that participation doesn't always raise productivity, improve morale, or bring about greater efficiency. They even point out cases in which asking employees to express their opinions concerning a problem has caused hard feelings and a dissatisfaction with management's ultimate decision. It is obvious that many factors should be considered when deciding whether to adopt a participation style of managing.

1. The desire of workers to participate and the satisfaction resulting from doing so vary from group to group and even from person to person. Not all workers are enthusiastic about getting involved in what they think is a management function.

2. Even workers who have the temperament and personality required for giving their opinions and viewpoints do not particularly want to do so unless certain conditions exist. They feel that the problem must concern them and not others, and they must have something worthwhile to contribute.

3. Many workers, particularly those belonging to unions, don't want to become involved in something that might conflict with their own best interests.

4. Don't confuse participative managing with democratic managing. The latter means that majority rules; you can imagine what that would do to the efficient and orderly conducting of your department functions.

Participation is not the answer to all your problems. However, it works under certain conditions, with certain workers, and when you know what you're doing.[6] Here are the steps you must take to make it work:

1. Make sure the problem is related to your workers' situation.

---

[6]T. R. Weiss, "Participative Management," *Foremanship*, January 14, 1985, Dartnell, Chicago, IL 60640.

2. Be convinced that your workers have the knowledge and skill to be able to make a worthwhile contribution.
3. Determine if participation will benefit the department.
4. Consider participation only if the situation is free of catches or gimmicks.
5. Be sure there is sufficient time for you to obtain and consider workers' suggestions before you ask for them.
6. State the problem and explain why it must be solved.
7. Give your own answer or opinion and ask for comments.
8. Consider all suggestions and recommendations regardless of who makes them.
9. Announce your decision and explain how you reached it.

GUIDELINES FOR EFFECTIVE TEAMWORK

High productivity in your department depends greatly on your ability to promote teamwork among your workers. Here are some guidelines on how you can achieve it.

- *Be an effective communicator.* Most conflicts are created because workers don't understand the true meaning of others' words. Keep your communication channels open.
- *Criticize only in a way that is kind and helpful.* It takes effort to keep criticism constructive. Wait for the proper time and place to give it. Focus on behavior, not the person. Be specific with how the problem should be dealt with, and try to end the discussion positively.
- *Prefer assertiveness to aggressiveness.* You can resolve conflicts and satisfy your own needs without dominating anybody. Aggressiveness is a battle tactic; assertiveness is a skill that uses honesty and truth to help persons make their point.
- *Stay open and receptive.* Most workers get defensive when they feel threatened. The best way to keep defensiveness from growing into conflict is to make sure you are not threatening. While some workers may get defensive without reason, if you stay open and receptive, you may be able to defuse the situation.
- *Don't gossip.* Spreading hearsay about others' business doesn't help you one bit. If you have a comment to make, make it to the person, not to others.
- *Refrain from belittling.* Everyone has an achievement or possession that he or she is proud of. Belittling others' accomplishments brings about group apprehension. On the other hand, sincere compliments promote group cohesion. Support your workers and they will support you.

- *Avoid arguing.* Not only is an argument a waste of time, it proves nothing and can cause dissention in an entire group. If an argument is going nowhere, resolve it or forget it.
- *Keep cool.* Tension breeds tension within a group. If you feel that a situation is getting out of control, either end the discussion or take a break. Reorganize your thoughts, and give others the opportunity to release their own tensions.
- *Be an optimist.* If you're usually a pessimist, keep quiet about it within your work group. Pessimistic viewpoints are bad for group cohesion. They also are a drag on group energy and productivity.

TIPS ON HOW TO AVOID COMPLACENCY

Complacency on the job is an attitude that you must avoid at all costs. Yet one of the most difficult feelings for supervisors and managers to overcome is treating their job responsibilities as routine matters. This attitude is difficult to forbear because most persons tend to follow routine procedures in their way of doing things. It's part of their way of life; it's normal for them to act that way.

But being complacent about your job is not good for you. You get in a rut, and, when you do, it's hard to get out of it. One of the worst outcomes of being complacent is that you begin to think that problems in the plant will eventually solve themselves.

You can, however, do something about complacency. If, for example, you want to avoid crises in your department:

- Try to anticipate foul-ups and breakdowns.
- Don't sit idly by and wait for human relations problems to come up.
- Look ahead and be prepared to handle the unexpected.
- Vary the ways you handle your job.

This malady is most likely to appear when your job no longer seems a challenge, when your work starts to become boring or monotonous, and when you would like to inject some life and variety into your responsibilities. This is the time to take a few minutes to consider what you are doing and whether you are doing it the best way.

Ask yourself, "What part of my job could be improved? How is it incomplete?" Once you have answered these questions, list the possible ways you can make your job better or improve your performance. The next step is to start to do the items on your list.

If your plant is to continue to make a profit and expand, all employees must continually be looking for ways to improve the product manufactured or the service performed. They must anticipate problems before they appear and take steps to either minimize their impact or prevent them from happening. They must be creative and innovative, and they must do everything they can to improve the operation.

Consider the number of supervisors and managers working in your plant. If each of these leaders concentrated on just one part of their job that could be improved every month, imagine the possible effect that could make on the profitability and growth of the plant. If a company expects to keep up with its competitors, none of the managerial people should ever be considered complacent about their jobs.

UNDERSTANDING WHY LOYALTY IS IMPORTANT

Every employee should be loyal to his or her superior and the company. Loyalty is one of the most notable attributes you can have in regard to your job, and one criterion an effective leader can't do without.

Supervisors who hope to move up in the plant never degrade or speak slightingly about their superiors. Nobody appreciates spiteful remarks about others. Besides, word will eventually get back to the slandered person.

You win loyalty by looking out for people and their interests, and by defending their actions to others who may try to discredit them. Loyalty is also promoted when you show workers your own loyalty to your superiors.

If you vent personal complaints and dissatisfactions to workers or run down the company or its products, your workers will never again have much respect for you. Loss of respect seriously undermines your effectiveness.

Some employees do not understand that loyalty is a mutual issue. They tend to be concerned only with the company's loyalty to its employees, rather than their own loyalty to their company. They feel that an employer should show its loyalty by its willingness to help employees meet personal needs and by providing benefits. Employees can show their loyalty by doing a fair share of the work and cooperating with fellow workers, supervisors, and other management people.

When you feel that an employee is being disloyal to you or the company, you must first make the employee realize it, and then determine how that realization affects the employee. If the person doesn't care, you must decide whether to keep him or her. Performance appraisal meetings are good for discussing attitudes and feelings about the company and the job.

TIPS ON THE ART OF NEGOTIATING

Would you prefer to avoid negotiating? Do you avoid it because of the confrontation, haggling, and risk taking it supposedly entails? Successful negotiating can:

1. Gain support for your project.
2. Improve your chance for success on the job.

It pays to see negotiating in a positive light. Decide right now to become skillful at it. Begin by considering the following factors that affect most negotiations and usually determine their outcome.[7]

- *The time and place.* To win (or get your way), you've got to be prepared both mentally and physically. Suppose, for example, you are asked a tough question, and are expected to give an immediate answer. You know you can come up with a more complete and better answer if you have time to get all the facts and figures together.

  Don't be pushed into giving a poor answer or an inadequate one. Instead, say, "I'm in the middle of something urgent. Can I drop by your office in an hour or two?" No reasonable person would be upset by such a request, and you will have time to get the information you need. You'll also enjoy the advantage of presenting it at a time and place of your choosing.

- *Policies can be changed.* Don't let anyone tell you that certain company policies and procedures are unchangeable. The fact is that nothing is unchangeable today. When the plant can benefit, show a profit, or help out a worthy, loyal employee, a policy can be changed.

- *Facts and figures.* The best way to prepare for a discussion is to collect all the facts, figures, statistics, reports, and other evidence supporting your position. Remember, printed material is especially impressive and convincing. Many people who are skeptical of oral arguments or someone's word will accept as true the words printed in an article, report, or book. The more material you can put your hands on, the more support you can produce when you feel you are losing an argument.

  While you may not need all the facts and figures you have acquired in your preparation, you'll negotiate with more confidence knowing it is available. History has shown that individuals who make out well in negotiations are usually the ones who have collected and can present the most facts.

- *The human aspect.* Don't forget that you're dealing with human beings, not machines, when you get into a serious discussion or a negotiation. Humans have foibles and weaknesses, are subject to persuasion, and have feelings. You'll find an advantage, too, if you recognize the personality and make-up of the individual you're talking to.

---

[7]W. H. Weiss, "Get Ahead by Negotiating," *Successful Supervisor*, February 8, 1988, Dartnell, Chicago, IL 60640.

Top managers and executives, for example, usually want to get to the bottom line in a hurry. They are concerned with a project as a whole and don't want to spend time discussing details. Middle managers and staff people, on the other hand, like to show you that they are aware of the latest developments in the industry. Before they approve your project, they might want you to explain every detail down to the last nut and bolt.

Before you start to negotiate, have three ideas in mind:

1. Have a picture of exactly what you want to accomplish—your optimal goal.
2. Have in mind the minimum goal you would settle for—the least that you would be agreeable to accepting.
3. Have a realistic picture of what you have a good chance of accomplishing.

Try for your top goal when negotiating, but be ready to accept any offer between the minimum and the maximum. Sometimes you may be surprised to find that the maximum is agreed to without argument. At other times, you may not be offered even the minimum. If this happens, you may decide to take more drastic action, such as going over the head of the other negotiator—or approaching the problem differently.

PROVEN BENEFITS OF PERFORMANCE APPRAISALS

In performance appraisal, employees are told how they are performing on the job and what they can do to improve their performance. When you make correct preparations for appraisals and are careful in implementing them, both the company and employees benefit.

Most managers have found that periodic interviewing of their people brings about an improvement in their work. The interview has proved also to be an effective way to keep up morale as well as raise the interest of workers in their jobs.

Some managers, however, are reluctant to give appraisal interviews. They feel that their day-to-day contacts with their subordinates do what interviews would do—that there is no need to make separate issues of their superior/subordinate relations. They fail to realize that interviews can provide the opportunity to promote the improvement of the performance of employees, and that not taking advantage of them deprives employees and the company from the good that results from people bettering themselves.

You might also shy from interviews because you may consider them as occasions when you are expected to reprimand or discipline workers, and you dislike having to do that. This viewpoint is not realistic, however, in that if counseling or criticism is due an employee, you would be shirking your responsibility if you don't face the problem.

Don't overlook the fact that a performance interview gives you an opportunity to commend and compliment a worker for good work, a practice too often neglected by supervisors. Most individuals want to know how they are doing on the job and what they need to do to be promoted. You should not deny them this information.

When receiving appraisals, employees gain in several ways:

- They learn what is expected of them and whether they are meeting those expectations.
- They learn where they are weak and what may be hurting their overall performance.
- They are told their deficiencies and what they need to do to appear better in the eyes of management.

Managers conducting performance appraisals also gain from the experience:

- They are able to get higher quality and quantity output from their workers.
- They can measure the growth of subordinates.
- They can get agreement and confirmation on responsibilities and their relative importance.
- They are able to review *who* is responsible for *what* among their workers.

Appraisals are a means of motivation in that workers can get a push, along with recognition from you. Some workers feel no news is bad news; periodic meetings allay this. Both parties in a discussion can also use the interview to relieve tension in their personal relations. Talking out matters clears the air and results in mutual understanding.

HOW TO GAIN PLANT WORKERS' SUPPORT

You can gain your workers' support by making them feel they are important to your department and to the company. Individuals back organizations in which they feel they truly belong. Because you are a member of management, this relationship may also gain you their personal loyalty. Personal loyalty usually evolves from being fair and honest with workers, treating them as equals, and offering to help them with their problems.

Getting support, however, is not always easily accomplished. Experienced managers say that you must attend to three matters to obtain it. Each is important in itself, and each is a requisite for success.

- *Keep people informed.* The most common ways of keeping employees informed are by means of the company newspaper, bulletin board notices, and plant meetings. While each of these is important, they are not by themselves sufficient.

  The best way is to inform people *directly*. This is usually an informal procedure, consisting often of at-the-moment conversations with individuals or small groups in the plant. To be most effective, however, supplement such contacts with more formal meetings held in conference rooms.

  To make meetings productive, call them for specific purposes. Be careful, however, not to define or limit the data and information too narrowly you give people. Telling individuals only what they need to know to do their jobs is not enough. You should let your people know about the work and problems of other departments in the plant, including the problems and accomplishments of people at higher levels in the company. Most plant employees arc interested in such matters and feel more like members of the family if they know about them.

- *Make people feel they are involved.* You can makc people feel they are participating in decisions by seeking their advice and asking for their answers to problems facing the department or the company. Do this either informally by discussing matters with individuals singly in the plant or more formally in a group meeting.

  Group meetings are a good way of getting workcrs involved in their jobs and in the problems of the plant. But some workers will fail to contribute unless conditions are conducive to it. To make this a reality, seat them in such a way that eye contact can be maintained between each person. Place the chairs facing each other or around a table.

  Make the atmosphere of the meeting one that encourages participation. Try not to dominate the meeting or use your position to restrict free discussion. Also, avoid doing most of the talking or responding in a negative way to comments from any member of the group. This behavior on your past will tend to make employees feel that their ideas and opinions are truly valued and that they are making worthwhile suggestions and comments.

- *Acknowledge contributions.* Acknowledge all ideas, recommendations, and comments received from employees either in casual conversations or in meetings. How you do this depends on the nature of the offering and its value to the company. Simply thanking a person is often enough. Saying you appreciate the contribution lets the employee know he or she has been recognized as a member of the team.

Individuals deserve recognition when they put a lot of time and effort into a project. Sometimes a short article concerning the employee and the idea or suggestion is published in the company newspaper, or an aware is made at a luncheon or social gathering. Whatever the form of recognition, you can be sure that the honored individual will be forever loyal to the company.

Tips on Running a Productive Meeting

Although many factors are involved in conducting a productive meeting, you should be skilled in the procedure if you expect to move up in your plant. The first of those skills is knowing when you should call a meeting.

- Avoid holding meetings when they are unnecessary. Maybe individual conversations are more appropriate. Remember that a meeting takes your people and others away from their jobs. You and the company may lose if an important activity in the plant is interrupted by your meeting.

- Make your meetings timely by holding them promptly after receipt of important information or requests for decisions, and always soon enough to ensure proper and adequate action. Plan to keep your meetings small by inviting only those persons who are directly involved and able to deal effectively with the matters to be discussed.

- After you have selected a convenient time and location for the meeting, inform participants in advance about the purpose and the agenda so they can come prepared. Get ready yourself by gathering as much information as you can on the subjects you plan to discuss. Try to limit your meetings to one hour, preferably less. Recognize that fatigue and boredom affect the efficiency and value of contributions of the participants.

- Open the meeting at the time you said it would start, thus not letting latecomers steal time from those present. Introduce individuals if they do not already know each other to ease tensions and make attendees feel welcome.

- Focus on the meeting's objectives and avoid discussing subjects that are not on the agenda. Meetings are fine for identifying and recognizing problems, but they are not always good for trying to solve them. To help you project the best image, go light on humor; you want to appear responsible and businesslike. Do not treat a company meeting as a social event, yet be relaxed and friendly.

- Do not preach or criticize, and try not to do most of the talking. The more you can draw out information and ideas from others, the more productive your meetings will be.

- Resist any attempt of the participants to confuse the objectives or to broaden them, even though this may introduce complications since people may be looking out for their best interests. While most attendants at meetings usually try to be constructive, their motives may lead them to obstruct as well as to introduce side issues.

- Keep the meeting on schedule, but periodically pause to review what has been discussed. There is no need for a "break" if you limit the meeting to an hour or less.

- Problems often encountered in a meeting are those concerning when and what decisions should be made. Attendants usually have several courses of action available to them, any one of which would probably lead to the desired objective. In such situations, it is often better to select one and go ahead with it rather than continue the discussion in hopes of finding a perfect answer.

- As for when you close a meeting, if you have an agenda to work from, you simply adjourn after you've handled the last item. Without an agenda, it's not so easy because people are inclined to go on until the leader announces the meeting is over. You can signify the end by saying, "That's all I have to discuss today. Thanks for coming."

HOW TO PREVENT SMALL PROBLEMS FROM BECOMING BIG

Most of the major problems you experience in the plant start out small. They are usually not recognized as having the potential to become serious; yet just about every such problem should have been solved shortly after it started. It takes perseverance from you in searching for the causes of abnormal and unusual occurrences and incidents, plus a determination to not tolerate irritants and minor problems. Such items too often grow into big problems. They must be corrected and handled as soon as they are detected. Following are some typical situations that occasionally arise, along with suggestions on what you should do about them.[8]

- *A slowdown begins in one of the routine procedures of the department.* Unscheduled delays in established procedures for doing jobs are indications that something has happened to upset the normal activities. Attack this problem by talking to workers about their jobs. Listen to their complaints. Find out if rumors are circulating through the department. Determine if one or more individuals are unhappy or dissatisfied with some recent turn of event.

    While most complaints and ill feelings of workers have no real

---

[8]Parts of the following section are from subjects discussed in the article "Keep Small Problems from Becoming Big," *Foremanship*, Feb. 9, 1987, Dartnell, Chicago, IL 60640.

basis, you may be able to quickly fend off their becoming serious problems once you learn of them. It pays to be alert to what is happening in the plant. You can't do this, of course, if you spend most of your time at your desk.

- *You see an increase in operating costs that cannot be attributed to normal inflation or more work being performed.* Several matters should be checked out immediately:

     Take a look at utility costs and maintenance expenditures. Determine if a wasteful practice has recently developed such as an undetected leak.

     Investigate if equipment and machine failures are occurring more frequently, thus increasing the maintenance costs.

     Find out if some jobs must be handled more than once. This would tell you that something is wrong with either materials, process procedures or workers performance.

- *There is a lack of interest in a new procedure or process.* This can spell failure for an idea or innovation if a turnaround in thinking and performance of employees isn't soon in coming. Although there may be several reasons for a lack of enthusiasm on the part of the employees involved, it's up to you to start searching them out before it's too late. Start by talking to the employees who are directly involved. Ask the following questions:

     Were they consulted about the venture or project?

     Did they contribute to its installation or implementation?

     Were they informed about the upcoming change before it was made?

     Are they working harder now than before?

You probably will learn why your department is not having success with the new procedure. If you are an astute supervisor, you will take the action necessary to keep this problem from getting out of hand.

- *There is an abnormal increase in the use of a certain storeroom item.* It's apparent that something isn't working properly or being used correctly. But since a single item is being questioned, it should be easy for you to figure out the problem.

     Look for a change in procedure or in the way a machine is operated. A speedup in an operation may produce strain on both workers and machines. Such stress can account for a greater use of a tool, office supply item, or a machine part. Whatever the cause, the problem deserves your attention so that consumption of the item and accompanying high costs do not continue.

GUIDELINES FOR MANAGING BY OBJECTIVES

Generally, medium-sized and large plants today are reasonably well managed. Despite the ups and downs of the business, the complaints of a few employees, and the changes in managers and executives with time, these plants make the most of their managerial talent. While some managers are more effective than others, comparatively few fail to survive periods of austerity.

It follows that managers at all levels in such plants are usually satisfied with their performance. They adapt well to the changes and problems of conducting their plant's operations. However, a few managers have been unwilling to settle for reasonably effective organizational performance. They have looked for better methods of managing.

Management by objectives has evolved as one of the methods, and it is practiced by supervisors as well as upper-level managers. An assertive attitude is an essential ingredient for the managing by objectives style. The assertive manager focuses on objectives as a natural way of doing business.

Before presenting the concept of management by objectives, let's discuss managing by control. When you manage by giving detailed step-by-step instructions to workers, the workers depend on your presence to know what they must do. Further, when workers finish the assigned job, they must solicit the next assignment from you.

This procedure does not require that workers know or agree with the purpose of the work. You simply tell them what to do and imply that they are not to do anything else. Basically, you are managing by control.

However, when you go to the trouble of explaining to workers the reason for the work they are doing, and how it fits into what other workers are doing, then workers can quite readily show an interest and desire to do a good job. In addition, when they understand the purpose behind the work and the objectives of the company, they can go ahead with further work.

Workers can proceed toward the objectives to some degree even without your presence. By explaining the overall objectives to them, you free yourself from the need to provide continual direction and guidance and liberate the workers as well. This is management by objectives.

The successful use of management by objectives depends on two assumptions:

1. Workers do better on the job if their work has meaning to them, if they can see the reason for doing it.
2. Workers generally will work to achieve objectives if they know what those objectives are and they can expect to be rewarded for helping to reach them.

You manage by objectives when you look ahead, determine where you want to go, set a means of measuring your progress, and communicate with your people in terms of the total project.

Yet there is more to the concept. As in all goal-directed efforts, follow-up is essential to evaluating accomplishments. Such an assessment is also valuable as a precedent when setting future goals and performance levels.

An assessment of performance is beneficial to both you and workers because it provides a totaling of accomplishments, a forum for airing problems, and an opportunity to refuel motivational drive.

HOW TO HANDLE COMPLAINTS IN THE PLANT

When a complaint is handled properly, the person making the complaint is satisfied enough so that he or she harbors no resentment or desire to seek revenge. Although the person may not entirely agree with how the complaint is settled, he or she doesn't permit the problem to build up feelings of anger, spitefulness, uncooperativeness, or disloyalty.

Too many plant supervisors are frequently guilty of being thoughtless and in too much of a hurry when dealing with their workers' complaints. Here are some suggestions on how to handle them:[9]

- *Take any and all complaints seriously.* Don't shake your head, look off in the distance, or act surprised when someone is telling you about a problem. These mannerisms tell the person that you think the complaint is unimportant.

  Remember that many workers will not come to you unless they believe they have good justification for doing so. Thus, if one of your workers feels strongly that he or she is not being treated fairly, you owe the person the courtesy of being interested and wanting to straighten out matters.

- *Be available and easy to see.* Even though you may have many duties and there are many demands on your time, you've got to make yourself available to your workers. Meetings are important, of course, and so is the paperwork on your desk. But to an employee, the grievance is just as, if not more, important. If you won't see one of your workers, who will? Turning away someone is asking for trouble.

- *Give a person your full attention.* It's not enough to only let someone tell you his or her story. You must carefully listen to every word. You would be very discourteous if you asked someone to talk to you and then shuffled papers, worked on your files, or took telephone calls while he or she was speaking.

- *Make a record of the complaint.* Some complaints will be given to you when you are walking through your department or other parts of the

---

[9]"Handling Complaints Properly," *Successful Supervisor*, Feb. 27, 1984, Dartnell, Chicago, IL 60640.

plant. Just because they were presented in an impromptu manner is no excuse to forget them. To be sure you don't, make a record of them.

That way you can act on them when you have time. Carry along a handy notebook for just this purpose, and have a pen or pencil at all times too.

- *Do a thorough job of investigating.* Put a lot of effort into getting all the facts and the complete story. Talk to individuals who may know something about the complaint. Look up records and other documentation and check your manager on company policy. If you fail to be thorough, you give the person who is complaining the impression that you want to prove him or her wrong.

- *Decide only after deliberation.* Avoid reaching a conclusion too quickly. Giving your opinion before you have all the facts makes you appear impatient and unreasonable. Workers have little respect for a person who lacks the ability to apply the basic principles of supervision.

- *Bypass politics and red tape.* Appealing to bureaucracy to handle a grievance smacks of upmanship. It also is seen as a delaying tactic, particularly when it takes time to fill out forms or get a ruling from a higher authority.

    While you may temporarily put off answering a complaint with such a maneuver, you still will have to contend with it later. Worse, you may arouse the anger of the person complaining to the point where he or she becomes more determined to fight and win the battle.

- *Avoid procrastinating.* Putting off the answering of a complaint only makes matters worse. You know that the person complaining will not give up until he or she has your answer. When you drag your feet in handling a complaint, you infer that the matter and the person complaining are not very important. Treating a person in such a manner may adversely affect morale, performance, and loyalty.

- *Tell the person the status of the complaint.* Keep the person up to date on what's being done about his or her complaint. The matter is very important to the person. Recognize that and keep it high on your list of priorities.

- *Follow up on the settlement of a complaint.* It isn't enough to just answer it. See that it is resolved by either removing its cause, paying for it in some way, or proving to the person's satisfaction that the complaint was unwarranted to begin with.

TIPS ON COMBATTING ABSENTEEISM

Supervisors and managers can put several methods into practice to help alleviate absenteeism. Among the most common are providing awards for employees and departments with regular attendance records. Departments receiving the award for a given period can earn the special additional privilege of offering individual prizes to members.

Another method of combatting absenteeism involves implementing a point system for regular attendance. When sufficient points are accumulated, employees may select gifts from a catalog supplied for this purpose. Additionally, outstanding attendance records can be recognized in the plant's employee service awards program.

Some plants put on special absenteeism drives during the month or months that have historically shown the poorest attendance. Departments with the best records are given coffee and donuts on company time and congratulated by the plant manager who makes it a point to be present.

It pays to give considerable publicity to such campaigns and drives. Personal recognition from management in letters, on bulletin board announcements, and in company newspapers are usually effective.

But when management realizes that people who enjoy their work seldom are absent from the plant, a strong course of action can be adopted to cut absenteeism. Communicating concern combats absenteeism better than any other method. Promoting personal participation in the activities program of the company goes a long way toward communicating management concern for employees.

Employee services including recreational activities are the backbone of such programs. In addition, a safety drive, suggestion contest, the United Way, and a Red Cross blood drive all support a sense of common purpose that causes people to want to show their loyalty.

Most employees want to be considered important contributors to their company's progress. The more that management—especially supervisors—indicate an appreciation of their efforts, and interest in them as individuals, the fewer personnel problems arise.

GUIDELINES FOR HANDLING EMPLOYEES ON PROBATION

Some plants require that all new employees serve a probationary period. The managers of these plants feel that a 30- or 60-day period would give their supervisors time to orient the new hires to their jobs and evaluate their performance.

However, plants with such policies often sacrifice an important aspect of effective labor management by not taking full advantage of the probationary period. Proper management of such periods can reduce turnover rate as well as break-in time. Here are some guidelines for successful handling of employees on probation:

1. *Orientation.* See that a systematic and thorough orientation is given employees after they have had a few days to adjust to the job. Recognize

that persons may be overwhelmed by the newness of the situation and not perform at their best during the initial time on the job.

2. *Attention.* Show an interest in the new employee by going beyond the explaining of start and quit times, lunch hours, coffee breaks, and similar matters. Give the person a quick tour of the plant and introduce him or her to fellow workers. Stay close the first day or two to answer the person's questions and periodically check on progress.

3. *Training.* Set a probationary period of sufficient length to ensure that the employee receives adequate training and is able to adjust to the plant working conditions. See that the established principles of job training are followed so that he or she has every opportunity to perform the job satisfactorily.

4. *Deciding.* Terminate without delay the employee who is unable to meet the work standards of the job by the end of the probationary period.

5. *Recognizing.* Treat the occasion upon which an employee is accepted as a permanent member of the plant as a significant event in his or her career. Take advantage of this opportune moment to give the employee positive feedback.

CONTENDING WITH THE SOCIALIZING PROBLEM

Should supervisors socialize with subordinates away from the job? On the job friendliness is not the issue.

Personnel experts pretty much are in agreement on how they see this problem. While the road to success in management/labor compatibility may be the maintaining of good relations, if your social life contains the same people as your business life, you may have trouble ahead.

There's no problem in being a good socializer; unless you're a bore, you're readily accepted. The difficulty is that such relations often cause on-the-job problems.

The experts recommend that you carefully limit your social relationships with employees outside the plant because such mixing adversely affects objectivity. For one thing, favoritism in making job assignments becomes a problem even though you may consciously try to avoid it.

For another, discipline on the job becomes difficult to administer. There's no denying that you occasionally must discipline someone. But that someone may be the fellow you were bowling with the night before.

An additional objection to maintaining social relationships with your workers is that they weaken leadership. Chain of command tends to be ignored if employees from several plant levels belong to the same social group. It is very easy for a person to overlook or forget job responsibilities as well as authority in an eagerness to get jobs done or reach personal and company goals.

Yet socializing away from the plant is acceptable, and in some cases recommended, as a means of learning the other fellow's problems and getting along with each other because of mutual interests. All groups of people like to get together to celebrate an occasion or simply enjoy each other's company.

Although office and plant parties are not as popular today as they once were, you should consider them a "must"—to a point. If you don't participate, you're regarded as rude. You must have the good sense to come in, be friendly, have something to eat and drink, and leave.

If you become overly friendly, you're going to have problems. You've got to use good judgment and discretion. Supervisors who let down their hair at a party on Friday may be willing to be tough on Monday but subordinates won't expect it.

How close, human to human, should you be to the people who work for you? Close enough to know their families, their hobbies, and their interests, but not close enough to play a game of poker with, have an afterwork beer with, or borrow money from, say management experts. This seems good and fair advice, especially if you want to stay out of trouble in the plant.

UNDERSTANDING CLIQUES

Small groups of employees who band together are very common today in plants of all sizes. Workers who have similar interests make up such groups. For example, if your workers belong to a union, its leaders may likely form such a group.

Other informal groups are composed of individuals who are avid sports enthusiasts and persons who are active in social programs, both inside and outside the plant. Sometimes you can identify group members by observing who works with whom, who consider themselves as oldtimers, and who joins whom for bull sessions.

Employees who aren't members of these informal groups, or "cliques" as they are sometimes called, may look upon them with either envy or suspicion. An outsider may claim that clique members get all the breaks. Another may say that members try to make themselves look good by brewing up trouble for employees who are not members.

While most such claims are unfounded, they result from conditions and situations that are very apparent to outsiders. For instance, clique members often have more experience than other employees. This enables them to do their work easier and faster.

Or they may be more familiar with the company's rules and regulations. Thus, they may seem to get more privileges than others. Whatever, employees who try to join cliques are either accepted or turned down, depending on how the clique feels about them.

As a supervisor, the existence of a clique among your people or in another department of the plant can give you both an advantage and a disadvantage in carrying out your responsibilities. The advantage arises when you are able to persuade and sell clique leaders on something you want to do such as improve safety, productivity, or workmanship. If members of the clique go along with you, outsiders will likely be influenced to follow.

The disadvantage is evident when the clique opposes an idea or request of yours in spite of everything you do or say to sell them. Outsiders may or may not be influenced, but you can count on being made aware of their feelings.

What can or should you do about cliques? Basically, you may as well accept their existence and not try to do anything. For certain, you can't break them up unless you transfer their members out of your department. And if you do this, another clique would probably soon appear; it would be composed of employees who would now consider themselves a grade above the new persons who are brought into the department. While employees who do not belong to a clique may look upon one with more disfavor than favor, cliques really aren't all that bad.

Your preferred course of action should be to try to get along with them rather than attacking them, because they can help you if you get them going in your direction. You can best do this by discussing your work-connected problems with the person or persons who seem to lead a group. Explain what you want to accomplish and ask for suggestions. If you do not get an immediate answer, bring the subject up again later after the group has had time to talk about it.

WHEN AND HOW TO DISCIPLINE PLANT WORKERS

Despite the fact that workers are better educated today and aware of the need for harmony and cooperation on the job, many supervisors continue to encounter worker behavioral problems in the plant. Personnel experts say that lack of respect for management is the major reason for workers' getting into trouble and requiring discipline.

Once a worker disdains authority, the person seems to become committed to breaking company rules and challenging you. Such confrontation requires you to take disciplinary action.

Unfortunately, many plants have not found good ways to solve disciplinary problems. The threats of supervisory personnel to irresponsible employees frequently go unheeded, and rewarding the employees who meet or exceed standards of performance does not affect trouble-makers. To make matters worse, many supervisors dislike meting out discipline intensely.

Some supervisors feel that disciplining workers is the toughest part of their job. Yet if they use discipline properly, their job should be easier, not harder. It depends on how supervisors see the role they play. If you see yourself as a boss rather than a leader, you become a person who assigns jobs to your people; you rule by authority and you use discipline to enforce it.

But if you see yourself as a teacher or instructor, you become a guide. By indicating what behavior is desirable and what gets positive results, discipline becomes just a matter of correcting deviations.

Surprisingly, some plant employees appreciate discipline. They actually welcome it because it tells them how far they can go in ignoring the rules, and they learn how they must behave.

One explanation for irrational behavior of some employees is that the employees misbehave not from lack of respect for management, but from lack of self-respect. Workers who cannot accept their own weaknesses unconsciously blame their failures on their supervisors. With such situations, supervisors should take a more objective attitude toward their problem people.

Instead of feeling that you are being personally challenged, look upon these people as having personal problems of their own. Of course, this view still does not permit you to abstain from taking disciplinary action when it is called for.

You must recognize that failure to use discipline when it is called for promotes a breakdown in the department. If some employees see an individual getting away with behavior that is forbidden, they may try it too. At this time, you may have to make up for past lapses unless you are willing to give up control entirely.

You should explain the rules at the start so that workers know what is expected of them. Then, discipline is simply a matter of pointing out deviations.

Discipline is easier to apply if you mete it out in small doses. Given that way, it makes correction easier and avoids major confrontations. It also makes your job easier and your people feel more secure.

You are effective in your use of discipline when you consider the rights of employees. You reprimand in private and you know that irregular enforcement of the rules is a suitable defense for breaking one.

You never make an example of a one-time offender, especially when chronic violators of the rules escape from being disciplined. You feel that setting a trap whereby a situation is created to cause a breaking of a rule is an underhanded tactic and never deserving of discipline.

Guidelines for Using Positive Discipline

In recent years, several companies have recognized that there is a need for a better way of administering discipline to employees requiring it. The traditional ways (warnings, suspensions, and probation) have many disadvantages in that they tend to cause resentment, hostility, and ill feeling toward the company; in addition, they often do not bring about a desired change in the behavior of those disciplined.

Other weaknesses with so-called punitive discipline are that supervisors frequently hesitate to apply it, resulting in unresolved situations. Also, there are usually inconsistencies in its application, which bring on complaints of favoritism and unfairness.

Many plants have found that an alternative, more positive approach to administering discipline can bring about fewer disciplinary problems and terminations, better employee morale, and greater supervisory self-confidence in the system. The two basic differences between positive and punitive discipline are:

1. Early discipline steps with the positive system are oral and written reminders instead of warnings.
2. The adoption of a so-called "decision-making leave" (explained shortly) is the final disciplinary step with the positive system.

Both of these differences contribute to improved relations between management and employees.

Oral and written reminders, instead of warnings, tell employees the work and behavioral standards of the company and their responsibility for meeting them. Most employees like this approach for several reasons:

- It helps in communicating with their supervisor; supervisors talk to their people more frequently. Workers are not ignored and left to shift for themselves.
- Employees are treated like adults and as individuals. This boosts their morale and self-esteem.
- Supervisors talk *with* employees rather than *down* to them. Job levels are deemphasized.
- It is direct and clear. The procedure demonstrates that supervisors want to help employees rather than punish them for rule violations and poor performance.

The decision-making leave as the final disciplinary step makes a tremendous impact on employees. Instead of being suspended without pay for a varying number of days, the time off is only one day, with pay.

The paid decision-making leave is to be used by the employees to decide whether they can and will follow the rules of the company and do what is expected of them, or voluntarily quit. Employees are made aware that a failure to go along with any of the commitments may result in discharge.

The paid decision-making leave provides many benefits:

- It confirms the company's and the supervisor's sincere interest in seeing the employees solve their problems and remain productive members of the company.
- It reduces, if not eliminates, the anger, resentment, and desire for revenge that commonly follow an unpaid suspension.
- It is by far the least costly method of handling a serious disciplinary problem. The true cost of discipline is not in the cost of the day's pay, but in the feelings and actions of an angry individual who holds back on effort and output, infects others with resentment toward the supervisor and the company, and may try to "get even."

A not-to-be-overlooked benefit of positive discipline is the improved supervisor/employee relationship of the great majority of employees who are often forgotten; these are the steady, reliable, and good workers who never cause trouble or require counseling or discipline. When a company adopts the principles of positive discipline, supervisors pay at least equal attention to employees doing good work as to the few having performance, attendance, or behavioral problems. The increased "stroking" and commendation for work and jobs well done bring on more good performance, unasked-for productive contributions, and happy people who are satisfied with their work.

Although positive discipline will not correct every and all discipline problems, because some employees simply will never become useful and must eventually be discharged, it still provides a systematic procedure that provides many benefits and advantages to both employees and the company.

HOW TO HANDLE TEMPORARY AND PART-TIME PLANT EMPLOYEES

Two conditions exist to help you handle temporary and part-time employees:

1. Both you and the new workers have the same objective. You want them to do well because you know from their interviews they are the right person for the jobs. In addition, you sorely need them to fill temporary jobs or to assist in meeting seasonal increases in production quotas.
2. The new workers also want to make good. They've taken the jobs knowing that if they do well, they may become full-time employees or that they may be hired again sometime in the future.

It pays to take a few minutes before such employees arrive to plan and make a few preparations. Realize that temporary and part-time employees, no matter how experienced, will have some anxiety when they report to you on the first day. Just like new employees who are destined to be permanent and full-time, they will be wondering if their jobs will be difficult, whether they'll be able to get along with you, and whether they'll be accepted by other employees.

There are several good ways you can help persons with such concerns:

1. Review their résumés so that you'll remember their names, experience, and background.
2. Tell other workers about their coming and encourage a good reception.
3. Have orientation manuals and rules and regulations available to be handed out.
4. Check the workplaces and tools they will use to be sure everything they need is furnished.

The more you prepare for these employees, the better you'll be able to make them welcome and relieve the stress they'll undoubtedly feel the first day on the job. After you greet them, you'll probably spend some time talking about the company and the work procedures. But what you say isn't nearly as important as how you present yourself.

By all means, be friendly and sincere. You want these workers to be productive and cooperative. You want them to like their jobs and get satisfaction from their work. If they achieve these goals, they may become valuable additions to the company.

Because there are so many things that new employees have to learn, you may decide to make a list to help you remember them. Be sure you do the following:

- Take them on a short tour of the plant. Include their personal work areas, the department as a whole, restrooms, storerooms, and canteens. Point out emergency exits, fire extinguishers, and safety equipment.
- Introduce them to other workers, but keep this short. You primarily want to have them meet the persons they will be associating with and those whose jobs are similar to their own.
- Review what is expected of them on the job. Describe how their work will relate to that of others in the department, and explain the jobs of those persons with whom they will work most closely.
- Emphasize when they are to report for work and when they are to leave at the end of their work day. State the amount of time permitted for rest and coffee breaks, and mention the arrangement they may have to make with others concerning the lunch period.

It's a good idea to periodically visit temporary and part-time employees at their workplaces their first few days on the job. You will see for yourself how they are doing, and you can ask them if they have any questions or need any help. This is also a good time to assure them they are off to a good start and to tell them you feel confident they'll do well.

ADOPTING FLEXIBLE WORK HOURS AND JOB SHARING

A Conference Board study in 1990 revealed that flexible scheduling is on the increase in business and industry. Also known as flextime and gliding time, such programs consist of required "core" work hours with flexible hours either before or after. All employees must work during the core hours, usually 9 A.M. to 3 or 4 P.M. In the flexible period, employees may arrive and depart at times of their own choosing with the approval of their supervisors.

Companies surveyed said the major advantages of flexible work hour programs are they improve employee morale, decrease tardiness, and accommodate working parents. Major disadvantages include lack of supervision during all hours of work, the unavailability of key individuals at certain times, and difficult-to-plan work schedules.

The Conference Board study found a significant workforce trend to companies' desire for a two-tiered workforce. The first tier is made up of salaried employees who are accorded a relatively high degree of job security, perquisites, and benefits. This is the group eligible for the flexible schedules. The second group, the "contingent workforce," includes trained workers, many of whom are not on the company payroll, who are hired as contractors, temporaries, or casual part-timers.

As for other flexible job programs, there is also a trend today toward job sharing, a work program whereby more than one employee may share a single job. Some plants allow two or more part-time employees to share one full-time job with one employee working mornings and the other working afternoons. The majority of plants with job sharing give these employees the same fringe benefits as those available to other part-time employees.

HOW TO AVOID CHARGES OF DISCRIMINATION

While it is well known that you cannot discriminate against anyone because of color, race, religion, or sex, reverse discrimination that favors a minority person over a more able majority person is equally wrong. Simply stated, you need to take every precaution to avoid charges of discrimination in the treatment of all employees in the plant.

However, under no circumstances should you put up with incompetence or rule breaking to avoid discrimination charges. The best way to help workers who perform unsatisfactorily is to counsel them and give them a chance to meet standards. No one benefits if standards are lowered to make it easy to get along with poor performers. Here are some ways that will help you avoid charges of discrimination:

1. Set performance standards for workers and explain what you expect from them on the job.

2. Warn persons when they do below average work. If they cannot improve, try to find jobs for them that they can handle.

3. Watch workers for tendencies to bend the plant's rules and regulations. Remind them of indiscretions; treat everyone alike in this respect.

4. Offer a second chance after a poor performance. But do not be more lenient with either majority or minority workers.

5. Tie wage increases to performance, not to any other characteristic or behavior.

6. Keep records of performance on each worker. Also document discussions you have with persons about their performance.

7. Discuss serious nonperformance of a worker that could result in the individual's termination with the personnel department. Make sure your records are accurate, complete and dated.

Most workers are unhappy and dissatisfied on jobs they cannot handle. They usually will do and feel better on more suitable jobs; other co-workers will also benefit from such a change. Although you may risk a charge of discrimination now and then, it's a good move to rotate assignments and put workers on jobs where they will do their best. You are responsible for keeping up the efficiency and productivity of the persons who work for you.

HOW TO GET ALONG WITH THE PLANT'S STAFF PERSONNEL

You and other managers whose responsibilities are to see that things get done are considered as belonging to the *line* organization. Other company people who help you to decide what to do and how to do it, assist in coordinating the efforts of all employees, or provide service are considered as *staff* personnel. Each function, line or staff, contributes in its own way to the company, even though they compete with each other for credit and recognition.

Plant staff personnel are almost entirely dependent upon you and other supervisors for cooperation. If you are compatible and agreeable with these people, their jobs are made considerably easier. Management judges them by their success in getting your help and cooperation, and on how much you accept and act on their advice. You can be fairly sure that they'll help you look good on your job if you make them look good on theirs.

As you get to know some of them better, you'll recognize their professional nature. Professional people are different from other employees in that many of them feel they are highly skilled and knowledgeable; therefore, they resent any treatment that suggests they are thought of as ordinary workers. You should be aware that the key to getting along with them is to treat them as special people. Because many of them want to be recognized as members of a profession, they are often more career oriented than company oriented. So remember that their job titles are important to them and they are jealous of their own ideas and accomplishments.

UNDERSTANDING YOUNG PLANT EMPLOYEES

You may often find that your younger workers have different values and aspirations than your older ones. Supervising them may be frustrating until you discover what makes them tick. The difficult to understand workers are usually of two kinds:

1. Those under 25 who come to the plant with a bitter or prejudiced attitude toward business or what is called the establishment. Their distinguishing characteristics are a preoccupation with themselves as persons with unique prerogatives and a rejection of everything traditional.
2. The disadvantaged workers who are distrustful of the establishment's intent. They begin working with several handicaps, most of which are neither of their own choosing nor of their own making. Their distinguishing characteristics are a disbelief in the possibility that business will ever provide an honest opportunity for them to succeed, and a hopeless feeling that the odds are against their succeeding.

It is a mistake, however, to believe that young employees do not want to work. They want to hold a job and work provided they have the proper incentive, but the incentive isn't always financial. Social and economic changes have taken place that explain why young people today want more out of a job than just the pay. For one thing, they are better educated than their parents. For another, their aspiration levels are higher. They become bored more rapidly with routine work; thus they shun such work for that which is different and challenging.

GUIDELINES ON SUPERVISING YOUNG EMPLOYEES

Although it may seem to be a challenge to motivate some of your young employees and enable them to get satisfaction from their work, you should consider this one of your responsibilities. If you are an astute supervisor, you can use their values and aspirations to help them do a better job. Here are some guidelines on how to do this:

- Avoid placing young employees in extensive training programs. Since they want to be where the action is and to participate, move them along fast to get over such hurdles quickly.

- Don't expect most of your young employees to place a high value on the security of rigid job descriptions and standards unless they have played a part in developing such things.

- Try to give them big jobs and assignments to feed their egoes and maintain their interest. Show that you are confident that they can handle important projects.

- Recognize that young employees will not be motivated to go beyond what is expected of them unless the extra work and effort offer them some promise of personal recognition or growth.

- Don't be overly concerned if they occasionally make mistakes and fail to reach objectives. They have to lose a few times to know what success really means and to learn to accept failure.

HOW TO HANDLE THE EMPLOYEE WHO PREFERS TO WORK ALONE

In getting to know your workers, it's worthwhile for you to learn if a person is most suitably a "group" worker or a "loner." Such knowledge helps you in motivating the person, in deciding what are the best assignments for him or her, and in assessing the capabilities of your work crew.

Although many production operations are carried out by teams, and maintenance repairs often are performed by pairs of craftspersons, some employees prefer to work alone. Don't think of these individuals as being persons who want to be physically separated from others. While some are of this nature, most loners simply prefer not to interact with others or be team members. They want to be inconspicuous on the job.

You should accede to their desires, as much as company regulations and work situations will allow, to enable them to like their jobs and be productive. Promotional moves as well as transfers to other environments should be carefully thought out and discussed before being made. Loners may leave the company rather than make a change, even though the change may appear to be in their best interest.

2

Conveying Company Policy and Plant Procedures to Workers

UNDERSTANDING COMPANY POLICY

Company policy is an understanding among members of company that makes the actions of each member in a given set of circumstances more predictable to other members. Yet it is one of the most impersonal elements in any company.

Policy statements are usually limited in distribution to those people with an established need, but all employees should be able to locate any particular policy quickly. You should have a complete and current set of policy statements directly affecting your functions, and you also should have a member of management available to confirm that questionable decisions do not conflict with policy.

Although company policies usually originate with top management arising from a need of middle or lower management, they also may be implied from the actions of managers; in addition, they may be required to comply with trade associations or government agencies. Policies may apply to all departments of a company or only one, yet they are generally considered to be the company's most important decisions.

Policies may have limitations as well as faults. Lack of understanding of a policy is the greatest limitation on its effective use faced by a company and its management people. A given policy may be unsound in concept or incorrectly stated, thus hindering achievement of company objectives. The climate and environment of business operations may change calling for a policy change that is not made; left as it is, the original policy will be misleading and will inhibit effective planning and action.

If you get into the habit of referring to a company policy as the only reason for your action, you are using the policy as a crutch and defeating its intent. Although policies support and provide direction to the actions of all management people, if a policy remains in existence long after conditions have changed, it can impede progress. If policies are stated in broad and clear terms, they may tend to encourage managers to avoid responsibility for their own decisions.

Rigid adherence to policies often leads to unforeseen and unwanted consequences. People are different, one from another, and the situations they get into are seldom exactly alike. However, the person who originated the policy or made the rule had to assume that all the situations covered by that rule in the future would almost exactly duplicate the specific one he or she had in mind when framing it. This is why the rules found in policy manuals may sometimes seem unrealistic or impractical to the persons who are asked to follow them. A supervisor coming across such a rule might be heard to say, "I can see that whoever made that rule never worked as a supervisor."

Policy manuals can be of great help to you if the statements and guidelines are presented in terms of goals and objectives. Manuals should simply outline the ways and means that users should consider in managing. In this form, a policy manual would be looked upon as standard practice instructions designed to ensure consistency and uniformity in handling most standardizable work.

Guidelines for Critical Company Policy

Status in the community and the well-being of a company are closely related to a plant's ability to provide products that are not only useful, but durable, reliable, and dependable. There may even be a number of public laws that define a plant's obligations.

Product quality and safety are so important to customer relations and to a company's reputation that the company may create a department in the plant whose sole responsibility is to oversee those functions. One of its responsibilities is to monitor the company's performance and assure that it is always in compliance with the law and the company's quality standards.

In carrying out this responsibility, the department may periodically issue letters to officers and employees of the company stating the company's policy in specific areas. Typically, a letter may read as follows:

> No matter what your job is—salesperson or secretary, repairman or researcher, production worker or trainee—you share the responsibility of immediately reporting to your superior whenever you know, or even suspect, that a company product is unsafe or inferior.
>
> The rule of thumb is this: if you have only the slightest doubt, report it to your superior, who, in turn, has the responsibility of reporting the information to the Quality Control Manager having direct responsibility for the product in question. A safety-related defect is admittedly difficult to define. A generally accepted rule is that a product defect that creates a risk of injury to anyone is considered a safety-related defect.
>
> In all our relationships, we strive to act as responsible corporate citizens in matters of product quality and safety. You are directed to give complete dedication to this policy.

Evaluating and Promoting Company Policy

Since management and employees may not tell you directly what they think about company policies, you must read and interpret various sources of information to gain this knowledge. Here are a few matters you can attend to in this respect:

- Study performance appraisals to learn what other supervisors are saying about subordinates.
- Analyze grievance complaints to identify areas where policies and procedures are being tested.
- Review reports of training programs to tell you where there are weaknesses or deficiencies.
- Critique the feedback that the company received from outside consultants.

All of this feedback will help you evaluate existing policies and procedures and pinpoint areas which some day may become problems or at least require revision.

The ability to "sell" company policy is critical. By being an advocate of the policies, and showing employees precisely what they do to improve the company, you contribute to the company's success. Whether it be improved productivity, better quality, more job satisfaction, reduced stress, or smoother operations, all help the company's image in the community and enable it to grow.

HOW TO EXPLAIN COMPANY POLICY TO PLANT WORKERS

You as a supervisor are responsible for explaining and carrying out company policy. When all employees are aware of the company's practices and rules, and follow them, everyone goes in the right direction, workers cooperate with each other, and employees are well organized. Here is how you should explain company policy to your workers:

- Tell them that company policies are guides or broad rules that cover the company's objectives and how the plant is to be operated. The guides and rules are intended to help managers at all levels to get their jobs done.
- Point out that some policies are based on regulations that you must follow if you are to run the department in harmony with other departments in the plant.
- Say that the plant may have a policy to cover almost every important part of its operation, from how it purchases materials to how it gives employees vacation.
- Tell them that not all policies are written. But both employees and supervisors recognize that matters affected by such policies must be handled in a certain manner and usually do so.
- State that you set policy at the department level. The application of policy is your interpretation of how the broader company policy should be carried out for plant employees.

Tip: If you do a good job of convincing plant workers that you fully represent the management of the plant, your actions and company policy will be the same thing in their eyes. Of course, you will sometimes have to carry out policy that you don't completely agree with. Resist the temptation to criticize the policy to workers. When you do, you weaken your position.

HOW TO SELL CHANGE EASILY TO PLANT WORKERS

You can sell a change in the plant much more easily if you explain why it is needed. When you tell workers why a change is to be made, you help them to understand it. Besides, explaining strengthens your selling message. Here are some tips on selling change:

1. Don't announce all the details of a change at one time. Furnish only enough information so that the workers can see what you're thinking about, but not enough for them to put up a strong argument against it.

2. Start your selling program by talking to only one worker initially, and by giving that individual time to think before you bring up the subject again. Plant workers usually need time to adjust to a new idea before they will completely go along with it.

3. Observe a worker's reaction, particularly the person's body language, to see if you are getting agreement with what you're proposing. Feel your way if you sense resistance or opposition. Tactfully probe for what the worker does not agree with or thinks is wrong.

4. Listen carefully if a worker objects. Recognize that you may have to alter your idea, that it may not be perfect. Try to learn how you might improve it or make a different change so that it is more acceptable.

MAKING CHANGES EFFICIENTLY[1]

Making a change in a process or procedure doesn't have to be something you dread because of automatic complications, loss of production, and general frustration with the delays. You can avoid these if you plan for the change and then implement it in the most expeditious manner. Both steps require the cooperation of people, and you must pay close attention to details, but the benefits you derive are well worth the time you put into it.

Hold a special planning session in advance of making a change of any significance. Invite all the people who will be involved, including both management and staff. Attendees should discuss the procedures or steps that need to be taken in the changeover. Most important is that each step should be discussed *separately* with the objective of trying to foresee and solve as many problems as possible before actually making the change.

A negative approach sometimes works. With such thinking, you study every event or step that could go wrong and set up alternate procedures should this happen. Studies have shown that unforeseen delays result when the *possibility* of the failure of a step has been overlooked. It's better to adopt the "it could happen" viewpoint than to be smug and rule out any such eventuality.

Where employees will require new skills because of a change, it pays to formulate plans for acquiring those skills as soon as possible. Employees can then be trained just prior to the change. There are at least two advantages to such action:

1. Employees will accept the change better when the fear of not being able to learn the new procedure has been overcome with time to spare.

---

[1]Reprinted from *Foremanship*, Dec. 1, 1986, Dartnell, Chicago, IL 60640.

2. Unfamiliarity with the new procedure will not be a disrupting factor on "C-day."

By selecting a period of minimum activity in a process or procedure for making the change, you minimize the loss in production or output. Check the records to determine that period and make plans accordingly.

Some companies assign a special group, either employees or outsiders, to plan and carry out a changeover. With this procedure, people's capabilities can be utilized to the maximum resulting in a quick and less disruptive change. This is a good idea particularly where special skills may be involved in the changeover.

Before you undertake a complete shutdown of a system or process and perhaps suffer the consequences of lost production, disruption, or other frustrations, consider whether it's possible to set up a procedure of gradual phaseout of the old system and blending in of the new. In some cases, the end result may be the same as though a complete shutdown were taken but with the difference that losses and disruptions are held to a minimum.

The optimum time to build up an inventory or surplus of whatever is after the changeover is scheduled and the change period is near. This buildup should compensate for any loss during the changeover period.

When a changeover can be broken down into its elements, with each handled separately, you can simplify the entire operation. In some cases, disruption will be so minor that it is of little consequence. Thus, if examination of what is involved in a changeover reveals that you can perform the change in steps, by all means do so. Carrying this idea further, you may be able to handle a few of the steps independently and thus only the remaining steps may be a problem.

Sometimes it's possible to shift work loads to different areas while a change is being made. In addition to relieving the pressure of keeping productive facilities in operation, such moves also serve as "balancing" aids in day-to-day activities. The knowledge of their existence can be valuable to you when problems come up involving maintenance or equipment.

GUIDELINES ON INTRODUCING NEW PROCEDURES

If you are adept at introducing and selling new procedures, you can help your company by making a process or equipment change take place smoothly and easily. But you need to recognize that you'll be most effective if you introduce change in three steps:

1. *Preparing.* Employees will more readily accept change if they know it's coming. It's natural to fear change if you don't know what to expect. Choose the time to talk about a new procedure carefully, preferably when employees are fresh and relaxed.

Anticipate questions and objections that will come up and be ready to answer them. Handling objections before a new procedure is put into effect will make acceptance much easier and assure good results much sooner.

Provide the tools, materials, and supplies that will be needed and work out transportation and storage details. Consider what skills and techniques must be learned by workers and arrange for training if this is needed.

2. *Explaining*. When everything is ready, explain the new procedure step by step. It is easier for workers to learn one thing at a time. Take plenty of time to define and clarify new terms and operations as they come up. Give a reason for each new step; reasons help workers to understand why something is necessary. Encourage questions by pausing periodically to ask if what you have said is clear.

Keep your explanation on your listener's level of understanding. Be aware that backgrounds and knowledge vary in terms of education and training. Use charts, diagrams and flow sheets if they will clarify matters and aid understanding.

Connect and relate the new procedure with the old as much as possible. This gives workers a base on which to build. Also, try to simplify your explanation. The simpler you can present a new method, the more readily it will be understood. Expect some steps that are clear to you to be hard for others to quickly pick up.

3. *Promoting*. You can promote and sell a new procedure most easily by pointing out its advantages over the procedure it replaces. But you should also stress increases in productivity, the ease of doing the job, reduced boredom, and more enjoyable work. However, it is wise to delay setting standards of work output for at least several days. Some workers take longer than others to get used to the new procedure.

Avoid high-pressure tactics when promoting something. They can cause friction and resentment. They certainly will not help to gain acceptance. Also, don't say that you expect increased productivity immediately. This puts persons "under the gun" to learn the new procedure quickly and accomplish more than they are accustomed to do. Your own attitude of confidence in the new procedure, shown right from the start, will help to bring about its overall acceptance.

TECHNIQUES FOR IMPROVING COMMUNICATIONS

Today's plants could not operate efficiently or productively without continual communication between management and employees. Both downward and upward communications are required for a smoothly functioning organization to maintain operations and be profitable.

Verbal communications include information and instructions, meetings, and announcements via the plant's intracommunications system. Written communications are disseminated through operating procedures, specifications, plant regulations, bulletin board notices, safety and other handbooks, and the company newspaper.

Communicating with Your Staff

To communicate effectively with your subordinates, keep in mind the following criteria:

1. *Be specific and straightforward.* If an order or instruction isn't meant to be followed, it shouldn't be given. If it is important enough to be issued, it should be enforced.

2. *Be consistent.* You can't vacillate one day and be stubborn the next. If you are easygoing one time and tough another, you cause uncertainty and anxiety among the people who work for you.

3. *Don't give conflicting instructions.* Telling an individual to do something that isn't standard practice or is against plant rules can get you and the individual into real trouble. The same advice applies to telling one person to do a job a certain way and the next person a different way.

4. *Temper your instructions with reason and practicality.* Giving too many instructions or too many details at one time confuses people. Limit your orders and make them short and to the point.

5. *Be complete.* The type, amount, and completeness of information and instructions that you provide workers greatly determine their safety on the job, the quality of their workmanship, and the extent of their productivity.

How to Promote Upward Communication from Your Staff

Your job as a supervisor is much easier if your workers keep you informed. You will have information and data that will help you make decisions, and you will be able to foresee problems that could arise. For these and other reasons, it is to your advantage to promote upward communication from your workers at every opportunity. Here are some steps you can take that will achieve it:

- *Be available and receptive to persons who want to talk.* Listen to all your workers' ideas regardless of how illogical or impractical they may sound. If you suspect that passing a worker's good idea up the line will somehow reflect poorly on you for not having thought of it yourself, dispel that notion.

- *Develop informal relations with workers.* As you walk around the plant, make contact with workers, either singly or in small groups. Take these opportunities to find out what individuals are thinking. You may decide, however, to treat what you learn with confidentiality if you want to pass such information upward.

- *Recognize all contributions with feedback.* Workers appreciate their bosses telling them that their ideas were discussed in management meetings. Also, always thank workers for their suggestions, whether or not they are adopted.

GUIDELINES FOR SELLING SUGGESTION SYSTEMS IN THE PLANT

Every plant should have a suggestion system if for no other reason than to raise the productivity of its employees. The most common system found in plants is one in which employees write their ideas on a printed form and put them into a suggestion box. Each suggestion is reviewed by a committee, and, if it is accepted, the employee is given a cash award or a percentage of the cost savings for a fixed period.

To raise productivity, you've got to promote efficiency and be cost conscious of all the operations and services your workers perform. The best way to do this is to ask your workers to think of better ways to do their jobs. Here is what you should do to sell them on submitting suggestions:

- Start by explaining the company's interest in suggestions from employees. Suggestions from workers help to increase safety, reduce costs, and make work easier to perform.

- Point out some of the problem areas where improvements are needed. Talk about the need to reduce waste, eliminate a bottleneck, and simplify some of the process steps.

- Raise enthusiasm by mentioning the awards that are made for good suggestions. Tell workers that they have a lot to gain with nothing to lose by participating.

- Say that you're available to answer questions and to help anyone in writing up suggestions.

You should, however, be aware of a caution concerning suggestions. When you promote them, be sure you make it clear that turning in suggestions is an entirely voluntary matter. Suggestions are not a requirement of the job, nor are you telling people that they should be submitted. Some workers are more likely to participate when you discuss the subject this way. Also, you avoid any arguments that may arise concerning pay for time spent developing an idea on nonworking time.

HOW TO MAKE SURE YOU'RE UNDERSTOOD[2]

One of the requisites of being a good communicator is having your message understood. You might just as well not say anything if your listeners misinterpret your words. Worse, not being understood can result in workers making errors or in their simply not doing a job.

Fortunately, there are a variety of ways that you can determine if you've communicated well and your instructions have been understood. It pays to use most if not all of them to verify that workers understand you before they start carrying out your orders to start work on a hazardous, major or complex job. Here are the ways to do that:

- *Ask them if they understand.* Although this is the most frequently used method, it is not the best. Few workers feel comfortable in admitting they do not understand directions given by their boss. As a result, the positive shake-of-the-head response to "Do you understand?" has gotten more supervisors in trouble than any other response. What has happened is that instructions have been carried out incorrectly or not at all. Except for workers you have directed a long time or in low-risk situations, you are better off with another way.

- *Have them repeat your directions.* Don't be concerned that they will think you don't trust them. This may be true only if you use the method with every little direction you give. It is a good procedure if used sparingly, especially when communication is vital such as when safety is at stake.

- *Ask them about key points.* Effective carrying out of instructions often hinges on a key step or point. Rather than have all your instructions repeated, it's more practical as well as effective to ask only about the key point. For example, if you've given a lot of directions to a worker on the completion of a plant cleanup project, ask the worker only to confirm the date you said the job should be finished.

- *Ask a question about a procedure.* How well a worker understands how a job is to be done can be demonstrated by what steps the person intends to take to do it. Rather than focusing directly on the decision to get the job done, determine the extent of understanding from the worker's plan of action. A side benefit from this method is that the worker will feel more "in" on the project when he or she explains his or her intentions.

[2]W. H. Weiss, "Make Sure You're Understood," *Foremanship*, June 18, 1984, Dartnell, Chicago, IL 60640.

- *Have them paraphrase your directions.* By having workers feed back your directions in *their* words, you can check for accuracy and understanding. In addition, ownership of the job is increased when workers put it in their own words. The only problem with this method is that it is not natural to restate in another form someone else's words. If you have many situations where accurate communications are required, it may be worthwhile to train persons to paraphrase because it is probably the most accurate verification technique.

- *Have them explain your directions to someone else.* This method of communicating is appropriate when more than one worker is involved in carrying out an instruction. You can listen to the explanation and add encouragement if it is correct. Should the worker doing the explaining leave out something important, you can add it. By having one employee explain to another, both become more involved. Not only that, but the chance to share directions with their words may strengthen commitment to do the job.

You may wonder if employees will become suspicious if you start using one of these methods of communicating, especially if you adopt one or more every time you give directions. The answer to this is to introduce them slowly and in the proper situations. When used cautiously and correctly, few employees will become concerned or disturbed. You may find that as you begin to favor verification methods, workers will begin to use them also. This will improve communications among all the employees in your department.

How to Write Memos

Although you may prefer to minimize the amount of paperwork you must handle in carrying out your responsibilities as a supervisor, don't let this feeling deter you from writing memos.

There are many times in supervising plant operations that you should write a memo. You should communicate policies and procedures to your staff by memo—to be sure that each employee has a written record. You may also want to report an unusual incident, point out a condition that should be corrected, or comment on a statement by one of your staff.

Memos should be avoided if you're angry about something. That's one time when you don't want to go on record because you'll sound irrational or overly emotional.

Even if you feel you're an experienced memo writer, the following tips could make you a better one:

- Make sure your memos match the style and tone of others written in the plant. Some plants have special forms for memos while others indicate how memos should be structured. By all means, follow them.

- Keep your memos short and to the point. Shorter memos have more impact. Don't try to cover every detail. Also, limit a memo to just one subject.

- Keep them simple. Before writing them, organize your thoughts. Decide what you want to say, and how you want to say it. Avoid awkward language.

- Be factual. Provide figures, if possible, and examples of what you are saying. Make your memo sound unbiased and unprejudiced.

- Be careful about stepping on people's toes. Check your words to be sure they aren't offensive, abusive, or fault-finding.

- Avoid writing self-serving memos. They become rather obvious after a while, and may try the patience of your readers. Some superiors may even feel that you shouldn't have written them.

- Limit the distribution of a memo. Think carefully about who should receive it.

- Keep copies of all memos you write. The permanent record potential of a memo is no good if you don't exercise it.

Developing Your Communication Style[3]

Workers need to know what is expected of them if they are to perform their jobs safely and efficiently. The burden of having them understand instructions and directions is with their supervisors. This is why it is so important that you be a good communicator.

The words you use in giving orders may be the difference between understanding and not understanding. How you say something and the conditions under which you say it also contribute to your message. In many situations, body language may have more meaning than the words you say.

In both formal and informal communication situations, you run the risk of being misunderstood because of a poor choice of a word or combination of words. Since there are so many words in our language and each one may have several meanings, you cannot hope to master all of them.

What you must do is try to know the common meanings of most of our often-used words. Just about every supervisor has overheard two people arguing over a point expressing their ideas in different words while they are really saying the same thing. Because the speakers place different meanings on various words, they feel only disagreement.

---

[3]"Gaining Understanding From Your People," W. H. Weiss, *Successful Supervisor*, Sept. 2, 1983, Dartnell, Chicago, IL 60640.

How to Effectively Communicate with Plant Workers

The proper use of language is a measure of your training, maturity, and egotism. It's also a measure of your interest in your listener. To be a good communicator, you must:

1. Combine the expectations of the person listening with the requirements of the orders and instructions you give. To achieve this goal, you must be a good observer.
2. Note your listener's reaction to your words. If you get too absorbed in what you're saying, you risk becoming boring. This is true whether you're giving instructions to one of your workers or talking about an on-the-job problem with another.
3. Pause now and then to let your words sink in and to give your listener a chance to comment. Pausing helps in assuring that you are getting through.
4. Maintain your composure regardless of the situation. You'll do a better job of communicating by not being moody, irritable, or easily upset.
5. Recognize that workers dislike questioning and will often say they understand when they don't rather than risk an emotional response.
6. Discount some of what is said by a worker who is clearly angry. To get a better idea of how the angry person really feels, bring up the subject again when he or she has calmed down.

In addition, you should be familiar with the nonverbal ways that workers communicate their thoughts and feelings. For example, when a person drums his or her fingers as you talk, he or she is impatient. The person may want to say something, may wish you'd get to the point, or may just wish you'd finish talking and leave. A worker who frowns is either puzzled by what you're saying, expected to hear something else, or doesn't like what he or she is hearing.

You may learn a great deal if you watch worker's eyes. Their eyes involuntarily express pleasure, displeasure, inquisitiveness, boredom, understanding, or bewilderment. By being alert to catch these nonverbal ways that workers communicate, you can better understand their words. More important, you can tell whether you are getting through with your message.

Tips on Using Nonverbal Communication Techniques[4]

Skill in reading nonverbal cues delivered by workers during a conversation or meeting will help you to be a more successful manager and communi-

---

[4]T. R. Weiss, "Utilizing Nonverbal Communication Techniques," *Successful Supervisor*, May 15, 1989, Dartnell, Chicago, IL 60640.

cator. Among the benefits gained from learning to read so-called "body language" is the growing sensitivity you gain in understanding the many needs of those you supervise.

To understand nonverbal communicating is essentially to recognize and interpret the meaning and significance of body movements, gestures, and facial expression. It's also necessary to see and comprehend the distances workers will keep between themselves and others as well as to know who is sensitive to touch. There are those who want to touch and those who want to stay away.

What some workers do with their hands, for example, is considered especially revealing. Aggressive individuals often will wave them about, using this way to show interest and enthusiasm for what they are saying. Reserved, meek, and shy persons seldom do more than raise a hand or point a finger when speaking.

There are those who use their hands to describe something in particular, using cutting and hacking motions when they converse on most any subject. In contrast, others use their hands only to emphasize words.

Nodding is another common way of communicating nonverbally. When you are speaking and your listener nods, you are encouraged to continue talking and to expand on a subject. However, if your listener shakes his or her head, you may lose confidence in what you are saying or be distracted. Thus a nod is usually a sign of agreement. As a supervisor, you may want to use the nod to encourage workers when they are talking.

The nervous habits of some workers in the plant confirm that they are concerned or worried about something, although they may also be impatient. They show their uneasiness by tapping their fingers, squinting, adjusting their eyeglasses, and pulling on their ears.

Other gestures portray various feelings. For example:

- Big smiles and hearty handshakes depict jubilance; you may soon hear some good news if someone greets you in this manner.

- Frowns, downcast eyes, and drooping shoulders tell you that a worker is either displeased or discouraged; so prepare yourself to hear a sad story. If you suspect you know the problem, start thinking about how you can perk up or console the person. A kind word or a pat on the back may do it.

Touch plays a big role in nonverbal communication because it tells you if someone is tense or relaxed. You may want to touch one of your workers to show that you appreciate what he or she has done or to assure the person. A simple clasp of the worker's hand or the placing of your hand on his or her shoulder will do this. Although some supervisors prefer not to touch someone for fear the person will withdraw or be annoyed, touching, if done gently and casually, carries with it your personal approval.

When workers move about, they often tell others nonverbally what space around them they feel belongs to them. Whether or not they do this intentionally, the message they send out is usually clear: "Don't you dare get any closer." It follows that how close you can stand to a person often is a measure of your friendship or how well you know the person. However, well-mannered persons seldom encroach on someone else's space.

In the plant, you may use a desk to keep individuals at a distance. But if you wish to establish rapport with workers, talk to them while you are standing or meet them at their workplace. Still, don't be surprised if you find that some will try to keep their distance by taking a step or two backwards. Territory or personal space is rigorously observed, especially if they don't want to appear too forward.

HOW TO ISSUE PLANT OPERATING SPECIFICATIONS AND GET WORKERS TO IMPLEMENT THEM

To assure that processes and operations in the plant are carried out safely, efficiently, and productively, management must issue a collection of standardized procedures for all employees. In many plants, these are known as *plant operating specifications*. The procedures are written as a description of the machines and equipment and include instructions on how to operate them. This enables the workers to know what is to be done and how to do it.

Verbal instructions on procedures are inadequate because they are too easily confused, misinterpreted, or forgotten altogether. Besides, there is a need for keeping the procedures up to date. Process methods, machines and equipment, and step sequences undergo change with time. Revisions will be necessary—issue revisions at the same time as the changes requiring them.

The best way to get workers to implement operating specifications is to base their training on them:

1. Use the operating specification in explaining the step-by-step procedure.
2. Call attention to critical steps and to any limitations or tolerances.
3. Demonstrate by performing the operation yourself.
4. Allow the worker to practice the operation.
5. Follow up later to see that the workers are performing the operation according to specifications.

OVERCOMING BARRIERS TO EFFECTIVE COMMUNICATIONS IN THE PLANT

To be a successful supervisor, you must be an effective communicator, but becoming one is not always easy. Those who have succeeded have overcome the barriers that prevent workers from understanding them and from being fully informed.

Communications within many plants today could be much improved. Not only do workers fail to always understand their supervisors, they also are sometimes not told everything they need to do their work. Some supervisors seem unable to get their messages across.

A weakness in human relations skills on your part is one barrier. Others can be traced to bias and prejudice that creep into your messages. Some can be attributed to your personal style and manner of communicating. Whatever the reason, you should recognize that such barriers exist and that they prevent you from doing a good job of communicating. Three barriers in particular deserve your attention:

1. *Considering the listener.* Communicating is much easier if you reckon with your listeners. Consider the experience and knowledge of your listeners in choosing the words to be said. You must also beware of being indifferent. Persistence and patience may be required to get your message across.

   You must realize that your people will not always respond to your messages no matter how clear you make them if you disregard their thoughts and feelings. Never use your authority to give orders that are unfair or that infringe on an individual's personal rights.

   You should also be aware that the same words may mean different things to different people, and that the same idea can be stated in different words. We express ourselves in our own ways for several reasons. Our backgrounds and education vary. Our training and experience determine the words we use and the meanings we attach to them. Under such circumstances, it's really a wonder that we don't have more misunderstandings.

2. *Giving information.* Managers sometimes withhold information from subordinates, thus hindering them from carrying out their job responsibilities. Right or wrong, they do this with the pretense that subordinates will learn better if they are required to dig out facts for themselves.

   But managers may not communicate fully for other reasons. Managers who feel they are going to move up in the company may willingly communicate upward but not so willingly downward. This is often an attempt to gain power and command admiration.

   Contrarily, the managers who feel they have reached their peak in the company may freely communicate downward. They realize they must work closely with others in order to remain where they are and not drop lower in position. At the same time, they are not eager to communicate upward because they feel they have nothing to gain by doing so.

   Misleading or inadequate communicating can sometimes be attributed to psychological factors. Fear, for example, can be a deterrent—fear of being criticized, disciplined, or denied promotion. Fear of displeasing a superior may be enough to cause information to be presented in an understated form or covered up completely.

3. *Calling on higher authority.* Using the name of a higher authority for leverage is a weak way to request that something be done. If you resort to such tactics, you show that you don't have enough confidence in your own authority, and must use that of a person whose name carries greater weight.

    For instance, you should support management decisions on policy when communicating with workers. When you give orders to them, word the orders in a manner as though the policy were yours, even though you may not be fully in agreement with the action to be taken.

    Handle your requests for information similarly. Avoid the unauthorative way, "The Boss wants to know . . . ." Obtain the information for the boss without using the boss' words and position as a means.

3

Techniques for Effective Training and Instructing Manufacturing Plant Workers

HOW TO DETERMINE EMPLOYEE TRAINING NEEDS

Plants of all sizes are placing increasing emphasis today on training and retraining their employees. The American Society for Training and Development (ASTD) has stated there currently is a workforce crisis because more than 4 in 10 U.S. workers are not trained for the demands of their jobs.[1] Contrasting U.S. technology advances with its training efforts, the ASTD believes that "the result is an enormous lack of competitive muscle."

In many plants, the responsibility for creating and conducting formal training programs is assigned to the Personnel Department. Depending on the size and type of company and its training resources, formal training may be given to employees by an in-plant training staff, first-line managers, or outside service organizations. Regardless of which is selected, it is essential that you establish the scope and purpose of a training program for

[1]Reported in *Modern Materials Handling*, January, Cahners Publishing Company, 1991, p. 7.

your workers at the start to ensure that the training is carried out successfully.

The need for training plant employees arises from two situations: either the employees' performance is not adequate or satisfactory for the job requirements, or the employees are not capable of performing the future requirements of the job. You have several sources of information available to you to determine employees' training needs:

- *Have your workers fill out questionnaires.* Ask them to respond to a training needs checklist or tell you what type of training they need.
- *Make personal observations.* Examine workers' performance over a period of time. Your observations should be both random and frequent in order to be accurate.
- *Review performance appraisal data.* Check the forms on which you or other managers have indicated the training needs of specific workers.
- *Test the workers' skills.* Develop and administer tests on workers' skills and abilities to identify their strengths and weaknesses.
- *Study exit interviews.* Determine if poor performance was the reason for an exit; you may uncover a training need that was not met.

ESTIMATING THE COST OF UNTRAINED WORKERS

A few years ago, Fischer & Porter Co., a manufacturer of valves, controllers, and recorders, wanted to promote its training programs to industry. One of their selling points consisted of listing what an untrained worker in a plant cost a company. The performance of the worker on the amount of lost time incurred in one day read as follows:

• Work habits. Worker left tool box in shop.	15 minutes
• Premature failure of equipment. Pump bearings burned out twice in two weeks; overtightening by worker was the cause.	30 minutes
• Correction of errors. Worker installed incorrect part in recorder.	10 minutes
• Time spent finding help. Valve operator was disassembled but worker was unable to reassemble.	10 minutes
• Miscellaneous lost time. Worker was unable to find adjustments on controller.	20 minutes
Total time lost/day	85 minutes

Translating these incidents to weekly cost:

Cost of the untrained worker/week = $(^{85}\!/_{60} \times 5) \times \$20/\text{hour} = \$140$

Although this may appear to be insignificant, the actual cost to the plant in lost production time is much more costly, depending on the particular process and output of the plant.

Tip: Training is a one-time expense that can reduce or remove the recurring problem of lost time.

WAYS TO GET PLANT WORKERS TO WANT TO LEARN

You can use several techniques to motivate workers to learn:

1. Show them that the information and training being presented are relevant to their work. It will benefit them in making their jobs safer and easier to perform.
2. Point out that the training is interesting and stimulating. Assure them that they will not be bored and that they will get more satisfaction from doing their work effectively and efficiently.
3. Give them rewards based on how quickly and completely they learn. The rewards depend on the individuals as to their effectiveness. Research shows that slow learners respond to praise and encouragement best, or to small monetary rewards for good performance. On the other hand, superior learners often respond better to mild reproof for unsatisfactory performance, rather than praise for good performance.
4. Set goals they can achieve only by taking the training. Although competition may be very positive, the trainee who learns fastest and most completely will need no other reward than being the best.

How to Sell Plant Workers on Training

Even though you are aware of the many benefits the company gains by having trained workers in the plant, such is not always the case with some workers. You may have to conduct an extensive selling program to convince them of the advantages of being trained. Here are some ways to do it.[2]

- Tell them that trained individuals are more likely to succeed in their current jobs and in their careers. Provide proof of this by referring to one or more of the managers in the plant.
- Point out that trained workers are more self-reliant and self-confident. They will be more at ease on the job and enjoy their work.

[2]Louis V. Imundo, *The Effective Supervisor's Handbook*, (New York: AMACOM 1980).

- Assure them that trained employees usually are more conscientious workers and take more pride in what they do. Insecure and unconscientious employees often try to protect themselves by hiding their own insecurities and inefficiencies.

- Mention that trained employees have more job security, opportunities for advancement, and a higher probability for wage increases.

HOW TO DEVELOP PLANT TRAINING PROGRAMS

In the development of a sound training program, it is essential that you take three basic steps:

1. *Determine and define the objectives of the program.* State what the trainee should be able to accomplish after the training is completed. Remember that an important objective of training is being able to perform a task safely, not just knowing how to do it.

2. *Establish the program content.* The content consists of the information, know-how, or experience that the worker needs to gain in order to perform the job safely and efficiently. For example, if the objective includes operating a band saw without injury, one element of the training program must be how to operate a band saw safely. Another element must be how to use the equipment efficiently.

3. *Select the instructional procedures to be used.* While you may have a choice of several procedures, the one you select should effectively tell and show the worker what to do. It should also motivate him or her to adopt this procedure in performing the job.

Meeting Three Objectives in Training Plant Workers

Regardless of the type of training you give workers, you must meet three objectives if you are to train and develop them successfully:

1. Give them the information, facts, and ideas to enable them to see what it is they must do and why it must be done. When workers understand more than how to do a job, they are better able to handle nonroutine problems. They are also better able to adopt the methods and procedures that improve their job performance.

2. Teach and instruct them in the technical skills, such as tool and equipment operation, so that they can perform jobs safely, proficiently, and efficiently.

3. Help them to acquire and maintain proper attitudes toward their jobs, the work, and the company. The right attitudes are conveyed and established not just by what you say, but also by what you do. The more

interest you show in your workers, the easier it will be for you to motivate them to think positively and optimistically.

Four Ways to Evaluate Plant Training Programs

All plant training programs should be periodically evaluated to ascertain if the programs as they are presented satisfy the needs of the workers being trained. Even if an evaluation does not indicate that a program should be changed, you should continue to evaluate it from time to time to assure that the original objective is being achieved. There are four ways you can evaluate a training program:

1. Have the trainees fill out questionnaires. These are good for learning the general feelings of workers about a program's adequacy and appropriateness.
2. Obtain verbal feedback from the trainees. While this direct response is of value, it does have a drawback; it may be slanted because some trainees may be reluctant to say that the program is of no value or that it does not meet their needs.
3. Give before-and-after tests. Such tests reveal the extent of learning that resulted from completing a program.
4. Make workplace studies. They should consist of determining the training program's effect on productivity, amount of waste created, number of accidents, and number of errors made.

EFFECTIVE TRAINING METHODS AND HOW TO USE THEM IN THE PLANT

Although you have many methods by which you can train plant workers, the ones you use must be those that would best enable you to meet your objectives. If, for example, the purpose of a program is to train employees to operate complex machinery, hands-on or demonstration methods are better than study assignments or classroom lectures. Following are the most common methods used in manufacturing plants:[3]

- *On-the-job training.* With this method, you teach trainees job skills while they are working on the job.

Tip: To avoid problems with this method, you should be compatible with the trainee in personality and background. Specific work procedures should

---

[3]Marc A. Dorio, "How to Establish and Evaluate Employee Training Programs," in *Personnel Manager's Desk Book* (Englewood Cliffs, NJ: Prentice-Hall, 1989).

be understood beforehand, and adequate time made available for the training.

- *Study and reading assignments*. Ask the trainee to read articles, manuals, and instructions. Follow up by giving the trainee oral or written tests to confirm that the assignments were completed and understood.

Tip: You must research and come up with appropriate assignments to make this method work. In addition, you need to make sure that the trainee is aware of the objectives.

- *Programmed instruction*. This method involves self-instruction in which the trainee studies a sequence of designed steps. The procedure enables a trainee to gain the knowledge or skills related to the instructional objectives of the program. The method also requires that a trainee be able to read at the level required for full understanding.

Tip: You must know the programmed material well so that you can assist the trainee at any point in the sequence steps. In addition, you should be able to motivate a trainee to complete the program.

- *Case studies*. This training method involves group discussions of the real-life plant situations described in the cases.

Tip: The more closely cases are connected to the plant, the greater the trainee's interest and participation. You must also carefully control discussions to assure that all trainees get a chance to express their thoughts.

- *Tutoring*. You provide individualized training with this method.

Tip: You must be able to provide selective training based on the trainee's needs. In addition, you should be skilled in diagnosing and correcting learning problems.

- *Role Playing*. This method requires a trainee to act out a real-life situation in which the person plays a role you assign. Thus, it gets the trainee quickly involved in the learning process.

Tip: You should pick a role-playing situation related to the job of the trainee to help the person get into the role. In addition, you should supply feedback and play up the learning from the experience.

GUIDELINES ON USING VIDEOS TO TRAIN PLANT WORKERS

Videotape technology has been a real boon to supervisors for training workers in recent years. Many high-quality videos are available; they have been made by professionals in several fields of industry and manufacturing, and they cover numerous subjects. What makes them so popular as training tools is that they are easy to use and flexible. A tape may be used with a group as large as 20 trainees or on a one-on-one basis.

Videotapes can complement your training program in a variety of ways. They can:

- Present information and data clearly, quickly, and in an interesting manner.
- Hold the attention of trainees almost as well as an instructor or trainer.
- Illustrate subjects that are difficult to understand, and show processes that are too dangerous to view live.
- Demonstrate correct and incorrect procedures.
- Motivate workers and change their attitudes.

Even the most effective videotapes, however, aren't complete in their training capabilities. For example, a video can't depict each and every situation experienced by each worker. Nor can it answer every question that can come to the mind of a trainee. Thus, videotapes can't replace good instructors.

Tip: You can get the most out of this training tool by preparing trainees to view a tape and discussing it with them after it has been shown.

Determining How Much You Should Teach Plant Workers at One Time

You'll do a better job of training if you consider a few factors when determining how much you want to teach your workers at one time:

1. *The type of job to be taught.* Teach jobs in their entirety if they are short and simple, or if they involve highly related operations that fit together in a definite sequence. Teach jobs partially if they are long and complex, or if they involve loosely related operations that can be performed independently.
2. *The learning conditions.* Conditions are best for teaching a job in its entirety when the material to be taught is challenging rather than boring, but not so difficult to cause learning problems.

3. *The capabilities of the workers.* Fast learners do better when you teach the entire job at one time. Slow learners do better when you break the job down into several steps and spread it out over more than one session.

POSITIVE WAYS TO TRAIN THE SLOW LEARNER

If you see that a worker is a slow learner, coaching is an appropriate course to follow. It provides an approach for taking immediate action to solve the problem. With coaching, you discuss the situation with the worker and provide personal instruction. Following are the positive steps to take when coaching:

1. *Be honest with the worker, but don't destroy the person's self-image.* What you say can bear on how effective your coaching will be in improving and speeding up the learning process.
2. *Don't say, "Why is it taking so long for you to get this?"* Instead, tell the worker that some individuals find this particular job skill difficult to learn. Ask if the worker has any suggestions for possible answers. This approach cuts the potential for excuses from the worker. It also focuses on the problem, not the worker.
3. *Listen carefully to the worker's ideas and suggestions.* Faster learning and better performance is more likely to occur if you can get the worker involved. Further, you may discover that the cause of the slow learning is beyond the worker's control.
4. *Make sure that the worker accepts the training objectives.* Repeat what they are before ending your conversation with him or her.
5. *Follow up on what you and the worker agreed to do.* This should include setting a deadline by which you expect the worker to have corrected the problem.

Tip: Recognize that coaching a slow learner involves criticism. Use it sparingly and carefully. You do not want to cause the worker to develop a negative work attitude. The key is to keep emotions out of your coaching.

HOW TO SUPERVISE INEXPERIENCED PLANT WORKERS

To effectively supervise inexperienced plant workers, you must first see that they receive training on the task involved. In a manufacturing plant where job skills are very important, you must provide training in both safety and productivity.

Although the training in most cases must be highly specific, it may involve the process of learning something in one situation and then transferring the learning to another situation. Thus, learning can be transferred from the classroom to the job or from one job to the next. To get started on training:

1. *Check that the training situation is similar to the job.* If you're going to train a worker on how to operate a machine, for example, use the material involved and the machine controls that the worker must operate.

2. *Motivate the worker to want to learn.* Generally, slow learners respond to praise and encouragement best. Superior learners often respond better to mild reproof for unsatisfactory performance, rather than praise for good performance.

3. *Explain the theory and operating principles of the machine.* Point out its components and say how they function. Describe the procedure that enables the worker to get the desired results.

4. *Make sure the basic tasks are learned and understood.* Give the worker time to become familiar with the machine and learn its capabilities.

5. *Provide feedback as guidance in both learning the operation and developing skills.* Continuous feedback throughout training is essential to ensure that the worker knows the safety rules and masters the necessary skills.

6. *Direct the worker to the right procedure.* Catch and correct a wrong act, such as the violation of a safety rule or an incorrect operation of a machine control, before the act becomes established through repetition.

7. *Encourage workers and give them sufficient time to practice.* Don't assume that the combined basic tasks require less practice, or that time on the job will provide additional practice. Doing the job without supervision doesn't supply the opportunity for feedback.

HOW TO MAKE SOUND WORK ASSIGNMENTS

Even enthusiastic and well-trained plant workers need guidance if they are to be productive and do good work. When you are skilled in giving instructions and making sound work assignments, you can expect jobs to be handled willingly, promptly, and correctly. Here are some guidelines on how to go about it:

1. Decide beforehand whom you are going to assign a specific job and plan how you're going to explain it to the worker. Determine how the job should be done, and check to see if materials and tools are available.

2. Promote receptiveness for your instructions with a friendly approach and by considering the timing; one time may be poor while another more appropriate. Ask a question to determine the worker's attitude

and emotional state. Knowing this helps in choosing your tone and what words to use.

3. Give clear and specific instructions. Use simple words and talk at a speed that gives your listener time to understand. If the assignment is complicated and long, break it up into small steps and put them in logical order. Be consistent: If you call something by a certain name at one time, use the same name when you refer to it later.

4. Tell a worker the *right* way to do a job rather than *not* to do it the *wrong* way. You are more convincing and persuasive when you instruct positively because what you say is more credible and authoritative. Positive instructions are more readily accepted than negative ones.

5. Talk about ideas. Ideas make assignments more interesting. They also cause workers to think, thus aiding understanding and promoting acceptability. Ask for a worker's opinion. When you do this, you appeal to the worker's knowledge and judgment, making the person feel appreciated.

6. Let workers know what's in it for them by pointing out benefits. Do this by mentioning their benefits and the company's in the same statement. For example, tell workers they will be safer, the quality of the product will be better, and the work will be easier if they use the right tools. Listing benefits results in better attitudes, more cooperation, and higher productivity.

7. Give instructions with a smile instead of a frown. Show that you are confident your assignment is clear and can be safely carried out. Indicate that you know a worker has the capability and wants to do the job.

TIPS ON TRAINING MACHINE OPERATORS

An excellent way to start training a worker to operate a machine in the plant is to use a model. Although modeling is not necessary for learning, it makes learning easier. To use the model method, you may:

- Demonstrate yourself how workers are to operate the machine.
- Have the workers observe another employee performing the job.
- Show the workers a film or videotape of the operation.

When training workers to operate machines, give them lots of opportunities to practice. Plant workers generally learn best by doing. Most workers must practice to develop a skill and some skills are developed slowly. Since the amount of practice needed may vary from worker to worker, permit them to practice until overlearning occurs or until operating the machine becomes second nature.

Feedback is necessary for learning how to operate a machine. Watch your workers while they are practicing so that you can supply feedback:

- Let them know when they operate the machine incorrectly and tell them what was wrong.
- Look for opportunities to give them positive reinforcement.
- Tell them when they did the job correctly or when they are improving.

WAYS TO TRAIN MAINTENANCE WORKERS

Maintenance workers and maintenance jobs are continually changing in today's manufacturing plants. Once members of a traditional craft or trade, maintenance workers now are highly skilled, knowledgeable, and technologically astute individuals. Further, the maintenance operation in the plant today is part of the system created to achieve a common goal—not a group of employees working independently of the manufacturing operations.

Since high-quality products cannot be produced efficiently with improperly maintained machines and equipment, it is up to you to see that your maintenance workers are properly trained. Training maintenance workers is covered in greater detail in Chapter 13, but basically you have three ways to improve the effectiveness and efficiency of the plant's maintenance group:

1. Train and develop workers on the skills they need in the plant.
2. Improve workers' technical abilities, knowledge, and effectiveness.
3. Motivate and encourage workers to be productive and innovative.

These approaches to the maintenance function focus on keeping the plant and equipment running efficiently with a minimum of downtime. To implement them, you need to develop specific improvement strategies:

- *Strengthen the basic skills of the workers*. Workers' abilities to read, write, and calculate may not be up to the levels needed for efficient maintenance of the plant. Since weak basic skills in the workplace significantly reduce the desire for technical training, you must provide the workers basic training in reading, writing, and math.
- *Update the training procedures*. Technological changes today require new approaches and different workers' skills than those in the past. Take advantage of equipment manufacturers' and vendors' on-site training programs. Purchase training systems that focus on critical maintenance procedures.

- *Overcome resistance to change.* Resistance not only prevents implementation of improvements but also discourages new employees from joining or remaining with the maintenance department. Point out how change is beneficial and worthwhile. Sell change on improved safety, greater efficiency, easier job performance, and higher productivity.
- *Boost understanding, trust, and commitment to improvement.* Make sure maintenance improvements address clear reasons to change. Listen to your maintenance workers. Involve them in department problems and promote team efforts.
- *Promote innovation.* Discourage desires to "not rock the boat." Too often, the best ideas go undiscovered because workers are not asked to find a better way. Recognize that individuals support what they help create.

Tip: At every training opportunity, ask workers what caused an equipment failure to occur. Although you want their theories, you also want workers to be able to look at a bearing, for example, and tell why it failed.

HOW TO DEAL WITH OBSOLESCENCE OF PLANT MAINTENANCE WORKERS

Today's advanced technology and complex production equipment have placed a burden on plant management to provide workers to service and maintain that equipment. The field of electronics is one of the most critical disciplines in this respect. But the problem may not be as difficult as it may seem.

Most maintenance supervisors and managers today feel that their workers need training and upgrading of their skills. If you feel the same, you have several ways to deal with the situation:

1. Send the workers to trade schools and educational institutions to receive the training needed.
2. Take advantage of the training courses offered by the manufacturers of the machines and equipment used in the plant. Instrument and computer companies are currently active in offering this.
3. Arrange for in-plant demonstrations of maintenance and repair work by equipment vendors and manufacturer's representatives.
4. Avoid maintenance and repair of complex systems by stocking spare components and units. When you have a failure, replace the faulty unit with a spare, and return the failed unit to the factory for repairs.
5. Purchase equipment and controls that are self-diagnostic when they experience failure. This gets around the problem of not having knowledgeable or skilled workers available to make repairs.

Tip: If you arrange for demonstrations of maintenance and repair procedures in the plant by equipment vendors or manufacturer's representatives, videotape the presentation. You will have a valuable training tool on hand for off-shift workers or new hires.

RETRAINING PLANT PRODUCTION WORKERS TO OPERATE NEW MACHINES AND EQUIPMENT

It is more cost effective for manufacturing plants to take workers in obsolete jobs and retrain them for new positions rather than hire skilled employees, according to a recent study.[4] The study, made by Work in American Institute, Inc., a New York research firm, confirms why it is common procedure today to retrain production workers to perform a different task or operate new machines and equipment.

"Retraining" is the word used to describe two procedures: (1) training in a different line of work, where a person's present job skills are of little or no use; (2) training in the modifications of a present procedure, where the job remains basically the same but the machines, equipment, or techniques are different.

How to Sell Plant Workers on Retraining

Before you try to sell workers on the need for retraining, recognize that some persons will resist it. You will have to persuade them that they have much to gain and nothing to lose. Then carry out your selling and subsequent retraining in steps:

1. Explain carefully why the retraining is necessary. Show how it will be of value and help the worker.

2. Point out what workers already know about the new job, and spell out what they will be learning. Often a person knows more than he or she realizes. This will come out in talking about the new job.

3. Don't accept the excuse that workers can't do what is expected of them. Insist that they try. Such resistance can be overcome only by actually doing the tasks.

4. Encourage the worker frequently as you start the retraining. Letting workers know that they are doing fine is a good way to motivate them and can spur them on to further learning.

---

[4]Reported in *Manufacturing Week*, April 6, 1987, p. 16.

Following Up

Testing, or follow-up, is an important step in retraining. Through it you learn if workers have acquired the knowledge or skill that will enable them to perform the new job successfully. Follow up by:

1. Observing the workers' performance carefully.
2. Recognizing that you may occasionally need to give additional attention to slow learners.
3. Not becoming concerned with initial failures. Simply determine what part of the retraining was inadequate for the particular individual, and alter it to suit the circumstance.
4. Correcting any reversals to old habits as soon as they appear. Old procedures are hard to forget. They often come up without the worker being aware of them.

Tip: Keep in mind that it's more difficult to retrain employees than to train new hires. Also, the time needed to retrain may be longer than the time needed to train.

PITFALLS TO AVOID IN TRAINING PLANT WORKERS

When you have the knowledge and skill to do a particular job in the plant, it's very easy to assume that you can teach workers how to do it. This assumption, however, can lead to many errors in the instructional process. The training mistakes you must avoid are:

- *Failing to prepare for the training.* An unorganized approach will create an image of unorganized supervision in the mind of the worker. Distractions and inhibition to learning occur when the instruction is not given in a logical sequence.
- *Failing to reduce tension.* Putting the worker at ease is essential in job training. Clear thinking is a must during the learning process. Tension inhibits learning.
- *Failing to establish clear training objectives.* There's more to the job than just pushing the start button on a machine. Safety ranks above the quality and quantity of output.
- *Failing to provide a means for seeing if objectives have been met.* You must have a way of learning if the worker can now perform the job safely and efficiently.
- *Trying to do too much.* Narrow the scope of your objective. Don't try to cover too much information. Limit a training session to just one subject.

- *Trying to train too fast.* Avoid the temptation to shovel information into the worker. Training too fast risks incomplete assimilation and misunderstanding.
- *Thinking that workers all learn the same way.* Trainees learn at different rates for different reasons.
- *Failing to follow up.* You must get feedback from the trainee during instruction. A crucial feedback technique after instruction is to have trainees perform the job two or three times to demonstrate their understanding of it.

4

How to Raise Productivity of Plant Workers

UNDERSTANDING PRODUCTIVITY

Productivity is not a simple thing. Here are some of the many definitions given to this interesting subject:

- It's the output of higher quantity and better quality products for the amount of labor and time spent.
- It's the research and development that result in better processing and manufacturing.
- It's the reduction of costs achieved by doing jobs better.
- It's the drive a person puts into work.
- It's know-how supported by motivation and put to work by machines and labor.

Many answers have been offered to why productivity in plants may decline. Poor management of workers is taking a lot of the blame. It is said that managers and supervisors are failing in their relations with workers.

Your workers want clean and pleasant workplaces, fair treatment, and recognition for work done. They want to become better at their work, to create, and to take responsibility by doing things their way. They are not getting as much of these as they think they should.

Too many employees have demeaning and uninteresting jobs, and quite a few are also being underutilized. In some plants, everyone is paid the same for like jobs; thus the incentive to do a better job or to do more is lacking. Plant employees need to be paid in accordance with their contribution, with rewards to those who do more.

A greater involvement of employees with their company in setting goals and reaching them would help. More spirit and enthusiasm could be generated if employees were shown how important their work is and complimented when good work was done.

Workers may restrict themselves by resisting change, by refusing to look for better ways to do a job. Management may ignore the suggestions of workers and thereby suffer a double penalty: the loss of the benefit that could result and the poorer performance of the worker because of the imposed demotivation.

How do you increase productivity? In plants, the answers seem to be simple. You cut manufacturing time and reduce direct and indirect costs. You see that operations are performed more efficiently. You achieve savings from value analysis, from automation and new technology, and from greater output of employees.

Although many increases in productivity are a result of actions taken by management through capital investment, productivity often rises when a change is made in a job condition or a procedure, even though the change may not be an improvement. This can happen when workers believe that a change is being made for their benefit.

They become enthused and motivated when management shows an interest in their welfare. A greater willingness to cooperate and to work as a team is the benefit of being treated as individuals and shown respect.

It follows, then, to increase productivity, management must provide job satisfaction to the workers on the production line. Management must also take more advantage of available technology.

BARRIERS TO ACHIEVING PRODUCTIVITY IMPROVEMENT IN PLANTS

Several years ago, a seminar on productivity improvement was held at the College of Business Administration at Texas A&M University. Sponsored by the Center for Technological Innovation, the program attempted to determine how management executives perceive current barriers to industrial productivity and technological innovation.

Management functions are far more likely to impede productivity improvement than nonmanagement functions, according to the perceptions of 36 management executives at the seminar. This group identified 16 major barriers to productivity, 11 of which are considered management functions. The most common of these are:

- Poor worker attitudes.
- Difficulty in obtaining, training, and developing supervisors.
- Poor objectives definition by management.
- Low quality of entry-level production workers.
- Management obsolescence.

The nonmanagement barriers included:

- Increased cost of energy, capital, and equipment.
- Government regulations.
- Tax policy.
- Machine obsolescence.
- Lack of adequate, useful control systems.

As for technological innovation, the executives felt that attitude and motivation were the most detrimental factors. The executives decided not to address the issues of government/state regulations and environmental laws and regulations because they can rarely be controlled on the company level.

HOW GOOD COMMUNICATION WITH PLANT WORKERS INCREASES THEIR PRODUCTIVITY

The effectiveness of plant workers depends on how you communicate with them because they must be informed, trained, and directed. Without good communication, they could not be efficient, work well together, or help the company keep up with the competition.

When you keep channels of communication open, you provide motivation, maintain interest, and promote cooperation. When workers know *how* to do their jobs and *why* they are doing them, they are inclined to do better.

Since the ambitions, hopes, and goals of workers are sensitive to motivation, you should do your best to encourage them to pursue their desires and try to gain satisfaction from their work. If you can inspire your workers, there should be practically no limit to the increase in productivity that can be achieved. One of the best ways to inspire them is to communicate with them personally.

Unfortunately, too many supervisors fail to listen; employees give up trying to communicate their concerns or ideas and remain silent. When employees don't talk about work-related problems, those problems usually become worse.

A worker makes a mistake or fails to complete a job, and this prompts a supervisor to criticize him or her severely. The worker who is criticized withdraws into a shell and won't even communicate with fellow workers. Other employees become disgruntled and the supervisor soon finds it difficult to motivate anyone. The result is a drop in productivity of everyone.

Most workers want to do a good job. It is much easier for them to accomplish their work if they know how they fit into the company's and department's plans. To the employees, the work seems more worthwhile, and the goals worth attaining, when they are well-informed and kept up to date. It usually follows that productivity will be better because the added interest leads to better performance and more efficiency.

Is there a limit to the amount of information that you should give to your workers? Yes, especially if the information is of little value in helping them with their work. In general, it is useful for employees to have information that affects their jobs and explains the goals of the company.

Since many workers also want to know what their peers and friends in the company are doing, this can be included. While company publications supply much of the latter information, it is still helpful for supervisors to have additional news that can be delivered on a personal basis.

Team effort, support, and agreement on goals are the normal result of cooperative efforts, but cooperation requires that people communicate openly. This is where you can participate by communicating matters relating to department functions and performance. In turn, workers can give their individual ideas on getting work done or on how bottlenecks can be reduced or eliminated. It begins with your willingness to communicate and it results in more productivity.

Alternative Methods of Improving Productivity

Over the years, managers at all levels have used various methods in trying to boost the productivity of their people. But it has sometimes been difficult to know when one way would be more appropriate than another, how all the ways fit together, and what combination of them would get the best results.

One approach to this problem is to recognize that only three variables are critical to the determination of the productivity level of a company's employees: motivation, ability, and technology. If any one of them is low, productivity will also be low. In trying to raise productivity, you should therefore use the methods that affect each of these variables.

THREE EFFECTIVE WAYS OF MOTIVATING PLANT WORKERS

Among the many ways you can motivate plant workers, three have proved to be the most effective in recent years:

1. *Management by objectives.* To use this method, you and a worker set performance-related goals for the worker for an agreed-upon period of time. Both of you also plan how these goals may best be achieved. At the end of the period, you evaluate the worker's performance with the intention of setting new goals plus making changes in the plan. Goal setting and reviewing a worker's progress towards them motivates him or her to be more productive by making the worker's progress and accomplishments more noticeable.

2. *Behavior modification.* With this method, you connect motivation to a worker's behavior. Behavior that appears to be due to a lack of motivation happens because it is rewarded in some way. To eliminate undesirable behavior, find and stop the reward, and replace the behavior with a desirable one. The lack of a behavior that indicates high motivation is attributed to no reward for that behavior. To increase its occurrence, reward a specific behavior that shows motivation with recognition.

3. *Job enrichment.* To use this method, you modify a job by increasing the variety of work performed and making the worker autonomous and independent. You also give the worker opportunities to make decisions and experience a sense of achievement. Workers who participate in job enrichment feel that they have completed a whole task rather than just part of one. The job itself becomes motivating.

When you cannot adopt any of these ways for one reason or another, training is an alternative way to motivate workers, especially if they are new employees. With equal opportunity and affirmative action regulations becoming more complex, less selection and more training are the best courses to follow. If you decide to combine selecting and training, select those who will benefit the most from training.

How Technology Raises the Productivity of Plant Workers

Don't overlook technology as a factor that determines the productivity level attainable in the plant. No matter how motivated or skilled, an employee's productivity will only be as high as the technology of the job allows. The term "technology" refers not only to machines, processes, and procedures, but also to such management activities as orientation programs, communication, training, and the like.

You can gain the benefits of technology for the plant in three ways:

1. Promote creative problem solving by your workers.
2. Give workers worthwhile rewards for good ideas and suggestions.
3. Provide workers with new and better designed tools.

POSITIVE WAYS TO MAINTAIN HIGH PRODUCTIVITY

Astute supervisors realize that the responsibility for maintaining productivity rests with management. In work output, quality, and attendance, management receives the work level it accepts. A lax management attitude will result in workers' performing only enough to get by, while high expectation and effort by management will produce comparable efforts from employees. Here are some steps to take to assure that high productivity is maintained:

- *Set goals.* Goals can be set for almost any type of work, ranging from production, to maintenance, quality, or other kinds of jobs. Goals should be attainable for the work group as a whole or individualized based on worker capability.

- *Expect good work.* When high standards exist, improved output will result. The example you set will be reflected in your subordinates' behavior.

- *Find better ways.* The individual who is never satisfied with the status quo and continually looks for a better way usually succeeds. Even a minor change to an established work procedure sometimes leads to a significant improvement in productivity.

- *Encourage employee participation.* Most productivity improvement programs focus on employee participation in solving problems that affect the employee's job. Keeping employees informed and involved in job issues increases their stake and interest in changes affecting them. Such participation leads to improved productivity.

- *Recognize results and give credit.* When you show appreciation for good work, you establish a work climate that encourages better performance among workers. Equally important, deal with poor performance by providing special training or corrective discipline.

SATISFYING EMPLOYEES NEEDS: A WAY TO MOTIVATE THEM

Of the many personnel problems that supervisors are expected to solve, the ones involving motivation are often the most serious. Motivating your workers is probably the most difficult job you as a supervisor can ever attempt to accomplish. Begin by trying to understand what employees want from their jobs. By identifying their needs and desires, and trying to fulfill as many of them as you can, you will take a big step toward motivating these employees. Motivated workers are almost always more productive than unmotivated ones.

Here is a list of the wants and desires of most plant employees. They want:

- *Praise and recognition.* Many feel that only the things they do wrong are noticed, not the things they do right.
- *Job security.* They want to believe they will continue to hold their jobs.
- *To be treated fairly.* This applies particularly where pay and the opportunity to advance are concerned.
- *To be kept informed.* They want to know where they stand and how they are doing on the job.
- *To be involved.* They like to be "in" on things and to take part in making decisions, especially when the decisions concern their jobs and the work to be performed.

Today's plant employees expect more from their jobs and their employers than ever before. This is a result of their being better educated, better informed, and more knowledgeable. To motivate such persons you must be aware of and concerned with their problems, and you must do what you can to act on those problems.

HOW TO EFFECTIVELY DELEGATE JOBS TO PLANT WORKERS

The more responsibility you have, the more you'll find you need to delegate some of your duties and tasks. Here are the steps to take to be an effective delegator:

1. *Decide which parts of your work you can delegate.* Obvious choices are jobs your workers can do as well or better than you can. Reserve for yourself those tasks that require the experience, skill, and training that only you have.

2. *Delegate to more than one worker, if possible.* Carefully select the person for a specific task by suiting the task to the person. By spreading assignments among all your workers, and especially among those who have the ability and desire to get ahead, you enable them to demonstrate their potential as well as gain recognition for getting a job done.

3. *Be clear and concise when you delegate.* Also, clarify what decisions you are delegating and what you are reserving for yourself. Delegating isn't successful when the person to whom you have delegated a task fails to do it or makes a decision beyond the limit of authority granted.

4. *Tell other persons in the plant about your delegation.* If you don't let them know what and to whom you've delegated, you make it difficult for your helpers to get cooperation and to avoid resentment when making decisions.

5. *Follow up on the persons to whom you've delegated work.* Even though you may have delegated some decision-making responsibility, you still have the total responsibility. Keep up to date too, on what you have delegated by asking the persons involved to report to you from time to time.

Tip: Be careful when you delegate that you don't overdo it. Some of your duties and responsibilities should not be delegated. Plant management expects you to handle such matters as planning, scheduling, coordinating, control, and supervision.

Tips on Talking to Plant Workers About Their Jobs

Most workers can do above-average work if they are motivated and if they help each other. Your success as a supervisor is determined by how well you bring about both of these conditions. When you talk to them about their jobs:

1. Be aware that each person is different in terms of thinking how the job appears and what that person considers a fair day's work. An average person is capable of doing much more than you realize.

2. Recognize that to make a point, you may have to be lavish with praise for one person, and appeal to pride with another. With a third, you may need to push and plead.

3. Spend more time with the workers who need to be encouraged. Those who like challenges will move ahead without a lot of your attention. Learn where you must put your effort, and spend most of your time in that area.

HOW TO PROMOTE COOPERATION AND TEAM EFFORT

The key to getting cooperation is being available and ready to help. By letting workers know this and by showing them you are enthusiastic, you provide an impetus to team effort.

Whenever you assign jobs to individuals, look for how you can get them interested in a team effort. This should be relatively easy since most workers want to know what's going on, whether they are directly affected or not. By keeping them informed, you can make them feel they are part of an important group rather than just individuals who work in the plant. There are three good ways to promote cooperation and team effort:

1. *Encourage workers to help each other.* Show them how cooperation enables work to be done faster and more efficiently. Always refer to their efforts and yours and accomplishments in *we* terms so that they will think in those terms.

2. *Look for opportunities to show individuals how to do someone else's work.* They will learn to appreciate their fellow workers' problems and see that some jobs are not as easy as they appear. This training will pay off, sooner or later, in that your efficient team workers will help others when they get behind.

3. *Let workers share in the making of some decisions.* They will get satisfaction in helping to decide what is to be done and how it is to be done. They will begin to think of the company's goals as their goals. This will lead to pooling their abilities and skills to benefit everyone.

USING WORK SAMPLING TO RAISE PRODUCTIVITY

Work sampling, or the random observation of personnel, is a technique whereby you can effectively determine how much time workers actually spend on the job. From a work sampling study, you discover how productive they are and how they spend their unproductive time. It is possible to determine whether workers are as efficient or inefficient as they appear.

The laws of probability provide the basis for work sampling. These state that a large number of observations made at random intervals and classified into distinct activities will provide a fairly reliable account of how often specific activities occur. A requisite of a work sample study is that observations must be made randomly if unbiased results are to be obtained.

When work sampling individuals in a plant, you should measure the following:

• *Direct work.* Performing specific work duties at the work site such as operating machines or equipment, repairing them, or handling materials.

- *Receiving instructions*. Conversation with supervisor. Some specific indication should be present such as tools or work papers so that there is assurance that more than a casual conversation is taking place.
- *Traveling*: Walking or traveling to a work area such as a machine *without* carrying work materials or tools.
- *Transporting*: Moving materials, instrument, or equipment within the work environment.
- *Preparing*. Getting ready to begin specific work or a job, getting out or putting away tools or papers, and cleaning up after work.
- *Idle-off-job*. Performing nonjob-related activities *away* from the job site, which cannot be classified in one of the other categories.
- *Idle-on-job*. Performing nonjob-related activities *on* the job site, which cannot be classified in one of the other categories.

You make observations with the following objectives:

- To measure the amount of control that you have over your people.
- To determine the percentage of time employees are working.
- To reveal the activities preventing employees from putting more time into their work.
- To provide a base against which future performance can be measured.

It would be unwise to work sample an individual worker's performance to use information as a disciplinary tool. You lose the trust and confidence of employees if you use it for this purpose.

A work study can be brief and simple or in-depth, depending on how much information about work habits is wanted. Size of the work force is also a factor in that large groups require more observers than small ones.

Some plant managers are not satisfied with simply asking supervisors to record observations while carrying out their normal responsibilities. While such studies can provide an indication of worker efficiency, it is felt they do not contribute much more for two reasons:

1. *Bias and prejudice tend to affect observations*. Supervisors know their workers quite well and have definite opinions of their productivity. Thus, observations may not be realistic.
2. *The study will not have the randomness in observation time that it should have*. Workers know the habits of their supervisors and when they would most likely be making observations.

Engineers and other staff people make good observers. They are often assigned studies of production and maintenance people. In many companies, observers are recruited from departments other than the one being studied.

To ensure success with a study, you should be sure to get the co-operation and participation of the workers to be studied. Knowing that work is to be investigated creates uneasiness and concern. You should fully explain the purpose of the study while also assuring workers that their jobs are not in jeopardy.

Questions should be solicited and answered so that the study is in no way secret. If this is not done, some may resent the observation and re-taliate by creating fictitious work, working faster, or working slower. Even with notification, it is advantageous to run a trial sampling period for a day or two until both observers and workers become accustomed to the routine.

After finishing the study, announce the results and thank participants for their cooperation. Later, if changes are made in procedures or work areas, workers will be more willing to accept them, because they will realize that it was a result of their own actions.

Procedures for Making a Study

If results are to be valid and reliable, definite procedures must be followed when making a study. Here is how to go about it:

- Predetermine what activities to look for so that observations can be classified. The greater number of activities you decide to use, the more you will learn about what your workers do during their workday.

- Make a tally sheet listing the activities with spaces for you to record each observation with a check mark. Take this with you each time you tour the plant.

- Determine the times to start trips by using random number tables found in the back of almost any statistics textbook. Make trips on a random time basis through the workday.

- Make observations in all areas of the plant or where employees may be working, covering the area entirely during one trip period. An observer must be able to distinguish the workers being studied from other individuals who might be in the work areas.

- Limit a trip period to 15 to 20 minutes. If it cannot be completed in this time, have one or more other observers help you. Vary your path so that you don't always enter a room from a particular door.

- Include the lunchroom and canteen in the areas to be observed. Do not include locker and washrooms unless you have a problem locating those being studied.

- Note the total number of workers to be observed on each trip, and compare the number of observations you make with the number available. Workers not observed should be less than 10 percent of the total or the reliability of the study will be affected.
- Make a minimum of 40 observations of each person over the period of the study. Total observations should be at least 40 times the size of the work group. The more observations you make, the more reliable the information.
- Record your first impression when you see a person—no additional observation time is needed. Don't be misled by what the person does after your presence is noted.
- Calculate the percentage of time you found workers taking part in each predetermined activity.
- Summarize the study and record the data so that they will be available for comparison purposes in future work sampling studies.

Reliability of Work Sampling Results

You should be sure that you make enough observations to give statistical reliability to the data developed. Although you may decide to vary the length of time devoted to a study, observations should be made for at least one week.

In applying the activity definitions, note that direct work is narrowly defined. Obtaining instructions, traveling to and from the job, and general preparation for work may be necessary elements of the job, but they do not get the job done and are not considered direct work.

Persons not familiar with work sampling may question the reliability of a study. They may ask why workers, knowing they are being observed, won't make an extra effort to keep busy and thus give a false picture of their normal behavior.

In general, plant employees do not behave that way. A few may deliberately attempt to cloud the issue by being overly industrious or by slowing down. But this attitude wears off in a day or two. It is difficult for individuals to change their normal behavior for any length of time.

Also, a worker soon becomes accustomed to the presence of the observer. If you notice that individuals are not behaving normally, the first day or two's observations should be disregarded.

When analyzing results of a study, note particularly the percent of time individuals spent in direct work, because this is the main indicator of productivity levels. But you must also take into account other activities to learn how to improve overall performance. If you find, for example, that a high percentage of time is lost in waiting for other persons, such as at a storeroom counter, then perhaps what's needed is another attendant, rearrangement of the facility, or a simplified procedure.

A work sampling study can also provide a comparison of activities of employees assigned to one supervisor with those assigned to another. This can give management insight into reasons for poor performance on the job. It may be possible to change a supervisor's work pattern to make employees more efficient.

The information and data obtained from a work sampling study may surprise you. Management often believes employees to be much more productive than they actually are. The facts are objectively revealed from the study. But the real payoff comes when you take action on your findings.

POSITIVE WAYS TO DEAL WITH UNPRODUCTIVE EMPLOYEES

Since unproductive employees are usually emotionally troubled, one of the best ways to deal with such persons is to counsel them. Handling problem employees isn't easy, but the sooner you face up to this responsibility, the sooner you can expect them to adjust to the job and become more productive.

Make your counseling session a positive and beneficial event by taking the following steps:

1. Start by putting the employee at ease. Then say that you see the employee has a problem and you want to help in solving it.
2. State what you feel is the problem, and tell the person what you and the company expect of him or her.
3. Assure the employee that you want the person to keep the job, that you are not looking for an excuse to get rid of him or her.
4. Listen patiently to what the employee has to say. Give him or her your undivided attention.
5. Avoid criticizing the employee or arguing with him or her.
6. Look beyond the words of what the employee says. Determine if the person is trying to tell you more than what the words mean.
7. Get the employee to agree on a course of action that will result in better performance.
8. Set a date at which you and the employee will again get together to discuss the person's performance.

EFFECTIVE WAYS TO USE PLANT EMPLOYEES' IDLE TIME

Although management may take all kinds of steps to prevent its happening, you must face the possibility that the plant may occasionally experience production delays due to such incidents as a power failure, a severe weather disturbance, or even a material shortage. Since such incidents drastically affect the plant's output and your workers' productivity, it's up to you to minimize an incident's impact. There are several ways you can use plant employees' idle time, depending on the circumstances and the length of a delay or shutdown:

1. Assign them maintenance and clean-up jobs. Even though you may have an excellent housekeeping program in which everyone participates, there probably are any number of small jobs that could be done at this time.
2. Show films or videotapes to the affected workers. You can never overdo health and safety training.
3. Train workers to do each others' jobs. Such training pays off when you need replacements for persons who are absent for short periods.

HOW COMPUTERIZED SYSTEMS IMPROVE PRODUCTIVITY

Computer systems are the major reason for the dramatic changes that industry is making in its plants and in the way it manages its operations. The concept of the automated plant depends on computer technology. So, also, are management information systems. Both of these developments are capable of increasing productivity significantly in those companies that use advanced technology effectively.

Yet the advantage and benefits of computers are not limited to companies that are actively involved in new technology. Computers also contribute to major improvements in the productivity of companies that are still taking steps to automate their plant processes and operations.

Automation is a proven way to higher productivity made possible and practical by computers. Microtechnology, in particular, has put automated equipment within the reach of many companies. It's not necessary to make a big investment to get started on automated systems. Management can develop a plan, then implement it in steps, meanwhile gaining the productivity increases that the program promises.

While computer systems enable plants to make worthwhile improvements in many functions and disciplines, their most important contribution is what they do to increase overall productivity.

How to Convince Plant Workers That Computerized Maintenance Improves Productivity

The opportunities for increasing productivity in the plant through computer systems fit into two well-known activities: planning and scheduling. Some maintenance workers, however, may have to be sold on how the computer can help them to be more efficient. To convince these workers, you should:

- Point out that the computer enables you (or a planner) to initiate and keep track of work orders.
- Explain how the computer aids in assuring that all the items needed to carry out a maintenance job are readily available.
- Tell them that the computer assists in scheduling and the setting of priorities for work orders.
- Show them that all the particulars of a repair job are contained in the computer data base. This information is available to them to help them when they are working on a machine that had previously been repaired.

HOW BETTER PRODUCTIVITY RESULTS FROM GOOD HOUSEKEEPING

Most plants recognize that good housekeeping is a necessary operation if employees are to be both effective and efficient. Successful organizations invariably have facilities that are well maintained, orderly, and clean, and that provide excellent working conditions for employees. Less successful plants often are characterized by general untidiness, carelessness in observance of order, and a lack of procedures.

Since all workers are affected by their surroundings, either consciously or subconsciously, disorderly and haphazard conditions are not conducive to quality workmanship. Even when a high level of precision is not required, carelessness and indifference can hurt production operations. Employees develop poor attitudes if management is negligent in seeing that buildings, workplaces and machines are kept clean and that working conditions are conducive to employee comfort and satisfaction.

On the plus side, the effect of good housekeeping on worker morale is encouraging. Employees certainly prefer to work in plants that are orderly, neat, and clean. Such conditions increase their safety and maintain their good health. Teamwork and cooperation become routine matters and people take greater pride in their work.

The cleaning up of personal work areas has usually been an employee responsibility in manufacturing operations. If supervisors follow up on this, the workplace should *always* appear as neat and orderly as it can under the circumstances of the job. Management's part should consist of the adoption of regular and systematic procedures for repairing, repainting, and renewing of the facilities. The overall image presented to the public is always enhanced if the company and the employees cooperate to keep facilities neat and clean.

Good housekeeping should not be a major problem for a plant if a few rules are established and enforced. All employees, of course, should be involved. Each person can contribute in some way or manner to this effort although responsibilities for certain jobs may be assigned. It is your responsibility to tell workers to do the following:

- Keep areas in and around buildings clear of wastes and debris by using approved receptacles for their disposal.
- Identify storage spaces and material confined within painted limit lines.
- Keep concealed spaces, attics, closets, elevator shafts, and penthouses free of extraneous material.
- Mark aisles and keep them free of obstructions.
- Remove empty and unused barrels, drums, and other containers promptly from the process or work area.
- Store materials and finished stock in such a manner that they will not obstruct a path to a fire alarm or fire fighting equipment.
- Keep machinery and equipment clean and lubricated.
- Provide metal drip pans at drum racks.

TECHNIQUES FOR REDUCING MACHINES AND EQUIPMENT DOWNTIME IN A PLANT

Downtime of machines and equipment is expensive to a plant. With no production there can be no sales, no income, and no profit. Worse, overhead costs continue. It's no wonder that a feeling of frustration comes over management when productive equipment is idle.

What can you do to reduce or minimize this downtime? Depending on your authority and responsibility, you can contribute in several ways to help your plant keep its equipment uptime figure high. Here are eight ways:

1. *Provide adequate training for production operators and maintenance craftsmen.* People who are trained to operate equipment and to maintain it will make fewer mistakes on the job. As a result, there will be fewer malfunctions, plug-ups, and shutdowns for adjustments. Maintenance work can be performed faster and more efficiently when craftspersons are familiar with the equipment.

If you participate in the training of operators and maintenance workers, you will become more knowledgeable with equipment functions, thus enabling you to recognize impending failures; you can then plan and schedule a shutdown.

2. *Plan and schedule maintenance and repair work.* Repairs can be made faster since people will be available to do the job, and they will have the required tools, material, and parts when they need them. Delays due to failure to satisfy any of these needs can be avoided.

   Planning and scheduling provides another benefit: The work may often be undertaken when the production line is down for cleaning or product change.

3. *Promote cooperation between production and maintenance departments.* When these two groups work together, they can significantly reduce equipment downtime. Replacement or repair of equipment is accomplished in three steps:

   The production people alert the maintenance people when equipment failure appears likely, or a machine is not performing up to standards. They also point out the nature of the problem and what is wrong. This enables the maintenance people to acquire the replacement machine or the parts which will be needed.

   The departments agree on a scheduled time for the equipment to be shut down and made available for replacement or repair.

   Both departments keep each other informed on progress of the work, anticipated time of completion, and releasing of the equipment for resumption of operation.

4. *Use value analysis when procuring equipment, materials, and tools.* See that more items are purchased for reasons other than lowest price. A value analysis study of proposed equipment purchases can be very revealing in answering questions on corrosion resistance, ease of dismantling, maintenance requirements, and the availability and cost of spare parts—all factors that determine or affect downtime of equipment.

   By paying a bit more for durability and better design, a plant can acquire machinery and equipment that will undergo a minimum of downtime over its useful life.

5. *Complete development and debugging work before putting new equipment into production use.* The petrochemical and chemical industries practice this principle by operating pilot plants where equipment and processes are studied on small scale levels. Problems of equipment performance are worked out before the large scale production line goes into operation.

   When a plant doesn't have such resources or when it lacks the time to use them, management should make a preliminary trial of the new equipment with staff and development people as operators. Operating characteristics should be charted, capacities tested, and reliability determined. Design changes can then be made, if required, before beginning production operations.

   A side advantage of such practice is that the equipment capability and performance constants can be recorded. The information is valuable later when questions of "performing up to standards" arise.

6. *Practice preventive maintenance.* Provide inspection and testing of machines and controls, particularly of critical equipment. The use of preventive maintenance enables management to reduce the number of equipment failures as well as their severity. Frequent inspection can reveal impending failure permitting repairs to be made during a scheduled shutdown rather than during a production run.

   Preventive maintenance also reduces and eliminates major breakdowns, whose occurrence results in long downtimes for equipment replacement or repairs.

7. *Take time to correct a problem rather than accept a quick fix.* The philosophy of management on how machines should be maintained is a factor in determining how much total downtime the machines experience over a production period. When a breakdown occurs, the machine can be completely overhauled or just the faulty component repaired.

   If you are not concerned, you can be caught in the current of making repetitive repairs of the same nature rather than taking time to upgrade or redesign the machine. Taking time to correct a problem rather than making a quick fix will reduce downtime in the long run.

8. *Keep good records.* Note causes of failures, their frequency, and the downtime incurred. You can more easily apply corrective maintenance when you keep records of performance variables and breakdowns. You can upgrade machines in areas where failures have occurred and thus bring about a reduction in the number of such failures in the future.

   In addition, prior knowledge of the downtime that will be needed to make repairs enables you to more efficiently schedule and carry out related process operations so that the effects of the failure are minimized.

HOW TO TRAIN EMPLOYEES TO AVOID PRODUCTION DISRUPTIONS

The more effectively you can train and instruct your production workers on how to perform their jobs safely and efficiently, the more productive they will be. Here are some guidelines on training employees to avoid machine shutdowns and operational delays:

- Tell them to plan their work to assure that machines, equipment, and tools are available when they are needed.
- Teach them to anticipate their material needs for the work they are performing so that they won't run short in the middle of filling an order or quota.

- Tell them to watch for abnormal performance of their machines. Ask them to inform you immediately of a change in speed or sound of any machine or equipment.
- Preach safety at every opportunity. Insist on your workers' confirming that controls and safety devices are operating properly before they begin a production run.
- Point out the importance of quality workmanship. When products must be reworked or waste is created, losses occur and production processes must be repeated.

(Training is covered more completely in Chapter 3.)

OPTIMIZING PRODUCTIVITY OF THE MAINTENANCE WORK FORCE

When you consider the seemingly endless list of functions performed by a plant's maintenance department, you can see why optimizing the productivity of maintenance workers is critical to the plant's financial success. The way you handle maintenance responsibilities affects overall plant performance in five prime areas—production, quality, cost, safety, and housekeeping.

Management control is essential to operating a cost-effective and efficient maintenance department. The major step in achieving control is the planning and scheduling of maintenance activities. To implement planning and scheduling, you need to:

1. Plan and schedule all maintenance work that requires two or more work-hours to complete.
2. Establish a priority system for all work orders.
3. Get agreement between the production and maintenance departments on which of the highest priority work orders should be put on a daily schedule.
4. Have the schedule duplicated, posted, and distributed to supervisors and managers of interested or affected departments.

Benefits from Planning and Scheduling Plant Maintenance

You get several worthwhile benefits from planning and scheduling maintenance activities:

- Planning enables you to get the most both from your workers and the time available to carry out maintenance functions. By thinking ahead, you can assure that labor, tools, and material are available when they are needed.

- You are given ample notice and time to shut down the affected machines and equipment, and have them properly prepared for maintenance work. You can also adjust production activities to the planned equipment downtime, possibly avoiding overtime labor.

- Planning and scheduling enable you to assign priorities in programming the work. You will also be aware of the labor requirements for particular jobs and can keep up to date on the backlog of jobs.

- When you plan and schedule, you initiate the implementation of a preventive maintenance program. Preventive maintenance must be planned and scheduled because it involves inspecting, adjusting, and servicing machines and equipment on a schedule acceptable to both the production and maintenance departments.

DEALING WITH PLANT EMPLOYEES' MISTAKES AND CARELESSNESS

With any kind of luck, nothing much happens when one of your workers makes a mistake. If you're the one that finds it, no one else may ever know. The cost may be small—just some of your time to correct it. But don't overlook some possible financial costs.

While some mistakes appear minor, the one your worker made may require that you or someone else work overtime. Or it may put another employee or your superior behind schedule. Or it may be much more serious.

Suppose for example, one of your employees types a letter you wrote to a customer. You don't get to sign the letter until late in a day which has been frenzied and hectic. You're tired and you're already working overtime. You expect that the letter is perfect, so without even looking at it, you sign it.

However, this letter has a mistake in it. You promised a May 1 delivery when the plant can't possibly ship before May 31. How will it make your company look when that shipment is "late"? How do you think you're going to explain that?

When the addressee gets that letter and sees the "mistake" in it, will the person recognize it? Will you be called, or your prompt response just appreciated? On May 2, how is the customer going to feel about your promptness?

Your letter becomes the company's image to the customer receiving it. That single error may cause the customer to stop doing business with your company. You simply can't afford that to happen.

The more mistakes that are made, the less able the department is to function efficiently and at full capacity. The fewer mistakes made, the better the department's productivity.

When a department can reduce rework, scrap, and overtime, it can cut costs. With lower costs, the company can sell a product at a lower price, beat the competition, and increase sales.

What's wrong with saying to your people, "Let's cut down on mistakes? Let's eliminate them entirely. If we can't do that, let's help watch each other to make as few as possible."

Tell your people to make a promise to themselves—*no more careless mistakes*. Stress better compliance with work rules. Concentrate on giving your people clear concise directions. If you do these things, and you all work together, you can count on having fewer mistakes in your department.

HOW TO HANDLE PLANT EMPLOYEES WHO WASTE TIME

Several studies have indicated that plants can place a fair share of blame for a mediocre or poor profit picture on the overall low productivity of employees. The surveys point out that ineffective performance of some workers is principally the result of an excessive waste of time. Recognizing this, you should continually be looking for ways to get your workers to put in more time on the job and less on personal matters.[1]

The waste of time by employees includes late starts, early quits, long lunch periods, and numerous talk sessions throughout the day. You can combat such behavior by:

1. Setting an example. Get to your desk early in the morning. Show by your actions and performance that you like your job and enjoy doing it.

2. Expecting workers to have a good reason if they're late very often, and asking them to promptly explain.

3. Making a tour of the workplace every morning soon after starting time to greet everyone, and noting who is not present. Later you can ask the late or absent individual for an explanation.

Slow starters invariably waste valuable on-the-job time. If you know that one or more workers have this problem, look for different methods of work assignment to alleviate it. Delivering reports that recipients need

[1]T. R. Weiss, "Time-Wasters Cut Back on Productivity," *Successful Supervisor*, Dartnell, November 3, 1986.

early, phoning information, or doing jobs for other departments are tasks that a person is less likely to procrastinate on; assigning them to slow starters may help them with their problem.

Although you know that nonbusiness conversations among employees can waste time, you may not know the best way to handle the problem. While you may not like to be labeled as a driver, you must limit such activities if you are to keep up productivity.

You can usually break up a session by approaching a group and asking for the help of one of the members on a special matter—help that requires the person to leave with you to go to some other area in the plant. Removing one person often tells the others that they should be getting back to their jobs.

Planning and scheduling of the work is a help in making sure that people have assignments with realistic due dates. Asking them where they stand on these assignments at opportune moments serves as a gentle prod to resume working.

By being alert, you can sometimes recognize the various ways that problem workers can waste time and cause jobs to take longer to complete than necessary. Here are some tactics to look for with plant workers who would rather drag out a job than try to finish it promptly:

1. Taking unnecessary trips to the storeroom for supplies.
2. Deciding not to start another step on a project because it's close to lunch time.
3. Going to the maintenance shop for a tool that was forgotten.
4. Waiting for a coworker to return from lunch or a break.
5. Being extra meticulous about unimportant details on a project.
6. Waiting for you to help with a problem or answer a question.

If you find that some of your workers are frequent offenders in wasting time in these or other ways, call it to their attention. A brief talk in private is usually all it takes. If you see no visible signs of change after a talk and/or some kind of warning, take further, more drastic steps.

UNDERSTANDING PLANT OPERATING COSTS

One of the ways you prove your worth to your company is by what you accomplish in cost control and keeping costs down. You can demonstrate this by becoming skilled in solving cost problems and preventing little costs from becoming big.

What you do about costs generally is not difficult because almost everything that you control is a cost to the company in one way or another.

While the ways by which costs can be controlled are many and varied, understanding plant operating costs is a requisite to doing something about them. Following are the most common manufacturing costs incurred in operating a plant:

Labor

1. Production
2. Engineering and maintenance
3. Shipping and receiving
4. Material handling and stores
5. Quality control
6. Training
7. Supervisory and administrative

Utilities

1. Water
2. Steam
3. Air
4. Electricity

Depreciation

1. Buildings
2. Machines and equipment
3. Vehicles

Raw Materials

Support Services

1. Fire protection
2. Guard service
3. Lunch/cafeteria
4. Medical and first aid
5. Cleaning
6. Waste disposal

Supplies

1. Production
2. Shipping
3. Engineering
4. Maintenance

5. Office

6. Janitorial

Taxes and Licenses

Insurance

How to Cut Labor Costs

If you are not getting the fullest potential from your workers, you are wasting one of the most costly items of running a business. Here are six ways you can hold down your plant's labor costs:

1. Control absenteeism and overtime—major reasons for excessive labor costs.
2. Stay on top of late starts and early quits, long breaks and lunch periods, and simple idleness.
3. Give clear instructions to all workers. They will be more efficient, work more safely, make fewer errors, and create less waste.
4. Assign only as many workers to a job as are actually needed.
5. Put skilled workers on skilled jobs and unskilled workers on unskilled jobs.
6. Provide enough workers on the job to assure that overtime work is limited.

Tip: You can minimize labor costs if you get the most from each person's ability, knowledge, and experience.

How to Control Material Costs

Positive ways to control material costs are to develop standards for their handling and use followed by training workers to meet them. Although training and instructing workers on how to properly handle materials may take time and cost money, the benefits will far exceed the costs. Here are six ways you can control material costs. Tell your workers to:

1. Avoid damaging containers, bags, and cartons in receiving and shipping operations.
2. Prevent loss in the warehouse and storerooms from poor stacking, inadequate protection, and failure of racks and bins.
3. Keep spillage to a minimum in handling and dispensing.
4. Protect materials from spoilage by aging or contamination.
5. Avoid wasting material by not taking more than needed for a job.
6. Maintain the quality of finished products; cut waste and rejects.

Tip: To do a good job of controlling material cost, you must continually stress three matters: care in handling, value, and conservation.

How to Hold Down Machine and Equipment Costs

Cost control of machines and equipment makes two demands on you: to keep these assets fully utilized, and to prevent malfunctions and breakdowns. The first is achieved by doing all you can to keep productive machines and equipment operating. The second is met by adopting a predictive and preventive maintenance program for all machines and equipment. Here are four ways you can hold down your plant's machine and equipment costs:

1. Recognize that the cost of energy to run machines depends on their design, the adjustments and control applied, and the condition of the machine's components.
2. Plan and schedule maintenance work to optimize running time of all productive equipment.
3. Adopt just-in-time procedures to minimize start-up and shut-down operations and smooth out processes.
4. Shut down machines, conveyors, and auxiliary equipment when they are not in productive use.

Tip: Care in handling and maintaining machines will not only make them more efficient, but also extend their useful life.

How to Minimize Utility Costs

The most accurate way of accounting for the use of utilities by various departments in the plant is to put meters on the steam, air, and water lines to them. Meters enable you to uncover excessive usage and tell you also where leaks may be occurring. To control utility costs, you must be concerned and constantly checking to see that:

1. Steam, air, and water leaks are repaired.
2. Insulation is used in adequate amounts to prevent energy loss.
3. Lights are turned off when not in use.
4. Machines and auxiliary equipment are shut down when they are not in productive use.
5. Heaters and air conditioners are not running in areas with doors and windows open.
6. Engines are turned off when motor vehicles are not in motion.

Tip: Projects that promote the reduction of utility consumption and saving of energy should be included in the plant cost reduction program.

HOW TO PREVENT LITTLE COSTS FROM BECOMING BIG

It pays to be alert and aware of the danger of little costs in the plant becoming big. If you see a machine or process slowing down or speeding up, or an omission or inclusion of a procedural step, immediately investigate to learn the reason for the change. The quality of the product or operating costs may be affected. Even if these changes don't affect quality, they may run up costs needlessly if they are not quickly diagnosed and corrected. Here are a few examples of such incidents along with suggestions on what you should do:

- An increase in operating costs occurs that is not explainable by current trends, rate increases, or new acquisitions. Look for work being repeated because of something being wrong with either equipment, materials, or procedures. Check also on customer complaints and returned goods.
- The accounting department bills your department for a new overhead item. Call the department for an explanation. It could be that your department picked up a research or development charge or that a new tax has been levied.
- An increase in the use of an operating item takes place as shown by excessive withdrawals from the storeroom, but there is no accompanying increase in product or work output. Since it is a single item, tracing it should be easy. The job deserves your attention to determine if a serious problem is behind it.

HOW TO DETERMINE PLANT OPERATING COSTS

Your involvement in costs and cost control is primarily with plant operating costs. You have two responsibilities in this area: to see that accurate cost reporting systems are being used and maintained, and to continually make an effort to control and reduce manufacturing costs.

The starting point for studying and controlling costs is to determine the type of expenditures with which the plant is involved. Any cost system is meaningless unless all the expenditures made by the plant, department, or other cost center are recorded and charged back to it on the company's cost report. This means that each of the manufacturing cost elements must be accounted for; it also requires the plant to use the following techniques on those elements:

- *Labor*. On the hourly time card, space should be provided for the account number to which the employee's pay is charged; several spaces will be needed if the person works for different cost centers.

  When hours worked by employees in one department must be balanced (often a requirement in a unionized plant), these hours are kept on a form designed for that purpose.

  Salary people do not ordinarily punch time cards, but may keep time sheets on which account numbers must be listed. Supervisors who work in more than one department or on special assignments are expected to distribute their time accordingly.

- *Raw materials*. Purchase price and freight charges may be obtained from suppliers' invoices and freight bills. Handling and production losses are determined by charging the quantities delivered to a department and comparing them to the amount in inventory and what went into the finished product within a fixed time period. Job tickets, shift logs, and intradepartment/plant receipts are used to keep track of material used and transferred.

- *Supplies*. Purchase orders, receiving slips, and suppliers' invoices are the key records. Company policy should dictate that nothing is to be bought without a written purchase order that is documented to show the account number to which the material is charged.

- *Utilities*. Although monthly bills sent to the Accounting Department provide the information needed to determine the total individual costs, there can be a problem with deciding how to distribute the charges among the various cost centers within the plant. The most accurate method is to put meters on the utility lines to each of the departments and distribute the charges according to usage. But this procedure can be expensive in the cost of meters, their installation, and their maintenance. Many plants, therefore, have their staff people estimate the amounts used by each department and charge the costs out on that basis.

- *Support services*. If these services are furnished by plant employees, the methods of allocating labor and supplies charges already discussed will suffice. If the services are obtained outside the company, purchase orders or service contracts will be the basic documents used for cost distribution.

SETTING UP AN EFFECTIVE ENERGY CONSERVATION PROGRAM

If your plant doesn't have an energy conservation program, you could be asked at any time to participate in or take charge of one. This may be a real challenge because such a project entails considerable study, investigation, and the introduction of change. In addition, there are many problems to solve if significant energy savings are to be realized. Here, for example, are the kinds of problems that you must solve:

- *Management problems.* Planning, scheduling, coordinating, and implementing all the operations to achieve the desired results.
- *Engineering problems.* Redesigning and replacing machines and equipment.
- *Maintenance problems.* Adjusting, repairing, and insulating energy sources.
- *Financial problems.* Capital investments and operating expenses.
- *Motivational problems.* Persuading people to make an effort to save energy.

Setting up an effective energy conservation program generally requires that you carry out five separate actions:

1. *Audit and survey energy use in the plant.* This consists of inspecting the plant to learn what kinds of energy are being consumed, the amounts, and where in the plant it is used. By studying the information and data, you can determine:
   - Which systems are operating at the lowest levels of efficiency and therefore offer the greatest opportunities for energy conservation.
   - Whether savings can be obtained by changing or adding to the types of energy being purchased by the plant.
   - Where meters or other instrumentation should be installed to measure the effects of energy conservation steps.
2. *Identify machine and equipment changes that will improve efficiency.* Typical examples of this include:
   - Modifying machines to use alternate fuel.
   - Replacing equipment that is not energy efficient.
   - Installing new equipment such as heat exchangers and capacitors to recover energy.
3. *Identify operating and procedural changes that can be made without changing machines or equipment.* Include:
   - Shutting down certain machines and equipment part of the time.
   - Operating machines and systems at lower temperatures or at slower speeds.
   - Modifying procedures and processes or combining them so that total energy use is less.
4. *Establish goals for energy savings.* State the reductions in energy use the program is expected to accomplish:

- Give them in clear, measurable terms (preferably in units of energy consumption).
- Include a stated time period for accomplishment.
- Make them realistic; if they are too difficult, people will be frustrated; if they are too easy, no one will be motivated to work very hard for them.

5. *Promote energy conservation among employees.* Make plant employees understand:

- What the program involves.
- Why it is being conducted.
- What it means to them to contribute all they can.

Tip: The better you are able to sell an energy conservation program, the more successful it will be in savings to the company.

TECHNIQUES FOR SAVING ENERGY IN PLANT OPERATIONS

Once you begin to implement an energy conservation program, you may be surprised to learn how many ways you can save energy. Reviewing the use of utilities alone can result in the adoption of procedures that can result in significant savings. Here are some techniques that will enable you to cut waste and improve efficiency of the plant's energy sources:

- *Electricity.* You can save electricity by shifting the load, correcting the power factor, using lighting more efficiently, and promptly shutting down unproductive equipment, among other ways.

    Fluorescent lamps provide the same illumination as incandescent ones for about one-third of the energy consumption. Reduced illumination in specific areas (warehouses) and use of "task lighting" at work stations also saves energy.

- *Water.* You can save water by using thermostatically controlled valves in piping that supplies cooling water to air compressors, condensers and heat exchangers. Waste of water in rinse or flush operations can be minimized with the use of conductivity-sensing flow controllers, and making sure that sanitary facilities are operating properly. There are also many operations and processes in the plant where water can be reused. Notably, there is a strong trend in this direction today.

- *Steam.* Conservation of energy derived from steam begins with how it is generated and distributed. Improper burning of fuel results in losses; substantial energy losses can also occur by discharging the stack gases to the atmosphere at too high a temperature. Using an economizer also results in less fuel being consumed per unit of energy generated.

Frequent inspecting for and prompt repairing of steam leaks in the plant is an absolute must. Implementing a steam trap repair/replacement program will save at least $10 for every $1 spent. Repairing, replacing, and installing insulation on steam piping and equipment will also prevent large losses of energy.

- *Compressed air.* Eliminating leaks on piping, equipment, and instrumentation not only saves air, it also results in more efficient operation of tools and controls. The best time to look for and correct leaks is when they can be heard, or when a machine or piece of equipment is down. Savings can also be achieved by using low-pressure blowers in place of high-pressure air, and using smaller compressors for off-shift or weekend operations.

Ways to Save Energy in Plant Design

You can save considerable energy by judicious use of the plant's heating and cooling systems. Here are three ways you can do this:

1. Adjust temperature settings in the unoccupied areas of the plant, or in areas only sparsely and intermittently occupied, during certain periods of the day. Lower the heat control settings and raise the cooling controls in such areas.

2. Adjust temperatures in the plant lower in the winter and higher in the summer. Try settings of 68 and 78°F, temperatures that most workers will not find objectionable.

3. Put all systems on preventive and predictive maintenance schedules. See that thermostats, dampers, control valves, drives, and belts are operating properly, that heat exchangers are clean, and that filters and traps are adjusted or replaced.

Reducing conduction/convection losses of heat through roofs, floors, walls, and windows are other ways to save energy. Here are the ways to accomplish this:

- Large amounts of heat are lost through the roofs of industrial buildings when insufficient roof insulation has been provided. It has been found that increasing the standard 1 inch of insulation to 3 inches can cut heat gain or loss by 20 percent. If incorporating more insulation directly into the roofing is not feasible, additional insulation can be provided inside.

- In buildings with high ceilings, a great deal of energy can be wasted when the warm air rises to the ceiling. One way to avoid this loss is to install a false ceiling at a lower height, cutting off the space above from the flow of air. Another is to install fans in the upper air space to direct the warm air to the lower levels.

- Uninsulated concrete floors laid on the ground undergo a heat loss of about 2 Btu per hour per square foot when the room temperature is 70°F and the ground is 50°F. Uninsulated concrete and brick walls will lose about 15 Btu per hour per square foot when exposed to outside temperatures of 0°F. These losses can be greatly reduced by using insulation thicknesses up to 5 inches, depending on the cost of fuel and the severity of the climate.

- Even if the thermal conductivities of glass and building brick are about the same, a 1/8 inch thickness of glass will conduct 96 times as much heat as the same area of a 12-inch brick wall. This explains why many newer plant buildings (especially if they are air-conditioned) are designed without any windows. Thermal pane (double glazed) windows, that consist of two or three sheets of glass separated by dead air space, can be used to reduce heat loss or gain, but their high cost has tended to limit their use in plants.

HOW TO SELL CONSERVATION OF ENERGY TO PLANT WORKERS

When your plant is making an effort to save energy, one of the first things you must do is pass this word to your people. Only with their cooperation can you accomplish a significant reduction except for shutting down parts of your department.

Although some of your people may see the situation as beyond their control, it's up to you to convince them otherwise. The way to do this is to explain how they are directly involved and what they can do to help.

Consider how you would feel if someone in authority were to talk costs to you, and let that guide you in what you say to your people. Suggest procedures and operations that should be looked at and changes that should be made. Talk about why energy must be saved and costs thereby reduced.

Workers often do not understand why their company makes changes in machines, equipment, or procedures because nobody takes the time to explain such matters to them. The key to selling conservation of energy is to give them the facts and point out how cutting the costs of operating the plant helps them. Talk to them in words and terms they understand.

5

How to Maintain Quality and Improve Employees' Work Performance

GUIDELINES ON PROCESS CONTROL

Process control in plants covers the disciplines, control systems, tooling, staff operations, and so forth necessary to assure error-free output of product without requiring excessive inspection. The function includes appropriately skilled and trained individuals serving as staff to assist line department workers.

Process control also provides for the correlation of measurement results between the plant and its customers. This consists of documentation from drawings and process specifications for all manufacturing and inspection procedures. Further, process control includes all the data collection and analysis, and auditing procedures needed to assure that a system or process continues to operate as planned.

Quality control systems based on process control differ considerably from systems based on final inspection. In many plants, however, inspection has been found to be both too costly and too inefficient a way to assure quality. The abandonment of heavy final inspection can be tolerated only if it is replaced with stringent controls at every step of the process.

HOW TO PERFORM STATISTICAL PROCESS CONTROL[1]

Statistical process control (SPC) is one of the most important parts of a process control system. The technique guarantees that unfavorable trends on a manufacturing process are detected and corrected long before any off-specification product is produced. Thus, it is a dependable way of determining that some factor is causing variations outside the normal variation of the process.

Statistical process control is a way of evaluating a process to identify both desirable and undesirable changes. Each characteristic that is measured is evaluated to determine if statistical process control methods can be used. Preliminary limits are set for each characteristic based on technical judgment, past experience, and/or the specification limits. These are the limits within which natural variation is expected to occur. Control sample size and frequency are also set.

Measurements are best taken in the workplace or on the process line by an individual assigned the job. This individual records the data and plots data points on control charts. See Figure 5-1 for a typical process control chart. It is critical that the person taking the samples or making measurements also do the analysis of the control charts since he or she needs to be continually up to date on the state of the process.

Once this system is underway, the process is monitored to determine if the process sample data stays within the control limits for at least 25 samples. If not, causes of the variation must be identified and eliminated until the test is passed. At this point, the process is stable enough to make a process capability study.

The purpose of the process capability study is to learn if the controlled characteristics falling outside the specification limits are below a predetermined limit. When a process capability study has been successfully completed, sufficient real process data will be available to replace the original preliminary control limits, with ongoing process monitoring limits statistically determined from the real data of the stable capable process.

In case a control chart sample point indicates that the process has gone out of control, the individual in charge of the process must immediately take two actions:

1. All output since the last in-control sample was taken must be examined to determine if it is in specification. Any deviant output must be either corrected or eliminated.

---

[1]H. James Harrington, *The Improvement Process* (New York: McGraw-Hill, Inc., 1987).

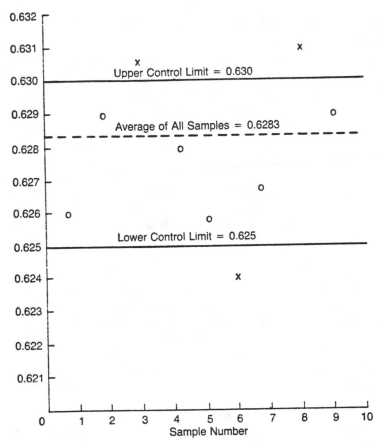

Upper and lower control limits are statistically determined limits of control.
All readings are taken at preset intervals using samples of output.
0 = readings falling within limits (variations due to chance)
x = readings falling outside limits (assignable causes to
   be corrected)

FIGURE 5-1
Typical Process Control Chart

2. The person(s) running the process must be notified immediately so that
   it can be stopped before additional off-specification product is produced.

   If there is a compelling reason to keep the process going, such as
economic necessity or customer demand, all output must be screened until
the process is back in control. In no case should the process be allowed to
continue in the hope that a few more samples will indicate that the process
has corrected itself.

Tips on Training Employees in Quality Control
Using Statistical Techniques

Statistical process control is founded on a philosophy of the need for continuous improvement. The concept of using statistical data on which to base decisions is a fundamental part of ongoing improvement. It starts with the premise that companywide productivity levels, good enough in the past, will not be good enough tomorrow. In that respect, SPC is a tool that companies use to develop ways to implement efforts and then measure their results. Supervisor-employee cooperation and involvement are the keys.

While the technical aspects of quality control, and of SPC specifically, have been well developed and perfected, training of plant employees is sometimes inadequate. In many plants, the engineers who set up processes and the workers who run them need to receive more training in the concepts and techniques.

Your primary responsibility to workers is to furnish the right tools for the job and an environment conducive to doing the job right every time. Training cannot be left to chance or to another employee who may be doing the job but is not trained to instruct a newcomer. Too often, plants do not have the in-house resources to provide the required training. However, consultants, training organizations, videotapes, films, and written instructional material are available on the subject. If you want to train employees on SPC, survey these sources for training material that fits your needs.

Among consultants, you could talk to The Leawood Group Ltd. in Leawood, KS and SORA in York, PA. The training organizations that provide videotapes, films, and written instructional material include Industrial Training Systems Corporation in Marlton, NJ, and NUS Training Corporation in Gaithersburg, MD. In addition, a Quality Assurance Bulletin is published semimonthly by the National Foremen's Institute in Waterford, CT and The Bureau of Business Practice, Inc. publishes literature on quality control.

In addition, review companies in your industry that have implemented statistical process control using a consultant or training materials. Ask for their experiences and recommendations. Don't be satisfied with advice from companies that have just sent a few employees to a class or rented a videotape.

Explaining to Plant Workers the Importance of
Quality Inputs

Acceptable quality of finished products depends on the level of quality in all the inputs to the process. Materials, equipment and tools, training, worker attitude, and supervision are among the major ones. They are interrelated to the extent that poor quality in one of them affects all the others. To get this information across to your workers, point out that:

- If the quality of materials is poor or low grade, defects will appear as the materials are being processed into a product. While these poor-quality products may be caught and removed, this runs up scrap or rework costs.
- If the equipment or tools used in the process are inferior or worn out, product quality is very likely to suffer regardless of the quality of the materials.
- If the workers aren't trained in the correct methods of handling the material, the quality of workmanship will be poor, even if the tools and equipment are in good shape.
- If workers are faced continually with shoddy or defective material, and/ or equipment that's difficult to use, and/or if workers haven't received sufficient training, they will soon develop a "don't-care" attitude. This negative attitude invariably results in their turning out defective and inferior products because of the lack of attention and carelessness. It is your responsibility to see that this doesn't happen.

When you explain the importance of quality inputs, resist the temptation to talk about "improving quality." Product quality is determined by one or more of the inputs you talked about. A defect anywhere along the process will undo all the good quality inputs that precede or follow it. To insure that the finished product meets quality standards, you have to maintain continuous quality control on everything that goes into the product.

POSITIVE WAYS TO GET EMPLOYEES TO HELP IN PREVENTING MACHINE DOWNTIME

Downtime of a machine in the plant has a negative effect on the plant's output as well as on employee's work performance. If it's a critical machine, matters could be worse; it could cause several other machines to be nonproductive until it's been attended to. By getting employees to help in preventing machine downtime, you will be benefiting everyone. Here are the ways to get employees involved in this effort:[2]

1. Discuss with them why machine downtime occurs in the plant. Explain that it's usually because parts and components wear out or need ad-

[2]*Supervisor's Handbook of Productivity and Quality Meetings* (Bureau of Business Practice, Inc., 1981).

justment. Mention which parts on the machines in your department are most subject to failure.

2. Point out that some parts fail due to excess stress or abuse. If the machines are not operated according to the manufacturer's recommendations, they may fail prematurely.

3. Remind them that all productive machines require preventive maintenance. This means that inspecting, cleaning, and adjusting schedules must be adhered to rigorously. Lubrication and adjustment prolong their service life.

4. Inform them about the signs of impending failure on machines. The most common symptoms are: excessive vibration or chatter, overheating, unexplained slowing down or speeding up, and inability to hold tolerances.

5. Ask them to report these signs and indications to you as soon as they notice or become aware of them.

Tip: Tell your machine operators that they are the experts when it comes to solving a chronic machine problem. They work with the machines every day, and know how they should be running. Your operators also know when the machines are not performing normally. By informing you of their observations, you can build on that knowledge and take the necessary steps to prevent or minimize machine downtime.

HOW TO SET AND IMPLEMENT QUALITY STANDARDS FOR EMPLOYEE OUTPUT

Ensuring that employees' output is of high quality starts with written guidelines specifying the standard of quality required. In some industries, standards are set by local, state, or federal enforcement agencies, such as the EPA. In others, standards are set by groups like the Food and Drug Administration or the various organizations that set standards for specific industries.

Your job is to make sure that employees know and understand these guidelines. You must also see that the required quality control checks are being made and that the tests are verifiable. Your first step toward reaching these objectives is to rewrite official and technical jargon into simple standard operating procedures. Then review them with your workers and quality control analysts to assure that they understand and are able to follow them.

Once these standards are implemented into your plant processes, you must now regularly confirm that all the plant's analysts are tested. Although it's more expensive to interject performance evaluation samples into the system of real samples, it's the best way to ensure a quality product.

If an analyst fails the test, consider all the possible reasons. An incorrect analysis could be due to an error in the system, such as a problem with the instrumentation. If the failure is due to an analyst's error, what you do is dictated by the experience level of the person:

- If it's a human error by an entry-level employee, additional training or coaching will help.
- If it's a human error by an experienced employee, it's probably due to a lack of concentration. Point out the problem in a nonaccusatory manner. Work with the person to determine the cause, and then do anything you can to improve the person's performance.

Answers to the Relationship Between Quality and Worker Productivity

The success of your company depends on both quantity and quality output of the plant. In many of the processes and operations, there is a close relationship between quantity and quality. But quantity can never be permitted to supersede quality. While workers may try to produce all they can, they must maintain quality. For the long term, the payoff is always on quality.

If you don't place quality ahead of quantity in directing your workers, products will eventually be rejected, piled up in the department, or sent back from later steps in the process. Other departments will complain, customers will stop buying, costs will rise, and profits will disappear. The result is likely to be neither quality nor quantity output from the plant.

HOW TO CONVINCE EMPLOYEES THAT HIGH QUALITY KEEPS COSTS DOWN

If any of your workers claim that emphasizing quality always causes costs to rise, correct the workers' thinking. Point out that, if high quality is maintained, the cost of the products is usually less. When a plant places a high priority of the quality of its products, operating and manufacturing costs are usually lower. But some employees may question that this actually occurs. You can sell the importance of the plant putting out high-quality products on an ongoing basis in a number of ways:

- Tell your workers that the best and most immediate way to reduce the cost of a product is to make it right the first time. When you produce scrap, costs go up because you are paid for your time on the job, machine costs are incurred, and productive capacity is wasted on something the plant can't sell. All those wasted costs are tacked on to the remaining good products.

- Convince them that it's to their advantage to do error-free work. Their chances to get ahead in the company are directly related to the high standards of work performance they set for themselves.

- Point out that when customers buy the plant's product, they expect it to be free of defects.

    If the plant ships some questionable or low-quality products, either inadvertently or to meet a customer deadline, and the customer detects the poor quality, your company has a real problem on its hands. The products may be returned collect—your company pays the freight costs. Then there's also the possibility that the customer may be lost and the company may never get another order. In such cases, poor quality can be very costly.

- Tell them that defects hurt the company's reputation in the marketplace. Customers won't buy the plant's product if they've heard it could be defective because other products the company has made have proved faulty.

- Emphasize that, if the products the plant makes bear a trademark, the symbol supposedly assures buyers of a certain level of quality. Advertising frequently mentions trademarks in telling and persuading customers that they can trust the product. But trademarks don't mean much if that trust is broken. The result is that the cost of advertising is for naught if the quality of the product is poor.

- Stress liability, which is a factor to be recognized and reckoned with. If the company is taken to court, subjected to government-mandated recalls, adjustments or other settlements because of product defects or failure to perform as claimed, making matters right can be very costly.

- Talk about pride. A serious as well as costly effect of turning out poor-quality products is what such workmanship does to you. You have no pride in your work. If you are determined to build quality into the company's products, you usually like your work. And when you like your work, your productivity is high. High productivity of employees means low operating costs for the company.

Tip: Tell a worker who is difficult to sell on quality that when a defect is traced back to him or her, and the cause is carelessness, the incident puts a black mark on the person's record that's hard to erase.

HOW TO PREVENT WORKER STRESS FROM AFFECTING QUALITY

Because quality of the plant product will not maintain itself, you must constantly put pressure on your workers to assure that it stays at a high level. This means that your workers may be under stress. But there's nothing harmful about the right kind of stress.

While any kind of stress will bring about a change in productivity, stress that induces fear, anger, or frustration will usually result in more negative than positive effects. Here's what happens:

- Workers who are in constant fear of a reprimand or of losing their jobs will waste productive energy coping with this fear.
- Workers who are angry because of an injustice or humiliation will experience a slow burn, affecting their performance on the job.
- Workers who are frustrated by inadequate time, tools, materials, or training vent their feelings by becoming destructive or simply by turning off.

Conversely, stress that challenges, arouses competitive feelings, or encourages initiative will be positive in its effect:

- Workers' who are challenged with a difficult assignment will call upon all their creative and innovative skills to come up with a solution that is both practical and cost effective.
- Workers who must use all of their knowledge and skill in order to compare favorably with others who are also putting out will excel both quantitatively and qualitatively.

There's nothing wrong with putting pressure on your workers to maintain or improve quality. However, to prevent worker stress from affecting quality, the stress should be positive. Encourage workers to achieve a quality level that may be hard to attain, but that is possible with the existing tools, time, materials, and training.

TIPS ON PREVENTING WORKER ATTITUDE FROM AFFECTING QUALITY

Some workers have a cheerful way of glossing over their shortcomings by saying, "Everybody makes mistakes." Yet if they were to look the truth in the eye, they would have to admit that mistakes are avoidable; they don't often make them when they are alert and paying attention. Here are some suggestions on how to deal with such workers to turn their thinking in the right direction. Say to them:

1. Keep your personal worries to a minimum. Stay rested and healthy, and maintain good relationships with others. A troubled mind will cut into quality workmanship fast.

2. Think quality whenever you start a new project or a new week of work. Stress the quality part of the work from the beginning; it will become a habit.

3. Learn where your primary quality weakness is, and figure out what you need to solve the problem. Inspect or check your own work.

4. Find out what happens next to the part, item, or material you work on. See what the assembly or finished product looks like. Your work will mean much more to you.

5. Remember the importance of quality and good workmanship. Dispel the idea that mistakes should be expected. Maintain a mental picture of doing the job right.

6. Set quality quotas for yourself. Life is more fun and work is more enjoyable when you try to reach your own goals.

HOW TO GET HELP FROM EMPLOYEES ON PRODUCTION QUALITY PROBLEMS

Employees often have ideas that can be of benefit when improvement is needed in the quality of the plant's products. But some employees have problems in organizing their thoughts and putting them across in clear and understandable form. Unless an idea is obviously good or has potential, it may be lost by the wayside and never tested simply because it wasn't presented properly.

There are three steps you can take to show employees how to go about developing quality improvement ideas and presenting them in suggestion form.[3]

First, explain why they should try to make improvement suggestions:

1. Ideas generated by employees generally cover ways that would make them more efficient.

2. Adopted suggestions enable the company to be more competitive.

3. The number of suggestions submitted are taken into account when management considers promoting or raising the pay of employees.

4. Submitters will receive awards from the suggestion department if their ideas are adopted.

Second, state the way to investigate an idea before submitting it:

[3]*Supervisor's Handbook of Productivity and Quality Meetings* (Bureau of Business Practice, 1981).

1. Describe the problem as simply as possible.
2. Estimate the cost of the current method of handling it.
3. List all possible courses of action, with the pros and cons of each.
4. Make a cost/benefit comparison.
5. Choose the best of the alternatives.

Third, tell them how to present their suggestions:

1. Summarize the current method.
2. Summarize the improvement idea.
3. State the cost of implementing the idea.
4. Give an estimate of savings if the idea is accepted.
5. Provide a detailed description of the idea.

HOW TO SET UP A QUALITY CIRCLE (QC) PROGRAM[4]

A quality circle is a small group of employees, usually 6 to 12, who meet voluntarily on a regular basis to solve problems related to the workplace. In most cases, the employees select their own chairperson, rather than have you or some other manager lead them.

Quality circles work on problems that directly affect employees' productivity. With management approval, the group is formed to solve a specific problem that the employees have identified. The quality circle is discontinued when the problem has been solved to the satisfaction of the employees.

Your employees are responsible for defining the problem to be solved, agreeing on a meeting schedule, and obtaining your approval of the project. However, if you see a quality problem in your department that lends itself to quality circle treatment, ask one of your group leaders to volunteer to organize one. Point out the benefits and advantages of quality circles if you sense any reluctance to do so.

How Plant Management Participates in Quality Circle Programs

In many manufacturing plants, a manager or facilitator is assigned to co-ordinate the quality circle program for the company. The responsibilities of the manager are to:

---

[4]H. James Harrington, *The Improvement Process* (New York: McGraw-Hill, Inc., 1987).

1. Direct the entire program.
2. Explain how a program functions and promote its advantages to management and employees.
3. Arrange for meetings to be held in a place that is free from noise and distraction. See that they are limited to a maximum of one hour.
4. Prepare and give training programs on quality circle procedures.
5. Help quality circle groups solve plant problems.
6. Serve as the leader of quality circle meetings until the chosen employee leader is ready to take over.

Functions of Quality Circle Meetings

The first few meetings of quality circle groups are usually training sessions conducted by a manager or facilitator. Employees are trained in:

- How to conduct and participate in brainstorming sessions.
- How to make cause and effect diagrams and analyses.
- How to make histograms, graphs, and check sheets for solving problems.

Following these introductory meetings, the next ones cover problem analysis that reinforces earlier training. In addition, the manager teaches:

- How to collect data, analyze it, and present it.
- How to use control charts and sampling for process control.
- How to make unstructured cause and effect diagrams.

Maintaining Commitment to Quality Circles

When quality circles are first initiated in a plant, enthusiasm among employees typically is high. Over time, however, both enthusiasm and commitment can decline considerably. If you wish to maintain support for a program, you should:

1. Avoid overpublicizing it. Too much publicity puts pressure on a new QC in its formative stage to show immediate results.
2. Make sure the objectives are reasonable and conservative. Discuss the feasibility of objectives with circle managers and leaders. Put the objectives in writing and distribute a formal statement of them.
3. Expand the training of QC members. Consider training them in group dynamics and motivational methods.
4. Report improvements resulting from solving problems in quantitative terms. To be able to do this, you must establish specific quality and production goals for each project.

Benefits and Advantages of Quality Circles

Since members of quality circles are responsible for collecting pertinent data, analyzing the problem, evaluating alternatives, and recommending solutions to management, they gain valuable training from these activities. Both management and members benefit also in that:

1. Only employees who want to be involved join a circle; as a result, members are highly motivated to participate.
2. Employees work on problems that are challenging and personally meaningful to them.
3. Quality circle members are committed to making their problem solutions work.
4. Members implement the solutions approved by management when they are within their sphere of control.
5. The program helps overcome resistance to change among all employees.

HELPING PLANT EMPLOYEES TO MINIMIZE REWORK OF POOR QUALITY PRODUCTS

You can reduce costs by talking to your workers about what they can do to decrease the number of defective products and thereby minimizing product rework. State by giving them reasons for defects. Tell them they are more likely to make mistakes when:

- They're in a hurry to finish their work for any of several reasons.
- They allow their mind to wander and don't give their full attention to their work.
- They're tired and unable to think clearly.
- They have a poor attitude, such as not caring if their work is not perfect.
- They use the wrong tool for the job or the right tool improperly.
- They've allowed their workplace to become messy and unorganized.
- They don't make an effort to be careful.

Tip: Tell your workers that absenteeism and tardiness also result in more rework of products. Explain that when workers are not at the plant, their substitutes are likely to make mistakes because of not being familiar with the job.

HOW TO ENFORCE EMPLOYEES' ADHERENCE TO PRODUCT INSPECTION PROCEDURES FOR QUALITY

An effective way to ensure that employees have adhered to product inspection procedures is to generate paperwork that accompanies material to each assembly point or step in the process during the manufacture of the product. Documentation is tangible proof of the operations that have been performed and verified on each part or subassembly. If there's no supporting inspection documentation, there's no alternative but to reinspect the whole product from A to Z.

Even if paperwork for your company's product isn't required by law, you will be satisfied with knowing you've carried out the process steps the proper way and can prove it. Documenting inspection throughout the process is well worth the effort and time to do it. Here are the steps you should follow:

1. See that the paperwork is developed and available. This is best handled by a staff organization, such as the Technical or Manufacturing Engineering Department.
2. Set up rules and regulations on what employees should do at an inspection point in the process.
3. Confirm that responsibility for carrying out the actual inspections belongs to the Quality Control Department.
4. Assign "check off" responsibilities to your workers. When they inspect and document each job in the process, they report that the job was done properly and according to specifications.
5. Route the paperwork to the Quality Assurance/Quality Control Department when the process is complete. This group audits it to ensure that the specifications have been met.

Tip: To remind employees about the importance of adherence to product inspection procedures, post signs at each workstation where paperwork is checked. State that employees who fail to inspect and document their work are subject to disciplinary measures.

8 WAYS TO IMPROVE EMPLOYEES' WORK PERFORMANCE

Your guidance, ability to evoke the competitive spirit in employees, and power to motivate them can prove to be effective ways to developing quality job habits. Here are eight ways you can improve employees' work performance:

1. Start new employees off right by setting high performance standards for them. Make sure they understand what you expect of them, and see that they get the proper training for their jobs.

2. Get to know each of your workers. Talk to them about how they are doing on the job. Tell them how they can improve and give them recognition when they do.

3. Don't accept less than the best from an employee. If a person's job performance is inferior, find out why. It may be that he or she needs additional training or individual coaching.

4. Encourage creativity and innovation. Give employees credit for suggestions; your recognition promotes pride which is the key to quality performance.

5. Focus on good workmanship and attention to the job. Quality-conscious workers realize they must make products that satisfy customers to maintain the company's competitive edge and to protect their own job security.

6. Do a thorough job of inspection. Careful inspection insures high quality in machine and equipment maintenance and in employee performance, provided you can trace problems to their causes and correct them.

7. Work closely with other departments and supervisors. A good plant quality control program requires the participation and cooperation of all employees and supervisors.

8. Promote quality performance of employees with top-notch leadership. As a supervisor, you set the pattern of attitudes in your work group. Once employees get the quality habit, they take pride in being part of a team that turns out high-quality products.

PITFALLS TO AVOID TO GET COOPERATION BETWEEN PRODUCTION SHIFTS

When departments on different shifts in the plant don't get along, or simply don't realize the importance of working together toward a goal, efficiency usually suffers. This leads to poor-quality, high-cost products. The problem often can be traced to dissention and an uncooperative attitude among the plant's supervisors. Here are some pitfalls that you and other supervisors must avoid if cooperation between shifts is to be a reality:

- In any plant, there are going to be supervisors who do their jobs differently. But a difference in supervisory techniques doesn't mean that one supervisor is wrong while another is right. Unfortunately, however, one supervisor may be disdainful of another because of disagreement over the way the other's department is run.

- If a supervisor says something to another that is misinterpreted as unwarranted criticism, friction between the two is bound to develop. When that happens, help and common effort become nonexistent.
- Supervisors sometimes don't work together because they fear helping someone else up the company ladder ahead of themselves. Thus, they may be reluctant to share ideas or answers to mutual problems if there is a possibility another supervisor could benefit from them.
- Some supervisors just want to be left alone. They believe their shifts are efficient and productive. Therefore, they see no reason to interface with other supervisors.

How to Get Along Better with Other Supervisors

Problems in cooperating with fellow supervisors can arise from several sources. But you can get along better with your peers if you:

- *Respect their authority.* Don't infringe on the authority other supervisors have over their own workers. Never ask workers in another department to do something; instead, ask their supervisor for help.
- *Recognize their position.* Avoid criticizing their supervisory methods in front of others. If another department makes a mistake that affects your workers or operations, go to the other supervisor to discuss the problem in private.
- *Accept their advice whenever possible.* Do it with the same willingness you give advice to them. By taking the time to listen and consider, you may learn something that will help you do your job better.

There are three benefits you can realize by maintaining good relations with fellow supervisors:

1. Each department performs more efficiently when everybody works together to make a quality product at minimum cost.
2. It's easier to solve big problems when they come up if cooperation is already common.
3. A pleasant work atmosphere in the plant leads to higher productivity and better workmanship among all employees.

How to Ensure Employees Use Computers for Operations and Control

PLANT USE OF COMPUTERS

Most plants today, at least the larger ones, are using computers to aid management in manufacturing operations and control functions. The information obtained from computers has greatly helped in product design and engineering, process and production operations, inventory control, quality control, robotics and machine control, maintenance, and the integration of manufacturing operations.

The Computer's Communication Capabilities

The importance of communicating data and information—not only to supervisors, but to all employees—cannot be overemphasized. Today, a company is successful in proportion to its ability to rapidly and efficiently gather, interpret, and transmit all information describing its activities.

The complexity and amount of data needed to conduct a business have greatly increased over the years. Yet many companies haven't changed their manufacturing control systems appreciably. Managers frequently are trying to control systems and operations with information that is incomplete as well as out of date.

Using the computer's communications capabilities helps managers and supervisors with this function. The application is through the use of the computer at the executive decision level to implement management policy, and at the operational level to monitor and control the operations and processing activities.

INSTRUCTING EMPLOYEES ON THE USE, TYPES, AND CAPABILITIES OF PLANT COMPUTERS

If your plant is relatively large, or if your company operates more than one plant, management has probably installed at least one mainframe computer. This is usually the largest computer the company owns in terms of capital cost and processing power.

The memory capacity of a *mainframe computer* is in the millions of characters, and its calculating speed is measured in millions of events per second. Most of these computers cost at least hundreds of thousands of dollars and the newer models are up in the millions.

A mainframe is used to store the company's most widely used data bases including financial and accounting information, personnel and payroll data, and sales and production records. In addition to the routine jobs, such as payroll preparation and monthly accounting statements, a mainframe is used to put out management reports on production, sales, and profits. Because of their high calculating speed and large memories, many companies also use them for research and development.

The *minicomputer* is the next largest machine in the computer family, and the one most likely to be used in plants where it processes data specific to the plant's needs. These machines usually have memory capacities of 8 megabytes up to 2 gigabytes and calculating speeds of approximately 100 megahertz. The price of a minicomputer is not likely to exceed $250,000.

Microcomputers include the personal computer (PC) and other smaller machines used for industrial process control. Typical memory capacities are 120,000,000 bytes/characters of storage and 4,000,000 in RAM.

Calculating speeds range from 10 to 100,000 calculations per second. Most of these machines, along with a keyboard, CRT screen, and printer, can be purchased for less than $10,000, including the software.

The computer component of a programmable controller is usually in the mini- or microsize range. Input devices for a controller include a keyboard and CRT screen, which allow a programmer to make changes and to see displayed the logic system created.

Additional input devices receive signals from the machine being controlled such as that an operation has been completed, or that a predetermined liquid level, temperature, pressure, or item count has been reached. Output signals from a controller tell machines to start or stop operating steps and cycles, to change the set points of control instruments, or to open and close control valves.

ENSURING DOCUMENTATION TO HELP WORKERS USE THE COMPUTER

If you participate in selecting and procuring a computer for the plant, make sure the system is supplied with adequate documentation. The degree to which it is supplied is the degree to which you will have confidence in the system and will experience smooth operations. This user's reference manual is the guide to successful productive work.

You will find that one of the first levels of documentation in the manual is referred to as *the system overview*. In this area, how the overall system works is explained. Each part of the system is considered separately and described functionally.

The functional description usually includes information on the module, the input that is expected by the computer at each step, and the output that the computer user can expect to receive at various times during the use of that program. Some description should also be furnished of the file layout and the records in each file.

The most important documentation for a computer system is called *the user documentation*. It is the most critical to the plant because it gives the persons using the computer system a detailed step-by-step procedure that must be followed in order to do each job function.

In addition to the instructions on all job steps in each functional area of a system are the optional responses that can be made by the person at the terminal or work station. Errors and how to correct them should also be discussed so that an operator can become truly independent after being trained.

Another level of documentation is known as *the programmer's reference*. This is a technical package that is provided for the programmer who is responsible for supporting and maintaining the software. Since it is meant to supply in-depth descriptions of logic flow and coding (programming) that make up the system, it is the documentation least likely to be furnished users of the computer.

If you find that your responsibilities require you to frequently use the computer, you will probably want to add some special step-by-step procedures to the manual. A few examples are start-of-the-day steps, end-of-the-month jobs, and backup procedures.

Make sure that each routine you wish to include in your manual is complete to the last detail. This will prove to be invaluable to you when some day you want to delegate a job. Anyone picking up your set of instructions should be able to follow your directions without asking you for any extra help.

HOW TO GET BUDGET APPROVAL FOR A COMPUTER

If you want the funds to computerize your department or plant, you must be able to give sound business reasons for your request, and then back them up with results that can be demonstrated. To justify the cost of the computer and its implementation, you'll need to prepare a proposal that is well thought out and planned.

You'll have to decide how to present your request, show the return on investment, and give a description of expected results. You should also have an implementation plan, describe how the system will work, indicate what it will cost, and give the expected effects on other functions in the plant.

The best way to start is to examine your operation to determine the benefits you can expect from computerization. The apparent benefits are reduced labor cost, reduced overtime, reduced energy cost, reduced inventory, and increased equipment uptime.

Other benefits that are not so obvious but are nevertheless just as cost effective are:

- Improved communications between departments.
- Reduction in the cost of purchasing spare parts and equipment.
- Reduction of scrap product from malfunctioning equipment.
- Faster access to production and machine performance records.
- Elimination of wasted time waiting at storerooms.

Collecting and Determining Current Costs

After listing the benefits to be realized through computerization, determine and collect the current associated costs of those operations and activities that will be improved. This information will serve as the base for calculating expected savings and lower costs.

You can most easily collect current costs from historical records. When such information is not available, a three- to four-month collection period should be used to establish the base data.

The base data can then be used to set goals. For example, you might expect to reduce the current weekly average of 80 overtime hours of employees to 20 within six months, or reduce the plant's stores inventory 10 percent in twelve months.

These expected results are more easily understood by management if you show them on graphs or charts. It's wise to also mention that the time required to achieve the improvements may vary from six to 18 months, depending on the commitment of management to make a successful implementation.

Showing How Computer Reports Help to Achieve Goals

Reports generated by the computer greatly aid in achieving goals. Here is an example of how this is done. One of the reports issued for the maintenance department will highlight the most costly equipment in terms of maintenance labor and replacement parts. This report may also rank the equipment by the frequency of corrective work orders issued for its repair.

Such a report enables a supervisor to determine the cause of excessive breakdown maintenance for critical production equipment, and then correct the cause. When this is done, increased uptime of machines and equipment will result.

Three benefits can be realized by using the report for making decisions:

1. Equipment that is most costly from either downtime or excessive maintenance costs can be given attention first.
2. The causes of the excessive costs are pinpointed.
3. The information could lead to a decision to replace equipment rather than continue to repair it.

Describing Your Implementation Plan

You should now state what software you will use with the computer. The software should enable you to realize the benefits that you expect from computerization. Make certain the software you selected can produce the reports you need.

Following this, describe your implementation plan—how you plan to introduce the computer in the plant and train employees to use it. Consult with vendors of the proposed hardware and software to get their input on the cost of your proposed system and its implementation. Confirm these figures by talking to customers of these vendors.

Calculating the Payback

To calculate the payback period, take the cost of the proposed system and its implementation, and determine the number of months it will take to recover this cost through the resultant savings. Another calculation in this area that often draws management's attention is as follows: Determine the company's profit margin on current sales and show how sales would need to increase in order to affect the company's bottom line in the same manner as the cost savings from your proposed computerization.

Making the Budget Request to Management

When you have completed your study and calculations, prepare a presentation for management.

- Be sure to include visuals (graphs or charts) and plan to make your presentation last no longer than an hour.
- Tell management you feel your department should be computerized, and state the reasons why it should be done. Give an itemized listing of your goals and the number of months that you think will be needed to reach them.
- Describe your implementation plan to show how computerization will take place. Talk about the roles the vendors and your department people will play.
- Discuss and illustrate how the information and reports generated by the computer will be used to achieve the cost reductions and more efficient performance of people and machines. Be conservative but realistic.
- Conclude the presentation by asking for the money to purchase and install a system. This final part of your presentation is the most critical. At this time you must show the expected return on investment and the payback period.
- Give management a reasonable amount of time to respond. If the request for funds is turned down, ask for a written explanation giving the reasons for its failing to be approved. Upper management usually will respect this request. Moreover, history shows that whenever such a request is made, management will more often approve a budget than not.

However, recognize that upper management may ignore requests for funding of a project if it is not vigorously pursued. All the more reason for you to do your best when making your presentation.

7 PITFALLS TO AVOID WHEN IMPLEMENTING THE COMPUTER

The successful implementation of the computer in a plant can change the plant from an inefficient, poorly managed facility to a highly organized and profitable one. Computerization, for example, can significantly reduce equipment downtime and make the most productive use of your people.

Don't, however, overlook the possibility of an unsuccessful implementation of a system, with the confusion and frustration that go with it. This can happen if you don't recognize the pitfalls present and take steps to avoid them. If you are given the responsibility of launching a system, you must contend with seven major pitfalls:

1. Don't expect that the computer will arrive at the plant completely ready to go and programmed to fit your needs precisely. Realize that your accounting books and maintenance records probably aren't exactly identical to that of any other company. To be more realistic, assume that some modifications will be necessary before the system fits in smoothly.

2. A very common danger is lack of upper management's interest and attention. Although the upper echelon may have been very involved during the selection phase, this often ends when implementation begins. Without management's guidance and support to resolve crisis situations or provide spare resources, the implementation may be more difficult.

3. Put aside any notion that you'll be able to anticipate your operating and maintenance needs, and take all necessary actions yourself. Face the fact that even the smallest computer is a very complicated gadget. Since, more likely than not, you have no idea of how it functions, how could you expect to foresee every detail of what's needed to keep it up and running? Find a source of expert advice and rely on it.

4. If you expect that all your workers will like the computer right from the start, you'll be sadly mistaken. Some plant workers may burn at the thought that a heartless piece of metal and plastic can take over and become your new favorite toy. They must be sold on the computer as a tool to make their work easier rather than as a threat to their job security or self-esteem.

5. A serious pitfall is the failure to come up with an effective implementation plan or to use a poor one. A plan is a predefined, mutually agreed-upon set of objectives and responsibilities for the implementation of the computer. There must also be a clearly defined timetable on the procedural steps, including a decision on when sufficient data have been loaded into the system to put it on line.

6. Another problem to contend with is to not conduct training sessions too early. If workers are trained on how to use the system in a formal training program, but are not called upon to use that knowledge for weeks afterward, much will be forgotten. Retraining will be necessary and cost overruns are inevitable. You must decide when the system will be started up and plan the training accordingly.

7. A frustrating pitfall to avoid is to set an unachievable start-up date. Several problems will arise including a lowering of morale if the date is not met. Additionally, the payback period for the computer installation, which was crucial to its justification, might not be realized.

COMPUTER PORTABILITY: A PLUS TO AUTOMATION

Recent improvements in technology have resulted in hand-held computer terminals that are powerful yet compact. In the process area, at the shipping and receiving dock, and in the warehouse and storeroom areas, portability is now automating jobs that have never been automated before. Moreover, these rugged tools can withstand extreme heat, cold, moisture, shaking, dust, or dirt.

Accompanying this advance—actually part of it—has been the growth of battery power to aid productivity. Although office workers can use two hands and a table top when operating a terminal, plant workers need systems that are truly mobile. The introduction of smaller, lighter, and longer-lasting batteries has enabled workers to use terminals in more challenging applications.

A good example of this is the hand-held, radio frequency, data collection terminal that a forklift operator uses. This device guides an operator to locations for picking and storing. It also collects data on-line each time material moves. In shipping and receiving areas, the terminal is used to scan bar codes that record changes to inventory. With such applications, UHF radio waves are used to transmit data to and from a host computer in real time, resulting in up-to-date control over material handling, warehousing, inventory, and similar operations.

Several benefits and advantages can be realized from the use of portable computer in plants:

1. Workers can stay at their workplaces rather than make repeated trips to a stationary computer or record information manually for later data entry into the host computer. Thus, workers' efficiency improves.
2. Accuracy improves, particularly when hand-held data collection is combined with bar coding and scanning, reducing the need for keypunching and the opportunities for human error.
3. Information management and daily decision making also improve. Hand-held data computers make current sales and inventory data available much faster than manual data collection methods.

Even though the information and data obtained from portable systems can be quite sophisticated, implementation of the technology by a plant's organization is most often trouble-free. Today's hand-held data computers can be programmed in standard programming languages and can run software packages that support specific applications.

HOW TO GET PLANT WORKERS TO CONQUER COMPUTER ANXIETY

As stated earlier, not all people readily accept the computer when it is first brought into the plant, and some people, including those in management, actually fear it. Yet many supervisors and employees have conquered computer fear and are communicating more effectively because of its use. Others, however, remain plagued with computer phobia.

Here are some computer-conquering suggestions that you should give your workers:[5]

- Be willing to admit your ignorance. Whether talking to a computer trainer or a junior clerk, don't hesitate to say, "Help me."
- Believe that the computer is not here to take your job away; it is here to assist you to do better.
- Dispel the myth that a person must be good at math to click with computers. What you need is to be very logical and very systematic.
- Begin with something that will guarantee small successes when starting to learn and when teaching others. Don't overreact when the computer tells you that you gave it an illegal command.
- Study the computer inside and out. Learn what it can't do. Remember, it needs your brains; you're the boss.

SELLING PLANT WORKERS ON USING THE COMPUTER

In many plants, the computer is fast becoming as indispensable as the telephone. Unfortunately, it is in no way as universally understood. This situation exists partly because computer technology has grown at a tremendous rate over only a few years. It has also come about because there has been too much mystery and too much distrust of this remarkable tool. For these reasons, many employees are alarmed when they learn that their company plans to install computers for conducting its plant operations.

Yet with the demand for computer services including data processing, software products and turnkey systems are expected to grow four fold by the mid-1990s. Many companies see the computer as an inevitable investment if a company is to grow, much less remain competitive in its industry. Despite this movement, however, some companies are concerned with selling the computer to their employees, realizing that if its introduction and use don't get off to a good start, the investment may not pay off.

Complicating the issue, acceptance of the computer must go beyond the line and staff people. Lower, middle, and upper management people are also involved. It's no disgrace to be confused by computer hardware and software. Even the best supervisors are mystified if they haven't had any training in this area or are unaware of the great value of management information systems.

[5]*Public Management* (1120 G. St., NW, Washington, DC 20005).

Whether you are a supervisor in production, engineering, marketing, purchasing, finance or any other field that relies on automated systems to an extent, you must become updated in this technology. Companies usually expect supervisors to play key roles in gaining the optimum benefits from its data processing equipment.

How to Promote Computer Use

When you study computers and their operation, you will see there are many factors to be considered and many matters to be attended to before, during and after a computer is brought into the plant. Since you are closest to the firing line, the success of a computer acceptance program is often your responsibility. However, you need to have the backing and support of management in this effort.

This backing should be in the form of publicity and promotion to show employees why the company is making the investment in computer hardware and software. Complementing this, you should point out the advantages and benefits of computer systems to both employees and management and follow this with listing the many operations in the plant where systems can be used. Here a just a few of the benefits you can list for your workers.

- Large-scale computers keep inventory, fill orders, make purchases, perform all accounting functions, and issue innumerable reports.
- In the control area, computers aid maintenance, processes and operations, quality control, cost control, and many other functions.
- Computers are being used for tooling and product design; they are also interfaced with numerical control equipment for production.
- In the design function, a computer provides instant feedback, speeding up the design process and making it more accurate.

Although a plant may install a computer to handle only one or two of these applications, management must know the capabilities and potential of any system before it is purchased. Presenting that information to employees then can help to sell it as well as promote its value.

TECHNIQUES FOR USING THE COMPUTER TO RAISE WORKER PRODUCTIVITY

Starting here and throughout the remaining chapters, you will see how the computer is rapidly becoming the major management tool in the operation and control of the plant. Not only has the computer raised productivity, it has also improved quality, reduced costs, and increased efficiency. You should stress these benefits when talking to your workers about computers.

While the completely automated computer-controlled plant is still in the future, computerized information for management is the forefront of this movement. Schedules, production reports, quality records, cost reports, inventory records and other data are playing an important role in the trend to plant computerization. When you instruct employees on the use of the computer, explain how the following techniques are currently being used in the operation and control of plants.

Material Handling and Inventory Control

Plant management has always been concerned with how much inventory the plant should carry. Since it costs money to carry it, the less the better. But too little inventory of raw materials or finished products hinders the plant's ability to serve customers quickly and thus be competitive. With the computer, inventory control has been made considerably easier.

Material handling and inventory operations are greatly speeded up by putting all the data and information in the computer. Calculations of net material available, the economic order quantity, the reorder point, and the value of the inventory can be made instantly. Thus the current status of the inventory is available to managers at any time. Either a mini- or a microcomputer has the capacity to make these calculations for thousands of items.

However, the computer can do much more on material handling and inventory control through a system called Material Resource Planning (MRP). With this system, the computer is preprogrammed to calculate the effects of a production schedule on raw material and parts inventory, and on purchasing. If there are enough material and parts on hand, the computer reserves them for this particular order; if not, purchase orders are issued automatically with delivery dates set to meet the schedule.

By adopting MRP, a plant can greatly reduce the amount of inventory carried. Plants using the system report that inventories can be reduced as much as 50 percent. In addition, inventories are more accurate and customer service is improved.

Manufacturing Operations

The use of computers to control manufacturing operations has been of great benefit to plants in two basic industries:

1. Mechanical fabrication plants in which machine tools modify solid materials, usually metals, into products or components of products.
2. Continuous process plants in which solids or fluids go through a series of chemical or physical steps resulting in intermediate or finished products.

Mechanical operations such as drilling, turning, grinding, broaching, and threading were automated as early as the 1950s with the development of numerical control (NC). This system involves use of paper tape with punched holes to instruct an electromechanical controller to run a machine through several operations automatically and in sequence.

If the machine is equipped with an automatic tool changer, the taped instructions will also call for tool changes, which are made much more quickly than could be accomplished manually. While NC increases production capacity, improves quality, and reduces labor costs, the computer can be used to further improve the system in two ways:

1. *By simplifying the tape preparation.* Originally, the tape is punched in a special machine operated from a keyboard; typed instructions show up as punched holes in the tape. The typist follows a set of instructions prepared by an engineer who has manually made the calculations required for positioning the machine tool so that it cuts, drills, and grinds in the right locations and to the desired depths. If the machining job is complicated, these calculations are long and prone to error.

   Simplification of this procedure is accomplished by putting a computer ahead of the tape puncher. The engineer, using special software and a high-level language, gives the computer only the basic instructions required to accomplish the machining operations. The computer makes the detailed calculations needed to guide the machine, and instructs the punching machine to produce a properly coded tape.

2. *By replacing the electromechanical controller.* There are two ways of doing this. With the first, the computer is put between the tape reader and the machine tool controls. The tape is used only once; after passing through the reader, its instructions are stored in the computer's memory. This eliminates the need to change tapes every time a new product or part is to be made. The instructions are sent directly to the machine tool from the computer.

   The second way of replacing the controller involves using a central computer to control a number of machines. No longer using punched tape, the central computer sends instructions to the machine's tools either through their own computers, or, if they are not so equipped, through a specially designed machine control unit. Instructions for various machining jobs are stored in the central computer's memory and fed to the machine tools as needed.

Each machine may be working on a different product at any one time, or all machines may be working on the same product. With this system, each machine tool tells the central computer when it has completed a job, when it is ready for another job, and the number of types of products it has made. This information enables the central computer to make the most efficient use of the machines available, virtually eliminating idle time waiting for instructions.

Process Control

Automatic control of process equipment is important to a plant for its advantages in upgrading product quality, smoothing production operations, and reducing production costs. Many of the larger installations of the process industries, such as chemical plants and oil refineries, would not be possible without automatic control.

With the computer playing a major role in the automatic control of continuous processes, high levels of accuracy, response speed, and sophisticated control are being achieved. Computers are being used at three levels of control to accomplish this:

1. *Control of instruments.* Electronic instruments are replacing pneumatic ones in many industrial plants because they provide faster response and more reliable operation. In addition, the electronic instruments are more readily converted to computer control. If closer control is wanted than is possible with a standard instrument, a microprocessor can be added.

   The microprocessor is a silicon chip that contains in its circuitry all the essential parts of a central processing unit—arithmetic, logic, and control. It has built-in instructions applying to its particular purpose; it also has the ability to perform calculations on data coming from the process to be controlled.

2. *Control of process equipment.* In conventional process control, the variable to be controlled is usually measured after it has passed through the equipment. But this results in over- or undercontrol if input conditions suddenly change.

   Installing a computer in the process permits much better control. The sensor of the variable to be controlled is moved to the inlet of the process, and a flow meter is installed with it. Factors affecting the variable are also measured and controlled. All the data are fed into the computer, which is programmed to solve the equation applicable to the system.

   The computer calculates what the variable will be if nothing is done. The control mechanism makes the necessary adjustments to the factors before the process system is upset, resulting in much closer control of the variable.

3. *Control of the plant.* Many plants try to optimize profits by adjusting the mix of products they make and the size of their production runs to current business conditions. Raw material availability and cost, sales estimates for each product, and prices that the products are expected

to carry are considered. While the product mix and size of runs could be determined from an operations model and calculated manually, a better way is to establish a computerized operations center for this purpose.

With this approach, a plant optimization model is constructed and programmed into the computer. When costs and other factors are put into the data base, the output consists of instructions to management on what products to run and how much of each. By following the instructions, management is able to maximize plant profits.

OVERCOMING COMPUTER OPERATOR FEARS

The attitude of employees toward the computer can make the difference between success and failure in its use. A typical operator fear is, "My job will be eliminated." If not that, a person may say, "The computer is going to catch every mistake I make."

Another fear often expressed is that the computer will take over their thought processes. This fear may cause anxiety and depression. Computer operators should be shown how a system will keep them from making mistakes instead of how it will keep track of the mistakes they make. Here are some ways you can help your workers overcome their fears of the computer:

1. Tell them that the persons who write the software for computers recognize that plant employees may have fears. They counter them by writing programs that make the computer "friendly." A friendly computer is one that is easy to operate and almost impossible to break. It has been known to say "please," provide simple and easy to understand instructions, and kindly point out errors to its operators. Here are the key features that make a system user friendly:

   • Simple menus.
   • Screens and reports that are easily customized by the user.
   • A lack of command language.
   • Speed between changes in functions.
   • Fast data retrieval.
   • Easy-to-read screens.
   • Easy input/output of files with other systems.
   • Minimal start-up training required.

   With today's software capabilities, all good systems should have these characteristics. Compare one system with another. Don't rely on a software vendor's guarantee that its system is user friendly.

2. Explain that a friendly system is programmed to alert the user to trouble ahead. For example, if the system is overloaded or unable to grant a user's request, it can so report or at least beep or blink. Friendly computers also say when they are "down" or out-of-service so that users don't get the idea they have made a mistake or are at fault otherwise.

3. Compare the computer to a new phone system: It may be strange and appear difficult to get used to, but only for a short time. Many workers enjoy using the computer and consider it fun, like playing video games.

How to Sell the Use of Personal Computers

Selling the computer to employees will be much easier if you install equipment that is designed and structured for the job it is to do. For instance, a microcomputer is much less foreboding than a mainframe. If a department or plant is relatively small, there is no need to confuse employees with complex equipment that will not be used.

Also, the computer terminal will be better accepted if human engineering is considered when installing it. For example, here are five steps you can take to promote the use of personal computers:

1. Provide seats for operators that are adjustable and comfortable.
2. Arrange the furniture so that controls are easily accessible.
3. Place work tables so that they are convenient for organizing computer output and supporting documentation.
4. Install soft and diffused lighting so that there is no glare on the terminal screen to cause eye strain of the operator.
5. Prevent reflection by making the angle of the screen adjustable. The more that you can do ergonomically for employees, the less likely there will be cause for complaint with the computer and the more readily it will be accepted.

Tips on Making Employees Computer Literate

To be computer literate, you have to understand what can be accomplished with a computer so you can take advantage of its capabilities not only for your job, but for other work as well. This, basically, is what you want to put across to your workers to make them feel they are in control of the computer. To make that point, here is what you should say:

- State that overcoming any fear of the computer they might have will enable them to become much more efficient and accurate in performing their jobs.

- Tell them that they don't need to know a lot about hardware, software, the computer, and the peripheral equipment. Explain that they should be able to turn a unit on and get results from their input efforts.
- Point out the value of knowing what the data base contains. Demonstrate how they can retrieve information themselves, and thus feel more self-reliant.
- Discuss menus and self-help functions. Show them the menus they must be familiar with and how to bring them up on the screen.
- Say that it's up to them if they want to learn more, but being knowledgeable on what the computer can do and on how to tell the computer to do it are of most importance.

HOW TO TRAIN PLANT WORKERS ON USING THE COMPUTER

Perhaps the best way to sell plant workers on use of the computer is to see that they are well trained in how to operate it. Workers lose much of their fear of computers when they know what they can and can't do with them. When employees build the confidence they need to deal successfully with computers and systems, they soon forget their initial fears. Knowing how to run a computer gives a person an ego boost, a sense of power, and a feeling of control.

Training programs that are two-fold in nature have proved to work best. The first part should be an awareness presentation that is designed to motivate users to participate in the system's success and to alleviate any apprehension that users who are new to the system may have.

The second part should consist of objective-based instruction on the functions and tasks performed by the employees on the computer. While the first part may be very general in nature and suitable for all employees, the second part must be selective and designed for the employee's specific application area.

Although trainers should be well versed in data processing and computer operation, they should also be good teachers. Trainers that are understanding, easy to get along with, and well liked provide valuable assistance in selling new systems. They usually have the patience to stay on the job until the trainees feel confident they can operate the computer by themselves.

Tip: When you decide to make the change from the manual or standard procedure to the computer, do it by operating the department "in parallel" (both ways) for a period of time. This not only gives workers more confidence that they will not make an uncorrectable mistake or error, but also enables everyone to work out problems that might arise. Within a short period, most if not all of the "bugs" will be eliminated and employees will agree that the computer actually does make their jobs easier.

7

Proven Techniques for Handling Plant Workers' Safety Problems

HOW TO CREATE EMPLOYEE INTEREST IN PLANT SAFETY

How do you get employees interested in safety? How do you motivate them to avoid accidents? Getting employees interested in plant safety can be a difficult job because many people think that accidents happen only to someone else. They feel that they're too careful and alert to make a mistake, that they will never get hurt. But an accident can happen to anyone, and this is what you need to get across.

One way you can create interest in plant safety is to give employees the responsibility of checking for hazards in the workplace. Workers get satisfaction and a sense of achievement when management takes action to correct a hazard as a result of their suggestion.

You should always listen carefully to the comments and suggestions on safety made by employees. After all, a person on the job is closer to the hazard than anyone. Some workers may have had near misses on accidents, or they may simply be aware of a hazardous condition from being exposed to it day after day.

Communicating About Plant Safety

Promoting awareness and motivating employees to work safely requires putting a lot of emphasis on communicating about safety. We learn to provide safe working conditions and to work safely by talking, listening, and reading about plant safety problems as well as by observing what's going on around us. The more thorough we are in getting and giving information about plant safety, the more we can help ourselves and others to avoid accidents. Operating procedures, specifications, and regulations for working safely must be written, distributed, and discussed. For example, you should see that the following information and similar instructions are provided:

- What to do in case of a fire.
- Where fire extinguishers and hoses are located.
- Whom to notify in case of a major spill.
- Where respirators and gas masks are located.

In addition, you must plan how you will give your safety talks, the words you will use, and how you will say them. You must know the attitude and experience of your listeners and tailor what you say accordingly.

But that's only part of the job of talking about plant safety and persuading employees to work safely. You must follow up, first, right after talking about safety to see if what was said was understood, and second, sometime later to see if your employees' attitudes are right and if their work habits are good.

Training for Plant Safety

Training workers also should be a part of every plant safety program. Instructors and trainers have the important responsibility of teaching the safe way to work and do jobs.

One of the best ways to train and instruct workers is with on-the-job training (OJT), a method by which you do the training, one on one. Whether it is called coaching, counseling, or educating, the critical element with this type of training is one individual helping another to work safely.

The method lends itself well to training plant workers on such procedures as:

- How to operate hazardous machines and equipment.
- How to handle fire extinguishers and hoses.
- How to deal with hazardous materials.
- How to handle gas cylinders.

Your safety training program should include viewing videos and films on head, eye, hands, and feet protection, and on how to work safely in the plant. Be sure you also give workers plant safety manuals and booklets on safe work procedures.

Successful managers of plant safety programs have learned, however, that handing out specifications, safety manuals, and job descriptions is not enough to assure that workers are being trained in plant safety procedures. For one thing, there is no way to be sure that the material is read. For another, if it is read, is it understood? Training is effective only if the sender (supervisor) gets through to the receiver (worker). If your employees only read or hear the words but don't understand them, then they won't get the message.

The surest way of finding out if your employees understand instructions on how to work safely is through feedback, either by their questions or by the answers to questions you ask them. At some plants, supervisors use a group of general questions that they ask employees after they have become familiar with the plant and their jobs, and have read the safety rules and regulations. If the employees can't answer the questions, the supervisor knows that they need more training.

How to Indoctrinate Workers in Plant Safety

Safety indoctrination is often thought of as putting up posters, posting notices on bulletin boards, holding safety meetings, and passing out safety rule books. Is it any wonder that plant safety is sometimes considered apart from getting work done?

Safety indoctrination should include making employees and management alike aware that their personal goals and well-being are closely related to the company's profitability. Safety efforts must pay their way as with any other part of the business.

Relating accidents and injuries to the sales or units of production required to pay for them will convince management as nothing else will that preventing accidents must be a major objective in running the business. Awareness of the extent to which production and sales must be increased to pay for accidents creates a situation in which most companies realize that management must take corrective action.

Although management's concern and awareness may lead to the adoption of an accident reduction and loss control program, more personal reasons must be supplied to employees to make them want to participate in the program. Few employees completely understand the extent to which their own future and that of their families' is tied in with the company's safety program.

Therefore, it is essential that you make employees aware of the extent and nature of the accidents happening in the plant and how workers are affected. The National Safety Council and several insurance companies have made films on this subject. You should consider showing these to employees as part of your plant safety indoctrination program.

Safety indoctrination should always be directed toward specific employees or departments based on their particular problems. For example, promote the wearing of safety glasses if the frequency or severity of eye injuries in the department is high. Generalizing on safety usually does not get results; besides, it can be costly.

Although more and more companies feel that their workplaces are environmentally safe and the majority of their employees are safe workers, companies have found that most of the accidents occurring in the plant can be attributed to a limited number of employees, a few unsafe practices, and a minimum number of physical facility inadequacies. Knowing who, what, and where the problems are can considerably reduce the cost of safety indoctrination.

You can play a major role in this effort by analyzing machinery and equipment accidents and investigating property damage accidents. By correlating this data with information obtained from first-aid and injury records, those individuals and departments with inefficient and unsafe practices can be brought to light.

The engineering department can help by assigning dollar cost figures to equipment and machine accidents, spills, and fires, among other accidents. Such costs should convince management that control measures are needed and will pay off. With this information, you can inform and advise those individuals and departments of the unsafe practices and conditions that are under their control. You can use costs to make the point that these practices and conditions threaten the company's and their own goals. At the same time, you should solicit suggestions for eliminating or controlling the causes of safety problems.

Of course, problems that only management can handle should be separated from those that the employees can control. For example, employees are unable to eliminate machines, equipment or tools that are hazardous or inadequate for the operations. What management does to correct these conditions, as well as adopting employee suggestions for eliminating causes, represents an effective form of safety indoctrination.

How to Personalize Safety Training[1]

Although recent accomplishments in plant safety have reduced the number of plant accidents, much remains to be done. As part of that effort, you must convince your employees that accidents are caused—they don't just

---

[1]Reprinted from W. H. Weiss, "Use Personalized Safety Training," *Successful Supervisor*, July 9, 1990, Dartnell, Chicago, IL 60640.

happen. Workers must stop believing that accidents happen because their number is up, it's the law of averages, it's the price of progress, or they are accident-prone.

These are all lame excuses for accidents and far from being logical explanations of why they happen. The accident-prone theory, in particular, has been harmful to plant safety progress. People accepting this idea have been led to believe that there is little that can be done to prevent accidents because accident proneness couldn't be cured.

Fortunately, the accident-prone theory is no longer accepted by most people involved in occupational safety. More and more agree that there is a great deal that can be done to *prevent* accidents and keep workers free from injury.

Leaders in promoting and implementing safety believe that there is a close relationship between good safety and good supervision. With proper and adequate direction, motivation, instruction and enforcement of rules, employees can work in environments filled with hazards without having accidents. When safety awareness is lacking, workers find numerous ways of getting hurt.

You can and should develop safety awareness in your employees. You can do this best by talking about safety at every opportunity. But you also need to recognize that even though you lecture to employees on safety, show them excellent safety films, and distribute the best safety booklets available, your employees still may fail to apply these safety lessons to the actual work situation. What is needed most is personalized safety training.

This type of training includes telling employees specifically what the hazards in the workplace are and how to avoid them. Talking in generalities about the need to be safe is not enough. Each employee must be taught what to do, how to do it and certainly what not to do.

When you personalize safety training, you, the supervisor, must do the training. You are most familiar with an employee's knowledge, skills and temperament. You also know the most about the procedures, equipment and machines that may be involved in the plant operations. While personal training will take more of your time than other training methods, the extra responsibility pays off because of your greater effectiveness.

In addition to personal training, you must enforce plant safety rules. Enforcement is an important element in all safety programs. You must also take corrective action whenever safety rules and regulations are broken. Further, you should carefully watch safety offenders after violations to make sure they are not repeated.

If your employees put on their safety glasses or replace a machine guard when they see a member of the safety department but have no hesitancy about working without eye protection or a guard when you are watching, it is obvious that you have not accepted your safety responsibility and are not enforcing the safety rules.

In developing sound safety programs, you should stress preventive action rather than after-the-fact remedies. Emphasize correcting unsafe acts and eliminating shortcuts in procedures. The same principles and concepts that apply to quality, cost and production control must be applied to safety. Use posters, contests, and presentations to stimulate safety awareness and motivate employees to work safely.

But these actions won't work unless you take full responsibility for safety. If you set a good example by following all the plant safety rules yourself, and if you are reasonable but firm in handling violations, a safety consciousness should gradually develop among your employees. Under such conditions, the chances for accidents and injuries are considerably reduced.

HOW TO IMPROVE YOUR EMPLOYEES' AWARENESS OF PLANT HAZARDS

No amount of plant safety rules and regulations can keep workers from getting hurt if they do not think of safety as their own responsibility. No amount of safety instructions, safety equipment and supervision can prevent them from being injured unless they are sold on safety. Accidents are not a matter of bad luck, nor are they cyclical in nature. They are controllable. Accidents are almost always the result of conditions and factors that can be perceived and either corrected or eliminated.

Having protective clothing available isn't the entire answer; employees must wear it when the head, eyes, body, feet and hands need protection. Workers who remember the instructions given and the rules that are laid down for working safely won't necessarily avoid an accident; they also need to apply those instructions correctly and follow the rules.

Too often an accident or injury occurs because the employees involved fail to think about the problems facing them and go blindly into an ordinary situation with their minds on something altogether different from the work they are doing; thus they fail to do the little things that are routine but necessary to working safely.

If workers want to keep from getting hurt—and certainly they do—then they must make safety a definite part of their life and work style. They must be aware when they are not concentrating completely and take that into account.

8 Ways to Help Your Employees to Think and Work Defensively

A corollary to being aware of dangers and hazards is to think and work defensively. This means that workers should not deliberately put themselves in positions or situations that could result in their having an accident or being injured.

There are several behavioral patterns that people can adopt that will help them avoid accidents and injuries. You, as a supervisor, should tell your employees how to think and work defensively. Point out that they should:

1. *Learn to deal with their emotions.* Rising tempers, get-even attitudes, and general emotional upsets make workers temporarily mindless of danger. When worry, frustration, and depression prevail, stress can become so great that they almost invariably get into trouble. Some workers hurry while others want to impress somebody with their abilities; the result is that everyone forgets about working defensively.

2. *Avoid the consequences of the errors of others.* A worker can be a victim of an error of omission by slipping and falling because someone spilled oil on the floor and failed to wipe it up. Another worker can be a victim of an error of commission by operating a machine from which the guard for a moving component has been removed.

3. *Acknowledge the reality of a hazard and take precautions against it.* Many accidents and injuries could be prevented if workers took the time to put to use protective equipment and clothing when they are about to perform a hazardous operation. A typical case is the worker who ignores the safety glasses or protective goggles available for operators of grinders and abrasive wheels. It's only common sense to put them on and not give in to a risk-taking instinct.

4. *Look for changes in the norm.* A worker in a chemical plant may be accustomed to finding all valves on piping and tanks closed when he or she comes on the job. One day, however, the worker on the preceding shift forgets to close one of the valves. Unless the oncoming worker checks all the valves and finds the open one, he or she might inadvertently spill a hazardous liquid or release an explosive gas.

5. *Plan new and unfamiliar tasks.* When starting a new procedure or process that is potentially hazardous, workers should plan it completely so they will know, within reason, everything they are going to do. They should also look into every possible outside influence that could suddenly change the safety of their situation.

6. *Correct bad habits.* If workers habitually postpone the cleaning and maintenance of their tools and equipment, they are simply testing their luck. Some day they will have an accident involving a dull knife or a mushroomed hammer. Similarly, wearing safety glasses or hard hats only when supervisors are around reduces their protection from airborne particles or falling overhead material.

7. *Heed near misses.* Everyone on the job has near misses. One worker may almost break something, another may trip on some steps. Whatever, workers experiencing near misses should ask themselves what they did wrong or what conditions were different that could account for the incident. Then they should adjust their future behavior accordingly.

8. *Avoid abnormal physical states.* Any factor that changes a person's normal condition creates the potential for an accident or injury. Employees who drink or use drugs and then operate machinery risk having a serious accident. Even excessive drinking the night before puts workers in jeopardy the following day at work because perceptual and motor skills are still reduced many hours after blood alcohol level has returned to normal.

PROTECTING WORKERS FROM MACHINE HAZARDS

Rules and regulations on the safe use of machines have existed for many years. The Occupational Safety and Health Act of 1970 mandated that certain methods be used to protect machine operators and nearby employees from hazards such as point of operation, rotating parts, and flying particles and sparks. Yet OSHA records indicate that machine-guarding regulations are among the most violated of all standards.

Machine guards generally fit into five major categories: barriers, pullbacks, presence sensors, brakes, and clamps. The protective strategies vary with these devices; some are sensitive electronic instruments, while others rely on principles of strength.

Basically, however, all machine guards are designed to restrain the machine, its operational by-products, or the operator. Following are descriptions of these machine guard categories; you can use these descriptions when training your workers in how to protect themselves from machine hazards.

Barriers

Constructed of plastics and metals in a variety of styles, barriers are made to either enclose the machine, intervene between a machine and its operator, or maintain a clear point of operation. Both fixed and adjustable enclosure guards protect workers from flying pieces of material, sparks, and even noise. The fixed guards prevent access to dangerous moving parts by admitting stock but not hands and fingers through fixed feed openings. Adjustable guards, such as saw blade shrouds, shield the moving machine parts.

Barrier gate guards protect punch press operators by automatically closing the die area before allowing the press to activate. If fingers or other material remain on the worktable, the guard will not drop completely, thus putting a "hold" on subsequent stroke or cycle completion.

An advantage of transparent shields is that they permit an unrestricted view of the worktable, thus enabling the operator to tool the workpiece or to direct material feeds. By being permanently mounted to the machine frame or column, they can swing across or down like a sun visor to protect against hazardous forces.

Barriers are also available in various types of panels and cages. Whether mesh or solid, they can cordon off an area or encircle equipment with exposed moving parts such as fans and air movers. Tint-windowed and solid panels find use in blocking out deleterious UV light produced by welding arcs.

Tip: Make sure your employees know the protective benefit of using barriers; they will be more likely to do so.

Pull-backs

Although workers may be familiar with the dangers of a particular machine, because of the complexity and speed of the motions involved, they must sometimes be physically reminded of the precautions they should take. This is accomplished by pull-back devices, which actively remove an operator's arms and hands from the paths of moving parts capable of bending, cutting, or pressing.

Pull-backs are commonly used in power press applications where they automatically activate just before the work stroke of the machine. This protective device consists of nylon straps attached to snug wristbands worn by the press operator. The straps trail behind the operator to overhead rings gliding on a shaft as the operator moves laterally across the face of the press. By means of a direct connection to the press slide, the motion of the descending slide results in a pull-back of the operator's hands. However, the actual pulling occurs only when the operator's hands are left in the machine's work area.

Tip: Watch workers when they start a machine equipped with pull-backs to make sure they don't forget to use this safety device.

Presence Sensors

Presence sensors are the newest and fastest growing machine guards now being used in manufacturing plants. Of the various types available, some emit white or infrared light through hazardous machine areas, while others criss-cross electromagnetic waves to detect hands or fingers. The detection disrupts the planar energy and automatically stops the machine. Some systems are equipped with alarms to announce the infraction.

Although presence sensors are very quick in their action, they are insensitive to ambient motions, vibrations, noise, and light. However, some sensors can be programmed to slacken their diligence during nonhazardous steps of a machine cycle.

Tip: Tell workers to get in the habit of testing sensors each time they start a machine equipped with them.

Brakes

Because coasting machines pose hazards if they are not equipped with appropriate deceleration or signal motion devices, machine manufacturers have added brakes or brake monitors. These devices along with other machine guards give additional protection on lathes, saws, grinders, conveyors, and presses.

Automatic mechanical braking is accomplished with electronic motor brakes; remote mounting can add protection where conventional brakes are impractical. In addition, controlled logic circuits, actuated by normal off switches, prevent restarts and reverses while applying the braking current.

Tip: Use electronic and electromechanical brake monitors as double-checks to monitor the performance of brake systems on presses and other machines. On-line monitoring indicates dangerous operation levels and prevents further operation until adjustments or repairs are made.

Clamps

Clamps or holding devices are often used on machines where the placing and feeding of material to a machine is required during several phases of an operation. These "substitute hands" hold workpieces perfectly still, thus freeing a worker to operate the machine. Usually found on drill presses and intricate process machines, they attach to columns and swing clear when not needed.

Tip: Never permit a worker to use his or her hands to hold workpieces if a clamp will do the job.

PROVIDING EMPLOYEES WITH INFORMATION ON SAFETY DEVICES AND EQUIPMENT IN WORK AREAS

There are several ways you can supply information to employees and put across the importance of safety devices on machines and equipment in the plant:

- Stress safety devices when training and instructing workers on how the machines and equipment perform and why the devices are in place. Point out what could happen if a device is inoperable or bypassed.

- Make workers members of the Plant Safety Committee, rotating them periodically so that everyone serves at one time or another. See that the committee faithfully makes plant, machine, and equipment inspections every month and participates in accident investigations. One of the critical functions of the committee is to inspect and test all safety devices.

- Show videos and films on the safe operation of machines, equipment, and tools. Attendance at these safety meetings should be mandatory. Many companies show films in the plant cafeteria at lunch time. You should be present to introduce and explain the program as well as answer any questions your workers may have.

How to Ensure That Plant Workers Use Protective Devices

You must use common sense in ensuring safety rule compliance by workers, including that they use protective devices. Although your job is to make sure that management views on safety are known by workers, this does not mean that individual responsibility can be dismissed. Noncompliance with sound safety rules and procedures can affect others in addition to the employee who violates established procedures.

An excellent way you can ensure that workers use protective devices is to incorporate the condition and status of a device in the logs or reports workers fill out in performing their jobs. For example, a log should request the following data be filled in by a worker:

- Date and time of day the worker tested the device.

- Response time for the device to function.

- Overall condition of the device (needs calibration, adjustment, or repair).

Also make a point of observing whether protective devices are being used every time you walk through the workplace. If you find a worker failing to use a device, immediately talk to him or her about the need to do so.

Tip: Don't be satisfied that one reminder ensures future and continual compliance. Return a few hours later and also check for several days to confirm that the worker is following the safety rules.

Perhaps the best way to ensure that workers use protective devices in operating machines and controlling plant processes is to make their use a requirement of the job. If a worker persists in unsafe behavior after warnings and discipline, dismissal should be a logical course of action.

HOW TO DEAL WITH UNSAFE ACTS OF EMPLOYEES

Under the terms of the Occupational Safety and Health Act (OSHA), plant managers are held responsible for eliminating unsafe conditions and unsafe facts that can cause accidents that injure employees. In addition, OSHA has specified codes for almost every conceivable type of work. These codes list the requirements for eliminating unsafe conditions.

Note, however, that even though a plant's management may comply with all the applicable codes, this is not enough. The law states that management must also protect employees against their own actions that can result in injuries. The law thus recognizes that it is possible for employees to injure themselves by an unsafe act, even when working with tools or equipment that meet all code requirements.

Data collected by the government over many years clearly show that unsafe conditions that code compliance should eliminate account for only 10 percent of all injuries.[2] With so many unsafe acts that it is almost impossible to codify them, you must determine what unsafe acts are likely to occur in handling the work that you are responsible for. Then you must see to it that your workers do not perform these unsafe acts.

At first glance, this might seem to be a formidable task; however, to help you with the job, the American Standards Association has come up with a list of nine types of unsafe acts:

1. Operating without authority.
2. Operating or working at unsafe speed.
3. Making safety devices inoperative.
4. Using unsafe equipment, using hands instead of equipment, or using equipment unsafely.
5. Failing to use personal protective equipment or clothing.
6. Unsafe loading, placing, mixing, or a similar act.
7. Taking unsafe position or posture.
8. Working on moving or dangerous equipment.
9. Distracting, teasing, abusing, or startling other workers.

---

[2]Since 1931, when H. W. Heinrich published *Industrial Accident Prevention*, many safety professionals have subscribed to his finding, derived from research on 75,000 accident cases, that 10 percent of all accidents are caused chiefly by unsafe mechanical or physical conditions, and 88 percent of all industrial accidents are caused by the unsafe acts of persons.

This list is helpful in two ways: It gives you a lead on what to look for, and it enables you to classify those unsafe acts that you find. Thus, by knowing which types of unsafe acts occur most often, you can go to work on the most serious problems.

Of all the various types of unsafe acts that employees might be guilty of, the one they do most often is taking an unsafe position or posture. Statistics confirm that more than half of the accidents in which the prime cause is an unsafe act result when the person involved takes an unsafe position or posture.

The position a person takes relative to the work being done makes that worker vulnerable to an accident. The way to be safe is to place yourself in the clear in the event of failure of the material being worked with, the tool being used, or the machine being operated.

The *posture* of a person is his or her body alignment relative to the load placed upon it. For instance, the correct lifting posture is to squat and lift the load with the leg muscles. Bending over the load and pulling up with the back muscles gives the mechanical advantage to the load, not to the lifter.

Since every job a person does has its own position or posture requirements, it's up to you as the supervisor to help your employees identify the one best way to handle each job. Then make sure that this way is the one that's used.

What to Do When an Unsafe Act Occurs

You must act quickly when you observe a worker committing an unsafe act. Here is what you should do:

1. *Stop the act immediately.* Do this consistently.
2. *Determine why the unsafe act is occurring.* If a worker commits the unsafe act because he or she thinks there is no other way to do the job, investigate the work method.
3. *Instruct the worker.* Once you decide how the job can be done more safely, explain the correct method to the worker. Show him or her by demonstrating. Let the worker try it.
4. *Follow up.* Check on the worker from time to time. Make certain he or she understands the correct method and does not go back to an unsafe method.

Preventing Slips, Trips and Falls

Falls are a leading cause of accidental deaths in manufacturing plants today. The National Safety Council estimates that 1,500 workers die each year in falls on the job and more than 200,000 suffer disabling injuries in slips, trips and falls. Yet most of these incidents can be prevented.

An excellent way to prevent accidental injury due to falls is to spot and correct environmental hazards. Here are some conditions and situations to watch for:

- Slick spots on floors caused by water, oil, and chemical spills.
- Hoses, paper, and small objects that present tripping hazards.
- Floor surfaces where varying amounts of friction are present.
- Obstacles that obscure vision.
- Dim lighting in stairwells, hallways, and aisles.
- Deceiving height.

Since our bodies can either work for or against us in a fall, learning how to fall correctly is a lesson that could help reduce serious injury.

With instruction and training, employees who fall are better able to protect vital areas such as the head, spine, and back. They can also learn to absorb the force of a fall by spreading the impact over as large an area as possible. Falling on soft tissue is always preferable to falling on bones. Training on how to fall should, naturally, be given by specialists.

HOW GOOD HOUSEKEEPING PROMOTES SAFETY

Industrial housekeeping can be defined as the conditions of arrangement, cleanliness, orderliness, efficiency, and facility that determine whether or not a plant is well kept and therefore well managed. With more than one-third of all on-the-job accidents and injuries linked to poor housekeeping practices, the consequences can be serious, and may eventually cripple an organization.

Housekeeping and maintenance in manufacturing plants should not only include the work area and material storage (both raw and finished), but also the equipment and tools used by employees. Good housekeeping is beneficial to the workers and cost effective for the company. Make sure employees perform the following housekeeping functions:

- *Stack material neatly.* This helps reduce struck-by hazards, which often account for a high percentage of a plant's injuries. Also encourage your workers to close drawers, doors, and cabinets to reduce this type of injury.
- *Use and care for equipment properly.* This is critical to employee efficiency and safety.
- *Mark clearly the assigned places for tools.*
- *Return tools and equipment to the proper places after use.*

- *Make a conscientious and constant effort to keep tools clean and maintained*. This increases tool and equipment life and reduces injuries caused by defective and worn out tools.
- *Dispose of trash properly*. Material should be deposited in proper receptacles that are emptied regularly.
- *Place oil-, grease-, or paint-stained rags in approved, covered metal containers to reduce the likelihood of fire*. All containers should be flame retardant with automatic closures.
- *Clean up spills of any kind immediately to prevent slips and falls*.
- *Keep all stairways, aisles, and other passage ways unobstructed*.
- *Make sure lighting is adequate in these and other walkways*. Replace bulbs to keep these areas safe.

Housekeeping is part of everyone's job, both labor and management. It saves time when the workplace is neat and organized because jobs can be completed without delays or obstructions. Besides, an effective housekeeping program will project a positive image to visitors and customers who deal with the company. But remember that good housekeeping is not just for good looks. It can prevent a fire or an accident.

Identifying Hazards by Color Coding Equipment

Although many supervisors probably think of on-the-job housekeeping as putting scrap in containers, wiping up spills, or stacking and storing materials properly, there is another aspect of housekeeping that prevents accidents and injuries by identifying both hazards and equipment or facilities to contend with them. You can identify such hazards by color coding them. Firefighting equipment, dangerous machine parts, physical hazards, and piping systems are some of the objects that should be easily recognized because they are color coded.

Color coding is a safety application that uses seven basic colors—red, orange, yellow, green, blue, purple, and black with white—to highlight specific hazards. These colors, combined with symbols and lettering, provide highly visible signs for employees' and visitors' protection.

Red has long been used to identify fire protection equipment, including alarm boxes, hydrants, extinguishers, sprinkler system piping and other indicators associated with fire. In addition, use red to mark danger areas, on exit signs and on emergency stop controls on machines. Danger signals are:

- Warning lights at barricades, temporary obstructions, and temporary construction sites.
- Stop lights.

- Running lights on machines and stop buttons.

Use red on safety cans or portable containers of flammable liquids that have flash points at or below 80°F excluding shipping containers. Use yellow with red—either as a band around a red can or to state a container's contents—to furnish additional identification.

Orange indicates dangerous parts of machines and energized equipment that may shock, cut, or somehow injure people. Use orange to call attention to open enclosure doors and open or removed gears, belts, or guards. Use orange also on exposed parts (edges only) of rollers, pulleys, gears, cutting and shearing devices, and power jaws.

Yellow means caution: Use it to mark physical items or material that could cause workers to slip, stumble, fall, trip, strike against or get caught between something. Yellow and black stripes or checkers, or yellow with a contrasting background draw attention and caution workers. Thus, use yellow for steps, guardrails, low beams, pipes, crane hooks and mobile equipment.

Green denotes first-aid and safety equipment. Use green for stretchers, gas masks, medical kits, respiratory and eye equipment, and safety showers.

Blue should be used for special machines and equipment to indicate that it should not be touched or used except by qualified personnel. Use blue on instrumentation and controls, for informational signs and to signify temporary repairs.

Purple warns of radiation hazards such as alpha, beta, gamma, neutron, proton, and x-rays. Use yellow with purple on tags, markers, labels, and signs.

Black used with white or yellow specifies traffic routes. Use black to separate process, storage, and housekeeping areas.

You may also want to indicate the contents of piping systems by color. The most common uses are:

- *Red* for sprinkler or other fire extinguishing systems such as carbon dioxide.
- *Yellow* and *orange* for materials that are poisonous, toxic, explosive, easily ignited, hot, or otherwise dangerous.
- *Green*, *black*, *gray*, *white*, and *aluminum* for safe and nonvaluable products such as water, air, and steam.
- *Blue* for protective materials including inert gases (nitrogen) that are used for purging.

GUIDELINES FOR SETTING UP A FIRST AID PROGRAM

One of the axioms for successful plant management is that the health and safety of employees must receive top priority. Because professional medical help is seldom immediately available, a comprehensive first aid program is a necessity. *First aid* is defined as the immediate care given to victims of injuries or sudden illnesses until medical help is obtained. It also includes prompt attention to injuries not requiring medical attention.

Although first aid programs vary from plant to plant depending on the number of employees, the types of operations, the legal requirements, and so on, all programs have a few basic elements:

- Properly trained individuals to administer aid on each shift.
- A first aid kit or equivalent supplies.
- A first aid manual.
- Emergency action instructions and emergency transportation instructions.
- A record-keeping system.

Employees trained in first aid can reduce work-related injuries significantly once they know what causes accidents and begin noting and eliminating the causes. If a full-time doctor or nurse is not on hand, trained first aid people play an important role in the first aid program.

Since improper treatment may compound an employee's injuries and also subject the company to a possible lawsuit, first aid people must be qualified, trained, and certified. They should complete an American Red Cross or Bureau of Mines first aid course or its equivalent and be trained in cardiopulmonary resuscitation.

First aid kits and supplies vary with the plant. But whether large or small, supplies and controls should be reviewed and approved by a physician to assure applicability and to prevent improper use. Control of medications is essential. Drugs should be administered only by a physician, nurse, or trained paramedic. Inplant first aid facilities should also have a centralized room or area that is convenient for employees.

OSHA requires plants to keep accurate and complete records, and to report work-related illnesses, injuries, and deaths. Records are used for accident analysis and control. Additionally, they are vital in the event of legal action.

HOW TO LIFT AND CARRY LOADS SAFELY

With improper lifting and carrying near the top of the list of industrial accident causes, it is evident that many plant workers either are careless when lifting and carrying or don't know how to properly lift and carry objects.

How do lifting and carrying injuries happen? A survey conducted a few years ago[3] revealed that objects weighing more than 70 pounds accounted for 28 percent of lifting injuries; those weighing between 41 and 70 pounds, 19 percent; and those between 11 and 40 pounds, 36 percent. Surprisingly, 17 percent of the injuries involved objects weighing less than 10 pounds.

What load should be considered too heavy? There appears to be no simple answer. The U.S. Department of Labor's Bulletin 110, "Safety in Industry—Teach Them to Lift," contains this statement:

> There are no simple solutions to the setting of maximum permissible weights to be carried by any one worker. Due regard must be given to the physiological aspects of lifting and load carrying. Externally, we must give consideration to the climatic conditions, as well as the degree of training and experience each worker has had in lifting and carrying. The setting of manual lifting and carrying limits must be predicated upon, among other things, the size and type of load to be carried (compact or loose), distance of lift, height and position of lift, the working or walking level, the incline of the surface, and so on.

Although physical differences among individuals make it difficult to set safe lifting and carrying load limits for all workers, training in these techniques can greatly reduce injuries caused by improper lifting and carrying habits. Here are some recommendations for how plant workers can lift safely:

- Be sure you can handle the load. Never attempt to lift something if you doubt your ability to do so.
- Before lifting, inspect the item for sharp edges, splinters, exposed nails, weak bottom, or slipperiness.
- Make certain you have good footing. Do not try to lift something on a slippery, steeply sloped, or cluttered surface.
- Place feet close to base of item to be lifted to prevent back muscles from taking all of load. Feet should be 8 to 12 inches apart to assure good balance and stability.
- Bend knees and squat.
- Keep back, neck and head straight and as nearly vertical as possible. Spine, back muscles, and internal organs will be in correct alignment, reducing compression of intestines and the possibility of hernia occurring.

---

[3]Reported in *Plant Engineering* (Des Plaines, IL: Cahner's Publishing Company, September 18, 1975), p. 139.

- Grip item firmly. If lifting a box, grasp it at opposite top and bottom corners with full palms.
- Hold arms and elbows as close as possible to sides of body. Arms lose strength if held away from the body.
- Begin lifting. Use arm muscles while simultaneously pushing up with legs. Continue lifting steadily and smoothly, keeping load close to body, until item is in a secure and comfortable carrying position.

Carrying can be safer if your employees observe the following rules:

- Allow a load to fall if you should lose your grip, or, if possible, ride it to the floor by body pressure, keeping hands and feet out of its path. A quick bending motion when trying to catch an item can cause a back sprain.
- Turn your body with changes in foot position. Do not twist if it becomes necessary to change direction while carrying the load.
- Hold the load close to body to better maintain balance.
- Keep front end of a long object such as a ladder slightly higher than rear end. Such loads are easier to carry if they are held a little toward the front end.
- Be sure you can see over and around the load, especially when walking up or down stairs.
- Use two or more workers to carry heavy loads and keep the load evenly balanced. When two people carry long sections of pipe or boards, they should carry the items on the same shoulder and walk in step.

Workers who are lowering a load should follow these guidelines:

- Turn the feet and entire body to face location where the item is to be placed.
- Place the load that is to be lowered onto bench or table on edge of furniture, thus transferring a portion of its weight. Then push load to desired position using arms or body.
- Reverse the lifting procedure when lowering an object to the floor. Keep the object close to body and bend the knees until the body is squatting. Keep the back straight, maintain balance, and allow leg and arm muscles to do the work.

TECHNIQUES FOR USING ERGONOMICS TO IMPROVE PLANT SAFETY

Ergonomics, sometimes called biomechanics and human engineering, is defined as a multidisciplinary science that combines engineering, medicine, and psychology to optimize worker performance, safety, and health. When ergonomic applications become part of a company's safety program, the design of the workplace and the procedures and tools used not only increase workers' skills and productivity, but safeguard them from overexertion and stress.

Ergonomic solutions to plant safety problems can be as simple as adding a footrest to a work bench or elevating the work surface to a comfortable height; they can be as complicated and expensive as providing ergonomically designed, adjustable workstations, altering material handling operations, or redesigning hand tools. The results are that the workers can see and feel the difference, and this benefits safety, labor relations, productivity, and product quality.

The practice of ergonomics more than pays for itself in manufacturing plants. Here are a few specific areas where ergonomic efforts have proved to be worthwhile.

Layout and Design

Many workers need more room than they have to move around as they do their work. Confined and tight work areas limit their freedom to shift their weight and relax their muscles. These situations cause tenseness and strain, conditions that lead to painful cramping and muscle spasms.

As women continue to work on jobs previously held only by men, the challenge for management is to design the workplace and furnish equipment safe for everyone. For instance, most equipment and machine design favors male physical attributes, such as strength, size, endurance, and body structure. Although much of the need for size and strength in plant workers has been reduced by more efficiently and effectively designed procedures, many of these adaptations have not yet been fully applied to tools, equipment, and machines used by women.

Making allowances for differences in worker heights can eliminate the need to stretch or reach unnecessarily. This may help alleviate sore muscles and back injuries. Workers who need to bend over often during a shift may tire quickly and be more prone to accidents. When workers have to devise their own methods of adjusting to awkward work positions, like standing on pallets or boxes to reach controls or material, the chance of accidents also increases.

Procedures and Tools

Although instructing and training workers on how to lift prevents injuries, a better answer to this problem is to install machines to perform lifting operations. Fortunately, several equipment and machine manufacturers have begun to do this.

When tools are ergonomically designed and easy to handle, workers are less likely to have accidents involving them. Using the proper tool for a job also lessens physical and mental stress. Studies have shown, however, that many traditional tools are not compatible with the body dimensions and performance characteristics of humans.

The traditional design of pliers, for example, requires a bent wrist with a grasping force at some angle of the arm. This fault has been remedied with a bent nose or pistol grip design, so the tool can be used without bending the wrist. Another point to be made here is that tool handles should be extended through the hand because the center of the palm does not bear stress well.

Computer Operations

By applying ergonomics to the design and construction of workplaces with computers, you can considerably improve the comfort and well-being of workers who spend much of the day operating a computer. A large amount of the stress suffered by computer operators is the result of poorly designed tables for terminals and seats for operators. If separate surfaces are provided for the screen and the keyboard, an operator has a choice of a wide range of adjustments that allow the operator to position the keyboard and screen to suit his or her needs.

Because almost all sustained terminal operation is performed from a seated position, seating posture deserves attention. Proper posture assures both comfort and accessibility to the keyboard. The seat and back of a chair must be adjustable, and the front of the seat, called the waterfall, should be rounded. If it's not, users may notice that their feet get cold when they remain seated for long periods of time. What really happens is that the pressure on their thighs causes the circulation to be cut off to the lower part of their legs.

Another ergonomic improvement that can be made for computer operators is to reduce the glare and reflection off the screen. This can be accomplished by using soft, even light such as that from fluorescent lights or some type of indirect lighting.

PROMOTING THE USE OF PROTECTIVE CLOTHING AND EQUIPMENT

Adopting a Hand Protection Program

Many injuries to the hands and fingers can be prevented by putting a hand protection program in effect. The key to an effective program is employee education. A successful program explains to workers the importance of on-the-job protection and furnishes information on the proper selection and use of protective gloves.

The best way to promote such a program is to post the hand safety rules throughout the plant. The rules should include information on the potential dangers in your plant such as pinch points, jagged edges, sharp corners, solvents, corrosives, exposed machinery, and others. The posters and signs should encourage plant employees to follow these hand safety rules:

- Inspect material for slivers, jagged edges, burrs, and rough or slippery surfaces before handling it. Wipe off greasy, wet, and dirty objects.
- Wear suitable hand protection when working with acids and caustics.
- Keep hands clear when handling material, pushing hand trucks, hooking up hoists and slings, or working with saws and other machines.
- Never reach into moving machinery to repair, oil, or adjust it.
- Keep hands free of oil and grease; they are often the cause of dermatitis because they pick up dirt which gets into pores.
- Wear safety cuff or gauntlet gloves around moving machinery.
- Since a knitwrist glove is held securely to the hand, if it is caught in machinery, it is likely to pull the hand in with it.
- Keep fingers away from pinch points when handling or setting down materials.

Selecting Appropriate Protective Gloves

In the past, hand protection in plants consisted of using three basic types of gloves: cotton, rubber, and leather. Cotton gloves protected primarily against dirt and minor abrasion. Rubber gloves were used to protect against water and other liquids, and leather gloves were used when handling rough, abrasive, and cutting materials.

But all three types had weaknesses and deficiencies for many manufacturing plant applications. Cotton lacked strength and durability, rubber couldn't be used with all liquids, and leather was uncomfortable and unwieldy. To solve these problems, the coated glove was developed. Coatings such as rubber, synthetic elastomers, and plastics are applied over fabric linings in various thicknesses to meet specific conditions. Numerous materials are used for lining gloves. Flannel, jersey knit, interlock knit, and thermal material consisting of jersey and waffle-weave fabrics bonded together to trap a layer of air are the most common lining materials.

Five coatings are used most often:

- *Neoprene-coated gloves* resist many chemicals, oils, and solvents; they also do not snag or puncture easily. Because of these characteristics, they are used widely in manufacturing processes involving paints, varnishes, lacquers, enamels, alkalis, and acids. They are excellent for performing general maintenance work in the chemical and petrochemical industries.

- *Gloves coated with natural rubber* are suited for handling food products because the rubber resists the chemicals and enzymes found in foods, especially meats. Because these gloves are also cut- and puncture-resistant, they can be used for handling glass, brick, wall and floor tile, wire and other abrasive material. However, natural rubber should not be permitted to come in contact with oil. Oil causes it to swell and to tear easily.

- *Gloves coated with polyvinyl chloride (PVC)* are currently the most commonly used type of coated fabric glove. PVC-coated gloves are highly resistant to acids, caustics, and solvents. In addition to being flexible and comfortable, they are ideal for use in both the chemical and petroleum industries to protect maintenance and production workers from most liquids.

- *Nitrile rubber coated gloves* are exceptionally tough; they are resistant to abrasions, cuts, and punctures. These gloves are also excellent for handling oily sheet metal or partially fabricated metal and well suited for tough mechanical jobs. In addition, they offer long wear because of the excellent adhesion of the nitrile coating to the fabric liner.

- *Vinyl-impregnated gloves* find use in plants as substitutes for cotton, canvas, or leather palm gloves. They repel liquids and are available in various strengths for general purpose use including buffing, assembling, racking, bagging, and other mechanical operations in many industries.

When you select hand safety gear, you should recognize that no one glove is suitable for all jobs in the plant. You should select gloves best suited for the various uses and you should also monitor their use. Worn gloves should be returned before a new pair is issued to reduce costs. If gloves are handed out at a tool crib, make sure the attendant knows what gloves are required for which operation. This person is an important link in a company's hand protection program and the worker's acceptance of it.

Protecting Against Eye and Face Injuries

Preventing costly eye and face injuries in the plant takes a lot more than buying protective equipment and telling workers to wear it. In addition, you should analyze your operations' potential hazards to workers' eyes and faces, and specify personal protective equipment that best safeguards workers from those hazards. Then, follow up with effective promotion and training techniques, coupled with enforcement procedures to make sure your workers understand why protective equipment is needed, how it's used, and the consequences of not wearing it.

Eye protection programs vary greatly from one plant to another depending on the nature of the hazards, the commitment of management, and the dedication of safety personnel and plant supervisors. The supervisor usually bears the burden of responsibility for making employees wear safety glasses.

For instance, after a safety audit, someone from the safety department might notify you that glasses are needed for employees performing certain types of work. If the company is safety minded and committed, make sure your employees understand that they have no choice: They either wear the glasses or they work somewhere else.

Because some employees don't like to wear glasses, you may have to sell them on it. But this may not be as tough as it first appears. Start by showing such employees one or more of the many films available on why eye protection is needed on most industrial jobs. You can obtain eye safety films from the National Safety Council, the E. I. duPont de Nemours & Co., and training companies that specialize in films such as Industrial Training Systems Corporation.

Point out that the latest safety glasses are stylish and light weight, that they fit well and won't leave dents in one's nose. As one supervisor aptly put it, "If allowing workers to choose fashionable safety eyewear will get them to wear it on the job, I'm all for it!"

Depending on the nature of the hazard in your plant, some employees may need more protection than standard safety glasses provide. You should issue the following types of glasses for each type of hazard:

- Safety glasses with wire mesh sideshields for workers exposed to large flying particles such as grinding debris, molten metal splashes, or welding sparks.

- Glasses with plastic sideshields for workers in electrical and machine shops, rolling mills, finishing plants, and other areas without exposure to large particles.

- Welders' helmets, flip-front goggles, or cup-type goggles for workers on welding and burning jobs to protect them from particles and ultraviolet light.

- Soft frame, nonchemical splash goggles for workers on especially dusty jobs such as cleaning operations.

- Chemical splash goggles for workers in laboratories, on pickle lines, in water treatment operations, and in other areas where chemicals are used. Also, clear and tinted plastic faceshields should be worn by workers exposed to chemicals and intermittent radiant heat.

In addition to insisting that employees wear personal protective equipment to safeguard them from hazards, make sure your plant contains other eye protection equipment. Emergency eyewash and shower units should be strategically located throughout the plant in areas where workers may be exposed to chemical splashes.

Safety Shoes: The Answer to Foot Protection

A recent study on foot injuries made by the Bureau of Labor Statistics revealed that less than 25 percent of the injured workers were wearing safety shoes or boots.[4] If the operations or processes in your plant expose employees to foot injuries, you should make sure that safety footwear is being worn. It is equally important that employees wear the right protective footwear.

Steel toe safety shoes are available in dress or casual oxfords, slip-ons, work or western boots, and a wide variety of other styles and materials. Whereas women workers were once relegated to wearing small men's shoes, they now have a choice of many styles designed specifically for them.

Today's safety shoes are much more comfortable than those of the past. This has been brought about by the use of lower-density materials and soling designed to give better cushioning and support for the foot. Additionally, synthetic materials, with minimal bulk and weight, prevent heat loss from insulated footwear.

Shoe manufacturers offer a range of outsoles to meet the requirements of industrial plants. These soles resist oil, chemicals, metal chips, or heat. Various tread designs and materials, including treads impregnated with abrasive grit, enable wearers to get good traction on wet, slippery surfaces.

Because most foot injuries are caused by objects falling on or rolling over the foot, the steel toe boxes in shoes are designed to protect from these hazards. To protect the instep and front of the ankle, encourage plant workers to wear metatarsal shoes or guards that attach to shoes. To protect feet from underfoot hazards (such as nails and pieces of metal), select shoes with flexible steel insoles with optional cushioned backing.

Three types of shoes are made to protect workers against various electrical and sparking hazards:

- *Conductive shoes* are designed to dissipate static electricity, thus preventing ignition of potentially explosive mixtures.
- *Nonsparking shoes*, constructed with nonferrous or plastic materials, are designed to prevent sparks in areas containing explosive materials.

---

[4]Reported by *Occupational Hazards* (Cleveland, Ohio: Penton Publishing, Feb. 1985), p. 61.

- *Nonconductive shoes* insulate workers from the ground and prevent electrical shock. These shoes are often worn by linemen and electricians. The soles and heels of these shoes are made of rubber; no metal parts (e.g., eyelets or nails) are used except for the insulated steel toe box.

Other special safety shoes are used in foundries and metal manufacturing plants. They have a tight closure at the top to protect against cinders and molten metal. Wooden sole shoes find use in extremely hot or cold work environments.

If you are involved in recommending or specifying safety shoes for employees, the shoes you select should meet the requirements of the American National Standards Institute's ANSI Z41-1983 standard for protective footwear. This standard gives the requirements for both men's and women's safety shoes in the areas of impact, compression, metatarsal, conductive, electrical hazard, and puncture resistance performance.

Providing Adequate Head Protection

According to the National Safety Council, about 70,000 disabling head injuries occurred in plants in 1988. Although little data on workplace head injuries are available, surveys have shown that many serious injuries could be avoided or minimized by the proper use of protective headgear.

Hard hats are the most common pieces of protective gear worn by industrial workers. It is estimated that about 10 million are bought each year, and that anywhere from 35 to 50 million are currently in use. Hard hats provide protection in two ways: by the outer shell and by the suspension of the helmet. The shell, most commonly made of polyethylene or polycarbonate, protects against penetration of sharp objects and against impact. Contributing to the impact protection is the suspension, which consists of a headband and strapping that is attached to the helmet.

When an object hits the hat, the shell flexes, absorbing part of the impact. Then the nylon strapping in the suspension stretches, absorbing more of the force. Further, the suspension distributes the force from the point of impact to each of the places where it is connected to the helmet. The following is a list of ways a hard hat protects against impact:[5]

- *Impact.* The shell receives the full force of impact.
- *Flex.* The shell flexes, absorbing part of the impact force.
- *Distribution.* The hard hat passes the reduced force to the energy-absorbing points where the shell connects to the suspension.

---

[5]Stephen G. Minter, "A New Perspective on Head Protection," *Occupational Hazards* (Cleveland, Ohio: Penton Publishing, June 1990), p. 47.

- *Stretch.* The suspension stretches, absorbing still more of the impact forces.

- *Redistribution.* The hard hat distributes force by the suspension evenly over a greater area of the head, reducing concentrations at any one point.

- *Force reduction.* The hard hat passes remaining impact forces (now diminished) to the body's natural shock absorbers.

Performance specifications for hard hats are given in the American National Standards Institute (ANSI) Z89.1-1986 standard. Helmets are designed to withstand an impact of 40 foot-pound, which is that of a 2-pound object dropping two stories onto the helmet. But ANSI cautions that this standard primarily ensures protection from "small falling objects striking the top of the shell and against light bumps." Hard hats cannot furnish complete protection from heavier impacts, nor do they offer equal protection against blows to the sides, front, or back of the head.

Hard hats also protect against electrical hazards to varying degrees depending on their rating. Class A helmets are required to protect against 2,200 volts for 1 minute, and Class B to protect against 20,000 volts for 3 minutes. Class C helmets do not offer any protection.

The ANSI standard also requires that helmets pass a penetration test. If a 1-pound dart dropped from 10 feet does not penetrate more than $\frac{3}{8}$ inch in a Class A or B helmet, the helmet shell meets the criterion.

You should inspect your workers' hard hats frequently for cracks, deep gouges, or degradation of the material indicated by color changes. A simple test of a hat's condition can be performed by squeezing it around the brim inward approximately an inch and then releasing it. A hard hat in good condition should bounce back to its original form quickly. If it cracks or does not respond, it should be replaced.

When inspecting the hat, you should also examine the suspension to make sure the straps are in good shape and properly connected to the shell. Some manufacturers recommend that suspensions be replaced annually because fraying or cuts in the straps could limit the level of protection in the hats.

Although workers often like to personalize their hard hats with stickers, you should discourage the practice; stickers can hide defects and damaged areas. Similarly, you should not permit workers to paint their hats, because incompatible paints could affect a hat's integrity. Also, drilling of holes is forbidden because it can affect the hat's strength.

You also want to require your employees to wear their hard hats with the bills facing forward. This requirement ensures that the suspensions fit workers' heads properly, and that the bills will deflect falling objects away from workers' eyes and faces. The practice also helps to keep hats on in the event of impact.

Guidelines on Avoiding Work Clothes That Are Dangerous

Be aware that built-in accident hazards can be present in work clothes. Poorly designed and ill-fitting clothing should not be worn on the job. It is false economy to wear worn-out or dirty clothing or to work in old clothing not designed for safety. Following are a few dangers in work clothes to guard employees against:

- Dangling ties, floppy pockets, loose apron strings, and missing buttons are accident hazards that may not be recognizable as such. If a button is missing on the cuff of a worker's shirt sleeve, the dangling cuff may easily get caught in moving machinery and drag the person after it.

- Tears and rips in work clothing permit it to get caught in moving machinery or on some projection.

- Dirty work clothing breeds accident and health hazards in that it often causes skin rashes, irritations, and skin abrasions or burns.

- Oil or chemical-soaked clothing (or clothing soaked with any flammable material) can lead to fatal burns. Such contaminated clothing may also cause painful skin irritations and rashes.

Tips on Selecting Protective Clothing

Do you have the responsibility of selecting and procuring protective clothing for employees? If you do, you will soon learn that you are faced with many choices. By following certain guidelines, however, you can select the right apparel for both the application and maximum safety. Here are some suggestions:

- *Consider the specific application first.* Heat, cold, weight, moisture, spatter, impact, chemical resistance, and flame resistance are all factors in assessing the right materials. Whether to use rubber, leather, or any of the many synthetics such as aramid for protection will depend on these factors. For example, if your workers are handling oily metal that has sharp edges and/or burrs, you should select work gloves that are coated with nitrile rubber.

- *Recognize that comfort is important.* It doesn't matter if the materials are right unless the employee feels comfortable wearing the coveralls, jacket, apron, cape sleeve, or glove. Investigate the various fabrics, linings, and insulations available, and try them out to find the feel that is most comfortable.

- *Think value, not price.* A cheap pair of gloves that lasts only a few days is not worth as much as a more expensive pair that will last much longer.

There are also hidden costs to consider, such as laundering, associated with frequent reordering and replacement of cheaper materials.

- *Look at style and fit.* Many protective clothing manufacturers offer sizes and styles specifically designed for men or women. With the assortment available today, you should not have to substitute a man's size and cut for a woman's.

Overcoming Workers' Objections to Wearing Protective Clothing

You can take several steps to make protective clothing more acceptable to employees:

1. Discuss the hazardous nature of their jobs and why they need to protect themselves from injury. Talk about the various kinds of protective clothing that apply to their particular hazard. Let them decide which kind of protection suits the situation best. Offer a selection, if possible.

2. Get support of the union or from the informal leaders in the plant in selling the need for wearing protective clothing.

3. Set an example yourself. If the workplace dictates wearing safety glasses or hard hats, make sure that you wear yours every time you enter the hazardous area.

4. Impose disciplinary action if you can't persuade employees to wear their safety clothing. If you're consistent with your efforts and the protective clothing is appropriate and suitable, you'll have the backing of safety and governmental agencies.

WHERE TO GET SAFETY DATA AND INFORMATION

Plant safety is a highly developed technology and has received a lot of publicity in the United States in recent years. Much of the effort needed to make our plants safe requires the application of specialized information. When developing a safety program, you as a plant supervisor and those you work with have several sources of information:

- *The National Safety Council*, a nonprofit, nongovernmental, privately supported organization, continually sponsors various programs to promote safety. This public service organization was chartered by the 83rd U.S. Congress to arouse and maintain interest in accident prevention. As such, the Council does not endorse commercial products nor does it lobby for specific legislation. Its policy is as follows:

  The National Safety Council, by virtue of its charter, its bylaws, and its traditional procedures, has established a wide field of competence. The overall function is to deal with the accident problem of America. The specific ranges of its field of activity are determined by the enormous toll of life, limb, and property taken each year by accidents on the highways, and in the work places, homes, farms, schools, public places, and transportation systems of our nation.

In dealing with the whole problem, the National Safety Council concerns itself, through study of the record and through research, with the initial facts of accident occurrence, and seeks to establish the ascertainable cause and practical measure of prevention. The Council is also properly engaged in determining engineering requirements, in helping formulate model safety legislation where the force of law is required, in participation in planning and executing educational programs, in disseminating accurate information to the general public, and in encouraging the establishment of community and state safety organizations.

In carrying out this policy, the organization publishes six safety periodicals, *Accident Facts*, an annual report of accident statistics, and several accident prevention manuals. It also conducts safety training courses at its Chicago headquarters and on-site at plants, and sponsors the annual National Safety Congress.

- *Many smaller organizations and trade associations*, formed to meet the general interests of their respective industries and member companies, also promote safety and supply good safety information. The International Safety Academy, for example, operates a training center designed for conferences, consultations, and professional development of individuals. Another is the Chemical Manufacturer's Association (in Washington, D.C.), which publishes a series of *Chemical Safety Data Sheets* covering the properties, hazards, and safe handling methods for specific chemicals.

- *Other educational societies and institutions* concerned with safety include the Institute of Safety and Management at the University of Southern California, the National Safety Management Society, and the American Society of Safety Engineers.

- *U.S. government agencies* publish information on safety subjects. The Superintendent of Documents, U.S. Government Printing Office (Washington, D.C.) prints subject bibliographies at no charge; these are lists of the various publications available. To get the bibliographies on industrial safety, write for SB-229, *Accidents and Accident Prevention*, and SB-213, *Occupational Safety and Health*.

- *State agencies* also issue and enforce industrial safety health regulations. Some also publish periodicals and booklets on safety subjects. You should be familiar with your state's codes and regulations because they state the minimum legal standards for conditions in your plant.

- *Insurance groups* and other associations offer plants a wide range of inspection, advisory, and educational services. For example, your company's fire insurance carrier probably furnishes inspection and fire protection assistance through the Factory Insurance Association (in Hartford, CT) or the Factory Mutual System (in Norwood, MA).

    In addition, The American Insurance Association (New York), Underwriter's Laboratories (Northbrook, IL) and the National Fire Protection Association (Quincy, MA) all conduct research and issue publications on a wide variety of fire protection subjects.

TIPS ON CONDUCTING SAFETY INSPECTIONS

Most plants today have an inspection committee, the members of which are appointed by management. A safety inspection may be done in conjunction with the regular plant inspection and maintenance program, or it may be an inspection where the primary concern is with accident prevention. The latter type of inspection is frequently made by the members of the safety committee.

Safety inspections should focus attention on those items directly concerned with accident prevention. Thus, participating in an inspection affords you an excellent opportunity to check all safety equipment and devices, the condition of machines and other equipment, and the status of your housekeeping program. We have already seen where good housekeeping pays off in accident prevention.

A systematic method of inspection is preferred to assure that nothing is missed. The inspection should include:

- Buildings and physical equipment.
- Machinery, guards, and electrical facilities.
- Materials handling and storage facilities.
- Special equipment such as pressure vessels, furnaces, dryers, process tanks, conveying systems, elevators, and lifts.
- Welding, cutting, and brazing equipment.
- Compressed gas and air equipment.
- Ventilation and pollution controls for toxic and hazardous substances.
- Walking and working surfaces and means of exit.
- Hand and portable power tools and other hand-held equipment.

As part of the inspection team, you should be familiar with the company's safety and health policies as well as the particular laws and regulations that pertain to your plant. Regulations frequently specify only minimum requirements, thus making it necessary to exceed them to achieve adequate safety. You should also have an analysis of all accidents that have occurred in the plant within the past year.

You should keep careful records of all inspections and the recommendations made in the inspection reports. This is especially important in the event of an accident that results in litigation. Some plants, immediately after an inspection, issue repair orders to correct or repair unsafe machines and equipment uncovered in the inspection. Putting such information in the inspection report accomplishes two objectives: It puts pressure on the maintenance department to get the work done, and it serves as a means of following up on an unsafe condition during future inspections.

HOW TO GET PLANT WORKERS TO SHARE SAFETY RESPONSIBILITY

As a supervisor, you are responsible for providing safe working conditions for your workers. To do this, you need to perform many safety functions including making workplace and equipment inspections, training workers on safe procedures, and seeing that the work is done in a safe manner.

Yet since safety should be everyone's business, why not ask workers to share these safety responsibilities? Workers are in better positions to spot safety hazards and to make sure that safety rules are not broken than are any other persons in the plant. Besides, you can't be in all work areas at the same time. Take the following steps to implement this idea:

1. Explain to your workers that management intends to meet all federal, state, and local regulations on safety. This means that safety devices will be provided and must be used, protective clothing will be provided and must be worn, and safe procedures will be established and must be followed at all times.

2. Say that you cannot enforce all the rules and check every machine, piece of equipment, and tool in the plant by yourself; so you're going to share this responsibility with them.

3. State, however, that you will see that each worker is well informed and trained on safety so that anyone can immediately report to you conditions and practices that are not safe.

4. Emphasize that you are serious about safety, and expect every worker in your department to be so.

ANSWERS TO PLANT ACCIDENTS THAT KEEP REPEATING

Accident repeaters, workers who continually have accidents, are usually well-known to supervisors. Most supervisors search diligently for the human factors to explain how and why these workers are so accident prone. Yet such is not the case with the accidents that keep repeating but involve a different person each time.

You should be just as concerned, if not more so, about those, especially because you can take definite steps to prevent them. For instance:

1. Get at the problem by analyzing all reported accidents for their causes.
2. Pick out the causes that are repeaters, and take action on them.
3. Tell your workers you want to hear about near accidents and other accidents, small and large, that don't result in injuries.

Correcting unsafe conditions and unsafe practices are sure ways to improve the safety record of your department. By following up on accidents that keep repeating, you will be able to learn of those conditions and practices.

SUPERVISING PLANT EMPLOYEES WHO DO DANGEROUS WORK

You are responsible for the safety of plant employees and for their behavior on the job. This duty dictates that you train and instruct your workers on the safe way to perform their jobs. You should be extra diligent when assigning jobs in hazardous areas or when the work to be performed is dangerous.

- Personally check the work site beforehand for adequate lighting, proper ventilation, and the availability and condition of safety equipment such as eye washes and emergency showers.
- See that a properly equipped first aid kit is in the area.
- Assure that equipment and tools to be used are safe to operate and run properly.
- Provide workers protective clothing, making sure it is appropriate for the work to be performed. For example, see that workers wear safety shoes, hard hats, safety glasses or gloves if the work to be done requires their use for safety.
- Discuss the safety rules and regulations applying to the job with the workers when you assign them the work. Confirm the procedures to be followed at the workplace.

- Obtain permits from other departments to perform hazardous work. Notify all departments including fire and safety personnel when the work will start and expect to finish.

- Oversee the start of the job and control the operation. Check constantly to see that there is compliance with all the safety rules and regulations.

HOW TO HELP PLANT WORKERS AVOID PITFALLS

To maintain safe working conditions and minimize the number of accidents in the plant, you must constantly remind workers to take control of their jobs in how they perform their work. Tell them that although taking control requires a conscious effort, they need to think through their work procedures from beginning to end, no matter how often they've done them.

While this may seem easy at first, explain that they must avoid three pitfalls:

1. *Boredom.* Workers who have lots of experience are more prone to succumb to this than younger, inexperienced workers because they have done a particular job hundreds of times. They know how to do it, how to control the machine and the material, and how to move their hands. Their eyes are open and they are seeing, but they aren't watching.

   The ways to avoid boredom are to break up the monotony and don't repeat the same task on and on. Tell your workers to mix in other jobs in their work routine and spell themselves so that they aren't lulled. Point out that they should realize they are subject to boredom; by focusing on it, they can avoid it.

2. *Haste.* Hurrying not only diminishes the worker's possibilities for perfection and quality workmanship, but it increases the risk. They risk not only the work, but also themselves.

   Inform your workers that most of their enthusiasm and satisfaction with accomplishment arise from how they work. They short-change themselves and their work if they hurry. They risk much more if they allow anxiety and haste to control their work.

3. *Timidness.* When workers are timid, they often find it difficult to concentrate on working safely. Timidity is a feeling that comes on somewhere between caution and fear. Caution permits them to proceed. Fear denies them access.

   Point out to your workers that for a tool to be used effectively, it must be used with confidence. But dangerous tools have to be used with confidence *and* caution. If a tool is new to them, they should look for its limitations. In this case, caution should be a little stronger than confidence.

HOW TO INVESTIGATE ACCIDENTS

Work accidents cause injuries and property damage and decrease employee morale; they also incur medical expenses, increase insurance costs and interrupt production schedules. Unless you investigate accidents and analyze the results, there is every probability that accidents will recur.

Many supervisors dislike investigating accidents. They will avoid the job if they can possibly do so. They are usually reluctant for one of two reasons: 1) They think an accident investigation reflects on their job performance, or 2) They believe its purpose is to find someone to blame. Neither of these reasons are valid excuses for not investigating an accident.

The argument that the safety director or engineer should investigate plant accidents because the supervisor is too busy with other problems also doesn't add up. Supervisors are responsible for the safety and health of their employees on the job. That responsibility includes preventing accidents.

But you must find the causes of accidents before you can prevent them. By investigating accidents, you can learn where, how, and why accidents happen, thus enabling you to take action to prevent recurrences. The best way to avoid writing an accident report is to prevent the accident in the first place.

When you promptly and thoroughly investigate an accident, you gain the trust and confidence of your workers because they see that you are looking out for their interest and welfare. Employees will not hesitate to do what you ask if they feel you are knowledgeable, experienced, and concerned with their safety.

Accident investigations can, of course, be made by the plant safety engineer or director. This is done in some plants. But the engineer or director doesn't know the process or the operation as well as you do. Neither the engineer nor the director train workers or have the authority to discipline them. Nor do workers look to them for leadership and guidance. Although the director may assist in the investigation and perhaps advise you, you have the responsibility to take whatever corrective action is necessary.

You must be interested in finding out how *any* accident happened, even the minor cuts and bruises that employees doing physical work often suffer. After all, an accident may not be minor. Its seriousness is not known until it is investigated. Many accidents appear to be minor at first glance but later show up to be serious and costly.

What an Accident Investigation Involves

Accident investigation involves reporting the incident and analyzing it based on the information that is available or that can be learned by examining all the factors involved. You must do more than simply report the explanation of the individual who had or saw the accident. Your report should also include recommendations for action to prevent a recurrence.

In reporting, distinguish between what you learn firsthand from the victim and what is someone else's view. For example, unless you *saw* a worker trip over some wood on the floor, you should report, "the worker *allegedly* tripped over some wood."

Proper investigation requires that you go to the place of the accident, verify that wood is on the floor, and then report that wood was on the floor. How it happened to be there should also be stated if this is known.

If no wood is found, your report should say that none was found at the area nor was any reportedly picked up in that area. A proper and complete investigation frequently uncovers accident causes that are not readily apparent.

You may be tempted to report the cause as employee "carelessness." But evaluation and study may reveal that the carelessness was the result of improper or inadequate job safety training. The carelessness could also have been the result of an unsafe condition that made the employee decide to do the job in an unsafe manner.

When to Investigate an Accident

Except for giving immediate attention to an accident victim, nothing else should take preference over an investigation. There are several reasons for making it as soon as possible:

- Conditions at the accident site are likely to be the same as those at the time it occurred. Equipment will not have been changed nor the area cleaned.
- Facts about the accident are more clear, and details are more likely to be remembered by everyone now than later.
- Witnesses may still be available for an immediate source of information.
- The cause of the accident should be remedied quickly to prevent a recurrence.

How to Investigate an Accident

How you investigate an accident may be a factor in preventing a similar accident from occurring. A thorough and complete investigation should be the rule regardless of how minor the accident appears. Talking to the worker who was involved in the accident is the first step you should take.

Try to put the employee at ease. Say that you want to prevent a recurrence of the accident and that you need help to do this. Point out that the purpose of the investigation is not to put blame on someone or to make an impression with your report. You only want to prevent a similar accident from happening again.

Go to the accident area, if possible, but do your talking in private. The employee involved in the accident will be more at ease if the two of you are alone; also, what you report will not be influenced by comments and opinions of others in the employee's presence.

Let the employee describe what happened without interruption. If you don't understand something, ask at the end of the description. Avoid judging what happened or what is said. You do not want to put the employee on the defensive.

Limit your questions to asking for facts rather than opinions. You want to learn what happened, what was done, and how it was done. "Why" questions may make the employee defensive. Ask questions in a friendly, helpful manner, and ask questions that cannot be answered with only a yes or no.

It's a good idea to repeat the account of the accident to the employee after you've heard and recorded it. This will enable you to correct any errors in the account and perhaps add something you omitted or did not mention originally.

Finish the investigation by discussing what should be done to prevent a similar accident. You thus confirm the purpose of your investigation and prove that you want to help.

How to Talk to a Witness

If the accident was a serious one, you may not be able to interview the employee involved and must rely on a witness for all information. In either case, you should always try to get an account from a witness.

Be just as tactful and sincere as you were with the employee involved. Witnesses may provide a more factual account of the accident since, not having been involved, they may not be defensive. Also, they may have noticed something that the employee experiencing the accident was not aware of.

When talking to a witness, recognize that nobody wants to get another person in trouble; a witness's account might defend the employee involved through sympathy. Witnesses need not necessarily have observed the accident. They could have been nearby, familiar with what was being done, or know the circumstances. Thus, they are capable of providing information about conditions that could explain the cause of the accident.

Writing the Accident Report

When writing an accident investigation report, you should be sure to do a complete job by including a recommendation for corrective action. Stating that the employee involved committed an "unsafe act" and not explaining that act is insufficient. Similarly, telling the employee to "be more careful" is useless in helping avoid an accident if you do not say what not to do and if you do not change conditions to make it easier and possible to avoid an accident.

Do not be negative in your investigation and your report. When you suspect or encounter management errors or deficiencies, report them in terms of problems with procedures. You can point out that procedures and methods are inadequate, improper, or lacking in practicality. They can be changed and made better without placing blame.

Human errors must be defined before they can be corrected. Recognize that mistakes can be made in job assignments, training (or lack of it), procedures, and job scope in relation to the equipment involved. You can resolve these issues easier than preventing an unsafe act caused by an emotion.

The Value of Accident Investigations

If you closely analyze accidents, you'll usually find that more can be attributed to management errors than to worker errors. If you investigate an accident and simply attribute the accident to human error, you will fail to discover the true cause and thus you won't see ways and means of preventing accidents. Accident investigations can be of great value if they are not sloughed off routinely.

Most workers want to belong, to be involved in how their company is managed. They want to be asked for their opinion. They want to have a voice in what they do and how they do their work. You must find ways to communicate with employees to show an interest in their welfare. One of the ways you can do this is through accident investigations. See Figure 7-1 for a typical accident report.

UNDERSTANDING THE FREQUENCY AND SEVERITY OF PLANT ACCIDENTS

The terms "frequency" and "severity" are used in determining a department's or plant's safety record. The *frequency* reports how often accidents have occurred, whereas the *severity* reports how long injured persons are unable to work. If an employee is injured but loses no time from work, the accident is not measured by either term; if the employee does lose time, it is.

OSHA uses a formula based on the assumption that 100 employees will work fifty 40-hour weeks, for a total of 200,000 hours annually. Thus:

$$\text{Frequency} = \frac{\text{Number of incidents} \times 200,000}{\text{Total hours worked}}$$

$$\text{Severity} = \frac{\text{Number of lost days} \times 200,000}{\text{Total hours worked}}$$

Example

Suppose your plant has 200 employees, each averaging 40 hours work per week. In 12 months, four workers are injured, resulting in 160 days of time lost.

The injury *frequency* is:

$$\text{Frequency} = \frac{4 \text{ injuries} \times 1{,}000{,}000}{200 \text{ workers} \times 40 \text{ hours/week} \times 50 \text{ weeks/year}}$$

$$= 10 \text{ lost-time accidents per million hours worked}$$

The injury *severity* rate is:

$$\text{Severity} = \frac{160 \text{ days lost} \times 1{,}000{,}000}{200 \text{ workers} \times 40 \text{ hours/week} \times 50 \text{ weeks/year}}$$

$$= 400 \text{ days lost per million hours worked}$$

HOW TO MAKE A SAFETY "NEAR MISS" REPORT

You can promote the safety of plant workers by incorporating a "near miss" investigation report in your safety program. The purpose of such a report is to prevent serious injuries from similar or related near miss incidents which might otherwise recur, by prompt and thorough analysis, reporting, and follow-up of all safety near miss incidents.

You are responsible for investigating, reporting, and following up to see that your recommendations are implemented. When conducting your investigation, look for and report:

- The circumstances surrounding the incident.
- The conditions around the incident site.
- How the incident happened.
- Why normal inspection didn't catch the potential hazard.

Also report which of the following contributed the most in causing the incident:

- Safety rule violation.
- Standard practice violation.
- Inadequate procedures.
- Lack of safety alertness.
- Equipment failure (design, maintenance, or malfunction).

FIGURE 7-1

F-153 (10-63) v

ACCIDENT INVESTIGATION

THIS REPORT IS TO BE MADE OUT IN TRIPLICATE. ORIGINAL TO LOCAL SAFETY DEPARTMENT, DUPLICATE TO COMPENSATION DEPARTMENT, TRIPLICATE TO DEPARTMENT FILE.

EMPLOYE NAME - LAST, FIRST, MIDDLE			PLANT (CITY, STATE)	
CC NO.	DEPT NO	DATE OF INJURY & TIME	DATE INJURY WAS REPORTED	STATE EXACT LOCATION OF ACCIDENT - BUILDING NO, FLOOR, ETC.
JOB INJURED ON (BE SPECIFIC)			NAME OF EQUIPMENT INVOLVED - IF APPLICABLE	

DESCRIPTION OF ACCIDENT	OBSERVE ACCIDENT SITE, ASK QUESTIONS, DETERMINE FACTS INVOLVED. DESCRIBE.
ACCIDENT'S CAUSE(S)	CONSIDER UNSAFE ACTS AND/OR CONDITIONS CONTRIBUTING TO ACCIDENT. IDENTIFY AND LIST.
CORRECTIVE ACTION REQUIRED	CONSIDER CORRECTIVE ACTION FOR PEOPLE, PREMISES AND MACHINERY. IDENTIFY AND LIST.
PLACEMENT OF RESPONSIBILITY FOR CORRECTION AND FOLLOW-UP	☐ IMMEDIATE ACTION TAKEN. DESCRIBE. ☐ ITEMS REQUIRING FURTHER ACTION. DESCRIBE.

REFERRED TO FOR ACTION	TARGET DATE FOR COMPLETION
SIGNATURE (SUPERVISOR)	DATE

FIGURE 7-1, cont'd

INVESTIGATION GUIDE

Investigation requires "looking into" all facts involved in the accident. You must determine:

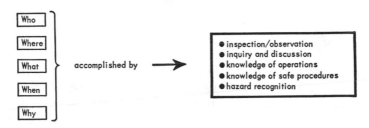

• • • • •

Since every accident follows a sequence, it is important to determine each step of the sequence:

PEOPLE	CAUSE	ACCIDENT, INJURY, OR DAMAGE

Was the person involved:
 	
1. Trained in safe working methods?
 	
2. Aware of the consequences of his actions?
 	
3. Capable of performing his job?
 	
   a. Were there physical limitations?
 	
   b. Were there external limitations?
 	
4. Aware of proper methods, consequences, and limitations and still took short cuts?
	1. What conditions of the plant, equipment, machinery, tools, etc. contributed to the accident?
	
	2. What employee actions contributed to the accident? (Note: both #1 and #2 are usually involved.)
		Describe the accident and injury to help:
		
		1. Identify the accident causes.
		
		2. Develop statistics that identify patterns, trends, or accidents of a repeat nature.
		
		3. Decide if the corrective action taken is effective or if it is still needed.

It is imperative that you don't stop at this point.

Corrective action is vital if similar accidents are to be prevented. After the cause is identified, select a corrective action. Does:

- Your recommendation involve the correction of an unsafe condition?
- Corrective action involve additional education or specific training of employees?
- Your recommendation involve different personnel selection and orientation?
- Your recommendation involve increased monitoring or supervision on your part?

Remember: Proper corrective action may involve a variation or combination of each step.

STEPS IN ACCOMPLISHING YOUR CORRECTIVE SUGGESTIONS:

- Select the person, department, or function that will best apply your suggestions and recommendations.
- Set dates.
- Follow up.

• • • • •

Remember: By removing the cause, you reduce the possibility of similar accidents recurring.

Make sure your recommendations cover all points brought out in the investigation. Check to see that they are positive, realistic, and compatible with the cause. Complete your report by determining a key safety lesson from the incident. See Figure 7-2 for a typical near miss investigation report.

WAYS TO PROMOTE ELECTRICAL SAFETY

You can prevent many of the electrical accidents resulting in injuries, fire, or damage to facilities by encouraging your employees to recommend safety procedures. For instance, all repair and maintenance work on electrical systems and equipment should be performed only by trained and authorized personnel.

In addition, when any electrical equipment is to be overhauled or repaired, the repair worker should check the main supply switches or cutout switches in each circuit from which power could possibly be supplied and should lock them in the open position and tag them. The tag should state why the circuit is locked out and who is in charge of the repairs. After the work has been completed, the same worker should remove the lock and tag.

Make sure workers keep fuse boxes and junction boxes closed, except when electrical work is being done. Further, workers should never alter or disconnect safety devices such as interlocks, overload relays, and fuses except when replacing them.

Protecting Plant Workers Against Electrical Shock

For a person to experience an electrical shock, there must be voltage across the person's body. But the resulting current flow is what is felt. The response of the body to alternating current has been graded into three levels:

- *Perception level* produces a slight tingling sensation.
- *Let-go level* is the maximum current at which a person holding a conductor can let it go by using muscles directly affected by the current.
- *Lethal level* causes chest or heart muscles to contract and breathing stops; if the current flow continues, the person loses consciousness and dies.

The extent of an electrical shock depends on the ratio of voltage to resistance, thus determining the current and the amount of the hazard.

- *Voltage* is the pressure required to provide the energy needed to do the work.
- The *current* is what does the work; it is forced from point to point by voltage.

- *Resistance* restricts the current and is determined by the size of the object through which the current flows; the larger the area, the less the resistance.

The current is determined by the resistance to ground of the human body and the working conditions. For instance, if hands or feet are wet, skin resistance will be lower and the current higher.

Three methods of protecting against electrical shock are commonly used: double insulation, grounding, and isolation transformers. These methods, however, are not foolproof. Double insulating a tool, for example, does not protect the user against cord, plug, or receptacle defects. Grounding a metal housing helps prevent shock when internal parts contact the housing, but human contact with the housing will result in shock unless grounding permits current flow. Isolation transformers may not work if the wiring is faulty or if the insulation is badly worn.

As for circuit breakers and fuses, these devices furnish protection from receiving too much current, but they do not prevent shock.

Grounding Equipment to Prevent Electrical Shocks

All new tools that are properly connected use the green wire as the safety ground. This wire is attached to the metal case of a tool and to the polarized grounding pin in the connector. The wire carries no current except when the tool insulation fails, in which case it short circuits the electricity around the user to ground, thus protecting the user from shock.

Some old electrical installations are not equipped with receptacles that will accept the grounding plug. With such installations, make sure your workers use one of the following methods to achieve a ground:

- Use an adapter fitting. Make sure employees know that they should not use the center screw that holds the cover plate on the receptacle but connect the ground lead extension to a good ground.
- Use the old plug and connect the green ground wire separately.
- Use an independent safety ground line. Where the separate safety ground leads are externally connected to a ground, first connect the ground and then plug in the tool. Likewise, when disconnecting the tool, first remove the line plug and then disconnect the safety ground. The safety ground is always connected first and removed last.

Using Ground Fault Interrupters to Prevent Electrical Shocks

A *ground fault* occurs when a circuit leaks current to a grounded conducting material. Although until recently there hasn't been a good method of

FIGURE 7-2

6–66

F-163 (6-82)　　　**SAFETY "NEAR MISS" INVESTIGATION REPORT**

TO: SAFETY MANAGER　　　　　　　　　　　　　　DATE_____
　　　DIVISION HEAD
　　　DEPARTMENT FOREMAN

WHAT HAPPENED: _____
_____
_____
_____

DATE, TIME & SHIFT OF INCIDENT: _____
TYPE OF POTENTIAL INJURY: _____
NAME OF EMPLOYEE(S) INVOLVED _____
LOCATION OF INCIDENT (DEPT. & WORK AREA): _____
MACHINERY OR EQUIPMENT INVOLVED: _____
_____

CAUSE OF INCIDENT: _____
_____

INVESTIGATION FINDINGS WHILE ON INCIDENT SITE: _____
_____
_____
_____
_____
_____

ACTION TO BE TAKEN: (CIRCLE ONE OR MORE)
ENGINEERING REVISION/TRAINING/CORRECTIVE　COUNSELLING　　Responsibility　　Estimated
　　　　　　　　　　　　　　　　　　　　DISCIPLINE　　For Follow-up　Completion Date

_____
_____
_____
_____
_____
_____

KEY SAFETY LESSON: _____
_____
_____

APPLICABLE TO FOLLOWING AREAS: _____
SAFETY TEAM INVESTIGATORS:

_____
_____
_____　　SIGNED _____
_____　　　　　　　　SUPERVISOR

CC Mgr of Engineering

FIGURE 7-2, cont'd

PROCEDURE FOR HANDLING SAFETY "NEAR MISS" REPORTS

OBJECTIVES:

To prevent serious injuries from similar or related "Near Miss" incidents which might otherwise recur, by prompt and thorough analysis, reporting, and follow-up of all safety "Near Miss" incidents.

INVESTIGATING AND REPORTING:

The prime responsibility for all "Near Miss" incident investigation and communication lies with the Supervisor. Specifically the Supervisor is responsible to insure that:

The investigation is conducted.
The investigation is thorough and complete (if not, he conducts his own investigation).
A clear and concise write-up is delivered to the Safety Office for publication within 3 working days from the date of the incident.

INCIDENT INVESTIGATION:

While conducting your investigation look for and think about:

The potential type of injuries possible from the incident.
Ask: Who, What, When, Where and Why of circumstances surrounding incident.
Ask: Who, What, When, Where and Why of conditions around the incident site.
Look for circumstances or conditions existing that set up the major cause of the incident.

Ask: Why didn't normal inspection catch the potential hazard?
Ask: Why or how did the incident happen?
Ask: Did the employee check for unsafe conditions before the job began?

Safety Office will determine areas that have similar exposure, type in under "Applicable to following Areas," and distribute to those areas. Engineering will get a copy of all incident reports. Every area in which incident is applicable must take immediate action to prevent a similar incident and respond to the Safety Office.

FOLLOW UP:

A thorough procedure should be in place to make sure the "Near Miss" preventative recommendations are implemented within the estimated time allowance.

INCIDENT CAUSE:

Report which one of the following contributed the most in causing the incident:

Safety rule violation (unsafe act)	Equipment failure:
Standard Practice violation	____Design of fabrication
Inadequate procedures	____Maintenance
Lack of safety alertness	____Malfunction

KEY SAFETY LESSON

A Key safety lesson should be determined from all "Near Miss" incidents.

ACTION TO BE TAKEN:

Are the recommendations complete? Do they cover all points brought out in the investigation?
Are the recommendations positive and realistic?
Are the recommendations compatible with the cause and investigation?

protection against fault current that is too small to actuate fuses or circuit breakers, that problem has been solved. The development and use of the ground fault interrupter (GFI) provides protection against this source of electrical shock.

After a GFI is connected between the power source and the load, it monitors current in the hot wire and grounded neutral wire. There is no fault as long as the current stays equal in both wires. But the instant there is a decrease in the amount of current in the neutral wire greater than a predetermined value, the imbalance causes the GFI to disconnect.

HOW TO ENSURE THE SAFETY OF PLANT WORKERS FROM ELECTRICAL HAZARDS

You can ensure the electrical safety of plant workers three ways:

1. *With safe wiring*. Determining whether wiring is safe involves electrical testing on a regular basis.
2. *By having workers adopt safe work practices*. Safe work practices evolve from a thorough electrical safety training program for all workers, combined with a continual respect for the dangers inherent in the use of electricity.
3. *Through preventive maintenance*. Practicing preventive maintenance prevents small problems from developing into serious ones resulting in injuries or deaths, explosions, or electrical fires.

This three-way approach to electrical safety translates into a safe working environment for workers as well as maximum production and the cost-efficient use of the plant's electrical facilities.

10 Safe Practices When Working with Electricity in the Plant

Your workers should have respect for the potential dangers of electricity. You can both educate and influence their attitude with a thorough safety training program that acquaints them with the importance of grounds and other basic principles of electricity. Too many accidents are caused by human error resulting from ignorance and carelessness. Tell them to follow these 10 safety rules:

1. Check that all portable tools are in good repair and there are no worn or frayed cords.
2. Do not make repairs to portable tools or electrical equipment unless it is part of your job.

3. Be sure your tools are grounded before you use them.

4. Do not change fuses or attempt repair work in a switch box unless this is part of your job.

5. Never store anything in a fuse box.

6. Operate safety switches and manual starters with your left hand. This allows you to stand to the right of the switch box.

7. Turn your head away when operating a switch. Wear eye protection.

8. Don't depend on insulation on wires to protect you; it may be defective.

9. Do not use foam or water extinguishers to fight electrical fires. Use carbon dioxide or dry powder.

10. Use the proper lock-out and tag procedure when your electrical equipment is down for cleaning or repairs.

Precautions on Supervising Employees Who Work with Electrical Systems

Your primary concern in assigning plant employees jobs on electrical systems and equipment is that this type of work should be performed by workers trained specifically in electrical functions and technology.

There has been a trend in recent years to employ multicraft workers in the engineering and maintenance departments of manufacturing plants, particularly the relatively small plants. The efficiency and productivity of workers is increased when a craft worker can do both simple pipefitting and mechanical work although the worker was trained as an electrician. But both management and labor unions are reluctant to accept the reverse of this thinking. As a step in the direction of safety, craft workers other than electricians and electronic specialists are generally not asked to do even minor electrical work in many manufacturing plants.

If you supervise plant employees who work with electrical systems, you should see that your plant's preventive maintenance program includes the regular inspection and cleaning of all switch gear, starters, controllers, circuit breakers, and similar electrical equipment. While some inspection and testing for loose connections by use of infrared instrumentation can be performed during normal plant operations, the cleaning of electrical facilities should be limited to partial plant shutdown periods when the pertinent system or equipment can be completely deenergized.

A good way to remove dust from electrical facilities and structures is to use a long-nozzled vacuum cleaner. Tell your electrical workers to wipe all bus insulation and bus supports with cloths moistened in a cleaning solution (preferred are heptane, Stoddard's solvent, or cleaners' naphtha). But because these solutions are flammable, good ventilation in the area where they are used is essential. In addition to good ventilation, avoid creating sparks and flames.

TIPS ON WORKING SAFELY ON VERTICAL STRUCTURES

Although most falls from fixed ladders and scaffolds are preventable, this type of accident is responsible for many reported plant injuries. Accidents occur most commonly on ladders, with accidents on stairs or steps second, and on scaffolds third. Proper maintenance procedures and common sense, however, can minimize accidents on ladders. Here are some suggestions for what you can do to prevent employee falls.

Set up a ladder maintenance schedule based on the four main kinds:

1. *Portable wooden ladders.* Check these at least once a month. Although they will not conduct heat or electricity when kept clean and dry, they tend to splinter, rot, warp, and absorb moisture.
2. *Portable aluminum ladders.* Examine these about every two months. Although this type is noncorrosive in most environments, aluminum ladders conduct heat and electricity, and they are not as stable as wood or steel varieties.
3. *Fixed vertical steel ladders.* Check these quarterly. Their major advantage is they will not absorb moisture, but they require protection from rust and corrosion, and they conduct heat and electricity.
4. *Fiberglass-reinforced plastic ladders.* Check these quarterly. The major advantage of this type are nonconductivity and resistance to corrosion and impact.

Establishing a System to Prevent Falls

Every climber should be protected against falls. When ladder cages are used on high ladders, platforms placed at 30-foot intervals are recommended to limit falls. Ladder cages provide protection in that if a climber loses a grip on the ladder but maintains footing, the person may be prevented from falling because his or her body comes to rest against the back of the cage. Also, if a climber slips, the person may be able to grab one of the horizontal cage supports until footing is regained.

Basket guards also protect against falls. A basket guard consists of a series of horizontal and vertical steel strips welded together in a crosshatched design to form a circular structure. The device is attached to a fixed ladder and surrounds the climber during his or her ascent and descent.

If workers under your supervision frequently work on vertical structures, look into positive-locking fall prevention systems for increased protection against falls. Two basic types are available.

1. *The cable system* uses a cable as a carrier. Safety is achieved through a locking sleeve that rides up and down on the carrier and is attached to

the climber's belt by a safety snap. The cable is secured at the top only and is restrained at the base. Guides, spaced at intervals, hold the cable parallel to the climbing structure. The sleeve operates when tension is applied, similar to a friction brake.

Cable systems have some weaknesses, however. The sleeves may fall below a climber's waist and make climbing difficult. The cable also tends to slacken with frequent use and may require adjustment. In addition, whenever the climber reaches a cable guide, the cable must be disconnected from the guide to allow the sleeve to slide by; it then must be reconnected.

2. *Fixed rail systems* use a tubular carrier rail attached to the center of the ladder with brackets at 6-foot intervals securing the rail. A sleeve with a locking pawl rides on the rail which is notched every 6 inches. Binding is eliminated by the use of roller bearings on the pawl. Double safety snaps attach the system to the climber's safety belt.

If the climber slips, the body weight forces the locking pawl into the notched rail, engaging the next notch down. This positive locking action prevents even an unconscious climber from falling.

WAYS TO ASSURE THE SAFETY OF PLANT WELDERS

Most industrial plants today must contend with the dangers of welding operations, whether they occur in production processes, installation or retrofitting of machines and equipment, or various maintenance and repair work that periodically must be done.

To make welding as safe as possible for the persons involved and other employees, you should see that steps are taken to provide adequate ventilation, protect against radiation, and guard against fires and explosions.

Welding operations result in the creation of gases and fumes from combustion products and heated metal. The amount and composition of these gases depend on the composition of the filler metals and base materials. Other factors affecting the type and amount of fumes developed are the specific welding process, the current level and the arc length. Exposure to these gases can cause nausea, headaches, dizziness, and metal fume fever.

Fumes and gases can be removed from the work area by furnishing ventilation or a method of exhaust. Numerous factors must be considered in determining the amount of ventilation needed:

- Volume and configuration of the area to be ventilated.
- Number and kinds of operations generating pollutants.
- Permissible level of specific toxic or flammable contaminants in the space.

- Location of welders' and other persons' breathing zones in relation to the pollutants or contaminants.

The recommended way to determine if adequate ventilation or exhaust is being furnished is to sample the fumes and gases to which personnel are exposed.

All kinds of welding produce radiation, but the amount and type of radiation exposure depends on the processes involved and the temperature of the materials. Since radiation is considered hazardous to one's health, safety glasses, gloves, and insulated clothing should be worn by the persons exposed to it.

Radiation may be ionizing, such as x-rays, or nonionizing. There are three forms of nonionizing radiation:

1. *Infrared*. This radiation emanates from hot metal, flames, or arcs, and feels like heat.
2. *Ultraviolet*. This type comes from welding arcs; while it cannot be felt by skin, it causes arc burns in the same way the sun causes sunburn.
3. *Visible*. This radiation comes from the bright light from flames. It can be harmful to unprotected eyes similarly to looking directly at the sun.

Fires and explosions caused by sparks and spatter are major hazards for welders. Because they wear eye protection or helmets when they weld, they are not always able to see where sparks and spatter land. The hot metal may fall through cracks in floors or just sit and smolder, causing fires to start long after they landed. For the safety of your welder and to prevent a fire, use a fire watcher or standby worker every time you assign a job to a welder.

This person can protect the welder from clothing or equipment ignition and put out any fires that start. He or she can also monitor the operation and prevent passers-by from getting too close.

Protecting the Safety and Health of Welders

To protect the safety and health of welders, you need to teach welders and cutters why and when to wear appropriate work clothing, gloves, and protective overgarments. Management should participate in this effort by seeing that these articles are made available to employees.

Welders need protection primarily from sparks and globules of molten metal. Trousers without cuffs, a long-sleeved shirt with a collar, shoes with safety toes, and cloth or leather-palm, cloth-back gloves are recommended. Cuffless trousers shed sparks; a buttoned shirt collar, as well as sleeves rolled down and buttoned, protects the upper body.

Denim and cotton duck are the best materials for trousers and shirts because they readily shed sparks. Synthetics should not be used because they melt where sparks land, letting the sparks burn through to the wearer's skin. For the same reason, shoe laces should be of rawhide, not of nylon or another synthetic.

The amount of sparks produced by welding varies with the process, electrode diameter, and procedure. The number of sparks striking a welder varies with the height of the job; overhead welding produces the most. For more protection, chrome-tanned leather is good for resisting heat and sparks. Alternatives are cloth woven from aramids and other temperature-resistant fibers.

To assure maximum safety, you should see that welders wear protective overgarments. Such overgarments include:

• Jackets, sleeves, and capes with sleeves that protect the torso and arms. The capes and sleeves allow body heat to radiate from the body, cooling the welder.

• Bib aprons and waist aprons to protect against sparks striking below the waist. Bib aprons work in combination with sleeves, waist aprons with capes.

• Pants that keep welders warm in cold weather. Chaps and leggings permit dissipation of heat from the lower body, thighs, and legs.

• Spats that protect the tops of shoes from sparks; they strap in place or come attached to leggings or trousers. Bib screens protect a welder's neck when they are attached to the back of a hard hat. Hoods with inset frame-mounted filters cover the entire head for protection from sparks.

The dexterity needed and the amount of heat and sparks generated by the welding or cutting process determine the type of hand protection that should be provided. Gloves allow the most dexterity, one-finger mittens (thumb and index finger individually enclosed) less, and regular mittens the least. The materials in a glove or mitten also affect dexterity, spark-shedding ability, and protection from heat.

Cloth gloves with short cuffs work best for soldering, brazing, resistance spot and seam welding, mechanized arc welding, gas tungsten arc welding, and low-amperage gas metal arc welding. For added protection against heat, a welder should wear all-leather gloves of deer-, elk-, or split (thin) cowhide. All of these materials aid sensitive touch and dextrous handling.

Gloves of thicker leather sacrifice dexterity for better protection from heat. Heavy linings or aluminized linings or pads protect from radiant heat produced by gas metal arc welding, multipass welding, air-arc gouging, or preheated parts.

Helping Plant Welders to Work Safely

Of all the protective clothing and equipment that welders wear and use, their welding helmets rank high in enabling them to perform their work safely. Helmets protect the eyes and face against the splashes of molten metal and radiation produced by arc welding.[6]

You can help your welder be safe on the job by seeing that the helmet and its components are properly designed and in good condition. Here is how to do it:

- Furnish the welder a helmet that resists sparks, molten metal, and flying particles. It should be a poor heat conductor and a nonconductor of electricity.

- See that the helmet has the proper filter to keep ultraviolet and visible rays from harming the eyes. Shade numbers recommended for various operations are given in USA Standard Z2.1. Since worker's eyes vary due to age and general health, two persons may require different shaded lenses when doing the same job.

- Make sure that the helmet has a headgear that permits the welder to use both hands and also to raise the helmet to position work.

- Supply the welder with impact goggles worn under the helmet to guard against flying particles when the helmet is raised. The spectacle type with side shields is recommended for protection from flash from adjacent work or from popping scale of a fresh weld.

- Provide the welder a hand-held shield for when the convenience of a helmet isn't needed. It can be used for inspection work, tack welding, and other work requiring little or no welding by the user. The frame and lens construction is similar to that of the helmet.

- Discard helmets that develop pinholes or cracks. Replace filter lenses that are cracked or chipped; otherwise they will permit harmful rays to reach the welder's eyes.

DEALING WITH THE HAZARDS OF WORKING IN CONFINED SPACES

Any tank, vat, manhole, silo, or enclosed or partially enclosed space should be considered dangerous and potentially lethal. Needless injuries and deaths occur each year in plants because employees are overcome by unrecognized hazards after entering confined spaces to do routine jobs or special maintenance work.

---

[6]*Supervisor's Safety Manual* (Chicago, IL 60611, National Safety Council), Chap. 7, pp. 144–145.

Most of these types of accidents are preventable. In some cases, workers are either forgetful or in a hurry. In others, poorly maintained or defective equipment may be at fault. Whatever the cause, you should adopt and enforce procedures for entering and working in confined spaces to help ensure employee safety.

The primary rule for establishing any procedure for entering and working in confined spaces safely is to assume that a hazard exists. Many workers are overcome because they ignore this possibility and believe a confined space is safe. Nobody should ever enter a space until tests for all possible gases, vapors, and other hazards have been carried out. This rule also applies to anyone entering an untested space to rescue a fellow worker. In many cases on record, multiple deaths occurred because this rule was not followed.

The hazardous conditions that could exist in confined spaces are of three types: oxygen deficient, combustible, and toxic. It is imperative that you tell your workers to test for all three conditions before entry. Testing for only one or even two of the possible hazards is not much better than not testing at all. A worker might learn that a tank contains enough oxygen and no toxic materials, only to have a spark from his equipment ignite an explosive gas.

The first concern when testing a confined space should be with its oxygen content. The level of oxygen in a confined space can become dangerously low in a short time. When it is insufficient to support breathing, it can kill quickly and without warning.

Oxygen deficiency is difficult to detect without instrumentation. With fresh air normally containing 20.8 percent oxygen, most safety standards require a minimum level of 19.5 percent. At this level, a person usually will experience no problems.

But at 16 percent, a slight difficulty in breathing may occur along with a ringing in the ears. The person may also be unable to think clearly and become sleepy. A worker who stays in such an environment for very long will begin to feel euphoric. At an oxygen level of 12 percent, a worker becomes unconscious and may die.

Combustible gases in confined spaces are a serious hazard. The vapors of liquid fuels and other hydrocarbons as well as naturally occurring gases can be a major problem in that a spark from an engine or a grinding operation, static electricity, or a cigarette can cause an explosion. Combustible gases and vapors often cannot be detected by sight or smell.

Toxic substances also may be encountered in confined spaces. These substances consist of two types:

1. *Irritants.* These include gases that act on respiratory and nervous systems at low concentrations and may cause death at high levels.
2. *Chemical asphyxiants.* These include gases that cause injury or death by preventing the body from using its oxygen supply. However, these

materials cause physiological damage long before they are concentrated enough to cause oxygen deficiency.

You should tell your workers that they must know the general types of hazards that exist in a confined space before they can develop procedures for safely entering and working in it. In addition, they must prepare for the unexpected. The only way to deal with the hazards to ensure a safe entry is to use instruments to evaluate a potentially dangerous environment.

Following Specific Entry Procedures

Although testing the confined space to be entered is necessary before entering and working in it, this is only part of a total program. After evaluating the environment and identifying the hazards, you must insist that workers follow certain procedures for entering and working within the space.

Safe practice dictates that an entry permit be issued each time entry into a confined space is planned. The permit form should contain a checklist for test and entry procedures, provide documentation for the entry, and alert other employees of what is being done. You should carefully check this form for completeness before you permit an entry.

Any confined space to be entered must be isolated from the entrance of all possible materials. In addition, all moving equipment or machines in or connected to the area must be locked up. If a space cannot be isolated from the possible release of hazardous substances, it must be treated as if it contained those substances.

The recommended procedures for isolating confined spaces have been published by the American National Standards Institute (ANSI) in standard Z117.1-1977, "Safety Requirements for Working in Tanks and Other Confined Spaces." These recommendations read as follows:

- Confined spaces should be protected against the introduction of hazardous materials before employees are allowed to enter them. This can be done by removing the valve or pipe fitting leading to the space and installing a blank on the open end leading to the vessel. An alternative method is to close, lock, and tag at least two valves in the piping leading to the space, and then install an open drain valve between the valves.

- All moving equipment within the space should be locked out and tagged; an open breaker or line switch controlling the equipment should also be locked open and tagged. The person entering the space should retain the key. If more than one person enters, each should lock the switch with his or her own lock and key. It's good safety practice to also block blades and rotors to prevent the weight of equipment from causing half revolutions.

- Nobody should enter a confined space without having another person familiar with emergency procedures standing by. Additionally, this person should maintain visible and oral contact with workers inside the space at all times, and should have access to immediate help.

Once a space has been isolated, it should be cleaned, purged, and ventilated. After purging with either steam or nitrogen, the space must be ventilated to eliminate oxygen deficiency and accumulated combustibles or toxic substances. The space should be ventilated to the point where the levels of combustibles do not exceed 10 percent of their lower explosive limit and the levels of toxic substances do not exceed their threshold limit values.

Tip: If working in confined spaces is a common occurrence for your plant workers, give each one a copy of *Working Safely in Confined Spaces*. This is an 8-page booklet published by the Bureau of Law & Business, Inc. Copies can be obtained by writing Order Department, Bureau of Law & Business, Inc., 64 Wall Street, Madison, CT 06443, or by phoning (203) 245-7448.

HOW TO IMPROVE PLANT WORKERS' SAFETY AT LOADING DOCKS

With 10 to 25 percent of industrial accidents occurring on loading docks today, companies that do not use accident prevention technology are taking a special risk. Three common accidents that happen at the truck dock interface are attributed to trailer creep, landing gear collapse, and premature departure.

- *Trailer creep* is the slight movement of a trailer away from the dock caused by the impact of a fork truck entering a parked trailer. If enough movement occurs through repeated impact, the dock leveler lip loses contact with the trailer causing the truck and driver to drop into the gap.
- *Landing gear collapse* is also caused by impact from the fork truck entering a parked trailer or by the gear sinking into soft apron pavement.
- *Premature departure* of the truck takes place when the driver, thinking the loading or unloading operation is finished, pulls the truck away from the dock. Unaware of what is happening, a fork truck driver may be spilled off the dock with the truck and load landing on him or her.

These three types of accidents can be prevented by use of a trailer restraint device attached to the dock. The restraint is attached to the ICC bumper on the rear of the trailer, holding it against the dock. A two-way signal light system tied into the restraint system further increases safety as follows:

- For dock personnel, a red light indicates the truck is not properly restrained; a green light indicates the restraint is attached, and it is safe to enter the trailer.
- For truck drivers, a red light outside the dock indicates the restraint is attached; a green light signifies the restraint is not attached, and it is safe to drive away.

Other safety devices for docks include safety stops on levelers, recycling levelers that return to a safe position after the trailer departs, and levelers with toe guards to keep persons' feet from being caught under the platform.

Accidents can be prevented also by installing ladders, stairs, and ramps at strategic places, thus providing persons access to ground level without having to jump down from the dock.

HELPING THE WAREHOUSE AND DOCK EMPLOYEE TO WORK SAFELY

Manual handling of materials in the warehouse and on the dock increases the possibility of worker injuries. To minimize injuries, materials handling should be done mechanically, insofar as possible. Much equipment has been developed for this purpose.[7]

- *Hand tools.* The crowbar is probably the most common tool. Because it can slip, tell your workers to never work astride it. They should so position themselves that they will not be pinched or crushed if the bar should slip or the object move suddenly.
- *Rollers.* These devices are used for moving heavy or bulky objects. Caution your workers to be careful not to crush their fingers or toes between the rollers and the floor. They should use a sledge or bar, not their hands and feet, to change direction of the object.
- *Hand trucks.* Two-wheeled hand trucks are very common in warehouses and docks. Tell your workers the safe procedures that must be followed with their use:
  Keep the center of gravity of the load as low as possible.
  Place the load so the weight will be carried by the axle, not by the handles.

[7]*Supervisor's Safety Manual* (Chicago, IL 60611: National Safety Council), Chap. 9, pp. 208–216.

Never walk backwards with a hand truck.

When going down an incline, keep truck ahead. When going up, keep truck behind.

- *Power trucks.* These trucks have either a battery-powered motor or an internal combustion engine. Only physically qualified operators, who have received training and are duly authorized, should be permitted to drive any industrial power truck. Since there are many safety rules involving the operation of power trucks, and they will be impressed on workers when you or someone else trains them, only the most critical are listed here:

    Stay within maximum speeds for trucks in your plant.

    Slow down or stop at intersections or blind corners.

    Face the direction of travel. Never back up without looking.

    Never drive a truck loaded so high that the view is obstructed.

    Never load a truck beyond its limit. The load limit is posted on the vehicle.

    Keep forks about 4 inches off the floor when traveling. When going downhill, keep the load last; when going uphill, keep the load first.

- *Conveyors.* Do not let anyone ride on conveyors. If employees must cross a conveyor, provide crossover bridges to eliminate their having to crawl across it. Furnish warning or protective devices on gravity conveyors to prevent people's hands from being caught in descending material or jammed between material and the receiving table.

GUIDELINES TO SAFE OPERATION OF ROBOTS

The key to developing a safe workplace where robots are used lies in developing respect for what a robot is, how it works, how it is controlled, and how it interacts with its environment.

Although robots can replace humans on dangerous or onerous jobs, they do not necessarily eliminate the hazards associated with the operations they perform. In some situations, they themselves present new hazards. Using a robot for spraying paint, for example, avoids worker exposure to paint vapors and fumes, but it doesn't minimize the risk of a fire or an explosion.

Unlike many plant machines, robots can do many jobs and do them in varying sequences. A robot may move its arm in one direction a certain distance, pause, then move its arm in a different direction. Anyone who approaches the robot, believing it is not working because of the pause, or that it can move only as it was seen to do, could be struck by the robot's arm and seriously injured.

All employees in a plant where robots perform must be protected from them because a robot that is programmed can malfunction and "desert," that is, do other movements than it was programmed to do. You have to confine a robot in what is called the "envelope of its movement"— inward, outward, and around the operation. You must train employees to be sure that they do not expose themselves to the envelope area where they could be trapped or struck by the robot.

Safety experts recommend that robots be totally enclosed in a chain link fence, and that any access ways be interlocked to the control panel. An advantage of a fence, rather than rails, for guarding robots that pick up objects is that the fence can stop any objects that may be thrown by the robot if it does not firmly hold it.

Probably the most dangerous part of working with a robot is programming it to perform its operation. Two persons working together should do this. While one maneuvers the robot's arm with a remote control device connected to the control unit through which the robot can be oriented to its task, the other should be stationed at the main control panel ready to use the emergency stop if it should be necessary.

How to Ensure the Safety of Workers Using Robots

Two design precautions are necessary to ensure that your workers are safe when working with robots:

1. Robots must be properly grounded. Confirm that this was done with the engineering department before you permit a worker to operate one.
2. Nonflammable hydraulic fluids should be used if an ignition source is present. In paint spray operations, where static electricity could ignite solvent-based paints, the robot should be designed with an explosion-proof electrical system.

Just as important as design, you must thoroughly train workers who work with robots:

- Make sure the workers are aware of what the robot will do and what could happen if the robot is not doing what it is programmed to do.
- Insist and confirm that the workers follow the proper lockout procedure if they have to make any adjustments or put themselves in a confined area. Remind them that they must also bleed off any residual force, such as compressed air or hydraulic fluid.

8

Ensuring Plant Workers' Compliance with OSHA and EPA Regulations

DEALING WITH PLANT EMPLOYEES' ADHERENCE TO THE OCCUPATIONAL SAFETY AND HEALTH ACT (OSHA)

Although the cliché *safety is everybody's business* has long been worn out because of overuse, it still holds true and should not be discarded. Safety is everybody's business because it is needed both on and off the job, and because of the general feeling that every individual must play a part in being safe, not only for his or her own good, but also for the good of others.

Safety is also big business. The great national impetus on safety began with the 1970 Occupational Safety and Health Act (OSHA). In broad terms, three out of four civilian workers come under its jurisdiction. Standards were set under OSHA in a voluminous document that listed in detail various requirements of design and operation of equipment, machines, facilities, and structures, as well as specifying safety training and equipment for workers. In an effort to update the original standards and make them apply more directly to current workplace conditions, the administration continually makes many revisions each year.

This law requires all employers in the private sector of business to provide their employees with workplaces free from those recognized hazards likely to cause physical harm or death. It does this through the publishing of volumes of the Code of Federal Regulations. These documents are available from the Superintendent Of Documents, U.S. Government Printing Office, Washington, DC 20402.

The two most pertinent publications for plants are the General Industry Standards and Interpretations, and the Construction Standards and Interpretations. The former publication is issued in two documents: 29 CFR Parts 1901.1 to 1910.441 and 29 CFR Parts 1910.442 to 1910.1000. The latter publication is issued in one document: 29 CFR Part 1926.

Achievements and Influences of OSHA

Despite the fact that some companies are not entirely in agreement with how the administration conducts its business, OSHA can save some companies money. Savings can be realized from lower worker's compensation costs because compliance with OSHA laws improves a company's accident record, thus reducing the cost of worker's compensation. OSHA also has other influences on industrial organizations.

Before OSHA, the management of a company could deny an expense for safety because it would put the company at a competitive disadvantage if a competitor chose to forego the same expense. With OSHA forcing all companies to spend money for safety, that argument no longer prevails. Better safety can result in other benefits. Changing a process to eliminate a hazard sometimes improves not only the safety but also the efficiency of the operation.

In addition, enactment of occupational health standards by OSHA has forced many supervisors to become involved in the evaluation and control of industrial hygiene problems in their facilities. For example, industrial hygiene factors must receive attention when operating and maintaining ventilation systems, makeup air, enclosure and/or isolation of processes using toxic chemicals, handling and storage of toxic materials, and cleanup of exhaust emissions.

Lastly, OSHA states that all employers must keep accurate records of work-related injuries, illnesses, and deaths. Any injury that involves medical treatment, loss of consciousness, restrictions of motion or work, or job transfer must be recorded. Required information must be logged and specific information regarding each case detailed. With this information readily available to management, there is no excuse for not knowing what has to be done to improve a plant's safety record.

HOW THE NATIONAL INSTITUTE FOR OCCUPATIONAL SAFETY AND HEALTH (NIOSH) FUNCTIONS

The National Institute for Occupational Safety and Health (NIOSH) is part of the Department of Health and Human Services. It was established by Section 22 of the Occupational Safety and Health Act of 1970. NIOSH conducts research and experimental programs for the development of new and improved health standards.

The Secretary of Labor looks to NIOSH results when formulating standards under the Act. NIOSH also develops criteria for handling toxic materials and aids in determining safe exposure levels for physical conditions involving noise, illumination, vibration, radiation, temperature and pressure.

In addition to its research and development activities, NIOSH inspects and investigates workplaces to evaluate and improve employee safety and health. Although it has no authority to enforce standards, its authority to inspect is established by Section 8 of the Act.

Thus, a NIOSH inspector may visit a plant for one of two reasons: Either a request for a Health Hazard Evaluation (HHE) has been received, or NIOSH wants to make an inspection as part of its general research responsibilities.

An HHE of a particular workplace may be requested by the employer or an individual employee. Whatever the reason, the HHE must give specific information about the plant, the process, and the substances or materials that are the basis for the request. Much of what happens after the request is similar to what takes place with an OSHA inspection.

WHAT PROMPTS AN OSHA INSPECTION

Because OSHA is able to inspect only about one out of a hundred workplaces under its jurisdiction in a given year, the U.S. Department of Labor uses a system of priorities in deciding which places get inspected. Following is a listing and discussion of the justification of these priorities:

- When there is a fatality or an accident that results in the hospitalization of five or more employees, the employer must report it to the nearest OSHA office within 48 hours. An investigation and inspection will then be made to determine if standards were violated and to find ways to avoid similar accidents.

- When OSHA is reasonably certain that a condition or situation exists in a plant that may cause death or serious injury immediately or before normal enforcement procedures can prevent it, an inspection will be made.

- When an employee believes that there is an imminent hazard or that there is a violation of a standard that poses physical harm, he or she may ask OSHA to inspect. Although OSHA will keep the employee's name confidential if so requested, it will not automatically inspect. OSHA will review the request and inspect only if it believes the complaint is justified or if it is in doubt; it would not inspect for obviously trivial or vindictive complaints.

- When death, illness, high injury rates, or known exposures of employees to toxic substances comes to OSHA's attention, it may target specific industries for concentrated inspection.
- When a plant has been cited for a previous serious violation, OSHA may reinspect it to see if the hazard has been corrected.

HOW OSHA INSPECTIONS ARE MADE

Since it is illegal for anyone to notify an employer in advance of an OSHA inspection, the visit of a compliance officer to your plant will be a surprise to management. OSHA itself may give such notice in certain circumstances but only within less than 24 hours.

Upon arrival, the officer will ask to see the plant manager. The officer will present his or her credentials, which are issued by the Department of Labor and include the officer's photograph and a serial number that can be verified by phone at the nearest OSHA office.

The officer will then explain the purpose of the visit and the scope of the inspection, and will give the plant manager copies of applicable standards, as well as a copy of any employee complaint. After this, the manager will be asked to designate someone to accompany the officer on the inspection of the plant.

Employees have a right to have a representative accompany the officer on the inspection tour. If there is a union, it usually will designate the employee representative; if there is no union, the plant safety committee may designate someone. In either case, plant management may never select the employee representative.

With the route and duration of the inspection determined by the officer, the group begins the tour. Expect the officer to check conditions for compliance with standards. In doing so, he or she may take photographs and test instrument readings. The officer will also want to see the files and records that pertain to OSHA regulations.

When the tour is completed, the officer will inform the plant manager of the apparent violations of standards that have been found. The manager can discuss the situation, show efforts that have been made to comply with the regulations, and give information to help OSHA determine how much time should be allowed for correction.

The officer then will either issue or recommend the issuance of citations; in either case, they must be approved by the OSHA area director. Only the area director also has the authority to assess penalties.

GUIDELINES ON OSHA'S VIOLATIONS AND PENALTIES

After the compliance officer completes the report of the plant inspection, the area director decides what citations, if any, will be issued and what penalties will be imposed. Following are the types of violations along with the possible penalties:

- An *other than serious violation* is one that is directly related to safety and health, but not likely to cause serious physical harm. While a discretionary penalty of up to $1,000 may be imposed for each violation, it may actually be much less in consideration of the employer's good faith efforts to comply, the size of the company, and the history of previous violations. No penalties below $50 are ever levied.

- A *serious violation* is one that has a strong probability of death or serious physical harm, and the employer knows, or should know, of the hazard. There is a mandatory proposed penalty between $300 and $1,000 for each violation. But the penalty may be lowered when considering the employer's good faith, history of previous violations, gravity of the violation, and size of the company, to as low as $60. Imminent danger situations are cited and penalized as serious violations.

- A *willful violation* occurs when the employer is aware of and/or commits an intentional violation of the Act and makes no reasonable effort to correct or eliminate it. There is a maximum penalty of $10,000 for each such violation, but the penalty may be adjusted downward. If a willful violation results in a death, a court may impose a maximum fine of $10,000, or a prison term of six months, or both. If there is a second conviction, these penalties may be doubled.

- A *repeated violation* (not necessarily the same equipment or location in the plant) calls for a maximum fine of $10,000 for each occurrence. The time limit in effect is 3 years from the date that the first citation became a final order or the date of final correction, whichever is later.

Additional violations and their penalties are as follows:

- Assaulting, resisting, opposing, intimidating, or interfering with a compliance officer could result in a $5,000 fine and maximum imprisonment for 3 years.

- Failure to correct a violation may be penalized with a $1,000 maximum fine for each day beyond the prescribed abatement date.

- Falsifying records, reports, or applications may bring on a $10,000 fine and 6 months in jail.

- Violation of posting requirements calls for a maximum fine of $1,000.

10 WAYS TO WORK WITH PLANT EMPLOYEES TO AVOID AN OSHA INSPECTION

If plant employees believe unsafe or unhealthy conditions exist in the workplace, they or their representatives have the right to file a complaint with the nearest OSHA office. Since a complaint very likely may prompt an inspection, or at least an investigation, you must do everything you can to maintain safe and healthy conditions in the plant. Unquestionably, you need the help of the employees in this effort. Here are ten ways to get them to work with you:

1. Create a safety committee whose responsibilities include making regular plant inspections, investigating accidents, and suggesting safety improvements in the plant, its machines, equipment, and tools. Ask the members to also help in developing and implementing safety rules. (For a more detailed discussion on safety, see Chapter 7.)

Tip: Rotate membership over time so that all employees have an opportunity to participate.

2. Promote safety contests and encourage all employees to participate. Give awards to employees who submit usable safety suggestions and to the department with the best safety record over a given period of time.

3. Hold safety meetings regularly making attendance compulsory. Use films, videos, slides, and other visual aids that show how to contend with hazards in the workplace.

Tip: You can also use these meetings to train employees to work safely.

4. Point out to employees the necessity of wearing protective clothing and using safety equipment and devices in the performance of their jobs. Follow up, if necessary, to ensure they do so.

5. Instruct employees responsible for maintenance and repairs of safety devices to install or replace them only as designed. No change is to be made.

6. Instruct employees responsible for maintenance of instruments and controls to regularly check and adjust them to within their specified limits. Insist that these items also be tested after they have been serviced to confirm that they work properly.

7. Promote good housekeeping and a clean environment in the plant. Explain how such conditions contribute to the safety and health of everyone.

8. Ask employees to report the presence of a hazardous material or gas to you immediately after they detect it. Then take steps to correct the condition and do what is necessary to prevent a reoccurrence of the leak or spill.

9. Ask employees to check ventilation, lighting, and noise levels to make certain they are satisfactory and do not cause workers to tire abnormally.

10. Ask employees to report any plant, machine, equipment, or tool condition which could conceivably cause an accident or injury. Then take steps to correct the condition to make the area or item safe.

RECOGNIZING PLANT EMPLOYEES' RIGHTS UNDER OSHA

The most important right of employees under OSHA is to be provided with a safe place of employment that is free from recognized hazards causing or likely to cause death or serious harm. Other specific rights are as follows:

- Employees are entitled to see and review a copy of the Act and relevant OSHA standards and regulations, and they may request information from you on safety and health hazards in the plant. They have a right also to review all logs and records pertaining to OSHA regulations and must be told if exposure to harmful substances has exceeded permissable levels.

- Employees may ask for locations to be monitored in order to measure exposure to toxic, hazardous, or radiation materials. They may be permitted to see the records of such monitoring or measuring, and have a record of their own personal exposure. They may also have medical examinations or other tests made to determine whether their health is being affected by an exposure and have the results of such tests furnished to their physicians.

- Employees may request inspections anonymously if they believe there are hazardous conditions or violations of OSHA standards in the plant. They also have the right to have a representative accompany the inspecting officer in the plant, to answer any questions, and to request a meeting after the inspection to discuss findings and decisions.

- Employees may have regulations posted to inform them of protection afforded by the Act. They may also request that any citations made to the employer by OSHA be posted on the premises.

- Employees may appeal any actions taken by OSHA or their employer, but they may not formally contest citations, penalties, or lack of penalties. However, they may contest the amount of time OSHA has given the employer to correct a violation. When an employer applies for a variance from a standard, employees have the right to testify at the variance hearing and to appeal the final decision. Employees may also bring an action against the Secretary of Labor to compel him or her to get a court order furnishing relief in cases of imminent danger when the secretary has arbitrarily refused to do so.

• Employees are guaranteed freedom from retaliation by employers for exercising their rights under the Act. Employers are forbidden to punish, discipline, or discriminate against any employee for participating in OSHA conferences, inspections, or hearings; for complaining about work hazards; for filing safety grievances; or for serving on safety committees.

POSTING AND RECORD KEEPING REQUIRED BY OSHA

All plants must post the Job Safety and Health workplace poster (OSHA No. 2203) shown in Figure 8-1, and it must be posted in a prominent location. Although the wording may be changed slightly from time to time, the portion that advises employees of the law and their rights under it remains the same.

If there are more than ten employees in your plant, records must be kept of occupational injuries and illnesses. The forms used must be maintained yearly and be available for inspection at the plant for five years; they are not sent to OSHA. Currently, two forms are being used:

1. The Log and Summary of Occupational Injuries and Illnesses (OSHA No. 200) is shown in Figure 8-2. Each recordable case of illness or injury is entered on one line on this form. At the end of the year, the number of fatalities, lost-time, and nonlost-time injuries and illnesses are summarized on the right side of the form. This portion of the form must be posted by February 1 of the following year and must remain in place until March 1. Definitions and instructions for filling out OSHA No. 200 are printed on the reverse side of the form.

2. The Supplementary Record of Occupational Illnesses and Injuries (OSHA No. 101) is shown in Figure 8-3. This one-page form supplies a history of each accident or exposure to illness. OSHA No. 101 must be retained for five years but does not have to be posted.

Any citations issued by an OSHA inspector must be posted at or near the location of the alleged violations for three days or until the violations are abated, whichever is longer. If plant management files a petition for modification of abatement, that also must be posted. Or if management decides to contest a citation, the employees' authorized representative (usually the union) must be supplied with a copy; if there is no authorized representative, the notice of contest must be posted. Similarly, if manage-

FIGURE 8-1.
Job Safety and Health Protection Poster.

JOB SAFETY & HEALTH PROTECTION

The Occupational Safety and Health Act of 1970 provides job safety and health protection for workers by promoting safe and healthful working conditions throughout the Nation. Provisions of the Act include the following:

Employers

All employers must furnish to employees employment and a place of employment free from recognized hazards that are causing or are likely to cause death or serious harm to employees. Employers must comply with occupational safety and health standards issued under the Act.

Employees

Employees must comply with all occupational safety and health standards, rules, regulations and orders issued under the Act that apply to their own actions and conduct on the job.

The Occupational Safety and Health Administration (OSHA) of the U.S. Department of Labor has the primary responsibility for administering the Act. OSHA issues occupational safety and health standards, and its Compliance Safety and Health Officers conduct jobsite inspections to help ensure compliance with the Act.

Inspection

The Act requires that a representative of the employer and a representative authorized by the employees be given an opportunity to accompany the OSHA inspector for the purpose of aiding the inspection.

Where there is no authorized employee representative, the OSHA Compliance Officer must consult with a reasonable number of employees concerning safety and health conditions in the workplace.

Complaint

Employees or their representatives have the right to file a complaint with the nearest OSHA office requesting an inspection if they believe unsafe or unhealthful conditions exist in their workplace. OSHA will withhold, on request, names of employees complaining.

The Act provides that employees may not be discharged or discriminated against in any way for filing safety and health complaints or for otherwise exercising their rights under the Act.

Employees who believe they have been discriminated against may file a complaint with their nearest OSHA office within 30 days of the alleged discriminatory action.

Citation

If upon inspection OSHA believes an employer has violated the Act, a citation alleging such violations will be issued to the employer. Each citation will specify a time period within which the alleged violation must be corrected.

The OSHA citation must be prominently displayed at or near the place of alleged violation for three days, or until it is corrected, whichever is later, to warn employees of dangers that may exist there.

Proposed Penalty

The Act provides for mandatory penalties against employers of up to $1,000 for each serious violation and for optional penalties of up to $1,000 for each nonserious violation. Penalties of up to $1,000 per day may be proposed for failure to correct violations within the proposed time period. Also, any employer who willfully or repeatedly violates the Act may be assessed penalties of up to $10,000 for each such violation.

There are also provisions for criminal penalties. Any willful violation resulting in death of an employee, upon conviction, is punishable by a fine of up to $250,000 (or $500,000 if the employer is a corporation), or by imprisonment for up to six months, or both. A second conviction of an employer doubles the possible term of imprisonment.

Voluntary Activity

While providing penalties for violations, the Act also encourages efforts by labor and management, before an OSHA inspection, to reduce workplace hazards voluntarily and to develop and improve safety and health programs in all workplaces and industries. OSHA's Voluntary Protection Programs recognize outstanding efforts of this nature.

OSHA has published Safety and Health Program Management Guidelines to assist employers in establishing or perfecting programs to prevent or control employee exposure to workplace hazards. There are many public and private organizations that can provide information and assistance in this effort, if requested. Also, your local OSHA office can provide considerable help and advice on solving safety and health problems or can refer you to other sources for help such as training.

Consultation

Free assistance in identifying and correcting hazards and in improving safety and health management is available to employers, without citation or penalty, through OSHA-supported programs in each State. These programs are usually administered by the State Labor or Health department or a State university.

Posting Instructions

Employers in States operating OSHA approved State Plans should obtain and post the State's equivalent poster.

Under provisions of Title 29, Code of Federal Regulations, Part 1903.2(a)(1) employers must post this notice (or facsimile) in a conspicuous place where notices to employees are customarily posted.

More Information

Additional information and copies of the Act, specific OSHA safety and health standards, and other applicable regulations may be obtained from your employer or from the nearest OSHA Regional Office in the following locations:

Atlanta	(404) 347-3573
Boston	(617) 565-7164
Chicago	(312) 353-2220
Dallas	(214) 767-4731
Denver	(303) 844-3061
Kansas	(816) 426-5861
New York	(212) 337-2325
Philadelphia	(215) 596-1201
San Francisco	(415) 995-5672
Seattle	(206) 442-5930

Elizabeth Dole

Elizabeth Dole, Secretary of Labor

Washington, D.C.
1989 (Revised)
OSHA 2203

U.S. Department of Labor
Occupational Safety and Health Administration

FIGURE 8-2.
Log and Summary of Occupational Injuries and Illnesses.

Bureau of Labor Statistics
Log and Summary of Occupational
Injuries and Illnesses

NOTE: This form is required by Public Law 91-596 and must be kept in the establishment for 5 years. Failure to maintain and post can result in the issuance of citations and assessment of penalties. *(See posting requirements on the other side of form.)*			RECORDABLE CASES: You are required to record information about every occupational death; every nonfatal occupational illness; and those nonfatal occupational injuries which involve one or more of the following: loss of consciousness, restriction of work or motion, transfer to another job, or medical treatment (other than first aid). *(See definitions on the other side of form.)*		
Case or File Number	Date of Injury or Onset of Illness	Employee's Name	Occupation	Department	Description of Injury or Illness
Enter a nonduplicating number which will facilitate comparisons with supplementary records.	Enter Mo./day.	Enter first name or initial, middle initial, last name.	Enter regular job title, not activity employee was performing when injured or at onset of illness. In the absence of a formal title, enter a brief description of the employee's duties.	Enter department in which the employee is regularly employed or a description of normal workplace to which employee is assigned, even though temporarily working in another department at the time of injury or illness.	Enter a brief description of the injury or illness and indicate the part or parts of body affected. Typical entries for this column might be: Amputation of 1st joint right forefinger; Strain of lower back; Contact dermatitis on both hands; Electrocution—body.
(A)	(B)	(C)	(D)	(E)	(F)

PREVIOUS PAGE TOTALS ➔

TOTALS (Instructions on other side of form.) ➔

OSHA No. 200   ✩U.S. GOVERNMENT PRINTING OFFICE: 1989 241-374/08097

FIGURE 8-2, cont'd

U.S. Department of Labor

For Calendar Year 19 _____   Page ____ of____

Form Approved
O.M.B. No. 1220-0029
See OMB Disclosure
Statement on reverse.

| Company Name |
| Establishment Name |
| Establishment Address |

Extent of and Outcome of INJURY							Type, Extent of, and Outcome of ILLNESS						
Fatalities	Nonfatal Injuries						Type of Illness							Fatalities	Nonfatal Illnesses				
Injury Related	Injuries With Lost Workdays					Injuries Without Lost Workdays	CHECK Only One Column for Each Illness *(See other side of form for terminations or permanent transfers.)*							Illness Related	Illnesses With Lost Workdays				Illnesses Without Lost Workdays

Enter DATE of death. Mo./day/yr.	Enter a CHECK if injury involves days away from work, or days of restricted work activity, or both.	Enter a CHECK if injury involves days away from work.	Enter number of DAYS away from work.	Enter number of DAYS of restricted work activity.	Enter a CHECK if no entry was made in columns 1 or 2 but the injury is recordable as defined above.	Occupational skin diseases or disorders	Dust diseases of the lungs	Respiratory conditions due to toxic agents	Poisoning (systemic effects of toxic materials)	Disorders due to physical agents	Disorders associated with repeated trauma	All other occupational illnesses	Enter DATE of death. Mo./day/yr.	Enter a CHECK if illness involves days away from work, or days of restricted work activity, or both.	Enter a CHECK if illness involves days away from work.	Enter number of DAYS away from work.	Enter number of DAYS of restricted work activity.	Enter a CHECK if no entry was made in columns 8 or 9.
(1)	(2)	(3)	(4)	(5)	(6)	(a)	(b)	(c)	(d)	(e)	(f)	(g)	(8)	(9)	(10)	(11)	(12)	(13)

INJURIES   ILLNESSES

Certification of Annual Summary Totals By _____ Title _____ Date _____

OMB DISCLOSURE STATEMENT

FIGURE 8-2, cont'd We estimate that it will take from 4 minutes to 30 minutes to complete a line entry on this form, including time for reviewing instructions; searching, gathering and maintaining the data needed; and completing and reviewing the entry. If you have any comments regarding this estimate or any other aspect of this recordkeeping system, send them to the Bureau of Labor Statistics, Division of Management Systems (1220-0029), Washington, D.C. 20212 and to the Office of Management and Budget, Paperwork Reduction Project (1220-0029), Washington, D.C. 20503.

Instructions for OSHA No. 200

I. Log and Summary of Occupational Injuries and Illnesses

Each employer who is subject to the recordkeeping requirements of the Occupational Safety and Health Act of 1970 must maintain for each establishment a log of all recordable occupational injuries and illnesses. This form (OSHA No. 200) may be used for that purpose. A substitute for the OSHA No. 200 is acceptable if it is as detailed, easily readable, and understandable as the OSHA No. 200.

Enter each recordable case on the log within six (6) workdays after learning of its occurrence. Although other records must be maintained at the establishment to which they refer, it is possible to prepare and maintain the log at another location, using data processing equipment if desired. If the log is prepared elsewhere, a copy updated to within 45 calendar days must be present at all times in the establishment.

Logs must be maintained and retained for five (5) years following the end of the calendar year to which they relate. Logs must be available (normally at the establishment) for inspection and copying by representatives of the Department of Labor, or the Department of Health and Human Services, or States accorded jurisdiction under the Act. Access to the log is also provided to employees, former employees and their representatives.

II. Changes in Extent of or Outcome of Injury or Illness

If, during the 5-year period the log must be retained, there is a change in an extent and outcome of an injury or illness which affects entries in columns 1, 2, 6, 8, 9, or 13, the first entry should be lined out and a new entry made. For example, if an injured employee at first required only medical treatment but later lost workdays away from work, the check in column 6 should be lined out, and checks entered in columns 2 and 3 and the number of lost workdays entered in column 4.

In another example, if an employee with an occupational illness lost workdays, returned to work, and then died of the illness, any entries in columns 9 through 12 should be lined out and the date of death entered in column 8.

The entire entry for an injury or illness should be lined out if later found to be nonrecordable. For example: an injury which is later determined not to be work related, or which was initially thought to involve medical treatment but later was determined to have involved only first aid.

III. Posting Requirements

A copy of the totals and information following the fold line of the last page for the year must be posted at each establishment in the place or places where notices to employees are customarily posted. This copy must be posted no later than *February 1 and must remain in place until March 1.*

Even though there were no injuries or illnesses during the year, zeros must be entered on the totals line, and the form posted.

The person responsible for the *annual summary totals* shall certify that the totals are true and complete by signing at the bottom of the form.

IV. Instructions for Completing Log and Summary of Occupational Injuries and Illnesses

Column A — CASE OR FILE NUMBER. Self-explanatory.

Column B — DATE OF INJURY OR ONSET OF ILLNESS. For occupational injuries, enter the date of the work accident which resulted in injury. For occupational illnesses, enter the date of initial diagnosis of illness, or, if absence from work occurred before diagnosis, enter the first day of the absence attributable to the illness which was later diagnosed or recognized.

Columns
C through F— Self-explanatory.

Columns
1 and 8 — INJURY OR ILLNESS-RELATED DEATHS. Self-explanatory.

Columns
2 and 9 — INJURIES OR ILLNESSES WITH LOST WORKDAYS. Self-explanatory.

Any injury which involves days away from work, or days of restricted work activity, or both must be recorded since it always involves one or more of the criteria for recordability.

Columns
3 and 10 — INJURIES OR ILLNESSES INVOLVING DAYS AWAY FROM WORK. Self-explanatory.

Columns
4 and 11 — LOST WORKDAYS—DAYS AWAY FROM WORK. Enter the number of workdays (consecutive or not) on which the employee would have worked but could not because of occupational injury or illness. The number of lost workdays should not include the day of injury or onset of illness or any days on which the employee would not have worked even though able to work.

NOTE: For employees not having a regularly scheduled shift, such as certain truck drivers, construction workers, farm labor, casual labor, part-time employees, etc., it may be necessary to estimate the number of lost workdays. Estimates of lost workdays shall be based on prior work history of the employee AND days worked by employees, not ill or injured, working in the department and/or occupation of the ill or injured employee.

Columns
5 and 12 — LOST WORKDAYS—DAYS OF RESTRICTED WORK ACTIVITY. Enter the number of workdays (consecutive or not) on which because of injury or illness:
(1) the employee was assigned to another job on a temporary basis, or
(2) the employee worked at a permanent job less than full time, or
(3) the employee worked at a permanently assigned job but could not perform all duties normally connected with it.

The number of lost workdays should not include the day of injury or onset of illness or any days on which the employee would not have worked even though able to work.

FIGURE 8-2, cont'd

Columns
6 and 13 — INJURIES OR ILLNESSES WITHOUT LOST
WORKDAYS. Self-explanatory.

Columns 7a
through 7g — TYPE OF ILLNESS.
Enter a check in only *one* column for each illness.

TERMINATION OR PERMANENT TRANSFER—Place an asterisk to the right of the entry in columns 7a through 7g (type of illness) which represented a termination of employment or permanent transfer.

V. Totals

Add number of entries in columns 1 and 8.
Add number of checks in columns 2, 3, 6, 7, 9, 10, and 13.
Add number of days in columns 4, 5, 11, and 12.
Yearly totals for each column (1-13) are required for posting. Running or page totals may be generated at the discretion of the employer.

If an employee's loss of workdays is continuing at the time the totals are summarized, estimate the number of future workdays the employee will lose and add that estimate to the workdays already lost and include this figure in the annual totals. No further entries are to be made with respect to such cases in the next year's log.

VI. Definitions

OCCUPATIONAL INJURY is any injury such as a cut, fracture, sprain, amputation, etc., which results from a work accident or from an exposure involving a single incident in the work environment.
NOTE: Conditions resulting from animal bites, such as insect or snake bites or from one-time exposure to chemicals, are considered to be injuries.

OCCUPATIONAL ILLNESS of an employee is any abnormal condition or disorder, other than one resulting from an occupational injury, caused by exposure to environmental factors associated with employment. It includes acute and chronic illnesses or diseases which may be caused by inhalation, absorption, ingestion, or direct contact.

The following listing gives the categories of occupational illnesses and disorders that will be utilized for the purpose of classifying recordable illnesses. For purposes of information, examples of each category are given. These are typical examples, however, and are not to be considered the complete listing of the types of illnesses and disorders that are to be counted under each category.

7a. Occupational Skin Diseases or Disorders
Examples: Contact dermatitis, eczema, or rash caused by primary irritants and sensitizers or poisonous plants; oil acne; chrome ulcers; chemical burns or inflammations; etc.

7b. Dust Diseases of the Lungs (Pneumoconioses)
Examples: Silicosis, asbestosis and other asbestos-related diseases, coal worker's pneumoconiosis, byssinosis, siderosis, and other pneumoconioses.

7c. Respiratory Conditions Due to Toxic Agents
Examples: Pneumonitis, pharyngitis, rhinitis or acute congestion due to chemicals, dusts, gases, or fumes; farmer's lung; etc.

7d. Poisoning (Systemic Effect of Toxic Materials)
Examples: Poisoning by lead, mercury, cadmium, arsenic, or other metals; poisoning by carbon monoxide, hydrogen sulfide, or other gases; poisoning by benzol, carbon tetrachloride, or other organic solvents; poisoning by insecticide sprays such as parathion, lead arsenate; poisoning by other chemicals such as formaldehyde, plastics, and resins; etc.

7e. Disorders Due to Physical Agents (Other than Toxic Materials)
Examples: Heatstroke, sunstroke, heat exhaustion, and other effects of environmental heat; freezing, frostbite, and effects of exposure to low temperatures; caisson disease; effects of ionizing radiation (isotopes, X-rays, radium); effects of nonionizing radiation (welding flash, ultraviolet rays, microwaves, sunburn); etc.

7f. Disorders Associated With Repeated Trauma
Examples: Noise-induced hearing loss; synovitis, tenosynovitis, and bursitis; Raynaud's phenomena; and other conditions due to repeated motion, vibration, or pressure.

7g. All Other Occupational Illnesses
Examples: Anthrax, brucellosis, infectious hepatitis, malignant and benign tumors, food poisoning, histoplasmosis, coccidioidomycosis, etc.

MEDICAL TREATMENT includes treatment (other than first aid) administered by a physician or by registered professional personnel under the standing orders of a physician. Medical treatment does NOT include first-aid treatment (one-time treatment and subsequent observation of minor scratches, cuts, burns, splinters, and so forth, which do not ordinarily require medical care) even though provided by a physician or registered professional personnel.

ESTABLISHMENT: A single physical location where business is conducted or where services or industrial operations are performed (for example: a factory, mill, store, hotel, restaurant, movie theater, farm, ranch, bank, sales office, warehouse, or central administrative office). Where distinctly separate activities are performed at a single physical location, such as construction activities operated from the same physical location as a lumber yard, each activity shall be treated as a separate establishment.

For firms engaged in activities which may be physically dispersed, such as agriculture; construction; transportation; communications; and electric, gas, and sanitary services, records may be maintained at a place to which employees report each day.

Records for personnel who do not primarily report or work at a single establishment, such as traveling salesmen, technicians, engineers, etc., shall be maintained at the location from which they are paid or the base from which personnel operate to carry out their activities.

WORK ENVIRONMENT is comprised of the physical location, equipment, materials processed or used, and the kinds of operations performed in the course of an employee's work, whether on or off the employer's premises.

FIGURE 8-3.
Supplementary Record of Occupational Injuries and Illnesses.

OSHA No. 101   Form approved
Case or File No. ....   OMB No. 44R 1453

Supplementary Record of Occupational Injuries and Illnesses

EMPLOYER
1. Name _____
2. Mail address _____
             (No. and street)   (City or town)   (State)
3. Location, if different from mail address _____

INJURED OR ILL EMPLOYEE
4. Name _____ Social Security No. _____
     (First name)   (Middle name)   (Last name)
5. Home address _____
      (No. and street)   (City or town)   (State)
6. Age _____   7. Sex: Male _____ Female _____ (Check one)
8. Occupation _____
             (Enter regular job title, *not* the specific activity he was performing at time of injury.)
9. Department _____
           (Enter name of department or division in which the injured person is regularly employed, even
           though he may have been temporarily working in another department at the time of injury.)

THE ACCIDENT OR EXPOSURE TO OCCUPATIONAL ILLNESS
10. Place of accident or exposure _____
             (No. and street)   (City or town)   (State)
    If accident or exposure occurred on employer's premises, give address of plant or establishment in which
    it occurred. Do not indicate department or division within the plant or establishment. If accident oc-
    curred outside employer's premises at an identifiable address, give that address. If it occurred on a pub-
    lic highway or at any other place which cannot be identified by number and street, please provide place
    references locating the place of injury as accurately as possible.
11. Was place of accident or exposure on employer's premises? _____ (Yes or No)
12. What was the employee doing when injured? _____
             (Be specific. If he was using tools or equipment or handling material,
_____
           name them and tell what he was doing with them.)

13. How did the accident occur? _____
            (Describe fully the events which resulted in the injury or occupational illness. Tell what
_____
happened and how it happened. Name any objects or substances involved and tell how they were involved. Give
_____
full details on all factors which led or contributed to the accident. Use separate sheet for additional space.)

OCCUPATIONAL INJURY OR OCCUPATIONAL ILLNESS
14. Describe the injury or illness in detail and indicate the part of body affected. _____
            (e.g.: amputation of right index finger
_____
           at second joint; fracture of ribs; lead poisoning; dermatitis of left hand, etc.)
15. Name the object or substance which directly injured the employee. (For example, the machine or thing
    he struck against or which struck him; the vapor or poison he inhaled or swallowed; the chemical or ra-
    diation which irritated his skin; or in cases of strains, hernias, etc., the thing he was lifting, pulling, etc.)
_____
16. Date of injury or initial diagnosis of occupational illness _____
            (Date)
17. Did employee die? _____ (Yes or No)
OTHER
18. Name and address of physician _____
19. If hospitalized, name and address of hospital _____
_____
    Date of report _____ Prepared by _____
    Official position _____

ment petitions for variances from standards or record-keeping procedures, summaries of the petitions must be posted.

HOW TO ENSURE THAT EMPLOYEES CARRY OUT THEIR OSHA RESPONSIBILITIES

The Act states:

> Each employee shall comply with occupational safety and health standards and all rules, regulations, and orders issued pursuant to this Act which are applicable to his own actions and conduct.

Many OSHA publications recommend that employees read the workplace poster, comply with standards, follow all safety rules, report hazardous conditions, job-related injuries and illness to their employer, cooperate with OSHA inspectors, and exercise their rights responsibly. However, there are no penalties for employees' not meeting these responsibilities. Yet you, as their supervisor, must insist that these responsibilities be met. Here's how to go about it:

- Question each employee on the contents of the workplace poster. Ask specific questions that cannot be answered with a yes or no. If you find that an individual can't answer a question, send him or her back to the poster with instructions to carefully study it. Make a note of your conversation and follow up by confronting the individual later until you are satisfied that familiarity with the poster's contents has been established.

- When you hand out a work assignment that includes an act or procedure covered by an OSHA regulation, call the employee's attention to that fact and state the safe way the work is to be performed. Look upon this guidance and direction as a critical part of your job. Not only do you help the employee to work safely, you also remind the person that you and plant management intend to enforce all government regulations.

- Whenever you observe an employee violating a safety rule or regulation, bring it to the employee's attention immediately. Depending on the seriousness of the violation, warn the employee or apply appropriate discipline. The points you want to make are that employees must follow all safety rules and that you intend to enforce them.

- Remind employees frequently that they should report hazardous conditions and job-related injuries or illnesses. Management must report injuries and illnesses to OSHA on forms designed for this purpose in addition to posting the information in the plant.

REPORTING SAFETY STATISTICS BY THE OSHA METHOD

Most manufacturing plants in the U.S. now use the OSHA method of reporting occupational injuries and illnesses. As a means of learning how often they occur, OSHA uses a statistic called "incident rate" for any given time period. The formula for calculating this statistic is:

$$\text{Incident rate} = \frac{(\text{Number of injuries} + \text{illnesses}) \times 200{,}000}{\text{Total hours worked by all employees}}$$

To calculate the incident rate for total recordable cases, the number within the parentheses is the sum of fatality cases, cases that result in lost workdays, and cases without lost workdays but that:

- Require termination of employment or transfer to another job, or
- Involve loss of consciousness or restriction of work or motion, or
- Require medical treatment by a physician.

Not included are first aid cases (minor scratches, cuts, burns, and splinters that do not ordinarily require medical care), even though treatment is provided by professional medical personnel.

To measure the seriousness of injuries and illnesses that occur, the number within the parentheses is replaced by the number of workdays lost.

HOW OSHA PROMOTES PROPER HOUSEKEEPING

Safety is a key reason for practicing good housekeeping. OSHA has the following to say about housekeeping:

1910.141 (a) (3) *Housekeeping—*
  (i) All places of employment shall be kept clean to the extent that the nature of the work allows.
  (ii) The floor of every workroom shall be maintained, so far as practicable, in a dry condition. Where wet processes are used, drainage shall be maintained and false floors, platforms, mats, or other dry standing places shall be provided, where practicable, or appropriate waterproof footgear shall be provided.
  (iii) To facilitate cleaning, every floor, working place, and passageway shall be kept free from protruding nails, splinters, loose boards, and unnecessary holes and openings.

HOW TO PROMOTE A WELLNESS PROGRAM FOR
PLANT EMPLOYEES

The Health Insurance Association of America considers wellness as a lifestyle that advances and maintains people's good health. In recent years, many companies have created and developed wellness programs devised to prevent illness and to contribute to good health among their employees. If you want to create, develop, and implement an effective wellness program, you must take five steps:

1. *Determine the health needs of the plant employees.* Do this by reviewing absentee and medical records to determine the types of illnesses that are most common among employees. Also examine the plant's medical department records to learn the most common complaints reported to the plant's doctor or nurse.

2. *Talk to employees about their needs and interests.* Investigate the availability, scope, and range of applicable exercise and fitness programs. Study other health programs such as alcohol and rehabilitation, nutrition and weight control, managing stress, stopping smoking, first aid, and specialized training in such techniques as CPR and the Heimlich manuever.

3. *Assess your plant's capabilities.* Determine whether you can carry out the wellness programs that employees want or need on the site. Check on the availability of conference, training, or classrooms that can accommodate health and safety programs. Look into the availability of space in which to conduct aerobics and exercise classes. Decide on the feasibility and practicality of constructing or remodeling plant facilities to furnish a jogging track, gymnasium, pool, locker rooms, and similar large scale additions.

4. *Evaluate local resources.* Research community health and fitness organizations to find out whether they can accommodate your employees or put on their programs in your plant. Check with organizations such as YMCA/YWCA, Alcoholics Anonymous, lung, heart, and other associations, the Red Cross, and physical education departments at colleges and universities.

5. *Submit your proposal for a plant wellness program to management.* Include an estimate of the cost of your plan and how long it would take to implement it. If you or plant management want more information about health and fitness-related services for employees, you can contact the following organizations:
   The Association for Fitness in Business
   965 Hope Street
   Stamford, Connecticut 06907   203-359-2188

The National Employee Services and Recreation Association
2400 South Downing Street
Westchester, Illinois 60153   312-562-8130

INCENTIVES FOR PLANT EMPLOYEES' COMPLIANCE WITH OSHA REGULATIONS

Just as companies provide incentives to employees for absent-free attendance and good housekeeping, incentives for compliance with OSHA regulations can prompt better and safer performance from them. The primary purpose of incentive plans is to reward above-average performance immediately and encourage continued good performance. Here are some ideas on how you can stress the importance of compliance to employees through the use of incentives:

- Offer rewards for acceptable suggestions that relate to OSHA regulations. Not only will such a program make employees feel they are being rewarded for their work, but it will show them that the company recognizes and appreciates their contribution.
- Point out that when the plant is in full compliance with regulations, the workplace is safer and healthier. This means fewer accidents, less exposure to hazardous and harmful chemicals, and cleaner working conditions.
- Explain that when the plant establishes excellent safety and health records, its products are more competitive in the marketplace because plant operating costs are lower; insurance rates, worker's compensation costs, and maintenance expenses are minimized.

WAYS TO ENFORCE PLANT EMPLOYEES' COMPLIANCE WITH OSHA AND NIOSH REGULATIONS

If you work closely with plant employees on the ways to avoid an OSHA inspection, you are taking the basic step leading to enforcing plant employees' compliance with OSHA and NIOSH regulations. It remains for you only to take a tough stand on safety.

To be effective, safety rules and regulations, including those given in OSHA and NIOSH publications, must be strictly enforced. This means that your company policy should provide for strong disciplinary measures with warnings, suspensions, and even termination for violations of safety rules. Here are some tips on administering discipline:

1. *Respond to violations immediately.* There are two good reasons for this: One, immediate action has a greater impact on employee behavior, and, two, conditions and details tend to be forgotten with time.

2. *Keep accurate records of violations.* Document the times, dates, and events of actions that warrant disciplinary action.

3. *Investigate infractions and their circumstances.* Certain infractions may be symptomatic of more serious problems. Uncovering mitigating circumstances can reduce the severity of the infraction.

4. *Give warnings first.* Except for theft or other illegal acts, it is common practice to issue warnings before taking formal disciplinary action such as suspension or termination.

5. *Inform the union.* Most management/union contracts require union notification whenever a warning is given or other disciplinary action is taken.

6. *Discipline in private.* Making a public example of an employee only destroys the person's dignity and breeds resentment among coworkers.

CONTENDING WITH EMPLOYEES' REFUSAL TO WORK BECAUSE OF "UNSAFE" CONDITIONS

The Occupational Safety and Health Act prohibits an employer from discharging or discriminating against any employee who exercises "any right afforded by" the Act. Among the rights that the Act so protects is the right of an employee to choose not to do an assigned job because of a reasonable fear of death or serious injury coupled with a reasonable belief that no less drastic alternative is available.

This OSHA regulation was challenged by an employer in a case that went to the U.S. Supreme Court for decision.[1] Two maintenance employees at a plant were ordered by their supervisor to perform a job which required that they step onto a steel-mesh net suspended 20 feet above the plant floor. Claiming that the net was unsafe, they refused to follow their supervisor's order. Two weeks before, another maintenance employee fell to his death through the net.

The supervisor sent them to the personnel office where they were ordered to clock out without working or being paid for the remaining 6 hours of their shift. The two maintenance men subsequently received written reprimands, which were placed in their employment files.

The Secretary of Labor sued the company charging that its actions against the two employees constituted discrimination in violation of OSHA. However, the company contended that the Secretary's charge was invalid. While the Supreme Court upheld the validity of the charge, it pointed out that the rights given to workers under the regulation are restricted. The

[1]Whirlpool Corp. v. Marshall, U.S. Supreme Court, No. 78-1870, 2-26-80.

regulation does not give any right to walk off the job because of potential unsafe conditions at the workplace. Ordinarily, a worker is expected to use the procedures set out in the Act, including a request for an OSHA inspection.

But the Court added:

> As this case illustrates, however, circumstances may sometimes exist in which the employee justifiably believes that the express statutory arrangement does not sufficiently protect him from death or serious injury. Such circumstances will probably not often occur, but such a situation may arise when (1) the employee is ordered by his employer to work under conditions that the employee reasonably believes pose an imminent risk of death or serious bodily harm, and (2) the employee has reason to believe that there is not sufficient time or opportunity either to seek effective redress from his employer or to apprise OSHA of the danger.

The Court ruled that the two maintenance employees had been discriminated against when they were given written reprimands, but it also issued a general warning to employees by stating, "any employee who acts in reliance of the regulation runs the risk of discharge or reprimand in the event a court subsequently finds that he acted unreasonably or in bad faith."

How to Handle the Problem

Although this case went to the U.S. Supreme Court more than a decade ago, the problem occasionally arises in manufacturing plants today. You may as well be prepared to handle it in your plant.

Note that while the Supreme Court upheld the validity of the charge, it pointed out that the rights given to workers under OSHA regulations are restricted. The regulation does not give any right to walk off the job because of potential unsafe conditions at the workplace. Here are some recommendations on what you should do:

1. Suspend without pay for the remainder of the shift any worker who refuses to perform a job that plant management considers safe. Also place a letter of the incident in the worker's employment file.

2. Recognize that the worker has the right to file a grievance on the matter if the plant operates under a management/union contract. (Whenever a member of a union disagrees with a work assignment, it is customary for the supervisor to try to persuade the worker to do the work first and then turn in a grievance for later retribution.) If there is no union, the worker has the right to request an OSHA officer visit the plant to

decide if the worker acted unreasonably. In neither case, however, should doing the work be postponed.

3. Call a local contractor to come to the plant to do the work as soon as possible. It is unlikely you will find a service organization that will turn down the job.

KEEPING UP WITH CHANGES IN OSHA

Recognize that OSHA represents a series of comprehensive federal laws that have been and will continue to be initiated to cover plant operations. As such, OSHA is subject to many influences and will continue to experience change. For one thing, Congress can curtail or encourage specific OSHA activities through annual appropriation bills. For another, as political administrations change, there may be greater or lesser emphasis placed on various aspects of the program.

For example, inspections were once made in as many plants as possible in high-hazard industries, but later it was decided to omit those plants with lower-than-average lost workday accidents. At another time, the agency exempted from routine inspections all plants with ten or fewer employees.

While plant management should keep up with the current status of OSHA through the news media and trade journals, the company can best reach its objectives by the adoption of an effective safety program, regardless of any legal requirement to do so.

Much of what has been presented in this chapter is quoted directly from the Act or follows closely the wording in OSHA publications. Regardless, nothing stated here should be considered as a legal interpretation of these laws. You and plant management should get professional help when interpretation is needed.

WAYS THAT ENVIRONMENTAL LAWS AFFECT MANUFACTURING PLANTS

The first law covering pollution control enacted by the federal government was the Rivers and Harbors Act of 1899. This legislation outlawed the depositing of refuse in the navigable waters of the U.S. without a permit from the Army Corps of Engineers. Modern pollution control began with the Clean Air Act of 1963, the Water Quality Act of 1965, the National Environmental Policy Act of 1969, and the Reorganization Plan No. 3 of 1970, which established the Environmental Protection Agency (EPA).

In addition to frequently amending these laws, Congress has enacted separate laws to deal with air pollution, water pollution, disposal of solid wastes, noise control, and toxic substances. Those laws most likely to affect manufacturing plants include:

- The Federal Water Pollution Control Act of 1972.
- The Federal Insecticide, Fungicide, and Rodenticide Act of 1972.
- The Resource Conservation and Recovery Act of 1976.
- The Toxic Substances Control Act of 1976.
- The Comprehensive Environmental Response, Compensation, and Liability Act of 1980 (Superfund).

Many other federal laws dealing with the environment, too numerous to be listed here, have been enacted; and most of these laws have been extended by Presidential Executive Orders, which state how federal agencies will carry out certain of their provisions. Environmental legislation continues at a rapid pace, and Congress constantly amends laws and enacts new ones.

Common Features of Most Environmental Laws

Most of the environmental laws contain similar provisions:

- Federal officers (usually EPA personnel) are granted the right to inspect plants contributing to pollution and to tell their managers to install monitoring equipment followed by keeping records of its operation.
- Enforcement clauses in the laws state both civil and criminal penalties for violators. Typical maximums are fines of $25,000 per day of violation and/or one year of prison.
- Employees are protected against discrimination or firing by employers as punishment for instituting or participating in any procedure covered by the law.
- The government must treat as confidential any information, upon a satisfactory showing by the person submitting it, which, if made public, would divulge trade secrets.
- Federal officers or administrators are authorized to bring suit in court to restrain polluters and seize hazardous materials in situations of imminent danger.
- Small businesses are given certain exemptions in several of the laws, and may also receive other forms of assistance.

Note that many of the environmental laws encourage states to establish their own pollution control programs. Federal grants are authorized to help them do that, and federal authority may be delegated to them when they have acceptable programs in place. Thus, if your plant has a pollution problem, management may work with state, rather than federal, authorities to correct it.

HOW THE EPA IS ORGANIZED

The EPA is organized to handle pollution control on what is being protected—air, water, or land. Under the Administrator in Washington is an Office of the Assistant Administrator for each of the following main functions:

- Water and Waste Management.
- Air, Noise, and Radiation.
- Toxic Substances.
- Enforcement.

There are also Offices of the Assistant Administrator for Planning and Management, and for Research and Development. In addition, there are Staff Offices for Legislation, International Activities, Environmental Review, Civil Rights, and Administrative Law Judges.

GUIDELINES FOR DEALING WITH WATER POLLUTION

Even though federal laws and EPA regulations set the goals and standards for controlling water pollution, states are encouraged to take as much of the responsibility as they are willing or able to. The Federal Water Pollution Control Act of 1972, also known as the Clean Water Act, established a national goal to eliminate discharge of pollutants into navigable waters.

This Act provides for research programs and grants to state and local governments for construction of treatment works. The EPA Administrator is required to sct effluent limitations and to outlaw the discharge of any pollutant by any person without an EPA permit. The Act also lists toxic pollutants and states that the best available technology be used to limit or eliminate them.

In addition, the Act created the National Pollutant Discharge Elimination System (NPDES), which establishes the procedure and requirements for issuing permits. A permit specifies the effluent quality limits that have been developed in one of two ways:

1. Based on one or more technologies that the EPA believes achieves the highest degree of control, or
2. Based on what the EPA determines is necessary to protect a designated use of the receiving water.

When EPA issues a technology-based permit, it limits the choices of the discharger since only a small number of technologies may meet the standards. The technology designations are not precisely defined in the

Code of Federal Regulations, and presumably will change as the technology improves.

Types of Pollutants

In one of the codes, the EPA defines *pollutant* by supplying a long list of them. Included are: solid waste, dredged spoil, incinerator residue, filter backwash, sewage, garbage, sewage sludge, munitions, chemical wastes, biological materials, radioactive materials, wrecked or discarded equipment, rock, sand, cellar dirt, heat, and industrial, municipal, and agricultural waste discharged into water. Various sections of the law also require EPA to classify pollutants and list them. Here are the main categories:

A. Conventional Pollutants
   1. Organic, chemical and biological material
   2. Total suspended solids (nonfilterable)
   3. Fecal material
   4. Oil and grease
B. Toxic Pollutants

   The Clean Water Act contains a list of toxic pollutants, but it is continually being amended by the Administrator.
C. Hazardous Substances

   The Act requires the Administrator to establish a list of substances which when discharged in any quantity would present a danger to public health or welfare, including fish, shellfish, wildlife shorelines, and beaches. Some materials are on both this and the toxic pollutants list.
D. Nonconventional Pollutants

   All pollutants not listed in the other categories are placed here.

Regulations on Effluents

Since you are responsible for seeing that the plant complies with EPA regulations, you must be knowledgeable with what plant effluents must be controlled and know how the plant is designed and operated to control them. But that is only part of your responsibility. More important is that you must ensure that workers control them so that the plant is in compliance.

EPA is required by the Act to publish regulations that serve as guidelines for effluent limitations and to revise them periodically as scientific knowledge and new technology permit. This has been done for the major industries and many of the minor ones; the list continues to grow.

These guidelines list the pollutants to be controlled for each industry, showing for each the amount that may be discharged in any one day and as an average of daily values for 30 consecutive days. The guidelines also regulate the pretreatment of wastes that are discharged into a Publicly Owned Treatment Works (POTW). For each of the industries mentioned, limits are not only placed on particular pollutants, but the discharging plant is required to meet a set of general requirements.

The purpose of the general regulations is to prohibit discharges that interfere either with the operation of a POTW or its capability to meet its own permit requirements to avoid polluting the receiving waters. For example, specifically prohibited are pollutants that create a fire or explosion hazard in the POTW, cause structural damage through corrosion, obstruct flow, or are hot enough to inhibit biological activity. Dilution as a substitute for treatment is also prohibited.

HOW TO ENSURE THAT WORKERS CONTROL PLANT EFFLUENTS

Although most manufacturing plants today have installed instrumentation systems on processes that result or could result in effluents, you need to confirm that the systems are functioning properly and accurately. To assure this, you must see that two independent procedures are carried out regularly and faithfully:

1. Set up an inspection, calibration, and maintenance schedule on the instrumentation and control system. Make sure that instrument and maintenance workers conscientiously do this work and that they provide documentation on it.

2. Require that workers on processes fill out logsheets hourly, listing the operating parameters levels of the process. Their initials on the log confirm they took the readings and saw that the process was operating satisfactorily and within control limits.

Tip: These records and paperwork are invaluable if your plant is visited by a government compliance officer and inspected. In fact, you can almost guarantee that the officer will ask to see such records.

GETTING PLANT WORKERS TO FOLLOW YOUR INSTRUCTIONS

At times you will learn that your instructions to plant workers have not been followed as you requested. Although you'll find that the reason is simply a misunderstanding rather than disobedience, you must take steps to prevent this from happening again. Most of the time, you must make certain your workers really understand what you want. This is not as obvious and easy to handle as it may seem.

If you spell out the details of assignments, you must leave nothing to the imagination since any step you omit could cause trouble. It's up to you to anticipate every contingency. But you can handle unexpected problems that accompany step-by-step instructions easier if you give assignments in terms of results you want.

For example, suppose a gas piping system in the plant has developed numerous leaks creating a hazardous condition. You assign two pipefitters to the job and start them off by telling them how to clear the system of gas to make it safe to work on. But you let them decide how the leaks are to be corrected. They may repair leaks and valves, change the type of connections (threaded or flanged), or install new pipe and valves. You simply tell them you want a leak-free system.

Speak the other fellow's language to get understanding, and don't assume that workers always understand what you say. If there is any doubt in your mind, ask them to repeat back to you in their own words what they are being asked to do. This gives you a chance to discover any misunderstanding and correct it.

OBTAINING AND USING DISCHARGE PERMITS

Since the EPA has delegated its permit authority to 35 states, management of a plant must apply to the regional EPA office to find out if its state issues permits. Even when it does, the state is required to forward a copy of every permit application to Washington. If the EPA feels that the permit conditions do not meet its regulations, it may order a change.

Any plant that discharges or proposes to discharge must obtain a permit. If the owner and operator of the plant are not the same person, the operator must apply. The permit must be signed by one of the principal executive officers (of at least the level of vice president).

The information that the EPA requires in the permit application includes:

- Complete identification of the plant and its operator.
- A list of all other environmental permits applied for or held.
- A description of the business or process and the activities that require it to apply for a permit.
- A topographic map of the area.
- A line drawing of the water flow and mass balances through the plant.
- Average and intermittent flow rates.
- Location of drain, sewer, or river being discharged into.

- Characteristics of the effluent including an analysis.
- A list of the toxic pollutants contained or expected to be contained in the effluent.
- Any other information that may reasonably be requested.

Small businesses may be exempt from supplying part of this information. For a complete listing of information requirements, see 40 CFR 122.21 in the Code of Federal Regulations, the rules and regulations through which EPA administers the environmental laws. The code may be purchased from the Superintendent of Documents, U.S. Government Printing Office, Washington, D.C. 20402.

Once a permit is issued, a plant must, of course, comply with all its conditions. Failure to do so can result in civil penalties of up to $100,000 per day and criminal penalties of up to $25,000 per day and/or a year in jail. Other duties of permit holders include to:

- Reapply before the permit expires.
- Stop or reduce plant activity if that is necessary to stay in compliance.
- Alleviate any adverse impact on the environment resulting from noncompliance.
- Operate and maintain properly all control and treatment systems.
- Provide information as requested.
- Let authorities enter the plant, take samples, inspect and copy records.
- Monitor conditions by taking samples and measurements and keeping records.
- Submit regular reports of monitoring activities and special reports of any actual or anticipated noncompliance, including a report within 24 hours of any noncompliance that may endanger health or the environment.

Permits are good for up to five years, but they may be issued for shorter periods. Although separate applications must be submitted for permits under the various water, air, and solid waste programs, they may be consolidated for processing by the issuing authority if they all apply to the same plant or activity.

RECOMMENDED WAYS TO CONTROL WATER POLLUTION

The equipment required and the methods used to control water pollution in plants are quite varied and may be complex, depending on the pollutants that must be dealt with. While the best course of action is to design the plant process to keep the waste out of the effluent stream, this is not always practical or economically feasible. To add to the problem, many of the treatments in use today only concentrate the wastes and remove them from the water; the wastes must still be disposed of such as by incineration or burial in a landfill.

Water treatment procedures are ranked by the extent with which they remove pollutants and the ease with which they do it:

- *Primary* treatment may consist of simply letting solids settle out in a tank or pond, or skimming oil and grease off the surface.
- *Secondary* treatment takes the discharge from a primary treatment system and subjects it to additional cleaning steps, such as adding chemicals to the water to precipitate dissolved solids, followed by removing the solids in a clarifier or thickener.
- *Tertiary* treatment takes the process one step further. For example, the secondary treatment discharge may be put through a filter for complete removal of solids, or polluted water may be passed through a carbon adsorption system to remove all but the very small amount of pollutant allowed by the permit.

Water treatment procedures are also classified by the type of the operation performed:

- *Physical* processes include settling, floating, clarifying, thickening, filtering, screening, adsorbing, and extracting with solvents.
- *Chemical* processes include oxidation, acid and alkali neutralization, ion exchange, coagulation, precipitation, incineration, and reverse osmosis.
- *Biological* processes include treatment with aerobic bacteria (which function in the presence of oxygen), or anerobic bacteria (which function in the absence of oxygen). Even though facultative organisms (those that can function with or without oxygen present) are sometimes used, the term "facultative system" refers to a treatment method in which the anaerobic first step is followed by an aerobic process.

Treatment Systems and Equipment

Four types of water treatment systems are commonly used in plants today:

1. Probably the most popular method is the one that involves the use of activated sludge. With this system, the waste water is mixed with a biomass of bacteria in a tank, which is fed air or oxygen to promote the breakdown process. The treated waste water containing the precipitated pollutants is then pumped to a sedimentation tank where the

sludge settles out while the treated water overflows to a sewer, drain, or river. The sludge goes to filters, thickeners, or centrifuges for concentration and is disposed of in a landfill or by incineration.

2. Shallow ponds or lagoons serve for the settling out of pollutants after both aerobic and anerobic biological treatment. These ponds are sometimes equipped with aeration devices to maintain dissolved oxygen levels. By proper sizing, the retention time of waste water flowing through the ponds can be made to vary from hours to weeks.

3. Clarifiers and thickeners are used for concentrating suspended solids in waste water. These are large-diameter, relatively shallow, cylindrical tanks with conical bottoms and equipped with rotating scraper arms. The solids accumulate at the bottom of the cone and are removed while the clarified effluent discharges at the top.

4. Filters remove more suspended solids than do clarifiers or thickeners. Filtering is accomplished by passing the waste water through a cloth or fine-mesh metal screen. *Plate and frame filters* contain cloth stretched over a metal frame with a number of frames combined so that the waste water passes through them in parallel. When the cloths become caked with solids, flow is stopped, the filter opened, and the accumulated solids removed.

   Rotary vacuum filters are constructed with the cloth wrapped around a cylindrical drum which is partially submerged in the wastewater. A vacuum, pulled on the interior of the drum while it rotates, causes the water to be drawn through the cloth, leaving a cake of solids on the outside. The cake is brought out of the water, as the drum rotates, and scraped off.

   In operating a *belt-press filter*, sludge is placed between two layers of cloth forming a belt that passes between rollers. The water is squeezed out through the cloth and the filter cake mechanically removed.

HOW TO HANDLE SAMPLING OF PLANT EFFLUENTS

A basic requirement for controlling water pollution is that the plant have accurate and complete waste water data obtained through a comprehensive sampling program. By sampling the effluent and having an analysis made, you can determine the concentration of various pollutants in a multigallon-per-day effluent stream.

Four reasons for implementing a sampling program on the plant's waste water are:

1. Your local EPA agency requires it.
2. The plant NPDES discharge permit requires it.

3. You need the analyses for process control purposes.
4. Sampling is a part of management's commitment to improve the environment at the plant.

For all of these reasons, sampling of the plant's effluent must be accurate, repeatable and reliable.

- *Accurate*, because you may be dealing with very small concentrations of pollutants, perhaps in the parts-per-billion range.
- *Repeatable*, because the analytical methods used require absolute precision.
- *Reliable*, because false or erroneous data can result in serious consequences for your company.

Methods of Sampling Effluents[2]

Taking a sample manually is the simplest method since all it involves is periodically "grabbing" a sample from the flowing stream. While this procedure is effective and inexpensive, it also relies, unfortunately, on an individual's attention to responsibility; the method also exposes the person taking samples to whatever biological or chemical hazard that may be present in the effluent.

The grab sampling technique is the only viable method of sampling when the pollutants are volatile organic compounds. These pollutants cannot be sampled by an automatic sampler because the device draws from the flow by producing a partial vacuum in the airspace above the sample; the pollutant turns to vapor in the vacuum and is lost.

Two types of automatic samplers are available for use in plants: peristaltic pumps and pressure vacuum devices. Both are made for either portable or stationary use.

For accurate and reliable sampling, the biological and chemical conditions of the sample should be maintained in a similar state to the way they were at the time the sample was taken. Biological samples, in particular, should be held as close to 4° C (37° F) as possible because, at this temperature, organisms are relatively stable. Thus, most long-term sampling installations are constructed with stationary samplers mounted on refrigerators.

Portable samplers, in contrast, are used for intermittent testing or where space is limited. They often are equipped to carry ice or dry ice in the bottle case as a means of temperature control.

[2]"The How's and Why's of Industrial Effluent Sampling," *Pollution Equipment News*, Aug. 1990, pp. 102–105.

Implementing a Sampling Program

Before you think about acquiring sampling equipment and assigning people to the job, you need to get the answers to several questions:

1. *For what purpose are you sampling?* Sampling for reporting purposes has different criteria than short-term sampling for process control or for conducting toxic pollutant studies.
2. *For what pollutant(s) are you sampling?* This information will help you decide the method, optimal frequency of sampling, and the equipment, material, and people to use.
3. *Where should you sample?* The locations will determine your procedures and equipment. If electrical power is available, you can use a stationary sampler.
4. *What procedure should you follow?* In addition to the physical requirements for each potential sampling site, you should use the best method for meeting the EPA requirements for the type of sampling involved.

To help you answer these questions, the EPA recommends several textbooks:

Pretreatment Compliance Monitoring and Enforcement Guidance published by Government Institutes, Inc. of Rockville, MD in 1989. Written by the EPA Office of Water Enforcement and Permits in 1986, this book serves as an excellent guide on compliance monitoring.

NPDES Compliance Sampling Inspection Manual, written in 1979 by the EPA Office of Water Enforcement. This manual details specific sampling requirements and the sampling methods available. It also tells how inspections are to be handled.

Handbook for Sampling and Preservation of Water and Wastewater, written in 1982 by the EPA Environmental Monitoring and Support Laboratory. This publication is one of the best on procedures for sampling water and wastewater.

Additional information is available from the Water Pollution Control Federation and the American Water Works Association, who jointly publish *Standard Methods for the Examination of Water and Wastewater*. This reference guide to laboratory analysis and sampling is compiled by the two largest associations of environmental professionals currently existing.

Since industrial effluent sampling is so critical to the control of water pollution, your plant should adopt and maintain the highest quality program possible. Remember, there are civil and criminal penalties for falsely reporting. Lawsuits, fines, bad press, and other complications can result from a poorly operated program, even when it is not deliberate. Further, inaccurate sampling can lead to serious environmental damage going undetected.

GUIDELINES FOR CONTROLLING AIR POLLUTION

With the large number of federal and state regulations now in effect on air pollution, many plants today find it difficult to learn what rules apply to their particular operation. To make matters worse, most of the regulations are complex and continually changing.

In recent years, Congress has repeatedly amended the Clean Air Act and the EPA has issued new regulations to implement the amendments. This has been followed by the states making revisions and changes to conform. The EPA may accept the state plans in whole or in part, but it may also substitute other regulations for the ones it does not approve.

Under such conditions, the best way for a plant to take steps to assure that it is in compliance with all regulations on air pollution is to consult with local or state authorities, first, as to what regulations apply, and then to verify that information with the regional office of EPA.

Air Quality Standards

To control air pollution, the EPA has issued primary and secondary air quality standards for the most serious air pollutants. Primary standards set the levels necessary to protect public health; secondary standards set the levels necessary to protect the public welfare from known or anticipated adverse effects of a pollutant. These pollutants and standards are listed in Figure 8-4.

The Clean Air Act requires the states to develop implementation plans that will bring the level of each of these pollutants (and any others added later to the list) within the limits of the national standard. The EPA monitors their efforts, and, for designated areas within each state, determines whether that area meets the primary and secondary standards for each pollutant, is better than the national standards, or cannot be classified. The data are published in 40 CFR 81.300 to 81.356 in the Code of Federal Regulations previously referred to.

By studying this reference, management of a plant anywhere in the United States can find out whether the area in which the plant is located does or doesn't meet the standard for any one of the pollutants. If it doesn't, it is in a nonattainment area for that pollutant. All plants in such areas can expect increasingly stringent state or EPA regulations covering emissions from their plants in order to bring the area within the standards.

FIGURE 8-4
National Primary and Secondary Air Quality Standards

Pollutant	Primary Standard	Secondary Standard
Sulfur oxides (Sulfur dioxide)	Annual arithmetic mean: 80 micrograms per cubic meter (0.03 parts per million) Maximum 24-hour concentration exceeded no more than once per year: 365 micrograms per cubic meter (0.14 parts per million)	Maximum 3-hour concentration to be exceeded no more than once per year: 1,300 micrograms per cubic meter (0.5 parts per million)
Particulate matter	Annual geometric mean: 75 micrograms per cubic meter Maximum 24-hour concentration to be exceeded no more than once per year: 260 micrograms per cubic meter	Annual geometric mean: 60 micrograms per cubic meter Maximum 24-hour concentration exceeded no more than once per year: 150 micrograms per cubic meter
Carbon monoxide	Maximum 8-hr concentration exceeded no more than once per year: 10 milligrams per cubic meter (9 ppm) Maximum 1-hr concentration exceeded no more than once per year: 40 milligrams per cubic meter	Same
Ozone	Maximum hourly average concentration expected to occur on no more than 1 day per year: 0.12 parts per million (235 micrograms per cubic meter)	Same
Nitrogen dioxide	Annual arithmetic mean: 100 micrograms per cubic meter (0.053 parts per million)	Same
Lead	Maximum arithmetic mean averaged over one quarter: 1.5 micrograms per cubic meter	Same

Source: 40 CFR 50.2

Maintaining the Standards

To prevent any worsening of air quality in the areas already in compliance with the national standards, EPA has come up with a set of regulations in 40 CFR 51.24. In this Code, every area of the country is designated as Class I, II, or III (unless an area is already a nonattainment one). Class I areas are those with the cleanest air; Class III areas are the highly industrialized ones; and Class II covers everything in between the other two classes.

EPA regulations require that state plans permit no more increases in the concentration of particulates and sulfur dioxide than those shown in Figure 8-5. Eventually, increments will be specified for all the regulated pollutants shown in Figure 8-4.

If your company plans to build a new plant or modify an existing one in an area designated for prevention of significant deterioration, the company must use the Best Available Control Technology in the design and operation of the facility. Management must also:

- Furnish continuous air quality monitoring data for the previous year.
- Show that the installation will not violate any national air quality standard or any allowable increase over baseline concentrations.
- Supply information needed to analyze and make determinations on the effect of the proposed installation on air quality.
- Provide an analysis of the impairment of visibility, soils, and vegetation resulting from the installation and growth associated with it.
- Meet all other local, state or federal requirements.

The reviewing authority will notify the EPA and other interested parties of the application, as well as the general public, enabling them an opportunity to comment in writing or at a public hearing. Plant management may also submit an alternative plan providing it would meet emission reductions equal to those obtainable with Best Available Control Technology without putting public health at risk.

The EPA does, however, allow exemptions to these procedures in 40 CFR 51.24 if emissions or potential emissions are lower than some stated level. Since the exemptions are very complicated, the best course of action for a company planning to build a new plant or modify an existing one is for management to consult with the EPA during the planning stages.

Standards for New Sources

In addition to the regulations for nonattainment areas and prevention of significant deterioration, the Clean Air Act requires that the EPA develop standards for all new pollution sources, or modifications of existing ones,

FIGURE 8-5
Allowable Increments for Area Classes

Pollutant	Maximum allowable increase (micrograms per cubic meter)
CLASS I	
Particulate matter:	
Annual geometric mean	5
24-hour maximum	10
Sulfur dioxide:	
Annual arithmetic mean	2
24-hour maximum	5
3-hour maximum	25
CLASS II	
Particulate matter:	
Annual geometric mean	19
24-hour maximum	37
Sulfur dioxide:	
Annual arithmetic mean	20
24-hour maximum	91
3-hour maximum	512
CLASS III	
Particulate matter:	
Annual geometric mean	37
24-hour maximum	75
Sulfur dioxide:	
Annual arithmetic mean	40
24-hour maximum	182
3-hour maximum	700

Source: 40 CFR 51.24

constructed after specified dates in various industries. Part 60 of the Code of Federal Regulations contains such standards for many industrial plants, and more will be published by the EPA in the future.

Each of these standards contain sections that give:

- Definitions of the terms used in the standard.
- Definitions of the category and the date after which a plant is considered "new."
- Emission limits for one or more pollutants.
- Rules for monitoring operations.
- Test methods and procedures to be used in collecting and analyzing emission samples.

Other Regulatory Techniques: Bubbles, Banking, Offsets, and Netting

Concerned that its rules and regulations for industrial expansion were too rigid, the EPA came up with a set of regulatory techniques to give plants more flexibility in expansion requirements. These regulations are described in the 13th Annual Report of the Council on Environmental Quality (Washington, D.C.: U.S. Government Printing Office, p. 8), an excerpt of which follows:

> EPA's emissions trading policy incorporates four . . . regulatory mechanisms, all of which take advantage of market incentives to reduce air emissions at the lowest possible cost. First, EPA's bubble policy allows existing plants, or groups of plants, to be excused from imposing controls on one or more emissions sources in exchange for compensating controls on other, less costly to control, sources. Second, the netting policy excuses plants from new source review requirements usually required when they expand or modernize, if any increase in plant-wide emissions is insignificant. Third, under EPA's emissions offset policy, new or modified sources in nonattainment areas may be required to secure surplus emissions restrictions which more than offset increased emissions, thus allowing industrial growth while improving air quality. Fourth, the emissions banking policy lets firms store up emissions reductions for later use in bubble, netting, or offset transactions, or for sale to other firms that cannot achieve the same level of reductions as cheaply.

These trade-off regulations are controversial, and will probably be changed as new administrations take office, Congress amends the law, or courts make decisions.

EQUIPMENT USED TO CONTROL AIR POLLUTION

Manufacturing plants use a variety of equipment and systems to prevent polluting the air they discharge. Following is a list and description of the most common types:

- *Filters*. These usually consist of cloth bags suspended in a tank or steel enclosure. As air flows into the tank and through the fabric, particulate matter is filtered out.
- *Cyclones*. The cyclone is a cylindrical tank with a conical bottom. When air carrying particulates enters the tank tangentially and is given a swirling motion, the particles are thrown by centrifugal force against the wall of

the cyclone and drop out the bottom cone; the cleaned air discharges out the top.

- *Scrubbers*. In these rectangular tanks or cylindrical towers, air containing particulates moving vertically upward is sprayed with a scrubbing fluid, which removes the particles and soluble gases. Another type of scrubber is the packed tower, which is filled with various shapes of solid material such as rings or balls. As the scrubbing fluid flows down over the packing, it achieves more extensive contact with the air flowing up through spaces between the packing.

- *Electrostatic precipitators*. These devices give the particles in air an electrical charge by passing them through an electrical field. When the air is then sent between flat metal plates with an opposite electrical charge, the particles are held on the plates while the cleaned air passes on.

- *Adsorption beds*. Air containing hydrocarbons or volatile chemicals can be cleaned of those pollutants by passing it through an adsorbing bed, often consisting of activated charcoal. The pollutants are adsorbed on the surface of the carbon from which they are later removed during a reactivation procedure.

MEASURING AND MONITORING AIR POLLUTANTS

Any industrial hygiene or safety analysis program conducted in a plant should include evaluating the environment and workplace atmosphere to define the exposure of employees to real or potential hazards. This is particularly necessary if plant operations involve potential air contaminants resulting from storing, handling, processing, or packaging materials.

OSHA has established permissable exposure limits for more than 700 toxic and hazardous substances. Specific requirements for air contaminants are listed in OSHA standard subpart Z, 1910.1000. The regulations require that plants first attempt to use administrative or engineering controls to guard employees against excessive exposures. When such controls are not feasible, protective equipment must be used.

OSHA listings include permissible limits for such widely used solvents as acetone, amyl acetate, chlorobenzene, cyclohexanone, dichlorobenzene, ethyl acetate, ethylamine, ethyl benzene, hexone (methyl iso-butyl ketone or MIBK), methy ethyl ketone (MEK), toluene, and trichloroethylene.

Several variables are present with measuring and monitoring air quality, and they all relate to sampling and data acquisition. The most important are where, when, and how the samples are taken. Sampling and monitoring require representative data for the environmental conditions, and accurate, reliable methods of analysis. Additionally, the time between sampling and analysis should be kept at a minimum.

Sometimes it may not be clear what substances the analyst should try to detect. You must decide what to look for and what concentration levels are dangerous in order to establish safe limits for exposure. The sampling and monitoring may be random throughout the plant, selective, or both.

Sampling Instrumentation and Analytical Devices

Because of the increase of corporate and public concern with pollution, along with greater emphasis being placed on worker safety, many instruments and analytical devices are available today for air pollutant and toxic gas monitoring. These range from centrally located data acquisition systems capable of monitoring numerous remote sensors from a control site to multichannel computational controllers designed to process analog outputs of toxic and combustible gas detection devices for data outputs and alarm controls.

Personal air samplers and air/gas sampling bags and collection systems for use by industrial workers are also available. Portable infrared analyzers permit solvent-containing atmospheres to be analyzed quickly and accurately by plant personnel. The equipment's compactness and light weight allow it to be easily moved to various locations. Since production or plant engineering personnel can be taught to operate the equipment in less than half an hour, skilled laboratory personnel are not required.

Stack testing and continuous emissions monitoring is often needed to furnish proof of compliance to air pollution codes; these systems measure the concentration of air pollutants in or from emissions sources. Typical parameters measured include particulates, sulfur dioxide, and oxides of nitrogen.

Information and data needed to evaluate a continuous emission monitoring system include:

1. *A process flow diagram*, which gives the parameters of rate, temperature, and pressure.
2. *A layout or plan*, which shows the location of sample probes, dimensions of stack cross-sectional area, and positions of flow disturbances, if any.
3. *A test procedure* for stratification checkup.
4. *A description of the monitor and its principle of operation.*

POSITIVE WAYS TO HANDLE PLANT EMPLOYEES' COMPLIANCE WITH EPA REGULATIONS

Since more than thirty federal laws deal with the environment, there is a good chance that a plant employee is violating one of them. While the person may be doing it knowingly or unknowingly, it is your responsibility to see that the violation is discontinued immediately.

To attack the problem of compliance, your first step is to research these laws to determine which apply to your plant and its operations. Contact your local regional office of the EPA for help. The agency will supply you with pertinent literature.

Here are the ways to ensure that plant employees comply with the environmental laws:

1. Inform employees of the EPA laws that affect your plant. Point out that federal officers have the right to inspect the premises for pollution sources and require management to install monitoring equipment for keeping records. And that, in situations of imminent danger, the administrator of the EPA is authorized to bring suit in court to restrain polluters and to seek authority to seize hazardous materials.

2. State that enforcement clauses in the regulations provide for both civil and criminal penalties for violators. Typical maximums are fines of $25,000 per day of violation and/or one year of imprisonment.

3. Stress that plant management intends to comply to all EPA regulations without exception. Give examples of how this already has been done such as the procurement of licenses and permits to carry out certain operations and the regular submission of records. Mention specific capital and expense investments that the plant has made to assure complete compliance.

4. Ask for employees' help in quickly reporting apparent or suspected violations of EPA regulations. This includes spills, gas escapes, leaks, and malfunctions of machines and equipment that could result in polluting the environment.

5. Emphasize the seriousness of violating federal laws. Say that employees who knowingly break EPA regulations are subject to severe discipline.

COMPLIANCE WITH THE EPA: A PRECAUTION

The same caution recommended at the end of the OSHA section applies to the EPA. Because we are dealing with federal law, much of what has been presented in this chapter is quoted from the Code of Federal Regulations published by the EPA, or follows closely the wording in EPA publications.

The information and data given here are only a small part of that contained in the many pages of laws and regulations. Any legal interpretation of this information should come from qualified professionals.

9

Ways to Help Plant Employees Deal with Hazardous Materials and Toxic Substances

HOW THE EPA PROTECTS THE ENVIRONMENT

A set of laws enacted by the EPA covers the disposal of solid wastes and toxic substances. The three laws contained in the Code of Federal Regulations are:

1. The Resource Conservation and Recovery Act of 1976 (replacing the Solid Waste Disposal Act).
2. The Comprehensive Environmental Response, Compensation, and Liability Act of 1980 (Superfund).
3. The Toxic Substances Control Act of 1976 (revised 1981).

Solid waste is described in 40 CFR 257.2 of the Code of Federal Regulations as

> garbage, refuse, sludge from a waste treatment plant, water supply treatment plant, or air pollution control facility and other discarded material, including solid, liquid, semisolid, or contained gaseous ma-

terial resulting from industrial, commercial, mining, and agricultural operations, and from community activities . . .

Recognize that the solid waste generated by your plant is going to be disposed of at a waste dump, even though the waste may have been compacted, burned, or converted chemically to reduce a hazard. Whether the dump is on your plant site or owned and operated by someone else at a different location, it will be classed as an "open dump" or a "sanitary landfill."

The purpose of the rules in 40 CFR 240-271 is to eliminate open dumps. Yours is an open dump if it fails to meet the many criteria listed in 40 CFR 257.3-1 through 8. Conversely, if your dump meets these criteria in a favorable way, it is classed as a sanitary landfill.

Tips on Disposing of Solid Wastes

Although most plants contract with outside firms to pick up and dispose of solid wastes, plant management should at least try to keep the disposal costs at a minimum. For example, here are a few steps that, when taken, would hold down the total cost:

- Keep wastes segregated. If paper, trash, food, and process wastes are allowed to be mixed, costly labor and equipment may be required to separate them later.
- See if some of the processing or manufacturing wastes can be recycled back into the process. If the costs of recycling are less than those of disposal, savings can be realized as long as the process itself lasts.
- Check the solid waste accumulation for materials such as scrap metal that can be sold or given away at no cost.

Tips on Disposing of Liquid Wastes

When Congress passed the Resource Conservation and Recovery Act in 1976, the Act directed the EPA to develop and implement a program for controlling liquid waste management. The EPA first focused on large companies because they were responsible for the greatest portion of waste. Thus, small quantity generators (SQGs) producing less than 300 gallons of waste per month were exempt from the regulations.

Over the years, however, we've learned that even the smallest amount of liquid waste can, if improperly discarded, seep into the earth and contaminate underground water supplies. As a result, rules are now in effect specifically for SQGs. Plants and businesses that generate between 30 and 300 gallons of waste per month must comply with EPA requirements or face legal action, fines, and imprisonment.

Two basic methods exist for disposing of liquid wastes: incineration and recycling. Quite a few companies use the latter method because they then can reclaim many wastes as usable products.

To recycle solvent wastes, for example, you can use a distillation process that heats the liquid to its boiling point. The vapor that boils off is collected and condensed as reclaimed solvent. In this process, solids and liquids with high boiling points, such as oil and grease, do not boil off.

This residue may represent up to half of the original solvent volume, depending on the amount of contamination and the efficiency of the distillation equipment. These "still-bottoms" remain as waste (which is usually hazardous) and must be disposed of as such.

While plants that generate large quantities of liquid wastes usually have staff and line employees to handle the problem, operating an in-house recycling facility has proven to be a major stumbling block for some SQGs. Even if you buy equipment and supply personnel to operate it, disposing of the residue is still necessary. The result is that it often costs as much to dispose of the residue as the original solvent—and sometimes more.

Contracting for Waste Disposal

A practical answer for the small quantity generator is to contract for outside treatment and disposal of the waste. The advantages include:

- The reclaimed solvent can either be returned to the original generator or sold on the open market.
- The recycling firm is better equipped to deal properly with the problems associated with liquid waste handling.
- The cost of contract recycling may actually be less than in-house recycling.

There are three types of firms with whom you can work to remove wastes or contaminated solvents from your plant. They are:

1. Transporters that pick up and haul wastes.
2. Transfer and storage firms (waste brokers) that collect wastes from several SQGs and combine material to make shipments large enough to take to other disposal firms.
3. Treatment, storage, and disposal firms that either dispose of, recycle, or treat wastes.

Before deciding which firm is best for your plant, realize that your company is ultimately responsible for it. Therefore, be careful when choosing a waste handling/disposal company.

TECHNIQUES FOR DEALING WITH HAZARDOUS WASTE

The EPA considers a waste hazardous if it has measurable, detectable characteristics of ignitability, corrosivity, reactivity, or toxicity, and the EPA finds that it may cause an increase in mortality or serious illness, or that it poses a hazard to human health or the environment if improperly handled. All of these characteristics and conditions are defined in 40 CFR 261.10-261.24.

A waste is also hazardous if it is one of the many materials listed in 40 CFR 261.31-261.33. Plant management should be sure to monitor these lists, either through the Federal Register or the annual editions of the CFR, since the EPA adds new items to the list periodically.

Most plants prefer to send their hazardous wastes to off-site disposal areas owned by others. If, however, your management decides to operate its own treatment, storage, or disposal facility, the plant must meet the standards of 40 CFR 264. These deal with administrative matters, record-keeping and reporting, preparedness and prevention, and contingency plans and emergency procedures. They also cover technical, engineering and operating factors including equipment and land management.

If your plant sends out its hazardous waste for treatment or disposal by others, management must meet the standards for generators as given in 40 CFR 262. After obtaining an identification number from EPA, the waste must be packaged and labeled, including placarding the vehicle that carries it, according to the requirements of the Department of Transportation regulations in 49 CFR 172, 173, 178, and 179.

Before shipping, a manifest must be prepared with a sufficient number of copies to provide one for the plant, one for each transporter, one for the owner or operator of the treatment/disposal facility, and another to be returned to the plant by the facility. The manifest must show:

- A document number.
- The plant's name, address, phone number, and EPA identification number.
- The name and EPA ID number of each transporter.
- The name, address, and EPA ID number of the disposal facility where the waste is being sent.
- A description of the wastes as required by DOT regulations in 49 CFR 172.101 and 172.202-203.
- The total quantity of each waste, with the number and types of containers in which it is shipped.

Record-keeping and reporting obligations include keeping copies of the manifests for three years from the date of receipt at the disposal facility, plus the results of any tests or analyses. By March 1 of every even-numbered year, the plant must submit a biennial report to the regional administrator of all waste shipment activity on EPA Form 8700-13A.

Waste Treatment Methods

Four methods of treating hazardous wastes are currently being used:

- Physical treatments are used primarily for volume reduction and separation; the most common are adsorption, distillation, filtration, flotation, sedimentation, and solar evaporation.
- Chemical treatments include precipitation for volume reduction and separation, and neutralization for detoxification.
- Thermal treatments call for incineration to accomplish detoxification and volume reduction.
- Biological treatments are used for detoxification; among them, activated sludge and waste stabilization ponds are the most common.

GUIDELINES ON DEALING WITH TOXIC SUBSTANCES

The Toxic Substance Control Act gives the EPA authority to:

- Prohibit the use of dangerous chemicals.
- Limit the quantities or concentrations to be manufactured, processed, or distributed.
- Require that dangerous chemicals be supplied with warnings and safe use instructions.
- Require manufacturers and processors to conduct tests and report data.
- Require advance notice of the proposed manufacture of a new chemical.
- Prohibit the manufacture of polychlorinated biphenyls (PCBs).

Most plants use chemicals in some way. If not as raw materials or intermediates, they are used as solvents, plating solutions, lubricants, cleaning agents, pesticides, and others. If your workers are handling chemicals for any reason, check OSHA and EPA publications to see if they are regarded as toxic substances. The worst tend to be insidious poisons. Exposure to them in low concentrations over long periods of time, without noticeable discomfort, can result in lethal diseases such as blood and nervous system disorders, leukemia, and cancer.

The worst ten are acrylonitrile, arsenic, asbestos, benzene, beryllium, cadmium, isocyanides, mercury, polychlorinated biphenyls, and vinyl chloride. All are regulated by OSHA or EPA. If your plant is using any of them without strict controls, you should correct the situation immediately.

RELIEVING EMPLOYEES' FEARS OF WORKING WITH HAZARDOUS MATERIALS

Teaching employees about hazardous materials and motivating them to follow rules when working with these substances are the best ways of relieving their fears. The more employees know about hazardous materials, the better they are able to protect themselves by taking precautions, wearing protective clothing, and using appropriate safety equipment.

There are other ways, however, you can assuage employees' anxieties:

1. Speak their language when talking about hazardous materials. And avoid highly technical expressions, which they may not understand.
2. Don't alarm them with words such as "fatal" and "deadly." Yet be honest with them on the dangers of these materials.
3. Point out that hazardous materials are safe if kept under control. Explain that controls include use of proper handling procedures, use of personal protective equipment, providing adequate ventilation, and incorporation of specific engineering systems in processes.
4. Motivate them to maintain a positive attitude toward their jobs, to be careful, and always to follow the manufacturer's recommended handling procedures.
5. Convince them that training is the key to working safely with hazardous materials. See that they get sufficient training.

CONTENDING WITH SPILLS OF HAZARDOUS MATERIALS

Hazardous material spill regulations were enacted by the EPA in 1979 and were published in the Federal Register shortly thereafter. These regulations apply to all facilities that could experience chemical spills including industrial plants, storage depots, and transportation vehicles such as trucks, railroad tank cars, and tanker vessels.

With these regulations, responsibility has been placed on plants to notify federal authorities, as well as state and local authorities, immediately when a spill or other illegal discharge occurs. Failure to report a spill or discharge of a harmful quantity could result in criminal penalties of up to $10,000, a year in jail, or both. The regulations also require those who are responsible for a spill to pay the costs of cleanup.

These hazardous material spill regulations do not apply to oil. Spill prevention regulations to stop oil pollution became law in 1974 at which time the EPA required that every company that handles oil or "oil-type" materials prepare and implement a Spill Prevention Control and Countermeasure (SPCC) plan.

The Clean Water Act also contains amendments covering spill prevention and control. These amendments to the Act resulted in federal regulations requiring secondary containment of hazardous liquids. Secondary containment means that equipment must be designed and installations made to prevent materials leaking from storage tanks, processing units, piping, and liquid transport equipment from leaving plant/buildings or premises.

Why Spills in Plants Are Serious Matters

The EPA is the source of an alarming fact concerning spills; about 75 percent of the liquids spilled end up in rivers, streams, lakes, and coastal waters. In other words, three out of four spills that occur in plants affect people outside those plants.

When a spill gets beyond a company's property, it has an influence on the health and well-being of people in the community and beyond. A large spill, for example, can affect the community's drinking water, bring on a fishing, swimming, and boating ban, contaminate beaches and shorelines, not to mention kill fish and wildlife. The government has and will continue to impose fines on the persons or companies responsible for spills when they affect society.

You should not overlook the danger to people on the job in a plant when a spill occurs. In most cases, these people must contain the spills as well as clean up and dispose of them. When hydrocarbons are involved, there is always the risk of fire or explosion. Hazardous chemicals are a danger to people's health.

Even small spills are a problem because they create slipping and falling hazards, delay production operations and cause housekeeping problems. Accidents often occur in a situation where a spill has taken place. In addition, there is always the cost of the material lost and the cost of cleanup operations to add to a plant's operating expense.

PREVENTING AND CONTROLLING IN-PLANT SPILLS

Plants are violating the law today if they store more than 1,320 gallons of oil or oil-type material without having a SPCC plan. They are also subject to a penalty if they discharge harmful quantities of one or more of the hundreds of hazardous chemicals specified by the EPA in the Federal

Register. Having a plan and carrying out its provisions can save a company a lot of grief and money.

The SPCC plan can be prepared by anyone but must be certified by a registered professional engineer. While the plan must be available at the facility for review by the EPA at any time, it is not submitted unless the facility experiences certain spills.

A facility is required by law to notify EPA and submit its plan if a single spill of over 1,000 gallons occurs or if two spills of harmful quantity occur within consecutive months. When the EPA regional administrator reviews a facility's plan, he may rule that it is not adequate and that a better, more comprehensive plan be made.

How to Prepare a Plan for Spill Prevention Control and Countermeasures

The EPA believes that most spills can be prevented by appropriate equipment and plant facility layout, good design, proper piping, valving and controls, frequent testing and inspection, and safe operating procedures.

You might think that's a pretty big order, but it really isn't. It's simply optimum engineering design and control, plus knowledge and practice of safe operating procedures with good supervision and record keeping.

The SPCC plan should foresee and recognize how spills can occur, and take steps to prevent them. It should explain what has been done to minimize them. And it should state what to do and who should do it when a spill occurs.

Although a spill prevention plan usually is prepared by technical and engineering staff, don't rule out the possibility that you may become involved. All departments of the plant should participate by contributing information on operating procedures, properties of materials, and plant design. As a supervisor, your input is needed.

All of the plant's process operations must be carefully studied to determine what controls are needed and what responsibilities should be assigned. Operating mishaps of the past should be reviewed to assure that corrective measures have been taken to prevent reoccurrences.

Spills are not limited to process areas, or course. A plant's shipping and receiving areas may experience them since much material handling goes on in those departments. Leaks and spills in warehouses and storage areas may be small but they still must be contended with, especially if hazardous materials are handled.

What the Plan Should Contain

The plan should contain a checklist of equipment, piping, valves, controls, and procedures for preventing and controlling spills. The EPA will help a plant with the plan if requested. Your local EPA agency has specific recommendations for your plant and process on design of storage tanks, heating coils, liquid level controls, piping and valving, tank car loading and unloading facilities, drains and containment facilities, among other things.

Instrumentation can be very useful in the detection of leaks and spills to avoid major losses. In the petroleum and chemical industries, for example, explosimeters do a good job of detecting dangerous hydrocarbons and chemicals in sewers, drains, and diked areas.

Plant effluents may be monitored by chromatograph samplers, which analyze the stream identifying specific chemicals. Such equipment often provides information that enables the operating personnel to quickly locate the plant area in which a leak or spill is taking place.

If you want to know how other plants are handling spill prevention and control, several good articles have been published on the subject.[1] These articles report in detail how and what industrial plants have done to solve the problem and also give details on their SPCC plans.

The responsibilities of plant personnel in the prevention and control of spills must be covered in a company's SPCC plan. Operating procedures and specifications should call for periodic monitoring and recording of tank levels, temperatures, and pressures in addition to reporting the contents of piping and vessels. Tanks and equipment subject to extreme changes in temperature, pressure, or vibration are most susceptible to developing leaks.

The inspection of tanks and piping must be assigned to specific individuals, and they must keep records. A plant's SPCC plan should also include the duties of individuals in the event of a spill. Instructions and directions on what to do, who should do it, and how to handle communications help to avoid confusion, minimize the hazard, and hold down costs.

Putting the Plan into Effect

Proper handling of spills depends on making good decisions. You and other operating people in plants need to have information and know what to do when spills occur. You must immediately learn what has been spilled, how much of it, the dangers involved, and the alternative courses and actions you can take for handling the material. Knowing where spills can be diverted, what standby equipment is available, how it operates, and where

---

[1]W. H. Weiss, "Spill Prevention and Control," *Pollution Engineering*, Nov. 1976, pp. 22–29.

[2]Lynn L. Bergeson, "SPCC Plans: Should You Have One?" *Pollution Engineering*, Sep. 1984, p. 56, 65.

[3]Thomas Dalton, "Plant Emergency Procedures for Hazardous Spill Cleanup," *Engineer's Digest*, Oct. 1986, p. 32.

to get help are vital bits of information to the people who must make decisions.

Records of tank and pipe contents are valuable sources of information to the person faced with handling and containing a spill. So is the knowledge of equipment capabilities, surge capacities in the process, and the availability of utilities. Much of this information can be documented in plant operating procedures and process log books. A plant that keeps good records will more easily be able to handle a spill.

Training Employees in Spill Prevention and Control

Your company's SPCC plan can only be effective and accomplish its objective if it has the backing and participation of management. Management needs to be involved to train personnel, keep records, and follow up to see that responsibilities are being carried out. Moreover, these functions must be performed continually. Spills can and do occur anytime, sometimes when least expected.

People need to be alert and up to date on plant procedures in order to cope with them. The EPA regulation states that a company's plan should be reviewed at least every three years to see if it needs revision. Equipment and processes change. The plan must be corrected and augmented accordingly.

Effective spill prevention and control depend on the educating and training of employees on leak prevention and correction, procedures to be followed when a spill occurs, and familiarity with equipment and facilities to contain spills. Communications are important to get help quickly in an emergency. Time is critical in that it may determine whether a spill is minor or major.

Two guidelines in the Federal Register in the Oil Pollution Prevention section are pertinent to the training of employees on spill prevention and control. One reads:

> Owners or operators are responsible for properly instructing their personnel in the operation and maintenance of equipment to prevent the discharges of oil and in applicable pollution control laws, rules and regulations.

The other reads:

> Owners and operators should schedule and conduct spill prevention briefings for their operating personnel at intervals frequent enough to assure adequate understanding of the SPCC plan for that facility. Such briefings should highlight and describe known spill events or failures, malfunctioning components, and recently developed precautionary measures.

HOW TO HELP EMPLOYEES TO AVOID SPILLS

Here are some practical ways you can effectively help employees to avoid spills. Tell them to:

- Be aware of conditions and situations that could lead to spills or accidents. A small leak today may be a big leak tomorrow. Ask them to immediately notify you of any leak, regardless of its size.
- Be conscientious and careful. Keep your mind on what you're doing when you're handling liquids:
    Check to see that the valves are properly set in the line you are going to use.
    Make sure that the tank you're going to fill will hold the material you intend to transfer.
    Be certain that the drain or discharge valve on the tank or container you're going to fill is closed.
    Stay at a tank while you're filling it. If you leave, it might overflow before you get back.
- Before moving filled drums, confirm that:
    The drum lift is securely fastened so the drum cannot fall off.
    Your moving path is clear and there is nothing that could cause you to slip or fall.
    The drum you move will stay where you put it and won't fall over or roll away.
- Be sure that you do the following when you finish a liquid processing operation:
    Turn off the pump.
    Close all valves that are involved.
    Turn off any steam, air, or water that you were using.
    Stop related equipment.

Tip: Add impact to your advice by reminding employees that avoiding spills protects their jobs, the company, and the environment.

MONITORING WORKERS WHO HANDLE HAZARDOUS MATERIALS

Although the training of workers in the prevention of spills helps to avoid accidents and injuries, it pays for you to periodically check their work habits. Observe whether they wear their protective clothing, use the equipment and tools recommended for the operation they are performing, and use care when they are handling the materials. In addition, periodically remind them of the importance of doing their work safely, avoiding short-cuts, and practicing good housekeeping.

A good way for you to augment your safety efforts is to make short presentations to your workers on what your plant has done and is doing to prevent spills and to handle those that occur. To expand and make your point, you can give them a handout letter afterwards that tells them the ways they can avoid spills on their jobs.

People learn from experience. When you have a spill in the plant, the incident should be publicized so that all employees can learn and be informed on what happened, why it happened, how it was handled, and what has been or is being done to prevent a reoccurrence. This is a good way to get across the seriousness of spills.

PROVIDING EMPLOYEES WITH INSTRUCTIONS ON HANDLING SPILLS

Before anybody can go near a spill, the proper personal protective equipment must be put on. Breathing apparatus, in particular, may be required in an area where a volatile or toxic chemical compound has been spilled.

After the spill area has been cleared of plant personnel and all possible precautions have been taken, members of a spill response team can approach the spill with some type of sorbent material. The type of sorbent used depends on the substance that has been spilled.

Two types of sorbent are in general use. One is the polymer type, which includes spill booms and socks. Some sorbents are treated with surfactants to enable them to handle aqueous solutions. Those that aren't work with oils and solvents. Granular materials are the other common sorbent.

Although the materials that are made specifically for spills, primarily the polymers, are more expensive than the granular materials, many plants prefer them. The problem with granular materials is that they are extremely dusty when used in large quantities. Also, a lot of the granular material is usually required for even small spills.

No matter what material you use to absorb the spill, it doesn't change the chemical nature of what was spilled. However, there are materials that can render hazardous materials neutral. For example, if the liquid spilled is acidic, using an alkaline material that neutralizes the acid makes the liquid much easier to handle and dispose of.

But be aware that the sorbent used to clean up a spill usually takes on the characteristics of the spilled material. If you pick up material X with a sorbent, that material is now classified as hazardous waste X, and may have to be sent to an incinerator. With EPA's land ban, landfill disposal of more than 400 untreated hazardous wastes is prohibited. Incineration or chemical treatment are the remaining options.

If all of these procedures seem difficult, dangerous, or too time consuming, there is an alternative. Investigate some of the private contractors near your plant who clean up spills at any time.

A large number of spill control and prevention technologies are available to industrial plants, and the number of products on the market pertaining to these technologies continues to grow. But the best spill control technology, and the least costly, is spill prevention with proper contingency planning for the times when the inevitable spill occurs.

HOW TO DETECT HAZARDOUS GAS AND WARN OF ITS PRESENCE

While the hazards related to the presence, or lack of, gas have been known for many years and equipment has been installed to monitor for problems, more emphasis has recently been placed on the use of gas monitoring systems. This emphasis is due to the publicity of a few major accidents and many lesser incidents.

Reducing the risks begins with understanding the hazards and the methods available for detection. It involves analyzing the technologies used, equipment selection, and development of enforceable procedures for operation and use during and after an incident.

Gas hazards generally fit into three groups:

1. *Combustible gas*, which could be the source of a fire or explosion.
2. *Toxic gas*, which could result in various levels of injury to persons who are exposed.
3. *Oxygen deficiency*, which could result in suffocation.

Combustible gas is typically measured as a percent of lower explosive limit (LEL) where the LEL is the lowest concentration required in air for combustion to be supported. Since the effects of toxic gases are usually related to the period of exposure and concentration, time-weighted averages and ceiling exposures are specified as necessary. Oxygen is considered deficient at 19.5 percent of air; lower concentrations cause impairment of the respiratory system.

Three sensor types are used for ambient monitoring for a hazardous change in gas concentration at a location. These are:

- *The hot wire*, used for combustible gas at concentrations approaching LEL.
- *The semiconductor*, for combustibles and toxic gases.
- *The electrochemical cell* for toxic gases and oxygen deficiency.

The best technology for any application is determined by considering several factors: the anticipated amount of exposure to gas, sensor life, cost of replacement, environmental conditions (temperature, humidity, and other gases), speed of response and calibration requirements.

While the sensor is installed in the location where the monitoring is required, the controller is installed where it can conveniently provide power to operate the sensor and it can receive data from it to initiate response activities. These activities range from simply turning on a warning light, to activating remote alarms, dialing a telephone, and shutting down equipment. More sophisticated controllers process the data for complicated alarm logic, retain data for later recall, print reports, or communicate with other computers.

GUIDELINES FOR HANDLING HAZARDOUS GASES

Every plant that uses hazardous chemicals in gas form and each employee who works with them has an obligation to take the necessary steps to prevent leaks, spills, fires, or explosions. While in some instances, accidents seem to be unavoidable, there are specific preventive measures that can be taken to minimize their likelihood. These are plant and equipment controls, monitoring, and training.

How To Assuage Employees' Fears Through Controls

It's no wonder that many plant employees are concerned with their safety and health. The list of hazardous gases and chemicals that can be found in today's plants is seemingly endless. Hydrogen chloride, ammonia, chlorine, arsine, phosphine, and others are some of the hundreds of potentially dangerous substances being used in manufacturing plants.

Plant and equipment controls vary from plant to plant depending on the products being manufactured and the operational procedures of the specific workplace. However, you can take some general steps to make the plant safer and to assuage employees' fears and anxieties. Here are six positive ways to do that:

1. Keep only minimum quantities of hazardous gases in a work area. This will reduce the potential for injury or damage if a leak or spill occurs that could cause a fire or explosion.

2. Make sure all gases are stored and delivered in the proper cylinders. Check to confirm that all equipment is certified and compatible with the gases in use.

3. Test all gas lines, regulators, and valves with inert gas for leaks before using them.

4. Provide air masks for use during cylinder changes and in cleaning areas where residual gas or hazardous byproducts may be present.
5. Dispose of empty cylinders promptly and properly.
6. See that the workplace is equipped with firefighting and spill clean-up equipment.

Tip: An important thing to remember is that many employees' perception of hazardous gases is synonymous with something almost immediately deadly. To counteract this, you must explain controls and conditions in language and terms all employees understand.

The Need for a Monitoring System

All plants that use hazardous gases or generate them in processes should have reliable and easy-to-maintain monitoring systems to detect and measure the level of gases in the workplace. A system must be specific and capable of measuring low parts-per-million or parts-per-billion concentrations of gas. It should also be designed to report air quality at regular intervals in a form that can be documented. Continual monitoring along with an alarm is a must in case of a serious spill or leak.

Training Plant Employees in Dealing with Hazardous Gases

One of your responsibilities is to train employees in all aspects of the handling and use of hazardous gases. To train them properly, you should:

- Show them the proper procedures to follow in case of an accident.
- Provide a detailed plan for what to do in an emergency.
- Tell them to respond quickly and thoroughly to a spill or leak regardless of how small it seems to be.
- Make sure they understand that unnecessary risks should not be taken under any circumstances.
- Insist on a "no heroes" policy when it comes to dealing with potentially dangerous situations.

HOW TO REDUCE EXPLOSION HAZARDS IN THE PLANT

Whenever electrical equipment is brought into the workplace where flammable gases are present, the probability of an explosion increases. The explosion potential of electricity and flammable gases cannot be overemphasized. Consequently, it is critical that management recognize the danger and take preventive and protective action. Explosion hazards can be reduced by:

1. Eliminating the source of ignition by removing the electrical equipment and devices from the area.
2. Preventing gases from reaching dangerous concentrations. This can be accomplished by installing purge systems and sealing equipment and wiring.
3. Using intrinsically safe equipment and wiring that is incapable of igniting a specified atmospheric mixture in normal and abnormal circumstances.
4. Increasing the safety features of electrical systems. Examples are:

   - Providing special closures to prevent unauthorized entry
   - Assuring adequate insulation of wiring
   - Protecting against the development of hot spots by maintaining tight connections.

PROTECTING PLANT WORKERS FROM RESPIRATORY HAZARDS

Two major types of breathing hazards exist in plants: contaminated air and oxygen-deficient atmospheres. The effects of breathing contaminated air range from minor irritation of the respiratory system to serious injury or illness, or even death. Without enough oxygen, a person can collapse and die in minutes.

There is, however, a wide range of protective equipment available to guard against these hazards; each type is designed for a specific danger. By selecting the appropriate equipment, accidents can be minimized if not prevented.

Air can become contaminated by particulate matter, gaseous material, or both. Particles of solids or liquids (aerosols) exist as dust, smoke, fog, fumes, or mist, or they can be living organisms. Depending on their kind and size, they may irritate the upper respiratory tract, cause allergies, fever, cancer, or damage to organs by systemic poisoning.

Threshold limit values (TLVs), the levels at which potentially toxic materials begin to cause adverse effects, are published by the American Conference of Governmental Industrial Hygienists. TLVs are placed in three categories:

1. *Time-weighted averages* are the levels to which workers can be exposed to a substance for an 8-hour workday or a 40-hour work week.

2. The *short-term exposure limit* defines the maximum concentration that is allowed above the time-weighted averages for up to 15 minutes.

3. The *ceiling level* is the point that should never be exceeded, even momentarily.

When oxygen deficiency exists, the atmosphere does not contain enough oxygen to support life. While air normally contains 20.9 percent oxygen, the safe limit varies with atmospheric pressure. Current legislation requires that oxygen levels in the workplace be at least 19.5 percent.

Using Proper Equipment for Protection

Engineering control is always the preferred way to handle respiratory hazards. Among the ways that this may be achieved are by isolation of the process or source, use of nontoxic materials, provision of suitable exhaust or ventilation, and installation of filters or scrubbers.

When none of these procedures or equipment is adopted or installed, respiratory protective devices must be used. They should be approved by the National Institute for Occupational Safety and Health. Respiratory protective devices are of three types:

1. *Air-purifying respirators* use filters and sorbents to remove particulates and gaseous pollutants from breathing air, but they can be used only when there is enough oxygen in the air to support life.

    To remove particulate hazards such as dusts, mists, metal fumes, and smoke, use a mechanical-filter respirator. The filter is composed of fibrous materials that permit gases and air to pass through.

    Chemical-cartridge respirators protect against light concentrations of harmful gases and vapors, but should not be used against small concentrations of extremely toxic gaseous material.

    Both the mechanical and the chemical respirators should have their filters changed regularly and frequently. Both respirators should be used with full face pieces if the particulates or gases are harmful or irritable to the eyes or respiratory tract.

2. *Supplied-air devices* furnish clean air from an outside source through a hose connected to a face mask, helmet, or hood. There are two types of supplied-air devices: air-line respirators and hose masks.

    Air-line respirators should not be used in atmospheres that are dangerous to life or health because, were the air supply to fail, the user would be without protection while trying to leave the area. The devices are also limited by the length of the air supply hose.

    Three kinds of air-line respirators are available: constant flow, demand, and pressure demand. The *constant-flow kind* require an adequate air supply such as from an air compressor. When used with a face mask or helmet and hood, they perform well for workers on sandblasting, shot-blasting, and lead grinding operations.

Demand and *pressure-demand air-line respirators* usually are furnished air from a compressed air cylinder, air being delivered only during inhalation. The user exhales to the atmosphere. Demand respirators are equipped with regulators to ensure the air is at the proper breathing pressure.

A disadvantage of demand systems is that a negative pressure always exists during inhalation; this could cause inward leakage. If leakage is unacceptable, or the relatively high air consumption of a constant-flow unit is also not wanted, a pressure-demand respirator should be used. This type maintains positive pressure during both inhalation and ex-halation.

Hose masks, the other type of supplied-air devices, are fed an outside source of air by a hand or motor-driven blower rather than by a com-pressed air system. When a blower is used, hose length may reach 300 feet. When used without a blower, the hose length is limited to 75 feet.

3. A *self-contained breathing apparatus* does not require an outside air supply. The user of this device carries an air supply with him or her at all times. Three basic types are oxygen-cylinder rebreathing, open-circuit demand and pressure demand, and self-generating.

Oxygen-cylinder rebreathing devices have either a constant flow or a "lung-governed" system that automatically compensates for varying breathing demands. These units include a small cylinder of compressed oxygen, reducing and regulating valves, a breathing bag, face piece or mouthpiece and noseclip, and a chemical container to remove exhaled carbon dioxide.

Demand and *pressure-demand breathing apparatus* operate similarly to air-line demand and pressure-demand devices. However, the complete system is worn by the user.

A *self-generating breathing apparatus* has no high-pressure cylinders, regulating valves, or other mechanical components. Oxygen is generated when chemicals in the canister contact moisture and carbon dioxide from exhaled breath.

TRAINING EMPLOYEES TO USE RESPIRATORY DEVICES

Plant management is responsible for seeing that you, other supervisors, and employees receive proper training in the use of respiratory devices. Training and instruction must be given by competent and experienced personnel. The training should include explanations of:

- The nature of particular hazards and what may happen if proper protection is not used.
- The purpose of a device and its suitability for a situation.
- Various devices' capabilities and limitations.
- How to recognize and cope with emergency situations.

During training, supervisors and workers should handle the respiratory protective device, have it fitted properly, test the seal between the face piece and face, and wear the device first in normal air and then in a test atmosphere. In addition, trainees should be told how to inspect and maintain these devices. See the next section for guidelines on the care of respiratory protective devices.

A satisfactory seal between the facepiece and the wearer's face is, of course, essential. Since long hair, sideburns, or a beard could prevent a good seal, they may be forbidden on plant jobs where workers must frequently use respirators. If a satisfactory seal cannot be obtained, the worker should not be allowed in the hazardous atmosphere.

You can contribute to the training of employees on respiratory protection by obtaining an excellent booklet on the subject, which you can hand out. Titled "What You Should Know About on-the-Job Respiratory Protection," it is published by Channing L. Bete Co. Inc., South Deerfield, MA 01373, phone 1-413-665-7611.

Training Employees in the Care of Respiratory Protective Devices

The objective with inspecting and maintaining respiratory devices is to keep them in the same condition in which they were originally manufactured. This can be done most easily by closely following the manufacturer's recommendations. To train employees on the use and care of these devices, tell them the following:

- All respiratory equipment should be cleaned and disinfected after every use. Although the respirator harness can be washed with a mild soap or detergent, commercial solutions should be used to clean and sanitize the face piece and hose.
- Inspect respirators before and after each use. All connections should be tight. The face piece, headband, valves, connecting tube, and canister should be operable and in good condition.
- Check to see that air and oxygen cylinders of self-contained apparatus are fully charged according to manufacturer's instructions.
- Replace regularly disposable items such as filters and cartridges so that they don't become clogged with particulates or chemicals.

- Don't attempt to repair or replace a part. All work of this nature should be done only by trained personnel who will use only parts supplied by the manufacturer.

Tip: Keep records of the dates and findings of all inspections and repairs or replacements. This information will enable you to confirm that the devices are receiving the proper attention. It will also enable you to follow up on any questions as to the condition of a particular device.

DEALING WITH MATERIAL SAFETY DATA SHEETS AND LABELS

Section 1910.1200 (g) (1) of OSHA's hazard communication standard requires chemical manufacturers and importers to obtain or develop a material safety data sheet (MSDS) for each hazardous chemical they produce or import. In addition, employers are required to maintain an MSDS for every hazardous chemical that they use in their plant, and to make the MSDS available to employees.

Unfortunately, MSDSs are not standardized. Suggested formats have been issued by OSHA, but no universal, easy-to-use format has been adopted. Usually, they contain the following data in this general order:

1. *Product identification* lists product name, and manufacturer's address and phone number.
2. *Hazardous ingredients* tells what the product is comprised of, and at what levels of material exposure might cause harm.
3. *Physical data* explains product appearance, smell, and other unique characteristics.
4. *Fire and explosion data* reveals the flash point and classification of the material and describes any appropriate firefighting procedure.
5. *Health hazards* reveals the effects of overexposure to the product, and gives emergency and first aid information.
6. *Spill or leak procedures* provides spill clean-up and disposal information, and the proper equipment and materials to use in such situations.
7. *Special protection* covers personal protective equipment information.
8. *Special precautions* details any other precautions to use when handling the material.

OSHA also requires that hazard warning labels be put on all original and storage containers of hazardous materials and toxic substances. The label must state the name of the substance, and furnish an appropriate hazard warning.

This warning should cover the hazard of both short- and long-term exposure, as well as the part or organ of the body that can be affected. Though not required by OSHA, good labels will include the manufacturer, emergency procedures, an emergency telephone number, and safe use precautions.

The labeling system your plant uses must be explained to the employees, including how they obtain further information, such as from the material safety data sheet.

PROVIDING WORKERS WITH INFORMATION ON MATERIAL SAFETY DATA SHEETS

Although plants are required to maintain an MSDS for every hazardous chemical on their sites, and to make the information available to employees, several problems on consistency and clearness of MSDSs have arisen. For example, there currently is no requirement that the eight information categories be presented on the sheet in a specific order. This inconsistency in format from one manufacturer to another has led to confusion among users.

Another problem is that some manufacturers don't provide enough information, especially in the area of personal protective equipment. An example of this deficiency is that the user of a chemical is told to wear gloves but not exactly what kind.

A third problem concerns the language manufacturers use on the MSDSs. There is a need for simplification as well as uniformity. Examples are using the word "ingest" instead of "eat," and giving the chemical name of a material rather than its trade name.

Here are a few suggestions on how you can ensure that your workers are provided with the information they need or ask for:

1. Read and study an MSDS carefully before you make it available to workers. If some information is missing or you have a question that is not answered, call the telephone number that is given on the sheet.
2. Meet with the workers who handle or use the chemical. Talk about the MSDS and the data it contains. Encourage questions, pointing out that it's better to be fully informed than to risk an injury or accident.
3. Provide three pieces of information to workers, making sure they understand:

   • The primary hazard of the material and when it is a hazard.
   • The proper means of protection.
   • The first aid and emergency response procedures to be followed in the event of a spill or exposure to the chemical.

Tip: Consider furnishing workers with some sort of MSDS supplement, such as plastic-coated fact sheets, which they can take with them to their workplaces.

EDUCATING PLANT EMPLOYEES ABOUT HAZARDOUS MATERIALS

In the past, employees who wanted to know more about the hazardous materials in their plant had to depend on the cooperation of their industry and the willingness of management to provide that information. But if a company wasn't willing to share information about its operations with employees, there wasn't much a concerned employee could do about it.

All that has changed. In November of 1986, Congress passed a law designed to help communities and company employees deal safely and effectively with the many hazardous materials that are used in our society. The law is called the Emergency Planning and Community Right-to-Know Act. It has two main purposes:

1. To encourage and support emergency planning for responding to chemical accidents.
2. To provide local governments and the public, including plant employees, with information about possible chemical hazards in their communities.

WHAT RIGHT-TO-KNOW LAWS ARE ALL ABOUT

Right-to-know legislation at all levels of government—city, county, state, and federal—has been enacted into laws covering companies that produce or use hazardous materials. The laws, designed to protect all employees, embody legislation that requires corporate employers to inform their employees of any chemicals or conditions in the workplace that have potentially adverse effects if they are not dealt with properly.

The Emergency Planning and Community Right-to-Know Act contains four major provisions:

1. Planning for chemical emergencies.
2. Emergency notification of chemical accidents and releases.
3. Reporting of hazardous chemical inventories.
4. Toxic chemical release reporting.

The law also deals with trade secrets, disclosure of information to health professionals, public access to information gathered under the law, and other topics.

How Plants Are Affected by the Law

A company's initial responsibility under the Act is to determine whether it has reporting and emergency planning obligations, and if so, to meet those obligations. EPA has prepared a number of guidance documents, a videotape, and other materials to help explain the Act's requirements and to assist companies in filing required reports and participating in their communities' planning process. Industry trade associations, such as the Chemical Manufacturers Association (CMA), also have been active in alerting their member companies to their obligations under Title III.

Besides meeting the strict requirements of the law, some chemical manufacturers and other industries have also taken steps to establish a dialogue with citizens and to involve the public as partners in planning for chemical emergencies and managing chemical risks in their communities. CMA's Community Awareness and Emergency Response program is an example of these efforts. EPA encourages all companies affected by Title III to consider similar programs.

The annual toxic chemical release reporting requirement applies only to manufacturing facilities (those in Standard Industrial Classification codes 20-39) with ten or more full-time employees. Therefore, many small businesses will not be subject to this requirement because they do not meet the manufacturing, processing, or use thresholds.

Yet all businesses, both manufacturing and nonmanufacturing, are required to report under the emergency planning, emergency release notification, and hazardous chemical reporting provisions of the Act if they have specified chemicals in amounts greater than the threshold quantities for those chemicals.

Beyond these requirements, some companies—large and small—have taken steps to improve community safety by reducing their stocks of hazardous substances in heavily populated areas. Others are attempting to substantially lower the levels of chemicals they release into the environment. In some cases, these "source reduction" or "pollution prevention" programs have as their goal the virtual elimination of hazardous chemical wastes through substitutions, changes in industrial processes, reuse and recycling, and the use of new technologies to reduce the quantity and toxicity of hazardous substances before they enter the environment.

To the extent that industrial facilities and other businesses pursue these efforts, they will be helping to achieve one of the major objectives of the Emergency Planning and Community Right-to-Know Act: a reduction in the amount of hazardous and toxic chemicals stored in the nation's communities and released into the nation's air, water, and soil.

10 STEPS TO ENSURE EMPLOYEES' COMPLIANCE WITH RIGHT-TO-KNOW LAWS

Employees also have responsibilities under right-to-know laws. These include being acquainted with the chemicals they use, knowing how to protect themselves when handling these chemicals, and making sure they properly use the appropriate personal protection equipment. Here are the steps you should take to ensure that employees comply with the laws:

1. Keep a list of chemicals and hazardous materials used in the plant. Make sure the names are keyed to those on the material data sheets (MSDSs).

2. Compare this inventory with OSHA's list of applicable chemicals to find those covered.

3. Use this information to determine which employees are routinely exposed, or may be exposed, to hazardous chemicals. Maintain a file of all exposures.

4. Make sure that containers of hazardous chemicals in the plant are labeled, tagged, or marked with the identity of the hazardous chemicals they contain.

5. Collect MSDSs for those chemicals. Make sure employees have access to the forms.

6. Post a notice advising employees of the hazard communication program and its requirements, how the program is implemented, and whom to contact for information.

7. Set up a training program for employees. The training program must explain:

   • How the hazard communication program is implemented.

   • How to read and interpret information on labels and MSDSs.

   • How employees can learn the available hazard information.

   • How the chemicals in the plant are physical and health hazards.

8. Schedule employee training sessions and implement the program.

9. Document all events and activities. Record the names of employees who have received training and which chemicals were covered.

10. Observe employees on the job to confirm that they are handling the chemicals properly. Warn any person who is not, and apply discipline if the individual still does not comply with the regulations.

HOW TO MOTIVATE WORKERS TO FOLLOW RULES WHEN HANDLING HAZARDOUS MATERIALS

Teaching workers and motivating them to follow rules when working with hazardous materials can be challenging. You want to inform without boring or scaring them, but you also want to make sure they treat hazardous materials with respect. Here are some recommendations on how to handle the problem:

- Know your workers and watch your language. While a safety professional doesn't think twice about words such as "toxic" or "hazardous," the average worker thinks "chemical" and believes that's bad. Too many workers have been conditioned by news stories.
- Be familiar with materials, processes, and equipment used in the plant. It helps your credibility, for example, if you know how to wear a respirator when demonstrating one.
- Expect to be asked some tough questions such as, "Why haven't you told me this before?" and "Does this mean I might get cancer?" If you anticipate that highly technical questions may be asked when talking about hazardous materials, try to have a technical support individual available.
- Avoid scaring workers. Since "cancer-causing" triggers an emotional reaction in many persons, informing them without alarming them may be difficult. Training experts suggest that health information be given in a calm, professional manner.
- Stress the importance of controls. Chemicals in the plant are safe if kept under control. Make sure workers understand that controls include the use of personal protective equipment, ventilation, and specifically designed equipment.
- Be honest. You gain workers' faith by being honest with them. They will never again believe anything you tell them if you lie to them.
- Don't bore them. Realize that technical words may not be understood. Try to speak your listener's language. For example, when talking about a material, realize that its trade name identifies it more clearly than its chemical name.

TRAINING EMPLOYEES TO USE HAZARDOUS MATERIALS SAFELY

Training and educating employees so that they will recognize the hazards they face in the plant and how to protect themselves is a responsibility you cannot neglect. As a supervisor, you play a key role in your plant's training program.

While you may have a detailed inventory with all of the MSDSs on file and an excellent labeling system, if you don't explain how the system works or that each employee is responsible for making it work, your efforts could be useless. On the other hand, if you take the time to do it right, your training effort will have a far reaching, positive impact on the safety and health of all employees. Here is how you should go about it:

1. When preparing the training program, make sure you have collected all the required information, put it in the proper order, and decided how you will present it.

2. Train each employee as an individual different from all others. Each learns through different methods of input (reading, seeing, and experiencing) and at different speeds.

3. Use several ways to train employees:

   - In a classroom, present the specific hazards and review the methods that your company uses to control the hazardous materials. Video tapes are excellent and booklets are also good since both can be used for discussion and then reviewed at a later date.

   - In the workplace, demonstrate how to use protective devices and equipment. Also show the correct and safe way to transfer, dispense, weigh and measure the materials.

Why Responsibility for Training Employees Is a Serious Matter

"Companies and management may be held accountable for the death of employees at hazardous work sites." That was the ruling of Cook County (Illinois) Judge J. P. Banks who, in 1983, sentenced two former executives and a foreman of a silver-recycling plant to 25 years in prison and fined them $10,000 each for the job-related cyanide death of an employee.[1] The judge said evidence presented during an eight-week trial clearly showed that the victim died from inhaling cyanide under "totally unsafe workplace conditions. His death was no accident."

The deplorable part of this incident is that all three managers were aware of the hazardous nature of the work, but had refused to even post appropriate warning signs within the plant. Also, management had failed to caution workers about the lethal cyanide, even though cyanide suppliers repeatedly warned the company. Employees were merely provided cotton gloves, useless against the corrosive chemical.

[1]Reported in The Safe Foreman, The United Safety Service, Inc., Dec. 1985.

Although the murder charge of the judge was the first in the history of the United States to be sustained against an employer, the Cook County State Attorney, Richard Daley, said that the verdict will have a "national impact." Ronald Allen, a professor of criminal law at Northwestern University said, "Over time, we will see more and more of these cases."

DEALING WITH ASBESTOS AS A HAZARD

The presence of asbestos in plants is causing headaches across the country as managements learn the impact asbestos can have on their plant's operations. Employees in the following industries are particularly likely to be affected:

- Construction and demolition.
- Automobile production and service.
- Mining.
- Shipbuilding and repair.

The plant workers exposed to the hazard include carpenters, electricians, insulators, pipe fitters, mechanics, and boilermakers.

In 1986, OSHA revised its safety standards for people who work with asbestos. The revised standards call for, among others:

- *A lower permissible exposure limit.* They now limit concentration of airborne asbestos fibers to 0.2 fiber within a cubic centimeter of air averaged over an 8-hour day. This means mandatory respiratory protection and the use of protective clothing.
- *An action level that's half the permissible exposure limit.* Concentration of asbestos fibers at or above 0.1 fiber per cubic centimeter of air, averaged over an 8-hour day, requires exposure monitoring, employee training, and medical surveillance.
- *Engineering controls.* To reduce airborne concentrations and exposure to asbestos fibers, plant installations should include ventilation, exhaust, and vacuum systems equipped with special filters that collect dust.
- *Safety practices.* Good housekeeping and hygienic operations are promoted along with the wetting down of asbestos-containing material; also, the use of cutting or abrasive tools that release fibers in an uncontrolled manner is prohibited.
- *Posting of hazardous areas.* Such areas must be marked with warning signs. When feasible, work areas should be enclosed.
- *Labeling of containers.* All asbestos containers, including waste bins, must be labeled.

The OSHA standards also cover respirators. They must be approved by the National Institute of Occupational Safety and Health, and must be fitted properly to ensure maximum protection. OSHA further specifies when respirators must be used, such as when:

- Asbestos concentration exceeds the permissible exposure limit.
- Controls and engineering work are being installed or performed.
- Maintenance and repair work are being done.
- Emergency conditions exist.

The type of respirator to be used depends on the concentration of airborne fibers. While air-purifying types may be used at low concentrations, supplied-air types are required at high concentrations.

Protective clothing complements the use of respirators when workers are exposed to asbestos. According the OSHA, the clothing should include coveralls, gloves, goggles or face shield, head covering, and foot covering. This protection must be used when the concentration exceeds the permissible exposure limit and when contact with asbestos may be likely.

The best approach to the asbestos problem is to have a plan that anticipates difficulties rather than reacts to them after they happen. To be effective, the plan must involve a plant's management, its owner, occupants, and visitors. It must include training, communication, safe work practices, respiratory protection, medical monitoring, and accurate, comprehensive record keeping.

Adopting an Asbestos Management Program

Although the preferred solution to the problem of asbestos-containing materials in a plant or occupied buildings is to remove them, this is not always practical for several reasons. Even aggressive abatement action can leave some asbestos.

Instead, a plant must be managed by following appropriate work practices and in accordance with applicable governmental regulations. Remember, too, that the mere presence of asbestos does not mean a health hazard exists; negligent management of asbestos does.

An asbestos management program should be set up in three steps: making a survey, evaluating or assessing the findings, and taking action.

1. The *survey* consists of identifying the asbestos-containing materials in the plant. This work should be handled by a consulting or contracting firm with experience in identifying asbestos-containing materials. Recognize that an incomplete or inaccurate building materials survey makes abatement planning and budgeting impossible.

2. The *evaluation* step studies the data and information obtained from the survey and lists the asbestos-containing materials according to their condition, location, and content. The assessment grades the materials on factors such as surface area, friability, water damage, and proximity to ventilation systems. As a result, a rank-ordered inventory of the materials is obtained showing which material is in need of immediate attention and which can be handled later.

Prioritizing the status of asbestos-containing materials enables management to plan the removal of these materials when conditions are optimal—during a renovation, reconstruction, or expansion period. Management's goal should be to have all asbestos-containing materials removed by a specific date.

3. The *action* step is the longest and most demanding of an asbestos management program. During this period, the asbestos-containing materials actually are brought under control, either through an operations and maintenance program or by removal.

Training and Communicating with Workers

From its beginning, an asbestos management program is difficult to carry out in view of the communication involved:

- Workers who come in contact with asbestos in their work must be trained on safe procedures.
- All employees must be informed on how the presence of asbestos in the plant affects their jobs.
- Voluminous records must be kept once a program gets underway.

To comply with OSHA, management must:

- Maintain health, training, and exposure records on staff employees, contractors, consultants, and building occupants.
- Document incidents involving asbestos-containing materials.
- Reinspect asbestos-containing materials and document their condition periodically.
- Maintain records of the building's air quality.
- Track the custody of any asbestos-containing materials removed from the plant and be aware of the details of its disposal.
- Keep up with changes in applicable laws and regulations, and file copies of all correspondence and reports regarding the program.

Work practices for dealing with asbestos are given in the OSHA Construction Standard (29 CFR 1926.58). They cover construction workers, custodial and service personnel whose work may expose them to asbestos-containing materials. The EPA believes that even short-duration exposures can be harmful.

In most cases, the engineering procedures to be followed with routine service work are simple:

- Plan and schedule asbestos work for after the plant is shut down.
- Discontinue operation of the HVAC system during asbestos work.
- Limit access to the work area.
- Use respiratory protection and protective clothing.
- Vacuum and wet-wipe exposed surfaces before and after the job.
- Dispose of asbestos-containing waste in an approved manner.

Many plants decide to use outside contractors for large jobs rather than tie up employees for long periods of time. If the work area is an occupied area, air samples should be take before, during and after the work. This enables the air quality in the area to be documented.

As a recommendation, if your plant contains asbestos, management should implement an asbestos management program, even if on a small scale. Its purpose should be not only for health and safety, but for risk management.

An asbestos management program means getting upper management involved in planning as much as possible. One obstacle may be management's unwillingness to accept how costly and disruptive asbestos abatement can be. Once the need is established, however, allocating funds and resources to the program is generally not difficult. The worst viewpoint is complacency; this must be discouraged in both superiors and subordinates. Environmental awareness is here to stay.

TIPS ON AVOIDING SKIN DISEASE IN THE PLANT

Skin disease incurred in the plant can be irritating in more ways than one. It is a source of pain, discomfort, and loss of income for workers, and it results in lower productivity of the workforce for management.

Yet much skin disease can be prevented if you initiate a strict personal hygiene program and see that your workers carry it out. To put it in effect, tell workers to:

- Keep their work areas clean and uncluttered. Poor housekeeping is the major cause of skin disease and injuries.
- Wear protective clothing, footwear, and gloves when the work they are doing calls for it.

- Wash often, using proper cleaners. Avoid gasoline and turpentine, which are notorious for causing skin problems. If an irritant gets on the skin, wash immediately, not on a break or just before lunch.
- Get in the habit of taking showers before leaving the plant. You will avoid bringing hazardous materials or chemicals home.
- Change clothes that come in contact with irritants; these substances could eventually come off the clothing onto the skin.
- Keep work clothes separate from other clothing to prevent substances from being transferred.
- Have cuts and abrasions treated promptly to avoid possible infection.

As an aid to your program, you must see that workers are supplied with the proper cleaning materials. Industrial skin cleaners should remove soil quickly and efficiently. They should also have good foaming qualities and be pleasant to use. Another step you can take is to furnish protective or barrier creams for employees working with solvents.

Tip: Help your workers to avoid skin disease by making sure that all materials that are irritants are stored and labeled properly.

HOW TO DEAL WITH PCB WASTE

In response to concerns regarding the toxicity of polychlorinated biphenyls, known as PCBs, Congress promulgated the Toxic Substances Control Act (TSCA) of 1976. This law requires the EPA to, among other things, regulate the manufacture, processing, distribution in commerce, and use of PCBs. Although PCBs were no longer manufactured after 1978, this toxic chemical is still in use in tens of thousands of transformers.

To monitor these transformers, the EPA has enacted stringent regulations on inspection, labeling, and reporting. But the resultant increase in PCB disposal activity has brought on the need for a PCB waste tracking system. In response, the EPA has promulgated new TSCA regulations that took effect February 5, 1990.[2]

The new regulations apply to handlers of regulated PCB waste, including generators, commercial storers, transporters and disposers. If PCB transformers are in your plant, you are considered a potential generator of PCB waste and are subject to this new set of requirements.

The PCB waste tracking system under TSCA is intended to assure EPA control over management of PCB wastes. The tracking system's com-

---

[2]Reported in "New TSCA Regulations Affect PCB Waste," *PLANT Services* (Putman Publishing, Sep. 1990).

bination of notification, manifesting, and record-keeping requirements creates a clear line of accountability among PCB waste handlers. The EPA can now track shipments of PCB waste from the point of generation to the point of disposal.

Notification, Identification, and Disposal

If you store PCB wastes at your site, you were to notify the EPA by April 4, 1990, to obtain an EPA identification number. The EPA has adopted the Resource Conservation and Recovery Act (RCRA) numbering system in order to maintain consistency and avoid assigning multiple numbers to those who already possess RCRA identification numbers.

If you do not store PCB wastes, you may use your current state or EPA identification number, and notification is not required. If you do not have a state or EPA identification number, you may use "40CFRPart761" (12 characters, no spaces) for manifesting purposes.

Under the new TSCA regulations, if you are not exempt from the notification requirements, you are prohibited from processing, storing, disposing, or offering for transport, PCBs after June 4, 1990, if an EPA identification number has not been obtained.

When you dispose of PCB waste, the new regulations require that you:

- Use a disposer, transporter, or commercial storer who has an EPA identification number.
- Prepare a manifest.
- Keep annual records and an annual document log.
- Under certain conditions, verify arrival of the PCBs at the designated facility.

For example, if you use an independent transporter to dispose of your PCB waste, you must verify that the waste was received by the designated commercial storer or disposer.

HANDLING SPILLS OF PCB MATERIALS

Cleaning up spills of polychlorinated biphenyls has become a major problem for plant management. The majority of PCB spills from electrical transformers take place on solid porous materials such as concrete and asphalt, as well as on hard surfaces such as metal and glass. PCBs have a strong environmental stability and have proven to be very resistant to effective clean-up and disposal methods. Given the amount of PCBs spilled and the stringent clean-up requirements, the cost of PCB cleanup continues to rise.

When deciding how to clean up a spill, the following matters should be considered: effectiveness, cross-contamination potential, extraction efficiency, waste treatment and disposal requirements, labor intensity, and total cost. Current chemical technology is concerned with cleaning up PCB spills and containerizing them for disposal or destruction.

The ideal chemical process for cleaning up PCB spills is one that extracts as much PCB from the surface with as little labor and chemical used as possible. Such a process achieves a number of cost savings:

1. Less material is needed to accomplish the clean-up.
2. Less labor is involved to perform the clean-up and disposal.
3. Less PCB-containing material is generated by the clean-up.

Currently, the clean-up of PCB spills has been accomplished primarily with the use of like polarity solvents such as hexane or trichlorethylene. The drawbacks of using solvents, however, are their volatility and the difficulty of applying and removing them. Solvents also increase the PCB's mobility in concrete, allowing them to migrate further into the concrete.

Detergents have also been extensively used for cleaning up PCB spills. These products work by cleaning up the soils that contain PCBs but have a low percentage solubility for PCBs.

One treatment method uses an aqueous-based solvent system that extracts PCBs from surfaces and then suspends and emulsifies them, thus allowing removal in water. The technique also has the capability of applying the formulation as a foam blanket on overhead, vertical, and horizontal surfaces.

This increases the contact time with the surface and increases extraction efficiency of the PCBs while reducing the volume of materials needed for cleanup. The product along with the PCBs are then vacuumed from the surface. The cleaned surface is then rinsed with water and re-vacuumed.

ENSURING WORKERS' COMPLIANCE WITH REGULATIONS ON HAZARDOUS MATERIALS

No one wants to suffer the tragic and costly losses that can result from an explosion, fire, spill, or leak. The best way to prevent such occurrences is to ensure that plant workers comply with regulations on hazardous materials. You must take a hard line on this since much is at stake. Here are the most important steps you should take:

1. See that your workers wear protective clothing appropriate to the materials they work with in the plant. Review the pertinent information

and recommendations on safety in Chapter 6 of this book; confirm that you have provided workers with their needs.

2. Make certain that workers are familiar with the plant's spill prevention plan. Confirm they know their duties and responsibilities in handling plant spills. Question them on their knowledge of how they should perform their work to avoid spills.

3. Check to see that workers know how to use protective devices and equipment. Learn if they know the correct respirator to use for the particular hazard they are exposed to. Test them on the care of respirators to assure that these devices are effective when they are needed.

4. Review with workers what they know about right-to-work laws. Make sure they read and understand material safety data sheets and labels on material containers. Sell them on treating hazardous materials with respect.

5. Insist that they follow all the plant rules and regulations concerning hazardous materials. Observe how they handle these materials, and immediately point out any deviations from correct procedures.

Ensuring workers comply with rules and regulations is an endless job and one of your major responsibilities. Remember that your workers depend on you for their safety. To lessen the load on your shoulders, persuade them to share that responsibility with you. Say that the way they can do that is to always comply with regulations on hazardous materials.

GUIDELINES FOR FIRE PREVENTION

Fire prevention means reacting to possible causes of fires to reduce the chances of a fire ever starting. Three elements are required to start a fire:

1. Combustible material in solid, liquid, or gaseous form.

2. Oxygen.

3. A source of ignition, such as a flame or spark caused by friction, static electricity, or electrical arcing.

Since all three elements must be present at the same time for a fire to start, the way to prevent one is to control all of them at the same time.

How to Avoid Accumulations of Combustible Materials

Poor housekeeping contributes greatly to the danger of spontaneous heating resulting in ignition when the materials involved reach their respective ignition temperatures. Accumulations of such items as oil, grease, and paint rags are especially susceptible to ignition. Following are some suggestions on how you can avoid accumulations of these and other combustible materials:

1. Set up a housekeeping program designed specifically for your plant and its operations and processes.
2. Arrange for regular and adequate disposal of all combustible wastes and rubbish.
3. Provide safe containers for all substances subject to spontaneous heating, and for prompt and regular disposal of their contents.
4. Institute a program of external housekeeping that will prevent the accumulation of waste around buildings and will not allow grass or weeds to serve the spread of fire to buildings.
5. Forestall spills of flammable liquids by controlling the methods of transfer from tank to tank and by regular maintenance of tanks, fittings, and pipelines.
6. Prevent flammable vapor accumulations by ventilating confined spaces, exhausting process areas, and installing flame arrestors on tanks to prevent ignition if venting does occur.

Controlling Oxygen

It is very difficult to control or eliminate oxygen as an element necessary for causing a fire because it is present in air at a concentration of 21 percent by volume. However, you can do something about the oxygen that is in empty and partially full tanks:

- Displace it from empty tanks by filling them with water or steam.
- Sweep it from the vapor space above flammable liquids in tanks by introducing gaseous nitrogen or carbon dioxide, neither of which supports combustion.

Techniques for Eliminating Sources of Ignition

Of many ways you can eliminate sources of ignition, the most common are:

- Prohibit smoking or the carrying of matches and lighters in work areas.
- Limit electric motors used in the plant to the totally enclosed type.
- Employ spark suppression systems on electric and gasoline driven lift trucks.

- Install electrical ground straps to dissipate a possible static potential difference between metal containers when flammable liquids are poured from one to the other.
- Ground tanks used for the storage and processing of flammables by burying a copper plate in the ground.
- Install static collector combs to draw off static potential created by moving belts.
- Carry out process operations that require the use of flame or that repeatedly produce sparks in isolated buildings or behind fire walls.

GUIDELINES FOR FIRE PROTECTION

The two aspects of fire preparedness—fire prevention and fire protection—need to be equally stressed for maximum effectiveness. The former means taking steps to minimize the chances of a fire starting. The latter deals with fighting an actual fire.

While preventing fires is the first priority, if a fire should start, most manufacturing plants are designed with systems to handle it. Should those systems fail, many companies rely on fire brigades. Fire brigades not only represent the final option in fire protection, but they also offer the best chance of minimizing fire-related damage.

A major requirement of protecting a plant from fire is to establish emergency procedures for the employees. A decision needs to be made by management on what employees are to do first—turn in the alarm and then leave the building, or fight the fire with hand equipment until it is out or too big to handle? The answer depends on the type of plant involved and the safety philosophy of management. But the important point is that these decisions should be made before a fire occurs, and the employees should be trained on the procedures to be followed.

Another question to be answered concerns whether the plant should be shut down in the event of a fire. If there is a fire in one process area of the plant, it would seem illogical to shut down operations in all other process areas until the situation is under control. But that may not always be wise for both safety and economic reasons. Since shutdown decisions can be more complicated than they first appear, many plants assign this decision to the plant manager or the person in charge when the fire occurs.

Establishing and Maintaining an In-Plant Fire Brigade

In today's manufacturing plants, the difference between a fire that causes minor property loss and one that is disastrous may be only a matter of minutes. A well organized, well trained in-plant fire brigade can use those minutes to minimize the threat to life and property.

To set up an effective fire brigade for your plant, you must determine the total requirements and then arrange for providing them. While no rules or guidelines apply to every plant, here are the main factors you must consider:

- *Staff*. Staff needs depend on a number of conditions including the size of the area to be covered, the types of fires and other emergencies that could occur, and where the manpower is likely to be located at the time of an alarm. Your choice of manpower is also important. Ideally, the brigade should consist of loyal, long-service employees who have demonstrated common sense in handling everyday problems and emergency situations. These individuals will know the plant and its equipment better than anyone else. Maintenance and tool-room personnel generally meet these requirements.

- *Equipment*. Although needs will vary from plant to plant, there is no substitute for properly sized and functioning equipment of the type needed by your plant. The methods of attacking fires depend on the raw materials being used, the productive machines being operated, and the products being manufactured. Once the types of fires that are possible have been identified, the appropriate firefighting equipment can be provided and maintained. Fires involving ordinary combustibles such as wood and paper are Class A fires and are extinguishable with water. Special agents (dry chemicals, multipurpose chemicals, and CO_2) are needed to extinguish Class B (flammable liquids), Class C (electrical), and Class D (metals) fires. Most plant fires are combinations of at least two of these types.

- *Communication*. An easily operated communication system is needed to assure the efficiency of the brigade and minimize misunderstandings. The procedure for reporting fires must be simple, and the alarm system should pinpoint the location of the fire. Some plants use a switchboard system to determine pull-alarm locations; others use an intercom to announce an emergency. Whatever the reporting method, all employees should be familiar with it. It pays to also ask the local professional fire department to visit and tour the plant. These firefighters want to be familiar with the plant's structures, facilities, and problem areas. They may also instruct the plant brigade on what type of assistance to provide during an emergency.

- *Training*. Establishing a fire brigade requires that members receive comprehensive training. All volunteers should be instructed in firefighting, first aid, and cardiopulmonary resuscitation techniques. Training methods should be determined by the plant's work schedules, availability of instructors and volunteers, and the extent of the required fire protection. While films, videotapes, and lectures are very helpful, drills and demonstrations are much better to acquaint volunteers with the equipment and procedures. In some plants, fires are set for training purposes with a professional fire-fighter on hand as an instructor/advisor. Thorough training gives the volunteers the confidence they need to combat inplant fires.

The requirements for establishing and maintaining an in-plant fire brigade are broad and extensive. Yet all the needs including manpower, equipment, communication, and training are interrelated and interdependent. Regular inspection, testing of equipment, and training will help ensure readiness.

TRAINING EMPLOYEES TO USE FIRE EXTINGUISHERS[4]

Every plant employee should know how to operate a fire extinguisher. The only way to really know how is through actual experience in using one on a real fire. The individual characteristics of fires are best learned through practice.

If you want to ensure that employees get that experience, arrange for your local fire department to conduct training sessions at the plant. In this way, you do not have to worry about special permits to burn materials outdoors, and you will be assured of adequate backup protection if for some reason the fire gets out of control.

Actuating and operating approved fire extinguishers is relatively easy. All of the extinguishers currently manufactured in the United States and Canada operate simply by pulling out the restraining pin and applying the extinguishing agent by squeezing the trigger. The trigger controls the on and off flow of the contents as desired.

Since the soda-acid, foam, and gas-cartridge type of extinguishers are no longer made, you would be well advised to begin replacing such types if they are still in use in your plant. As long as they are an approved type, however, and have been well-maintained, these extinguishers may continue in service.

To ensure that employees receive proper and adequate training, they should be taught to fight four types of fires. These are:

1. *Class A* fires consist of ordinary combustibles, such as wood, paper, or trash. They are generally fought with stored pressure, water-filled extinguishers. The water stream should be aimed from close range at the base of the flames. After the fire is out, the water should be used to

---

[4]Portions of this section came from information given in "If You Discovered a Fire, Could You Put It Out?" *The Safe Foreman*, 1984 (The United Safety Service, Inc.).

wet down any glowing embers or smouldering material. Multipurpose chemical extinguishers can also be used on Class A fires. The correct procedure is to start at the edge of the fire and sweep the nozzle of the extinguisher from side to side while moving forward.

2. *Class B* fires are flammable liquid ones. The liquids include oil, gasoline, solvents, and paints. Dry chemical extinguishers are very effective against such fires. Start fighting this type of fire from about 10 feet to avoid causing the liquid to splash. Then move closer using a sweeping motion. The fire is smothered and hot surfaces are shielded limiting radiation of the heat. Carbon dioxide extinguishers can also be used on Class B fires provided there is no wind or draft. The carbon dioxide reduces the amount of oxygen around the fire until the air will no longer support combustion.

3. *Class C* fires involve electrical systems and equipment. Carbon dioxide and dry chemicals are most effective on these fires. Carbon dioxide leaves no residue, and it is nonconductive and noncorrosive. While multipurpose extinguishers will put out the fire, the chemicals may leave a film that is difficult to remove.

4. *Class D* fires consist of burning metals. Special dry compound powders are available for controlling these fires, but care and skill are required in applying them. Never use water on burning metals; the reaction will be extremely violent.

In addition to being trained in knowing which type of extinguisher should be used and how to use each one, you should also provide employees other training. Tell them:

- If they are alone when they see a fire, a call for help could be postponed if in their experience they think the extinguisher could handle the fire. However, if after a few seconds, they make no progress in putting the fire out, it's best to immediately give up and call for help. If the fire is large, waste no time in calling for help.

- If there are several employees near, have someone call the fire department while the others start fighting the fire. All too often, employees who thought they could handle a fire have something happen that causes the fire to get out of control.

- Know the location of fire alarms and fire extinguishers in the area. They may lose valuable seconds in starting to fight a fire if they have to search for these items. The location of either can also be a determining factor in whether they give the alarm first or start using an extinguisher.

WHAT TO DO ABOUT RADON

Despite what you may hear or read, radon is not a new phenomenon. Miners have been known to die prematurely from what was called lung disease, now known to be lung cancer. The disease originated as a result of the radon they were exposed to while working in the mines.

However, radon didn't come to the attention of safety and health authorities until late in 1984 when an employee of the Philadelphia Electric Co. tripped a radiation sensor when he entered the plant. Although the problem was traced to radon in the employee's home, the EPA has since discovered that the presence of radon in buildings is severe and widespread.

Many building owners now are testing to protect their employees from the potential hazard. Liability is a concern because the EPA's involvement could lead to numerous radon-related lawsuits.

Radon gas is a colorless, odorless, tasteless, and radioactive material that occurs naturally in soil and rocks. While it is not a hazard outdoors, when it leaks into buildings, it can build up to dangerous concentrations.

Radon-decay products attach themselves to particles in the air. When these radioactive particles are inhaled, they penetrate some of the most cancer-sensitive cells in the human body and also damage lung tissue. Since damaged cells can multiply rapidly and uncontrollably, radon is the leading cause of lung cancer among nonsmokers. For smokers, the risk is ten times greater, according to the American Cancer Society.

Although health risk estimates for most carcinogens are based solely on animal tests, EPA's radon risk estimates are based on studies of about 40,000 humans (miners). Thus, scientists are fairly certain of radon risk estimates.

Here's how the risk from radon exposure compares with other risks:

- According to EPA estimates, asbestos will cause 25 to 45 deaths in 1990. Radon will kill approximately 20,000.
- The radon hazard is significantly more severe than all other environmental hazards (asbestos, formaldehyde, toxic chemicals, pesticides) combined.
- According to the National Council on Radiation Protection and Measurement, radon is the source of more radiation for the average individual than all other sources (x-rays, cosmic rays, and nuclear fallout) combined.
- EPA's action level for radon (4 pCi/L) is comparable to having 300 chest x-rays a year, or smoking half a pack of cigarettes a day.

But surveys have shown unpredictable radon levels. You cannot assume what the radon levels are for your plant by basing estimates on readings within your locality or by the construction of the plant. The EPA emphasizes that the only way to know radon levels for a specific area is to test that area.

Although testing for radon is fairly simple, it is recommended that you work with a contractor who provides radon consulting and testing services. If you do not select testing rooms properly, use the right detection equipment, and keep accurate records, your tests may be deficient if not erroneous.

Reducing High Radon Levels

The most practical way to reduce levels is to prevent it from entering the building. This is done by making the pressure within the endangered space higher than that of the ambient soil. A contaminated room may be under negative pressure because of exhaust fans or a system imbalance. But first check to see if air supply fans are operating properly; increasing the supply should also be considered.

If this doesn't help, look into depressurizing the area around the foundation or basement by applying suction beneath floors or walls and venting the air above the roof. This will prevent radon from entering the building.

Sealing cracks and utility line openings often is tried as a corrective measure but seldom is effective over the long term. Yet it may turn out to be worthwhile. For example, sealing may not only lower radon levels but also reduce energy costs and improve the appearance of some buildings and facilities.

Radon is undoubtedly an environmental health problem. But testing for radon and reducing high levels when they are found are relatively easy and inexpensive steps to take. The real danger comes from doing nothing.

10

Guidelines for Planning and Scheduling Work for Plant Employees

HOW PLANNING HELPS ORGANIZATIONS

Large organizations have become so complex that, without planning, they would be unable to efficiently operate, much less grow and prosper. Businesses simply can't afford capricious organizational change. Planning is essential to avoid unnecessary stresses and strains in their evolution. Every change has an impact on someone in an organization. Even the threat of change can cause concern and negative personal reactions.

To be effective, organizational planning must be wide in scope. Matters of authority, power, values, communications, industrial relations, and work or service to be performed must be considered. Planning must control and minimize conflict, and complement the style of administration. Equally important, it must facilitate coordination, control, and feedback.

In large manufacturing plants today, the production and maintenance departments often are served by a staff planning group, whose members are classified as planners. Their responsibilities require them to work closely with supervisors and middle management. In plants that have no such planning group, supervisors in both departments do their own planning.

TECHNIQUES FOR RECOGNIZING PEOPLE WHEN PLANNING

Good planning is not the result of technical analysis alone, but of a greater emphasis on human resources. Effective planning depends on a tie-in between programs and people, between procedures on paper and actual operations, and between planned goals and the proven abilities and desires of people. Unless you make these tie-ins realistically, all your projections, simulations, and schedules are of little value.

In the plant, planning is closely related to scheduling in that it usually involves work to be done within a time frame. If a supervisor is dealing with workers who will be directly involved in doing a job, both the supervisor and the workers should know specifically what is going to be accomplished.

There are five steps to formulating a plan that correlates procedures, resources, time, and workers:

1. *Define the job*. Make sure everyone understands it and there is agreement on the time frame.
2. *Assure that resources are available*. Check on materials, machines, and equipment.
3. *Consider alternatives*. Flexibility is necessary if you are to succeed under unexpected conditions. Be ready to change your plan.
4. *Select the course to follow*. Whether the decision is made by a majority or by group consensus, you are responsible to the company for the decision.
5. *Review all the details of the final plan with each person involved*. Get each person to describe his or her responsibility and how that responsibility fits with others.

Good planning is always worth the effort. You and all the workers will gain satisfaction with a job well done. Planning is a key management skill that will ensure coordination and teamwork, resulting in getting work done in the most efficient manner.

WAYS THAT PLANNING AND SCHEDULING PAY OFF

Planning and scheduling are among the most important of the many functions of management in both the production and maintenance departments. They consist primarily of analyzing the jobs and projecting the workload into the future. Thus, the work can be done at the right time and by the most efficient methods; staff, materials, and tools will be available for it. Following are a few of the major benefits of good planning and scheduling:

- *Work measurement.* A planning and scheduling program forces the application of work measurement in one form or another. An estimated time must be placed on each job or operation in order to fit it into the schedule intelligently. Once the time has been established, it is only one more step to compare that time with the actual time taken for the job.

  Wide variations from the estimated time call for an explanation from a worker or the supervisor. This highlights where additional training is needed. It also stimulates competition for high efficiency among supervisors, and provides a means of measuring their managerial ability. Thus, the estimated job times required for scheduling can be used in many ways to improve the efficiency of everyone.

- *Better methods and procedures.* A planner cannot establish a time for a job without first making a study to determine the best methods, the best tools and equipment, and the best material. This results in a complete job analysis.

  Too often a supervisor has to assign a job and let the worker do it the best he or she can. The supervisor doesn't always have the time to study all the possibilities. Consequently, the work may be done in a more complicated manner than necessary, or the worker may use more expensive material than is needed. Sometimes a worker may go only so far with a job, then wait for the supervisor to come along and explain how to proceed. If a job is well planned, these unnecessary expenses are eliminated.

- *Establishment of priorities.* A planning and scheduling program provides a means for making sure first things come first. For example, in a large plant, it is hard to determine the relative importance of various maintenance jobs.

  In a plant that does not plan and schedule the work, each production supervisor keeps pressuring a maintenance supervisor to get a repair job done ahead of another supervisor's. This pressuring is not conducive to good relations among supervisors.

- *Coordination of labor and materials.* A planning program results in better coordination of labor and materials. A complete analysis of a job before it begins reveals what materials are required. Those materials are ordered, and are on hand before the job is started. Thus, workers don't have to wait for a decision on what to do next because some item of material is not available when it is needed.

  A common cause of lost time on maintenance jobs is that one craft is kept waiting for another to handle its part of the overall project. Good planning eliminates this, and ensures that each craft is available when it is needed.

- *Preventive maintenance promoted.* A planning and scheduling program provides a system in which preventive maintenance procedures are carried out. Preventive maintenance is now commonly accepted as a must for production equipment. If preventive maintenance work is continually shoved aside in favor of other apparently "more important" work, the benefits of the program will not be realized.

As scheduling contributes to the success of preventive maintenance, so does preventive maintenance contribute to the success of scheduling. The greatest obstacle to an effective scheduling plan is the periodic need to make repairs on machines and equipment. By scheduling inspections and repairs when machines are idle, breakdowns can be nearly eliminated. Thus the cause of interruptions to the planned schedule is removed or reduced to a minimum.

- *Maintenance backlog.* Scheduling furnishes a means of determining the maintenance load. It provides an index of the backlog for each craft, and this information tells a supervisor whether to work overtime, increase the maintenance force, or allocate some of the work to contractors.

  It is much easier to make a decision if the backlog figures are on hand. It is also much easier to justify to top management the need for an increase in the work force or an increase in the overtime if a record of the work load is available.

- *Work order system.* Planning and scheduling force the use of a work order system, thus eliminating the many abuses encountered when production supervisors give jobs directly to maintenance supervisors. A work order system, in turn, supplies the structure for better job cost control, job progress reports, and records of machine repair.

  Planning and scheduling also force the use of written instructions for jobs, thereby eliminating the costly errors caused by oral orders. Use of drawings, sketches, and layout plans to guide the workmen in performing the job is promoted.

- *Help to you and other supervisors.* When planning is handled by a planner or member of the staff, you have more time for directing workers. Closer attention on your part promotes a better quality of workmanship and reduces idle time. You have more time to train and instruct personnel, and to build apprentices and less skilled employees into workers who are more likely to be error free in their performance.

You also have more time to practice good employee relations and to promote creativity and innovation. The resultant higher morale among the group represents the greatest contributing factor to an increase in productivity.

HOW PLANNING CAN HELP YOU CUT MATERIAL HANDLING COSTS

The lack of comprehensive planning is the single most important cause of high materials handling costs in industry today. This was the conclusion of a two-year study made by the British Department of Industry. This poor situation has been attributed to planners of material-handling equipment who failed to take productivity into account in providing for the material-handling function. As a result, there are many types of special equipment, handling methods that are noncoordinating, and innumerable different types of pallets, boxes, and containers.

High handling costs are due most often to:

- Moves of long distance.
- Congested and limited routes of travel.
- Cumbersome transportation equipment.
- Poor coordination with trucking personnel.
- Inadequate or improper scheduling.

These weaknesses and insufficiencies can be overcome by good planning.

Awkward and unsafe containers also lead to difficulties and unnecessary costs. While these things are typically problems for engineers, planners can contribute to solving particular problems. They can specify what and how much of each item has to move, where it is to move, when and for how long the moves are to be made, and what facilities are available to aid the handling operation.

Absence of comprehensive planning is a prime contributor to costly materials handling. It can be remedied by planning that incorporates appropriate handling methods, long as well as short range.

HOW TO OPERATE YOUR DEPARTMENT EFFICIENTLY AND AVOID WASTE

There is a lot of waste in many plants today. It shows up in several forms: damage to materials, defective products due to poor workmanship, and machine breakdowns, to mention only a few of the more common forms.

The planning and scheduling of production processes and operations in the plant is usually based on customer's orders or company needs. In addition, market research often provides guidance on what and how many items or how much material should be produced.

But regardless of how much planning you may get from your company's centralized department, you won't be able to operate your department efficiently and avoid waste without detailed planning and scheduling on your part. Planning and scheduling enable you to:

- Save time by anticipating and avoiding process bottlenecks and interruptions.

- Reduce material costs caused by spoilage or unnecessary inventories.
- Get better performance out of machines and equipment by operating them at optimum speeds and at appropriate times.
- Improve process control and avoid congestion by better coordination of incoming supplies and materials with outgoing products.

Increase Productivity of Employees by Keeping Them Fully Occupied

Another big waste is that of human effort caused by poor scheduling. Poor scheduling affects the performance of everyone in the plant, and it often seriously impairs direct labor output.

For example, setups and jigs may be broken up before they should be because of a lack of materials, a rush job, or wrong information. Whatever the reason, the result is that the output of both workers and machines is not what it could be.

Poor scheduling can also affect the efficiency of plant supervisors. This is a double loss. First is the loss created by emergencies that demand the supervisor's constant attention. Second is the loss created by the failure to realize the potential of methods improvements that supervisors could make if they had the time to work them out.

Plants that have adopted planning, scheduling, and production control systems have realized tremendous benefits. Management needs only to recognize the strong impact that good scheduling has on manufacturing productivity and to act upon that knowledge. When they do, they'll find that the potential for savings in the plant is enormous.

HOW PLANS AND SCHEDULES IMPROVE PLANT EMPLOYEES' ATTITUDES AND MORALE

Employees like to work for companies where their work is planned and scheduled. In addition, they have more respect for you, their supervisor, when you organize their work. Here are the reasons most employees like planning and scheduling:

1. *They dislike and fear change.* They would prefer that their work procedures remain the same and that the plant runs smoothly all the time.
2. *They feel insecure when the plant goes through continual crises.* Their morale is much better when, because of planning, there are few emergency situations.
3. *They want to go home at the end of the day fairly certain of the job they are going to work on tomorrow.* Good planning and communicating on your part make that possible.

4. *They like to feel assured of a regular paycheck.* Poor planning adds to the fear that something will happen to prevent them from receiving it.

5. *They want to feel that they know what they're doing each day.* If you show them that you can schedule work smoothly and effectively, they will be more willing to help when an occasional emergency arises.

GUIDELINES FOR EFFECTIVELY MAKING WORK ASSIGNMENTS

Although asking workers to do something seems simple enough, there is more to the art than is apparent. If you are an expert at giving orders, you probably are also good at planning, motivating, and persuading because those endeavors are prerequisites to making good work assignments. Since handing out work assignments is one of your main responsibilities, your success as a supervisor is measured by how skilled you are at it. Here are some guidelines to help you improve your technique:

- *Make your assignment appropriate for the worker and the situation.* Use different approaches depending on the current workload in the plant, the importance of the job, and the urgency with which it should be carried out. A request is always better than a command because it makes the worker feel that cooperation is being asked for rather than demanded.
  Tip: *Suggesting* that something be done is usually effective. Its success depends on the initiative and cooperative attitude of workers. Although the order is implied, it brings a positive response from conscientious individuals.

- *Make an assignment at an opportune time, such as when the worker is more receptive.* Avoid making it when the worker is very busy or engrossed in another matter. If the assignment is complex or detailed, pick a time when the worker is alert; there will be less chance of misunderstanding.
  Tip: Be aware that an assignment given just before lunch or at quitting time might be forgotten when the worker returns to his or her job.

- *Be sure your assignment is clear and complete.* While you should keep it as simple as possible, make certain it includes all the information needed for it to be carried out quickly and efficiently. If more than one worker is involved, clarify who is responsible for doing what. If time is critical, say when the job should be started.
  Tip: Check for understanding if you sense your listener is in doubt. Ask that your assignment be repeated back to you in the worker's own words.

HOW PLANNING HELPS YOUR PERSONAL DEVELOPMENT[1]

Although you can get many benefits from planning, a few may especially appeal to you because they can aid you with your personal development, a matter which should be of concern to you if you want to move up in your organization. Of course, being aware of these benefits will not guarantee your advance or promotion; you must commit yourself to planning in order to gain its benefits.

Planning gives you confidence and a feeling that you are in control. When someone else plans for you, goals may be set that you may not agree with, that you may feel are not practical, and that you think are too ambitious. You realize satisfaction and a feeling of power when an event or activity that *you* planned comes off the way you planned it.

An organization works toward an objective much better when the means for reaching it have been planned. People have the goal in mind constantly, know the sequence of operations, what part they play, and when to expect success. Managing people who are goal oriented is much easier than managing people who are working aimlessly.

Planning helps in making use of all available resources. You can assess the potential of individuals and aim to put it to its full use. You can evaluate each available resource to see if it can be applied to your operation, and you can assign unneeded resources elsewhere.

When you plan, you provide the basis for good communication. Getting along well with your manager and your subordinates may depend on how you interpret your organization's goals and what you are doing to reach them. Your manager prefers a written plan to oral assurance that you understand your job and that your operations are going well.

Plans also let subordinates know that attainment of the goals depends on their efforts and good performance. Subordinates can see that reaching the goals will result in their own development and recognition.

Planning enables you to have insight into your future financial needs. Managers frequently must prepare budgets. Your work plan supports your budget and lets management know what to expect of you.

You have a means for measuring a program's achievements when you do a thorough job of planning that program. Work plans should include time schedules, so that you can determine how much progress you have made at a given time—in addition to seeing where you are and where you should be. Measuring your effectiveness is important to you because it lets

---

[1]Portions of this section have been taken from W. H. Weiss, "The Value of Planning," *Successful Supervisor*, June 15, 1987, Dartnell, Chicago, IL 60640.

you know the extent of your effort and alerts you to what remains to be done.

TECHNIQUES FOR ESTABLISHING AND REVISING PRODUCTION STANDARDS FOR PLANT EMPLOYEES

A *control standard*, usually called simply a *standard*, is a specific performance goal that a product, service, machine, or an individual is expected to meet. In most cases, it is expressed numerically such as a rate (50 units per hour) or a target (98 percent within specifications). Many manufacturing plants allow a little leeway on their standards, identified as *tolerances*. "Allowing a tolerance" means that a performance or product will be considered in control or acceptable if it is within specified limits.

Standards in plants may be established by the Production Control Department for schedule quantities or by the Quality Control Department for inspection specifications. While it is typical for control standards in large plants to be set by staff employees, supervisors may set them in smaller plants. But even in large plants, you may have to take a department standard and revise it into standards for each employee. If you decide to do this, you should base your standards on one or more of the following:

- *Past performance*. Historical records provide the information you need. But the problem is that the method presumes what has been accomplished in the past represents good performance. Maybe a higher figure would be more realistic. This might be the case if changes have recently been made in the process or machines.

- *Desires and expectations*. Be wary of setting unreasonably high standards, hoping that employees can reach them. While you may want to present a challenge, standards should always be attainable with reasonable effort on the part of an average employee. If you set standards too high, some employees won't even try to reach them.

- *Study and analysis*. The best standards are established by studying a job and analyzing what it involves, such as by making a time study of each move and step. This permits consideration of all the factors that affect reaching the standard, among which are suitability of tools and equipment, training of the worker, material availability, and others.

How to Handle Employees' Complaints on Standards

Whether you or a staff analyst make a time study of a plant job, mistakes are possible that can lead to establishing a poor standard. Invariably, one or more workers may complain, especially if the standard is high. But since one of your responsibilities is to see that employees are not taken advantage of, you should take the following steps if an employee questions a rate:

1. *Listen to the employee with an open mind.* He or she may point out a condition that didn't exist when the rate was established.

2. *Get the facts and consider the employees' viewpoint.* Don't assume the standard is wrong, however, until you have checked material and machine specifications, availability of tools and supplies, and other matters that may be beyond the employees' control.

3. *Report your findings promptly to the employee.* If you find nothing wrong with the standard, encourage him or her to put more effort into the job. State that you're sure the employee can make and even beat the standard.

GUIDELINES FOR SHORT-INTERVAL SCHEDULING PLANT WORKERS' JOB ASSIGNMENTS

When you use the short-interval scheduling technique, you hand out several work assignments of relatively short duration at one time. This technique is currently popular in manufacturing plants where many of the maintenance and repair jobs can be handled in an hour or two. Basically, the technique requires you to assign only part of a day's work at a time to each worker rather than a whole day's work at once.

For example, you may give a mechanic several work orders that call for unplugging or cleaning spare pumps on a process line. When all of these jobs have been completed, you assign other jobs (that again can be finished within the shift) to the same mechanic.

There are several advantages to using short-interval scheduling:

1. Within a very short time, you know if a worker is keeping up or falling behind in output.

2. The technique requires you to estimate and enforce work and job standards. Thus you can maintain high productivity levels.

3. You can adopt the technique informally and on the spur of the moment, and still get unusually good results.

However, short-interval scheduling may not work well for you because whether it pays off depends on:

• How accurately you can estimate the time it should take a worker to do a job.

- How much time you can take to come up with good estimates and hand out multiple assignments.
- How much time you can spend observing workers' performance.
- How effectively you can motivate workers to accept a work pace that is higher than that associated with large and extensive work projects.
- How successful you are in training workers to apply specific skills with full attention until a job is completed.

TECHNIQUES FOR PLANNING, SCHEDULING, AND PROJECT MANAGEMENT

Operations management plans and controls the processes used to create products and perform services. Whenever production processes are planned, scheduled, and controlled, operations management is taking place.

The position of the operations manager in a plant is often identified by describing the process being managed, such as assembly-line manager, shipping manager, receiving manager, and service manager. To effectively and efficiently control a production process, the operations manager must have a plan for the use of materials, labor, machines, equipment, and information. Knowing whether the output of product or services is the right kind, of the right amount, at the right time, and at a minimum cost determines how capably the operations manager does his or her job.

While operations managers get satisfaction from seeing the tangible results of their efforts, they frequently suffer frustration from having to juggle and control many variables. In addition, they are continually trying to raise the productivity of employees and reduce plant operating costs.

Organization of Operations Management

It's common practice in today's plants to give each worker a single boss who coordinates all the functions of that worker. This first-line manager, or supervisor, assigns jobs and tasks to workers daily and on an individual basis.

In many industrial organizations and plants, further division of management and specialization results in higher-level management positions. Planning and directing the functions of the supervisor comes under the operation manager's jurisdiction, whose titles are often superintendents or general foremen. (First-line managers in some plants are titled foremen instead of supervisors.)

Operations managers plan a plant's activities on a weekly, monthly, and yearly basis. They plan material purchases, equipment and machine use, and assignment of labor. They also schedule the activities of their departments.

PROJECT ORGANIZATION AND MANAGEMENT[2]

When operations are extensive or important enough to be managed as one-of-a-kind jobs, they are designated as programs or projects. Responsibilities for management of a project are those of the project manager.

The schedule is all-important in project management. It defines, sequences, and times the activities that must be carried out to complete the project. The project manager is responsible for seeing that labor, equipment, and materials required to do each activity are supplied, and that the work proceeds on schedule.

Tips on Project Scheduling

Projects typically undertaken by plant management include the construction of a building on the plant site or the manufacture of a new product. To schedule such a project requires that the operations be broken down into three elements:

1. *The activities*. These are the steps or procedures that must be performed to complete the project. While a project activity requires materials, labor, equipment, and information for it to be carried out, only estimates of these are needed for the schedule.
2. *The sequence*. The order in which the activities are performed is determined from the relationships among activities and by their technical and physical characteristics. By defining the activities and knowing the technology involved with each, it can be decided which activities must proceed in a specific order, and which can occur simultaneously.
3. *The times*. The times are estimates of the time required to perform each activity. These times are based on estimates of the rate of use of materials, labor, and equipment. For example, the time estimate to electrify a new building requires knowledge of how many circuits and controls are to be installed and how many electricians will be assigned the job.

Guidelines for Scheduling

Scheduling is the planning for the sequencing and timing of work. From a schedule, the operations manager issues orders on when each part of a project is to be done.

- Control of *materials* focuses on the timing and release of orders for materials.

[2]"The Operations Manager: Role, Problems, Techniques," West Publishing Co., St. Paul, MN 55165.

- Control of *labor* focuses on using labor efficiently.
- Control of *cost* focuses on the efficient use of materials, labor, and equipment.

The objective in working out a schedule is to figure out the minimum total elapsed time needed to complete the project. Presuming that time is urgent, the objective assumes that time is money. Fast completion of the project saves time, money, and resources.

The project manager needs information to estimate the duration of activities. Collecting this information constitutes the major roadblock to the development of a detailed project schedule.

By specifying all the activities, estimating the completion for each, and developing a logical sequence of activities, a manager can get a good handle on the project. When this planning precedes the project start, the manager knows ahead of time what materials, labor, and equipment are needed. This information is used to anticipate and prepare for the difficult activities.

HOW TO MAKE AND USE A GANTT CHART

A Gantt chart provides a quick and easy way of scheduling small projects, as well as partly or ill-defined projects of any size. The chart graphs time on the horizontal *x*-axis and activities on the vertical *v*-axis. See Figure 10-1 as an illustration of the steps to be followed for installing a large, heavy machine in a plant production line.

When planning and scheduling this job, the project manager established the following activities as being required before the machine would be ready to operate productively:

- *Activity A*: Preparation of site where machine is to be installed, including dismantling of structures and equipment presently in that area.
- *Activity B*: Pouring of concrete foundations for the machine.
- *Activity C*: Setting the machine on the foundations.
- *Activity D*: Installing mechanical components and auxiliary equipment on the machine.
- *Activity E*: Installing piping and controls.
- *Activity F*: Installing electrical systems and controls.
- *Activity G*: Painting, lubricating, oiling, and other preparations for use of the machine.
- *Activity H*: Start-up and testing of operation and controls.

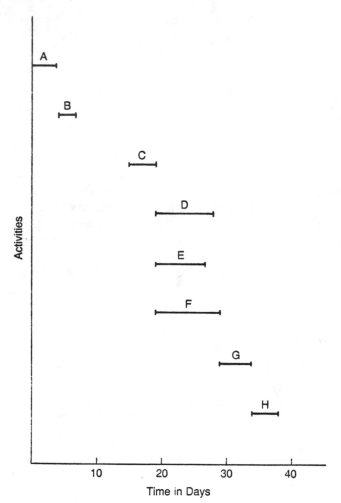

FIGURE 10-1
Gantt Chart for a Machine Installation

The first activity for the project, activity A, is scheduled to begin at time zero and be completed three days later. Activity B may begin when activity A is completed, and activity C may begin ten days after B is completed.

Activities D, E, and F can all start when activity C is finished, although some shop work and prefabrication of material may start a day or two earlier. Activity G follows when all other activities are completed, and the project is completed when activity H ends.

Note that the Gantt method starts activities as soon as possible—as soon as their predecessor activities end. The duration of each activity is scaled along the horizontal axis.

The project manager, or a planner, must periodically check the chart to assure that an activity is not started early; the chart shows which activities occur each day.

PLANNING WITH THE PROGRAM EVALUATION AND REVIEW TECHNIQUE[3]

A *network plan* is one of the best planning tools available to a project manager. With this technique, all the activities and events in a project are pictured graphically. The method makes it easy to visualize the events in a project that are interdependent. The plan also is of value in recognizing that some activities must occur in ordered sequence, while others can take place simultaneously.

The name for the network plan is *Program Evaluation and Review Technique* (PERT). With this plan, you can determine how a project is progressing, if it is on schedule, and if costs are in line. The system is also called the *Critical Path Method* (CPM). Although a few different terms are sometimes used, the basic concepts are identical.

Understanding the Basic Concepts of PERT

Use of the PERT system involves preparation of the network plan. It shows in graphic form what must be accomplished to complete the project. The chart provides information on two elements: activities and events.

Activities are time-consuming actions that must be carried out to complete a project. The PERT chart represents these activities by lines with arrowheads pointing in the direction of passing time (conventionally to the right). In the network plan, the activity arrows are not vectors; their length is not related to their duration, and their direction has no specific meaning.

Events are points in time, usually exact dates, that indicate the planned start or completion of activities. The PERT chart represents events by circles, which can be defined as either the beginning or end of one or more activities. The chart needs only one event circle between the two activities to indicate the end of one and the beginning of the other.

Figures 10-2a and b depict the relation among multiple events. The lines in Figures 10-2a signify that activities B, C, and D cannot begin until activity A is completed. The event circle that represents the finish point of activity A is the beginning for activities B, C, and D. Although the circle

---

[3]Marvin Flaks and Russell D. Archibald, a series of articles titled "The EE's Guide to Project Management," from *The Electronic Engineer*, Chilton Company, Philadelphia, PA 19139.

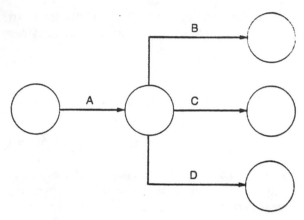

FIGURE 10-2α
PERT Network Chart

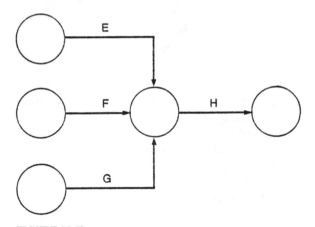

FIGURE 10-2b

could be for either the beginning or end of an activity, it usually indicates the finish.

Figure 10-2b shows activity lines where one event depends on the completion of three prior activities; activity H cannot begin until E, F, and G are finished. If E takes longer than either F or G, the beginning of activity H must still await the completion of E. This relationship can occur often during the life of a project.

The time required for the longest concurrent activity in Figure 10-2b is the quickest the following event can be expected to occur. No matter how quickly activities F and G are completed, the duration of activity E is the critical time—the time that must be used in establishing a schedule for the event.

Whenever there are multiple dependencies, such as those shown in Figures 10-2a and b, a critical path can be identified in the network along the lines represented the longest-time activities. Thus, the "least possible" time to complete the project can be determined from the event dates along the critical path.

USING THE COMPUTER IN NETWORK MANAGEMENT SYSTEMS

Network management systems can be handled manually only up to a certain point of complexity, one or two hundred activities. Beyond that point, the time involved may be prohibitive. Besides, there may not be enough experienced people available to keep all the detailed records. The speed and reliability of today's digital computers, however, are appropriate for the data accumulation and predictive simulation required with network analysis.

Software programs adapted to networking are available for most second- and third-generation computers. PERT analysis by the computer, therefore, can be made at a fraction of the cost it takes to get the same information manually. It's only necessary to select the right computer and program to fit the project in mind.

With complex operations, the whole network can be fed into and stored in the computer. The calculations needed to analyze and update the network are specified by the software, and are virtually automatic as updating information is added. Reports are available when requested, and they can contain as much detail as is desired.

Advantages of the Computer in Project Management

Using the computer provides several advantages to project managers, some of which are not always easy to see. While the most obvious savings are in labor because of the speed of the computer, here are a few other cost-saving benefits from computerizing a project:

- Many large projects are tightly scheduled. In such cases, a few days lost can cost hundreds of dollars in lost production. In addition, a delay in spotting an unexpected problem may cost much more, or even jeopardize the entire project. Because the computer can produce management information quickly, it is a valuable tool for staying out of trouble.

- The computer can be used for simulation, to set up hypothetical project situations and learn what could happen on the critical paths. Simulation permits study of the effects of such things as time, cost substitutions, and tradeoffs without actually trying them, thus eliminating costly mistakes.

- Computers are capable of letting management quickly study variables that are developing in a project plan, thus enabling a decision to be made on which of alternate actions is best. Speed of these analyses can be a critical factor—the computer is noted for its speed.

- Reports from computers are generally more accurate than those prepared by hand, provided, of course, that the input data are added carefully. When calculating critical paths, for example, the computer won't over-look a branch from among the hundreds as a human might.

- Computer reports are not only legible, they have a standard format with which everyone reading them can easily become familiar. This can be considered an asset in that the information presented at all levels of control is understandable.

- The computer can, to a degree, interpret data. With the right program-ming, any number of instructions can be given to the computer. For example, the computer can sort out activities that take more than two weeks to complete, rank them on cost, or report the information in bar charts or graphs. The possibilities are limited only by the capacity of the computer and the creativity of the programmer.

GUIDELINES FOR EFFECTIVE PROJECT MANAGEMENT

Project management is only one of a number of responsibilities of man-agement. Once the advantages of a system are understood, a manager is usually eager to put it into operation. Most plants that have complex projects and recognize them as such, use some of the concepts described in this chapter.

Successful project management requires that any and every project be planned, organized, directed, and controlled. When many specialized technologies must be coordinated and melded into a concerted effort, ordinary management techniques are inadequate.

Once a project is conceived, thorough and complete planning is the first step to take. Making lists of the activities and events preparatory to network construction is part of systematic planning. Without this planning, it is virtually impossible to effectively manage a project.

Grouping the project into its phases helps to organize it. All projects go through the phases of definition, design, development, and use. It is from these phases that the resources needed to complete it can be deter-mined. These resources consist of money, trained people, facilities and equipment, and materials.

Combining all these resources to get the job done is often an immense task, particularly when the time and dollar constraints that are inevitably forced on a project are considered. The resources must be made available, assigned in the right direction, at the right time, and in the right amount. Directing of resources is an important part of project management.

FIVE KEY ELEMENTS OF AN ACTION PLAN

If you must come up with a plan for completing a project in the plant, the best course is to take steps to assure that the five key elements of your plan are handled. You will have to:

1. Assign responsibility for a specific action to each person in your group.
2. Set a completion date for each major phase in the plan.
3. Identify the resources you will need in terms of people, equipment, outside services, and support from others.
4. Estimate the costs involved in each phase, both in expenses and capital investment.
5. Estimate the benefits you anticipate from completing the project.

No matter how skillful you are as a planner, realize that the future will probably be different from what you expected. For this reason, you must stay flexible and be ready to change your plan as you go along. The more flexible you are, the better chance you have of completing the project successfully. Always have alternative plans ready in case the unexpected happens; you'll be able to easily get back on track.

TECHNIQUES FOR COORDINATING WITH PRODUCTION CONTROL

Since you, as a supervisor, may become involved at one time or another with *production control* (PC), it's a good idea to learn its functions so that you can contribute and cooperate when called upon to do so. One of the primary functions of PC is to plan the fabrication, inspection, and timely delivery of a customer's order.

Cost is a significant factor in this process, particularly as it relates to materials and finished goods. So, based on a bill of materials, the first step is to make determinations of the most economical quantities and expenditures for material required to fill the given orders.

The orders for materials must be placed early enough to ensure delivery when they are needed. Time must also be allocated for processing or assembly, inspection, and the correction of deficiencies such as shortages and rework. In addition, there are often some design changes and combining of operations, among other problems, to achieve smooth performance and meet schedules.

Another responsibility of PC is to determine the maximum and minimum quantities of material required to maintain and sustain production profitably. To do this, the most efficient processes and operations to be carried out must be evaluated, and then specified in detail. Machines and equipment must be operated under conditions that will result in their maximum utilization.

This means that production or time standards must be brought up to date for each machine, operation, job or activity that will be involved with the customer's order. Since these standards are the basis of most cost estimates, budgets, and pricing, PC must avoid the possibility that they are artificial or out of date, or that they do not relate adequately to the current sales order.

The need for accuracy in this critical step of production planning and scheduling cannot be overemphasized. Yet it is frequently ignored or minimized with disastrous results. Because the plant capacity is based on the combined total of individual processes, multiplying an erroneous figure by other factual ones inevitably results in false data and misleading information.

Machine availability and capacity are determined and then coordinated to furnish the means by which the order will be filled. After routing and scheduling are finalized, a master schedule may be prepared to supply the beginning and end dates for each operation or process for all orders.

With this plan, it is possible to anticipate some problem areas. Uneven distribution of work may be apparent, areas susceptible to or capable of change are more evident, and areas requiring additional labor, material, and process time come to light. It is highly likely there will be many changes and additions to the master schedule before production actually gets underway.

After the entire project has been approved by management, the authorization to begin operations may be issued with work and production orders to the departments involved. Material is then drawn from stores, and individual machines or production lines begin processing. Work is inspected and the project continues to completion on or before the scheduled date.

Except for the excessive number of details to be handled, bottlenecks, the continual need for expediting, and constant feedback to facilitate control of the process, this is essentially the role of PC. Very few departments in a plant are not in some way affected by PC. You may be able to participate most effectively by adopting the following procedures:

- Get advance information on expected and actual sales orders with which your department will be involved.
- Try to anticipate any changes in the steps or sequence of your operations so you can contribute to the planning, scheduling, and carrying out of the process. Figure out what these changes will mean in terms of time,

machines, material, labor, work space and costs. Plan how you would make the necessary changes.

- Make notes of factors and variables that must be considered in your department's operations. Include elements such as time standards, deliveries of materials to and from your area, and quality control.

- Review with PC the rights and wrongs of your department's performance on previous production orders. You want to continue doing the right things and avoid doing the wrong ones.

REASONS FOR PUTTING PLANT WORKERS ON SHIFTS

Although numerous problems can arise when management decides to put workers on shifts, for many types of manufacturing operations, the need is compelling. There are four common reasons for doing so:

1. *High demand for the product.* When demand exceeds the one-shift capacity of the plant, the workday must be extended to a second and possibly third shift.

2. *Greater utilization of capital equipment.* Some machines and equipment, because of their high cost compared to profit realized from each unit of production, may have to be operated almost continuously to justify their use.

3. *Continuous rather than batch operations.* Complex chemical or petrochemical processes in which raw materials do not become finished products for one or more days after starting the process, are examples of operations that require shift work.

4. *Products or services cannot be stored.* Utilities are good examples of plants whose outputs must be used when they are created. Some food processing plants are in a similar position.

GUIDELINES FOR ESTABLISHING AND CONDUCTING SHIFT OPERATIONS

Setting up a plant for shift operations is a major undertaking because of the need to acquire additional personnel and provide support services. Here are some guidelines on the problems and how to go about handling them:

- *Selecting workers.* Most workers feel they can choose their shift on the basis of seniority. Management, however, would prefer to assign workers so that shifts are more equally balanced with experienced personnel. One way around this problem is to rotate shifts so that workers take their turns at night work. Whatever the distribution of senior workers, additional workers must be hired and trained.

- *Appointing supervision.* Just as more workers are needed, so must more supervisors be acquired. Many plants feel that it is easier and less costly to train an employee familiar with the plant and its procedures to be a supervisor than to hire a supervisor from outside and teach him or her the operations. Some plants rotate their supervisors differently than the workers, thus avoiding chances of personality clashes from having the same workers and supervisor together for long periods of time.

- *Minimizing night shift operations.* The fewer projects undertaken on the night shifts, the less need for staffing and management control. Unit costs of products may already be higher on the night shifts because of shift premiums paid to workers.

- *Providing production department services.* Very few plants are willing to accept the combined cost of lost production and maintenance expense caused by equipment and machine breakdowns on the night shifts. The only practical answer is to schedule one or more multiskilled maintenance workers to each of the night shifts, with fill-in work assignments to be carried out if production operations run smoothly.

- *Assuring food service.* Most workers will bring their own lunches to the night shifts and depend upon the plant's vending machines for beverages, snacks, and candy. A problem arises, however, when a worker stays over from one shift to another and has no opportunity to have a meal. Management has three options:

1. Permit the employee to go to an outside restaurant.
2. Arrange for catering service on each shift.
3. Stock frozen dinners and furnish a microwave oven at the plant to enable employees to serve themselves.

CONTENDING WITH PROBLEMS ARISING FROM MORE THAN ONE SHIFT

Shift work is very common today in manufacturing plants. By operating the plant "around the clock," management is able to get the most from the company's investment in machines and equipment. However, when the plant operates with more than one shift, you have some special problems to contend with:

- *Communicating.* Projects and jobs extended from one shift to another are susceptible to delays and getting off course because of poor or inadequate passing of information. You must be sure you give complete instructions in the logbook and include the status of an ongoing project at shift change time. What may be clear to you working with a process on your shift may not be clear to the supervisor who is going to take your place.

- *Safety*. Workers on night shifts are more prone to have accidents than those on day shifts. Not only are the former more likely to be tired and less alert, poor lighting may make working conditions more hazardous.

- *Worker attitudes*. Nightworkers frequently are less enthusiastic about their jobs. They may have been forced to work off-shifts because they didn't have enough seniority to hold a day-shift job. Some may also be working a second job to make ends meet. Whatever, they need more attention to ensure they maintain their productivity.

- *Experience and training*. When seniority prevails, workers on night shifts often consist of beginners or relatively inexperienced personnel. Recognizing this, you must try to keep those workers fully informed on plant rules and regulations, changes in operating procedures, and daytime activities in which they can participate.

  Tip: Showing films or videotapes in the plant cafeteria at lunch times are excellent ways to give nightworkers additional training.

- *Cooperating*. While promoting competition between shifts is a good way to increase productivity, gaining cooperation to smooth out operations and solve process problems is just as important, if not more so. At the end of your shift, always make an effort to leave the plant and the equipment in better condition than you found it. Make sure your workers clean up spills promptly and return tools and equipment to their proper storage places.

11

Guidelines to Plant Design and Material Flow to Improve Plant Workers' Efficiency

WAYS TO MAKE CHANGES IN PLANT LAYOUT

If you are asked to move your department to another area of the plant or to a different building, would you know how to proceed? Rather than just plan on moving everything from its present location to its same relative position in the new site, you should make a serious attempt to improve the efficiency and productivity of your department.

Among the benefits you could possibly gain through a better layout are improved safety and fewer accidents, less handling of materials, lower inventories, more efficient utilization of space, less work in process, and better morale of workers. To make these benefits a reality, you should start by doing the following:

- Map the flow of material and parts through the present area. Note any backtracking, bottlenecking, and process delay points that exist. Look for ways to eliminate or reduce them.
- Check for similar operations being performed in more than one area of the department. Determine if they can be combined or simplified.
- Study each operation and process step for its worth. Consider whether a job can be done another way or in another place.

By preparing a new flow chart based on what you have learned from your study, you will have a guide for setting up operations in the new location. The next step is to make scale model templates to represent each item to be moved, and give each one an identifying number. Now you are ready to go through the steps of making an equipment layout in the new location. Here are some suggestions on how to do it:

1. On a scale drawing of the new floor space, indicate the aisles, exits and entrances, building columns, and other basic features of the area. Allow a minimum width of 2 feet for pedestrian aisles; 3 feet for aisles in and around machinery; and 9 feet for two-way vehicular traffic such as lift trucks.

2. Place and move the templates within the boundaries of the proposed layout to indicate the new flow of material and work in process. When trying different arrangements, consider positioning several machines in such a way that one worker can tend more than one machine. Plan, if possible, to also have workers share the same work tables, feeders, auxiliary equipment, tools, and other common-use items.

3. Try to arrange work stations, machines, and equipment in a line that is conducive to even and smooth flow, reasonably compact yet accessible, and one that does not backtrack. Be sure to include ergonomic features in the design to reduce the number of movements of the workers and to make tools and controls easy to reach.

4. After the machines and equipment have been optimally arranged for safety and productivity, add walls, noise barriers, protective screens and other structures to provide safety, health, and industrial security. Mark the layout with each item's identifying number to facilitate recognition and later installation.

5. When the proposed layout appears complete, ask managers and employees to comment on it. Check out suggested changes for feasibility, practicality, and cost. Revise the layout accordingly.

6. Plan to relocate during low production periods or during plant downtime, as far as possible. Decide what equipment you need to purchase or rent for making the move, and make arrangements for standbys and replacements to minimize delays in moving and production.

HOW TO GET EMPLOYEES INVOLVED IN PLANT LAYOUT AND DESIGN

If plant management decides to add a new building, expand the existing facilities, or relocate particular machines and equipment, you should try to get employees to contribute to the appropriateness of the layout and design. You and the design engineer should ask for suggestions and recommendations from workers who will be involved and from personnel who will carry out various functions in the addition or relocated workplace.

Many helpful ideas on improving material flow can come from such discussions. Because an outside consultant, who has previous experience and a technical background, can recommend the most efficient layout, the plant engineer might consider employing one. However, the potential talent, capabilities, and direct experience of certain plant employees should not be overlooked. Here is how you can tap these valuable sources of help and information:

- Keep employees informed on proposed expansions, additions, and relocations. Not only do most employees want to be "in the know" about such things, they also may wish to participate in such ventures. This is especially true when their jobs or the work they do will be affected by the change.

- Ask for their suggestions and comments on proposed layouts and design, particularly as to positions of instrumentation and controls. Operators of machines and equipment know better than anyone else the critical operational steps, how machines respond, and what machines must be closely controlled.

- To sell them on becoming involved, point out how good design and layout can make their jobs easier. An example of this is the recognition of the need for service. For example, oil and lubrication points on machines must be easily accessible, or maintenance personnel may need considerable working room for making major repairs or for removing large machine components.

Tip: There is an additional benefit to be realized by getting employees involved in plant layout and design: it's an axiom that employees are always more cooperative and industrious on projects with which they have had an input. It's human nature to work hard to make such projects successful.

UNDERSTANDING MATERIAL HANDLING AND MATERIAL FLOW[1]

One of the clearest ways to get the true meaning of materials handling and material flow is to study the procedures and processes in a manufacturing plant. Such a study will reveal that four elements of a manufacturing process are involved:

---

[1]Portions of this section contain information and data presented in "What Is Material Handling?" *The Safe Foreman*, January 1986, The United Safety Service, Inc.

1. *Space.* Whether it's used or unused, storage space costs money. Materials and their flow dictate space requirements and control of inventory.

2. *Movement.* Raw materials, parts, in-process and finished products must be moved from one place to another. Material handling is the process of moving them in the safest and most efficient manner.

3. *Quantity.* The amount of material needed at each step in the manufacturing process varies with the type and kind of product. The purpose of a material-handling function is to supply each step with the exact quantity of the right material.

4. *Timeliness.* Materials and supplies must be available at the moment they are needed at each step in the manufacturing process. Material handling techniques must be such that no worker or process operation will be hampered by having material arrive at the workplace too early or too late.

These four elements should not be considered independently because each affects the others. To design an efficient material-handling system requires that you coordinate all the elements so that their overall performance results in smooth, effective, and safe material handling and flow.

HANDLING THE PROBLEM OF FLOOR SPACE UTILIZATION

The utilization of plant floor space is always a matter of concern to management. Like finished product inventories, too much or too little is costly. So designers and planners should target for the right kind of space of the right amount in the right place at the right time and for the right cost. But these objectives are seldom achieved in their entirety and also are very fleeting. The minute you attain them, conditions change, and you are then out of balance.

Large open spaces tend to improve the utilization of space. So do large column spacings, consistency of floor levels, and freedom from obstructions. Straight aisles generally improve space utilization, however, aisles against walls cost space because they serve only one side. Aisles against columns usually save space, except when the space along the column lines can be used effectively for built-in conveyors, storage of tools, or instrument panels, and they are better protected if backed out of the way against the column line.

In rapidly growing plants, it's often a good idea to provide more space than is currently needed. This reduces the frequency of building projects, the disruption of operations, and the likelihood of having to give up an opportunity to accept a large order or major contract. Additionally, empty plant space puts pressure on the company's marketing department to come up with sales orders that will fully utilize the plant's capacity.

Coping with Complaints of Not Enough Working Space for Employees

Whenever a new building is to be constructed, a department relocated, or a new process installed, the comments of plant employees should be solicited as soon as the project is announced. This procedure should also be continued during the planning and design steps of the proposed project.

You can get your workers to contribute to the development of such projects by having them review layout plans as they are developed. Studying these plans may reveal problems in the proposed design that can be eliminated on paper now, rather than in remodeling installations later. It is especially wise to investigate thoroughly any "not enough working space" complaints. Typical examples are:

- The complaint of the production worker that there is no place to store materials.
- The complaint of the maintenance worker about the limited accessibility of production machinery and building facilities for lubrication, repair, and removal.
- The complaint of the shipping and receiving workers who feel squeezed between the flow of incoming raw materials and outgoing products.

The best way to resolve such problems is to invite involved employees to group discussions with designers, engineers, and supervisors. If suggestions for changes are practical and feasible but involve additional expense, they should be passed to higher management for authorization to incorporate them.

MATERIAL-HANDLING FUNCTIONS AND OPERATIONS

If you were to observe material flow from where material enters the plant to where it leaves as a finished product, you would see that five different functions take place. These functions usually do not change or alter a material but are simply performed within the manufacturing process. As an example, many plants use various conveyors to move parts and products through ovens, dryers, paint booths, and other processing facilities. The material handling functions are:

1. *Receiving.* The activities that take place at the plant receiving dock such as inspecting, unloading, and moving materials to other locations constitute material handling.

2. *Storing and warehousing.* Material may be put in warehouses, store-rooms, or staging areas in preparation for immediate use. Material or parts being processed may be put in bins, or shelves, or temporarily on conveyors.

3. *Delivery to the process or worksite.* Material may be moved many times between departments, to process areas, and to individual workplaces. This may be done by lift trucks, hand trucks, conveyors, or other equipment.

4. *Handling at machines.* Manual feeding of material into a machine and disposal of the machine's output, in some cases, has accounted for more than half of the operations in a work cycle.

5. *Labeling and packaging.* These finishing operations represent the final step in material handling. The manner of their handling can have important effects on the ease and promptness with which products are shipped out of the plant.

HOW TO PROMOTE EMPLOYEES' UNDERSTANDING OF EFFICIENT MATERIALS FLOW

Using the right methods is the key to efficient materials flow. The methods should be selected on the basis of the materials' characteristics and flow requirements. But analysis and experience are required to design a system and select the best material-handling methods.

To ensure that plant employees understand the correct ways to handle materials and the importance of their correct handling to plant efficiency, call their attention to the following requisites:

• To provide the *right amount* of material, you must base lot sizes and load sizes on throughput and storage requirements. You must also minimize safety stocks and eliminate hidden stocks.

• To provide material in the *right condition* relates to control of quality. The materials-handling system must be designed to protect material and parts and to minimize damage and spoilage.

• To provide materials in the *right sequence* requires planning. For example, proper sequencing is critical to efficient order picking and palletizing.

• To provide materials in the *right orientation* requires physical positioning of material for both automated and manual transfers. Many of the warehouse operations are devoted to regaining proper orientation of parts, packages, and containers.

• To provide materials at the *right place* requires well thought-out storage systems and computer-generated locator systems.

- To provide materials at the *right time* demands precise scheduling. Furnishing them too soon can be just as disruptive and expensive as providing them too late.

- To provide materials at the *right cost* requires taking a systems view of economics. For example, minimizing materials-handling costs is the wrong objective of these functions. Maximizing profits is the right objective.

The Importance of the Right Place

For optimum use of floor space and efficient material flow, it is necessary that materials used in the process be put in the right place. You must make two decisions to meet these objectives:

1. *Where storage is needed in the process, if at all.* In a continuous manufacturing process, most plants prefer raw materials storage to storage of in-process materials, and in-process storage to finished products storage.
2. *Whether to use centralized storage or distributed storage.* Both have advantages and disadvantages depending on the application and the layout of the plant.

Customarily, arriving materials are placed in temporary locations or staging areas, and then later moved to storage. Regardless of whether they have assigned or randomized storage locations, for maximum efficiency, they should be placed in the right place. Equally important, locations should immediately be entered in the plant's locator system.

Assuring that materials are handy to workers is an example of why the right place is important. From an ergonomic viewpoint, when materials are placed within easy reach, stooping, bending, and stretching can be avoided. It is just as essential to ergonomically design a work station for a process worker as it is to assign materials to storage locations for an order picker.

Tip: Walk through your department periodically to look for instances in which materials are in the wrong places. Then take action to make matters right. You will be contributing greatly to the safety and productivity of your workers, as well as to the efficiency of your department's operations.

HOW ERGONOMICS IMPROVES PLANT WORKERS' EFFICIENCY

Ergonomics is the science concerned with the relationship of a person to the workplace. Known also as human engineering, it deals with the interactions between workers and machines, and their work environment. Two reasons why it has recently received so much attention in manufacturing plants are safety and efficiency.

Despite advances in automation, many material-handling procedures in today's plants still demand physical dexterity and skill on the part of the workers. Preparing solutions, for example, involves manual handling of bags and drums of raw materials. In addition, many packaging and warehouse operations include lifting, placing, and positioning materials on scales and conveyors.

Improper lifting technique and overexertion are common causes of back injury. An underlying cause of all too many back injuries is a poorly designed workstation or job method that forces the worker into a compromised lifting position. As a result, even seemingly innocuous lifting tasks take on increased factors of risk.

Fatigue from repeated motion is also common in many plant jobs. Not only is the worker's efficiency affected, the monotony of an effort becomes a problem because it may lull the individual into becoming careless. A worker may even become reckless, just to break the monotony.

Designing jobs to fit almost all employees and to reduce repetitiveness takes many forms. You need to design jobs for the best posture and avoid twisting and bending motions. That and teaching employees how to lift properly will enable you to improve their efficiency.

Why You Should Apply Ergonomics to Plant Workers' Jobs

It will be important in the 1990s to learn how to apply ergonomics to jobs in your plant. Here is what practicing ergonomics can do for you and your plant:

- You will be able to reduce injuries and illnesses of your workers.
- Your costs for workers compensation will drop with the reduction of injuries and illnesses.
- Your workers will be safer, healthier, and more productive.
- You will be complying with federal guidelines on ergonomics.

To assure that you are giving ergonomics the attention it deserves, start reading and studying publications on the subject. Also consider videotaping plant workers' jobs to analyze them for repetitive, stressful motions. Then take corrective action wherever it can be applied.

More than 50 books, courses, computer software programs, training videos, and other educational resources have been compiled and are available from the National Safety Council through its *Ergonomics Masterfile*. In effect, National Safety Council is providing a free, one-stop "shopping" catalog for ergonomics information. From wall posters on avoiding back injuries to a three-day intensive course on occupational ergonomics, if the organization has it, it's in this brochure. For your free copy of *Ergonomics Masterfile*, call 800-621-7619, ext. 1300.

IMPROVING THE SAFETY OF PLANT WORKERS WHO HANDLE MATERIALS

Manual handling of material accounts for more than 20 percent of all occupational injuries. Mechanical handling causes fewer accidents, but they are generally of greater severity. Adequate training of workers, proper selection of equipment, and careful use of space reduce the number of injuries when handling materials by either mechanical or manual methods. Here is how you can eliminate or minimize injuries from handling materials:

- Train workers how to correctly grip and properly lift loads.
- Caution them on lifting too heavy a load. Tell them to get help.
- See that workers are trained in the use of mechanical handling equipment.
- Provide them protective clothing and equipment appropriate for the jobs they are doing.

Since much material handling takes place in shipping, receiving, and warehouse operations, these areas deserve special attention. You should see that workers are trained in the proper and safe operation of lift trucks, hoists, conveyors, and dock functions. The best way to do that is to arrange for training and instructing of workers by the vendors and manufacturers of this equipment.

In addition to equipment-handling hazards, plant workers may be exposed to dangerous materials. The right-to-know laws require that all employees be made aware of hazardous materials to which they might be exposed. This is done through labeling of containers and the issuance of Material Safety Data Sheets. See Chapter 9 of this book for more information on handling dangerous materials.

BENEFITS AND ADVANTAGES OF EFFICIENT MATERIAL HANDLING

Although material handling is primarily a service function, it directly affects the cost of operating the plant. Thus, you should be continually looking for ways to improve it. Here are the major benefits and advantages to the plant and employees of efficient material handling:

1. *Safer working conditions.* Fewer injuries and accidents occur when workers use proper and well maintained equipment for handling materials. Efficient equipment and work methods reduce worker fatigue and stress, also leading to fewer accidents.

2. *Increased productive capacity.* Production control is easier and more effective when material flow is constant and smooth. Eliminating delays and reducing downtime in handling materials results in higher productivity of workers and increased efficiency of machines.

3. *Less scrap and waste.* Proper and efficient material handling cuts losses of material by minimizing spills, damage in transit or storage, and spoilage.

4. *Reduced operating costs.* Efficient material handling reduces the cost of space by enabling you to use it to the best advantage. When materials are handled efficiently, inventories are easier to control, resulting in fewer surpluses and less outages.

HOW TO SELECT A LIFT TRUCK

The lift truck is one of the most widely used items of material-handling equipment in today's plants. It evolved as a means of permitting individual parts and materials to be handled together as one large unit. Choosing the right lift truck for your department or the plant may not be an easy job because of the many factors involved. You have to decide which of the many features you need and what will work best under the specific conditions in your plant. But don't be in a hurry to call a lift truck dealer or manufacturer. You can save yourself time and be more assured of making the best choice by first assembling the following data and information:

- *The type of truck you prefer.* Determine, for example, how the truck will be powered. Environmental and economic factors may dictate the choice of electric or internal combustion power.

- *The conditions under which the truck will operate.* Consider whether it will operate indoors, outdoors, or both, and if it must be capable of traveling up ramps and inclines. Solid tires are fine on smooth indoor surfaces; however, pneumatic tires give better traction on rough or irregular terrain.

- *The loads to be moved and lifted.* Load weights and dimensions are critical to design, as is the height to which loads will be lifted. Capacity will be affected if load-lifting attachments are required.

- *The maneuverability and durability required.* Consider how many loads and lifts the truck will handle in a day. Look into aisle width and turning radius that will be required. Determine the height of the lowest overhead obstruction in the travel area.

After gathering this information, you will be better prepared to select the right lift truck for your plant.

TECHNIQUES FOR PROPER AND SAFE LIFT TRUCK HANDLING BY PLANT EMPLOYEES

By incorporating techniques for accident prevention and traffic control in operating lift trucks, not only will worker safety be increased, but plant operations are likely to be carried out in a more efficient manner. If you supervise drivers of lift trucks or are responsible for the maintenance and care of lift trucks, take steps to ensure the trucks are properly equipped for use in the plant. Also make sure that plant employees, and drivers in particular, understand the following:

- Lift trucks are generally steered by the rear wheels, thus demanding a special driving technique. Only the driver to whom a lift truck is assigned is permitted to operate it. Under no circumstances may other persons ride with the driver.

- When transporting a load, the forks should be within 2 inches of the floor. With this position, the driver has a better view and damage to materials that may be caused by stopping suddenly are prevented.

- Where a load obstructs the driver's view, the truck should be driven in reverse so the load is behind the driver. This is also the safest way to drive a truck down a steep ramp.

- Lift trucks should be equipped with backup alarms, which are activated either mechanically or electrically. A mechanical alarm is generally mounted on a wheel and sounds at every quarter turn. The electric type is wired directly into the backup light circuit and gives off an electronic sound when the vehicle is shifted into reverse.

- If the lift truck operating area is noisy, it's a good idea to mount revolving lights, horns, and other audible warning devices on the vehicle. These devices can help make vehicles more noticeable to other workers. Mirrors can also aid a driver to see more of the surrounding area.

- One of the most important features of a lift truck is its turning radius, which helps establish operational clearances such as at intersecting aisles. Small lift trucks need a radius of at least 6 feet to turn.

- A lift truck accident in the plant can cause just as much injury to the driver and other employees as an accident on the highway. Therefore, aisles, traffic lanes, and driving habits in the workplace should follow the same rules of the road used on highways.

MAKING SURE LIFT TRUCK OPERATORS RECEIVE TRAINING

Since accidents involving powered industrial trucks are both numerous and severe, you must assure that operators of lift trucks in the plant receive proper and adequate training before they are permitted to drive. Among other purposes, training is intended to:

1. Clarify the differences in handling between a truck and a car.
2. Develop safe operating habits.
3. Explain the consequences of taking certain kinds of chances.
4. Reduce the risk of injury to pedestrians as well as operators.

Regardless of how much experience a potential lift truck operator has, all new drivers should go through an initial training course, followed by a refresher course every two years. Most truck dealers can offer training or assistance in obtaining it. Vocational schools in your area may also offer training courses. In addition, you can obtain a training package from DuPont that combines videotape instruction with interactive, self-study training. Whatever, the training that operators receive should include:

- Inspecting the truck prior to use.
- The function and proper use of truck controls.
- General truck loading practices.
- Traveling and cornering speeds.
- How to load and unload highway trucks and trailers.
- How to load and unload railroad cars.
- Working in hazardous environments or with hazardous materials.
- Precautions when leaving a truck unattended.
- Refueling and recharging operations.
- Procedure when truck defects are found.

For maximum safety, trainees should also be instructed to:

- Stop at blind corners.
- Keep safe distances.

- Don't pass at intersections.
- Keep to the right of way without getting too close to other workers.

HOW ROBOTS AID IN MATERIAL HANDLING

Material handling is the most common of all robotic applications because it employs to its full advantage the flexibility of robots. Decisions about whether to install robots should be based in large part on the need for flexibility, along with dexterity and repeatability. Modern articulated robots are extremely dexterous, having at least five axes of motion. Fitted with the proper grippers, they can grab, hold, and transport many products and parts and manipulate them precisely.

Further, robots can be reprogrammed as material-handling needs change. This adaptability is vital when you realize that an all-electric robot can operate for an average of 10 years before it must be rebuilt. But this does not mean that robots are cost effective and efficient for all plant applications.

If a production run is complex with a low volume of finished products, manual labor is usually most efficient, especially if working conditions are comfortable. On the other hand, if a large volume of products with easy-to-handle parts and high speed essential, the robot is the answer.

Since electric robots can easily handle parts weighing up to 200 pounds, the decision of what size to install may be more a function of reach than of strength. Yet the need for repeatability and flexibility remains the primary considerations. This is especially true when a robot is not simply handling materials, but also transporting those materials to other machines. Then, tolerances are measured in thousandths of inches.

INSTRUCTING PLANT EMPLOYEES WHO WORK WITH ROBOTS

The highest percentage of robot-related accidents occur during programming, teaching, and maintenance. During these times, the accident risk is the greatest. Persons who perform these tasks are usually those who are most familiar with and comfortable around robots. Their danger awareness is low, and they ignore or circumvent established safety barriers or devices. Awareness, however, is vital to the safety of all employees.

Instructing plant employees who work with robots should begin with identifying the hazards and assessing the risks. Three types of robotic hazards exist:

1. Being struck by a moving part of the robot or items carried by the robot. This hazard is caused by an unexpected movement of the robot; it may be intensified by the robot's speed of operation.

2. Being trapped by movements of the robot in relation to fixed objects such as machines or posts, or by the movement of auxiliary equipment such as pallets, transfer mechanisms, or work carriages. If trapping points exist, they should be marked in an obvious way.

3. Being exposed to electric shock, burns, radiation, arc flash, and toxic substances. These hazards are those that develop from the application

Since the potential for creating hazards with robots always exists, safety planning and instruction should concentrate on the safeguards: any guard, device, interlock, or procedure that protects workers from the hazards associated with robots. The application and type of robot determines which ones should be used. For example, safeguards for hydraulic robots differ from those for electric robots. The danger of fire and pressure leaks is greater with hydraulic robots.

Your instruction should include a discussion of what a robot is, how it works, and what to do if a fault occurs. All training programs should stress the following:

- Do not assume a robot is not going to move at any time.
- Do not assume a robot repeating a pattern will continue to do so.
- Maintain an awareness of the hazards of a moving robot system.

See Chapter 7 of this book for more information on the safe operation of robots.

AUTOMATIC GUIDED VEHICLE SYSTEMS: INTELLIGENT MATERIAL HANDLERS

Automatic guided vehicle systems (AGVS) are a form of industrial automation that has proven its worth in thousands of plants worldwide. Today's AGVSs carry, transport, lift, transfer, position, and communicate. Through the use of electronic technology, they have become intelligent material handlers. Here are just a few of the ways they are used in manufacturing plants:

- To move incoming materials to remote storage points and picked orders to the shipping dock.
- To move parts between machining centers.
- To pick up and deliver pipe, structurals, castings, and other material in yards and warehouses.
- To supply kits and piece parts on assembly lines.

The trend of manufacturers today is to put more intelligence at the decision locations of AGVs. If the decision locations are static, you can put the intelligence in the floor. If they are mobile, you can put the controls on the vehicle. Also, the AGV manufacturers vary in the way they set up their systems for communicating from one vehicle to another and from the vehicles to the dispatch station, local control or central processor.

Barrett Electronics, for instance, uses one buried wire as both guide path and antenna for communications. The vehicles are in constant communication with each other, and thus don't run into each other at intersections or overtake one another on the same path. They also send a signal to the dispatcher or to a screen that shows their status on a path diagram.

There is also considerable sophistication in manufacturers' optical or chemical guidance systems in that much electronic know-how is put into the electronics that interpret the marks on the floor. Simple optical systems follow a white line on the floor that detects the difference between the white of the line and the dark of the floor. Other white marks are read as stops. Another optical method uses a chemical path or mark composed of a phosphorescent chemical. This is invisible under ordinary light but glows brightly when exposed to ultraviolet or black light.

The Litton Truckmobile's optical guidance system uses electronic proximity detection to avoid hitting obstacles, instead of a bumper system used on most wire-guided vehicles. Its proximity detection system uses a limited radio field to detect objects. The antennas are sensitive up to 18 inches ahead of the vehicle.

Some control systems are easier to upgrade than others. While many require simple programming changes that the user can make with the plant's dispatch keyboard, others require the system manufacturer to make the changes and incorporate them into a chip. The chip must then be added to the controller.

Advantages and Disadvantages of Automatic Guided Vehicle Systems

Properly designed automatic guided vehicle systems can result in substantial improvements in materials handling operations in manufacturing plants. The major benefits include:

- More flexible use of floor space, and freeing up of space previously dedicated to rigid handling equipment.
- Computer integration and control of the materials-handling function.
- Increased flexibility in the assembly process, resulting in improved product quality.
- Lower costs for unit material handling.
- Improved ergonomics for assembly workers and materials handlers.

- Reduced material-handling-related damage.
- Lower material-handling equipment noise.

Despite these impressive benefits and advantages, the plant may still have to contend with some irritations when the decision is made to install an AGVS:

- Control software for AGV systems may be very complex and difficult to implement. Reprogramming may also not be easily accomplished.
- Debugging time for AGV systems can take a long time, often more than six months.
- Getting help from the vendor with on-site debugging and training of plant personnel may be almost impossible to achieve.
- Some plant materials handlers may be reluctant to rely on the new system if it replaces lift trucks.

For an AGVS to be a success, everyone involved—managers, engineers, workers, and the system vendor—must take a clear interest in and responsibility for it.

PROMOTING EMPLOYEE INGENUITY TO SOLVE MATERIAL HANDLING PROBLEMS

Some employees think that being inventive and showing ingenuity is something mysterious, and to have those skills you must be born that way. They are wrong about that. Any person can be ingenious if the person sets his or her mind to it. Granted, getting ideas and solving problems is not easy, particularly when you're trying very hard to do so.

Nevertheless, it pays to encourage employees to be inventive and innovative, especially when the plant is experiencing material handling problems. Solving a problem not only helps the company, it gives the employee a great deal of satisfaction as well as heightens his or her status in the eyes of management.

Since a systematic approach to solving problems usually gives the best results, you should suggest that an employee attack a problem in that manner. Tell the employee to take the following steps:

Step 1. Identify the problem specifically. For example, "Cartons on the packaging line are failing to remain sealed after application of the adhesive."

Step 2. Collect all information pertaining to the problem. For example, look for data on the operation of the equipment involved, the adhesive being used, ambient conditions, and the operation of applying the adhesive.

Step 3. List as many possible causes for the problems as you can. Something must have changed in the equipment, material, conditions, or procedure.

Step 4. Pick the cause or causes that seem most likely. Do this by a process of elimination. To test a cause to see if it is a probable one, try thinking out what difference it would make if that factor were changed.

Step 5. Suggest as many solutions for removing causes as are possible. There may be more than one way to solve the problem. The point is to list all possibilities.

Step 6. Evaluate the pros and cons of each proposed solution. Some may be better than others in being faster, cheaper, or surer. Evaluation requires you to make judgments based on facts.

Step 7. Choose the solution you think is best or most likely to solve the problem. For example, if you think from your investigation that the adhesive may have lost its tackiness, try a new lot to see if the cartons then remain sealed.

12

How to Handle Plant Inventories and Promote Just-in-Time Operations

THE IMPORTANCE AND NECESSITY OF INVENTORY CONTROL

Although few plant functions are more difficult and challenging to perform efficiently and profitably then inventory control, few processes are more apt to limit the profits of the plant. If you underestimate your stores needs, you run the risk of stopping production because parts or materials are not available when needed. On the other hand, if you overstock, you pay the price in space, insurance, obsolescence, spoilage, damage, excess handling, and other inventory and maintenance costs. Tighter inventory management is necessary if manufacturing plants are to solve the problem, especially since it is more achievable than ever before through the use of computers.

One of the best ways to implement better inventory control is to adopt the Japanese approach referred to as *just-in-time (JIT) management*. This strategy, currently used by Ford, General Motors, Firestone, and other leading U.S. manufacturers, is based on stockpiling as needed. Materials and parts are scheduled for delivery by suppliers to fit scheduled units of production, such as cars, machines, or appliances with no extras.

The Japanese have learned that they can operate many of their plants with no warehouses and only small storerooms. Parts and materials are moved directly to processes and production lines as they are received; finished products go directly to retail customers or distributors. While this procedure requires more deliveries and higher delivery costs for supplies, the costs are minimal when compared to the savings realized.

An essential element for efficient just-in-time inventory control is close suppliers of parts and materials. Many Japanese plants are supplied from depots and parts manufacturers near their own manufacturing facilities. In the United States, we approach such arrangements with the numerous job shops and metal-working firms in Detroit and nearby cities to supply the automobile industry.

How to Improve Inventory Accuracy

In the last decade, many plants have been trying to improve the accuracy of their inventory records. The main reason for this effort is their attitude toward inventories. They have learned that much of their traditional attitude toward inventories is obsolete. Japan has demonstrated that many types of production can be carried out with very little inventory above current needs. Thus, most U.S. plants could cut their inventories drastically.

The easiest way to make reductions, both in purchased materials and work-in-process, is through better systems of production and control. Such systems, however, require record accuracy of at least 95 percent to be effective. To do that, you must make a major effort to update bills of materials, extensively train plant employees, and implement new procedures in stocking and picking. Your efforts should also include a complete analysis of the materials-handling system.

Advances in materials-handling technology have provided equipment and systems that improve inventory accuracy. Automated storage and retrieval systems, both for unit loads and small parts, are examples of this technology. So also are several other types of automated storage equipment, including case pickers and computer-controlled carousels.

These systems, by furnishing secure storage areas, virtually eliminate theft, lost materials, and unauthorized withdrawals. They also furnish up-to-date inventory information on every item in the system. The accuracy level is so high that, in many plants, systems such as these have eliminated the need for taking physical inventories.

Inventory accuracy has been improved also by the use of automatic identification systems. These systems can be used in receiving, storage, processing, or at any other point in the material-handling cycle to routinely achieve accuracy levels close to 100 percent.

GUIDELINES ON AUTOMATED STORAGE AND
MATERIAL HANDLING SYSTEMS

If your management decides to automate the plant's storage and material-handling facilities, there won't be any problem in finding a system that meets the plant's requirements. To handle unit loads, there are automated storage/retrieval systems (AS/RS), car-in-lane systems, stacker cranes, and man-ride machines. To handle small parts, there are miniload AS/RS, small man-ride, orderpicking machines, and horizontal and vertical carousels.

With the ever increasing need to reduce inventory levels, more and more plants are considering and adopting just-in-time (JIT) operations. The aim of these is to receive material at the plant as frequently as possible, one or more times a day if practical, to meet that day's or several hours' manufacturing needs.

Running the process or assembly line with JIT deliveries, however, does not mean there won't be a need to store materials in the plant. With few exceptions, plants simply can't operate without some spare or surge material, to keep production running when one or more machines or processes are down for a short time.

As you reduce inventories, you must be able to move materials from storage to the workplace in the plant very quickly. Thus, the connection between the storage system and the delivery equipment becomes critical. With systems that require workers for picking and stocking, they typically serve as the connection by placing tote boxes or containers on conveyors for delivery to the point of use. But in unit load AS/RS where no workers are needed, the connection should be automated, either through the use of robots, automatic guided vehicles (AGVs), or other automated transfer equipment.

The type of transfer equipment used in the plant depends on a number of factors: the size and shape of the parts, production rates, and the frequency of equipment changeover and setup to handle different products. Although the unit load AS/RS is usually associated with pallet load storage, these systems can store a wide variety of loads and large parts or products. They also can act on or communicate automatically with a number of different types of conveyors and other transportation equipment. Additionally, they can operate with a minimum of human supervision.

The only place a worker is needed is to enter load identification information to the system control computer through a keyboard or by using a portable scanner. Once that information is known, material can be routed from storage to production and back again, or to a different storage system, all automatically.

AS/RS is an efficient and relatively safe method of storing material. The labor cost per item handled is low, while the activity rate and the volume and weight capacity per square foot of floor area are high. Human contact with material in motion is limited, and reaching and bending is minimized.

The Role of the Computer

Automated storage and material-handling systems couldn't exist without the computer. Computers are the brains of automated plants. They keep track of what's going on where and when, picking up information from the plant work areas through scanners and other automatic identification equipment; they transmit information to production workers through printers and visual displays. In addition, they can also control the operation of the material-handling and production equipment.

Almost all unit load AS/RS in plants today are fully computer controlled. Usually the control systems consist of a combination of minicomputers and programmable controllers. Working with scanners, photoelectric sensors, and other devices, the computers track the flow of incoming loads across a conveyor, for example, assign a storage location to each load, and then control the movement of the AS/RS machines to put away and retrieve the loads.

INDUSTRIAL BAR CODING: AID TO MANAGING INVENTORIES

One of the most important advances in technology in American industry is the use of bar codes for systematic data collection. It is promoted by the need for accurate and timely data gathered from the manufacturing, inspection, transportation, and inventory cycles of a plant operation.

The black and white bars that you see on grocery and household items in your supermarket represent a unique identification for that product. This symbol, called the *Universal Product Code* (UPC) is the standard for the grocery industry and has been in existence since 1973. Bar codes have received overwhelming acceptance because they offer the simplest, most accurate, and most cost-effective approach for identifying objects by using reading machines (scanners).

One of the primary advantages of bar codes over other technologies is its low susceptibility to errors in data input. Most bar codes have built-in safeguards (check digits) to prevent incorrect scans from being entered, minimizing the possibility of errors.

Other advantages of bar coding are speed, timeliness, and cost efficiency. Scanning a bar code is faster than manually recording information or keying data into a terminal. Bar-coded information is often immediately transferred to a host computer. Real-time data collection enables timely information to be accessed almost instantly, when the data are still current. Also, improved efficiency can be realized by substituting bar code systems in place of manual systems, resulting in increased productivity and reduced labor costs.

Bar Code Scanner Applications in the Plant

There are many ways you can put bar codes to use in the plant, either with portable or stationary scanners. Portable units are powered by rechargeable or disposable batteries. Data is stored in memory for later transmissions by either direct link or phone line to a computer. The stationary contact scanners are often installed at work stations or assembly areas throughout the plant. They are usually connected directly to a master computer. Here are the most common bar code scanner applications in today's manufacturing plants:

- *Inventory control.* A computer can download a portable scanner with operator directives to facilitate activities such as order picking. By following the computer directives, an operator would proceed to the location displayed on the unit, use the bar code to scan the shelf tab item code, enter a quantity from a menu tablet and proceed to the next picking location. At the end of the picking cycle, the gathered data is transmitted to the main computer where inventory counts are updated and purchase orders to replenish stock are issued.

- *Property management.* This is another worthwhile application for a portable scanner. Operators using bar code readers can periodically walk through the plant and pass the wand over labels to establish and confirm current property. More and more accountants and property control personnel are doing this with the plant's machines, equipment, and tools.

- *Material control.* Stationary scanners can be used to perform work-in-process monitoring. A bar code label identifying each lot of material is attached to a container. As the material is processed through each workstation, the code is read and the process results are transmitted to a master computer. Real-time production information ensures that orders are delivered on time and that the product has been subjected to a thorough inspection operation.

- *Production.* Bar code labels located on parts being assembled can be scanned and the code numbers validated against an acceptable "build list" to insure the final product has all of its components.

- *Receiving/Shipping.* Scanners located at receiving and shipping stations can be used to record product movement. In addition, captured information at the point of transaction permits invoices to be verified and bills of lading generated that are based on actual quantities shipped. Back orders can be immediately routed to the shipping dock.

- *Job cost data.* You also can collect job cost data by scanning an employee's bar-coded ID badge, scanning a bar code menu of labor activities and scanning the unit toward which you direct the labor.
- *Tool crib management.* You can track who has which tool for how long and for what job. Knowing that the right tool is being used for a particular job and making sure that tools are returned are other benefits you gain from using bar codes. Engineering and maintenance departments also find bar coding very useful. Bar codes furnish information on replacement parts for machines, refueling, and preventive and predictive maintenance activities. You can be assured that the right part has been used for a job and that maintenance has been performed on a given piece of equipment.

Understanding Bar Code Label Standards

Label standards are different from other standards related to bar code that specify symbology and print quality. Label standards detail how the pattern of bars and spaces will express letters and numbers in a bar code symbol. Print quality standards state the minimum levels of reflectance, contrast, and other critical measures of printed bar code symbol readability. Information requirements covered by standards vary by industry. A serial number is important for some while a product weight is important for others.

Since more than 30 major industries already have written bar code label standards, at many companies a supplier's ability to meet the standards has become a part of its customer service. Label standards thus are becoming an important item in communicating data and information between a company and its customers.

When every shipment received at a company's dock carries the same information in exactly the same place on every package, you gain several benefits:

- Data collection accuracy is improved because workers know which bar code to scan at each receiving step.
- Labor requirements for data collection are lower.
- Time spent on receiving operations is less.
- Integration of data collection with other company operations is improved.

HOW TO GET PLANT EMPLOYEES' SUPPORT FOR INVENTORY MANAGEMENT

The better and more fully you explain inventory management to plant employees, the more effective and successful will be your effort to control it. To gain their support, you must ensure that they understand the principles and are knowledgeable with how automation and the use of the computer provide control. Make sure also that employees are aware of the justifications for computerizing the inventory management function. Supplying employees with such information will help you to get their cooperation in controlling the plant's inventories.

The best way to sell the importance of inventory management is to talk to employees about it at appropriate opportunities. Here are the important points you want to make:

- The ideal plant would operate with zero inventory. It would make products exactly when they're needed, even if each order called for only one item. While the ideal may be unattainable, anything that enables the plant to get closer to it is an improvement over present methods.

- Four steps that can be taken to manage inventory better are (1) improve scheduling, (2) shorten setup times, (3) upgrade quality, and (4) convert production operations to flexible manufacturing systems. Each step is important in itself, but the benefits from all increase significantly when programs are developed for each one.

- Technology is not a problem for U.S. manufacturing plants. They have the know-how to automate and create flexible manufacturing systems that are as advanced as those in Japan and anywhere else in the world.

- Up to the present, most of U.S. plant's efforts to reduce inventories have focused on better planning and better scheduling. But it is clear that much more needs to be done. Plants must be concerned with their total manufacturing systems and with new technologies. One of those is to adopt the principles of just-in-time operation.

CONVINCING PLANT EMPLOYEES THAT COMPUTERIZED INVENTORY CONTROL SAVES MONEY

Interest in applying the computer to inventory management in plants probably peaked a decade ago. Many hardware and software manufacturers have capitalized on this situation to the extent that there are many choices for both large and small users. Two points on this subject that you should make with employees are:

1. It is well worth the effort to computerize inventory management, even in small plants.
2. The return on investment and justification is quick and easy to realize in most cases.

Explain to employees that interest in control of the plant's inventory arose from the increased awareness of what it costs to carry or to stock inventory. Inventory represents idle money waiting for the opportunity to convert it back to cash. If the company borrowed money to manufacture or buy the inventory, the interest is also a cost.

It's easy to figure the cost of carrying inventory. Add up the plant's annual costs of space with utilities, taxes, insurance, obsolescence, and material handling. Divide the total by the average inventory dollars the plant carries during the year, and show the result as a percent. Add this percent to the current lending rate in the company's area. The resulting total is the plant's carrying cost. This percent—whether it is 30 or 40—converted to dollars, means that it costs the plant 0.30 or 0.40 dollar to carry each $1 of inventory. This is a good illustration of how the plant can save money by reducing its inventory.

To further promote the benefits of low inventories, say that both inventory and space values are subject to inflation; the plant can get in the position where more expensive materials take up more expensive space. In addition, the more inventory the plant has, the higher the handling costs.

Make a good closing argument for computerized inventory control by summing up the justifications: lower labor costs, improved throughput, better customer service, and easier inventory auditing.

HOW TO CONTROL INVENTORIES OF STORES MATERIALS

You can achieve significant savings in your plant by adopting good inventory control procedures in the handling of stores materials. Two points, however, should be understood by all persons concerned with developing and implementing inventory control procedures:

1. Inventory control does not necessarily mean keeping inventories at a minimum because the lowest possible inventory is often not the best or least costly in terms of total cost to the company.
2. Although the relative importance of various inventory control objectives may change with changes in business conditions, the need for effective control of inventories is constant.

The problems of inventory control are best solved by working out answers to the following questions:

• What items need to be ordered?
• When should an item be ordered?
• How much of an item should be ordered?
• From whom should the item be ordered?

These questions are not difficult to answer if you have specific data and information on each item stocked in the storeroom and you understand the various technical terms concerning its acquisition and replacement. The data and information on an item enables you to decide when an item should be ordered, and a formula can be used to decide how much should be ordered. What is required of you is to understand the technical terms and the reasoning that resulted in the formula. You also need to know what items are in the storeroom and what supplier will give you the best terms.

Understanding the Terminology of Inventory Control

Here are definitions of the most common technical terms involving stores and inventories, along with a short discussion on how these subjects fit into inventory control systems:

- *Annual usage.* The number of items withdrawn from stores over a period of one year. You need to know this figure in order to make an intelligent decision when to reorder because it takes time to get an item ordered, shipped, received, and put into the storeroom. Fluctuations in usage must also be analyzed. The more stable the usage rate, the less likelihood of a stockout.

- *Unit cost.* The price of an item at the time you order it. A formula that can be used to decide how much should be ordered includes its unit cost; you need to know this.

- *Lead time.* The length of time it takes to obtain a quantity of an item. It includes the time to process an order from when the need to reorder is identified, the time for the supplier to ship it, and the time you stock it in the storeroom. Lead time is not, as most commonly believed, the time from when the purchase order was issued to when the item is received.

- *Order cost.* The cost of issuing a purchase order for a certain quantity. It includes the cost of labor and overhead, paper, office machines, and postage (not only in the Purchasing Department, but also in other departments that go through the procedures of issuing the requisition, receiving the material, and delivering it to the storeroom).

- *Carrying cost.* The cost of storing an item in the storeroom. It includes the charge for floor space, depreciation, taxes, interest, and storeroom operating charges. The largest of these probably is the interest or the cost of money to the company. The next largest is the wages and fringe benefits of material control personnel matched by their overhead charges. The carrying cost figure is expressed as a percentage of the value of the average inventory on hand.

- *Safety stock level.* The amount of an item you have on hand to protect you from running out when the delivery of it is delayed or the usage is much higher than normal. Think of it as insurance: You don't want to use safety stock just like you don't want to use insurance. To determine the quantity of safety stock you want, consider the cost of not having it in terms of lost production and lowered maintenance craft productivity versus the cost of carrying the added inventory.

  The amount of material you would like to consider safety stock depends on the lead time for that item, its usage, and how critical it is to the production effort. If the lead time is very short, or the material is readily available from several sources and it is not critical to operations, you might opt for a zero safety stock level. If the lead time is longer and the material has only a few alternative sources in addition to having some degree of criticality, you should set the level at some minimum figure. If the lead time is relatively long, the material has a single source, and it is critical to plant operations (you can't afford to be without it), you would establish a maximum safety stock level.

- *Expedite point.* The point in the inventory level at which you begin to use your safety stock. At this point, you must follow up on delivery of an order previously placed to be sure it is received before you reach zero inventory. If you set the expedite point of an item at zero, you are saying that the item is not critical to the production effort; you are also making the decision that you don't need any safety stock.

- *Reorder level.* The low limit for the sum of the in-stock and on-order balances that is used to determine when to order another lot quantity. The reorder level is determined from data on usage and lead time. It is the lead time in months times the usage per month plus the safety stock level.

- *Reorder point.* The point in the inventory level when, if an order is placed, if the usage continues as expected, and if the lead time is as predicted, the order would be received concurrent with the inventory reaching the safety stock level.

- *Economic order quantity.* Calculated as the quantity that will result in the lowest total cost of ordering, making, or procuring the item, and carrying the resulting inventories. The theory of economical order quantity buying is that the cost of carrying inventory and the cost of buying are like balance scales: When one goes up, the other goes down.

- *Maximum level.* The sum of the stock on hand at the safety stock level (expedite point) plus the order quantity.

A pictorial illustration of many of these terms is shown in Figure 12-1. This is an order diagram showing actual inventory levels for a typical item that must periodically be reordered. A pictorial illustration of the reasoning

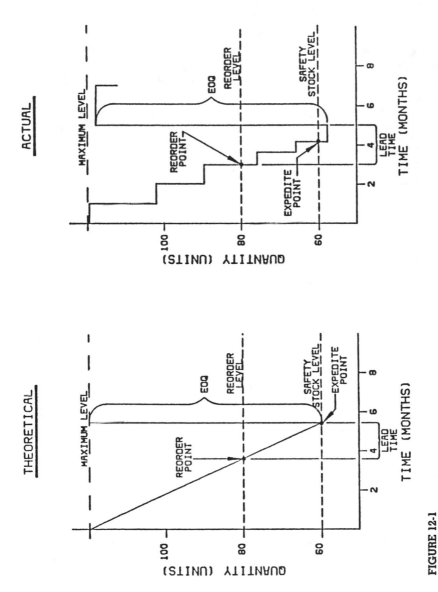

FIGURE 12-1

Theoretical and actual order diagram showing inventory levels for a typical item which periodically must be reordered.

behind the economical order quantity (EOQ) formula is shown in Figure 12-2.

Calculating an Economic Order Quantity

Note that the three curves in Figure 12-2 are identified as ordering cost, carrying cost, and total cost. What information was used to plot these curves? Here's an explanation: the *annual ordering cost* (OC) is equal to the cost for an order (A) times the number of orders in a year (S/Q). In other words:

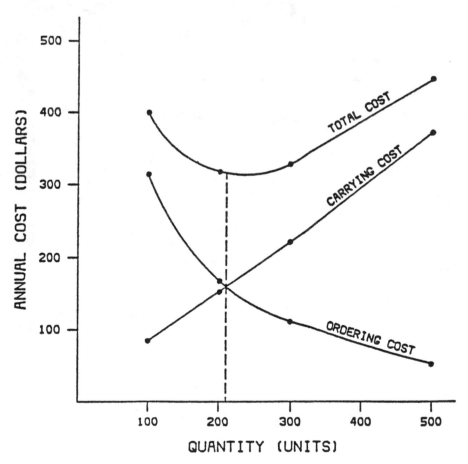

FIGURE 12-2
The interrelationship of ordering cost and inventory carrying cost as variations are made in the quantity ordered.

$$OC = A \times \frac{S}{Q}$$

where
OC = the ordering cost in dollars.

S = the annual usage in units.

A = the cost of issuing a purchase order in dollars.

Q = the quantity ordered in units.

If the cost of issuing a purchase order at your plant is $65 and the plant uses 500 a year of Item X, you could pick various numbers to order and get the ordering cost in dollars as follows:

S	A	Q	OC
500	65	100	325
500	65	200	163
500	65	300	108
500	65	500	65

By plotting OC against Q, you arrive at the ordering cost curve.

The *carrying cost curve*, actually a straight line, was derived in a similar procedure. The annual carrying cost (CC) is equal to the average quantity on hand ($Q/2$) × cost of carrying an item, where the cost of carrying an item is expressed as a percent of its value (IC). In other words:

$$CC = \frac{Q}{2} \times CI$$

where
CC = the carrying cost in dollars.

Q = the quantity ordered in units.

I = the inventory carrying cost as a decimal.

C = the unit cost in dollars.

If the inventory carrying cost at your plant is 30 percent or 0.3, and the unit cost of Item X is $5, you could pick various numbers to order and get the carrying cost in dollars as follows:

Q	C	I	CC
100	5	0.3	75
200	5	0.3	150
300	5	0.3	225
500	5	0.3	375

By plotting CC against Q, you arrive at the carrying cost curve.
    The total cost curve in Figure 12-2 is derived from the equation:

$$T = \frac{Q}{2} IC + \frac{SA}{Q}$$

where the symbols are the same as before. Thus,

$$\text{Total cost} = \text{Carrying cost} + \text{Ordering cost}$$

By plotting Ts, against Qs, you arrive at the total cost curve.
    Note that the minimum point of the total cost curve corresponds to a quantity where the carrying cost equals the ordering cost. This quantity is the *economic order quantity* (*EOQ*). When

$$\frac{Q}{2} IC = \frac{SA}{Q}$$

$$Q^2 = \frac{2SA}{IC}$$

$$EOQ = \frac{\sqrt{2SA}}{IC}$$

$$EOQ = \sqrt{\frac{2 \times 500 \times 65}{0.3 \times 5}}$$

$$EOQ = 208$$

Solving a Purchasing Problem

You have been buying maintenance materials for the plant. Periodically you have ordered some bearings to replace the storeroom stock as they are required on the pumps. The local vendor has been supplying them to you at $100 each when you order 12. But today when you phone him the order, he offers to let you have them at $90 each if you order 20. That's a 10 percent discount, but is it a good buy? How much would you save your company if you accepted the vendor's offer? To solve this problem, you should use the equation which applies to inventory control:

$$T = \frac{Q}{2} IC + \frac{SA}{Q}$$

You check the stores records to learn that the plant uses 25 of the bearings in a year's time. You know that it costs $65 to process a purchase order, and the inventory carrying cost in your plant is 30 percent of the value of the storeroom inventory.

Let T_1 = the total cost of your usual order

Let T_2 = the total cost of today's offer

$$T_1 = \frac{12}{2} \times 0.3 \times 100 + \frac{25 \times 65}{12}$$

$$T_1 = 180 + 135.4 = \underline{\$315.4}$$

$$T_2 = \frac{20}{2} \times 0.3 \times 90 + \frac{25 \times 65}{20}$$

$$T_2 = 270 + 81.2 = \underline{\$351.2}$$

Since T_2 is greater than T_1, the vendor's offer would *cost the company more*—you should turn it down.

How to Handle Lead Time Problems

Good inventory control depends upon setting realistic lead times. Establishing the right lead time is a cooperative effort between vendor and customer. If either attempts to impose a lead time on the other, the result will probably be both undependable and uneconomic.

Lead time problems arise because of interferences and misunderstandings. An example of an interference is the failure of a buyer to send information to the person who issues requirements for material. Another is not considering vacations or holidays in calculating time periods.

Examples of misunderstandings are using the same lead times for specials as for standard items, and confusing shipping dates with required delivery dates. Since you can't use a material until you have it, you should never be interested in a simple shipping date. Here are some suggestions on how to keep on top of lead time problems:

- Work closely with vendors when you issue blanket orders—those describing your needs over a stated period of time. Make sure both of you understand your liabilities concerning quantities, lead times, and prices. Clarify how you will notify vendors of your specific requirements, and make sure they understand when the blanket order agreement begins or ends.

- Keep a vendor performance record making a point to periodically update it. At least part of your orders should go to those who do what they say they will do when they say they will do it.
- Take time to find out why when a vendor performs poorly. Maybe the vendor is getting the blame for transportation companies' faults.
- Check also on the possibility you may have unintentionally misled the vendor.

HOW TO ADD AN ITEM TO STORES

A good procedure for adding items to stores minimizes material acquisition costs, ensures that proper quantities of materials are purchased, eliminates duplication, and furnishes a reliable method of information retrieval. Items are kept in storerooms for two reasons:

1. The item will be needed frequently for operation of the plant and equipment.
2. The item is critical to the process; a spare must be on hand to ensure against a loss in production if the item in use fails.

If it is obvious that an item will be used in large quantities, stocking it immediately pays off both operationally and economically. Decisions about adding to stock should not be handled by the materials control department alone, but also involve the purchasing department. The responsibility of the material control department should be to specify the factors that affect procuring inventory and maintaining quantities for all items on the stock list. These factors include the unit of measure, the unit cost, the economic order quantity, the reorder point, and the expedite point.

When you anticipate that an item such as a spare part should be added to stock, order it direct several times first. These direct purchases will give you basic information about the item such as its cost and which vendors handle it. With this procedure, you will also be able to examine the received item and approve or not approve it. This is good policy for several reasons:

- You have no positive assurance that the item will be needed in the future. New equipment in the plant may fail to operate as expected, processes may change, and an improved design may be available soon.

- At the time you place the order, you may know little if anything about what the annual use will be.
- You want to avoid the carrying costs of a high inventory.

Send the first requisition for the item to the materials control department rather than to the purchasing department so that the item can be coded (assigned an identification number). By coding the item now, it will be easier to later retrieve purchasing data and use data from the computer data base. Also, identify the item on the requisition form as potential stores material, and give a tentative date for the time when the item will be added to stock.

The materials control department should initiate a tracking procedure by putting a copy of the requisition in a reminder file. The purchasing department should aid the tracking by sending materials control a copy of the purchase order. When the item is received, materials control should notify you so that you can verify whether the item is what was wanted.

How to Handle Insurance Items

Items used infrequently in the plant are commonly called *insurance items*. Stocking them ensures against a loss that could be incurred if the item were not immediately available. The decision of whether or not to stock an insurance item should be based on economics. If stocking is a favorable move economically, the item should be put in the storeroom immediately.

The need to stock an insurance item becomes greater when it has a long lead time because the potential loss increases with time. But an alternative course is available to you: Ask the manufacturer or a vendor to stock the item for you.

Tip: Getting vendors to stock other than insurance items for the plant is becoming popular as an excellent way of keeping plant inventories to a minimum.

TRAINING PLANT EMPLOYEES IN THE USE OF INVENTORY MANAGEMENT TOOLS

With more and more emphasis being placed on the need to effectively manage inventory in the plant, it is essential that all employees be made aware of their responsibilities in this area. You can best accomplish this by providing them training on the techniques of inventory control. Although they may not be expected to perform the functions of the materials control or the purchasing departments, unless they are members of these departments, they should know how and why these procedures are carried out. Here are the major subjects you should cover in a training program:

1. Start by discussing the common technical terms involving stores and inventories. This can most easily be presented in a classroom or office.

2. Explain the part the computer plays in the various inventory procedures. Give examples of how the speed and accuracy of computers contribute to control.

3. Discuss automated storage and material-handling systems. State how far the plant has progressed on these systems and what management plans to do in the future.

4. Talk about bar coding and what this ingenious tool can accomplish. If your plant has adopted this tool for any of its many uses, show and demonstrate one of the scanners being used.

5. Give the benefits and advantages to the plant of the inventory management tools presently being used. Indicate how the employees you are training can contribute to the plant's inventory control program.

THE RELATIONSHIP OF INVENTORY TO JUST-IN-TIME PRODUCTION[1]

Soon after beginning to manufacture Toyota automobiles, Japanese plant management questioned the necessity for inventory in the manufacturing process. Toyota felt that it was being used as a panacea for most production problems such as:

- Inaccurate sales forecasts.
- Inability to schedule.
- Unreliable suppliers.
- Unsynchronized processes.
- Inadequate maintenance.
- Poor quality.

Parts and products were being made at the plant "just in case the forecast is wrong," "just in case the production machines break down," and "just in case the suppliers don't deliver." Toyota decided to manufacture *just-in-time* rather than *just-in-case*. This decision was based on the premise that inventory compensates for problems or shortcomings in the production process: If you eliminate or solve the problems, inventory is no longer necessary.

---

[1]Portions of this section contain information and data given in a presentation by Quarterman Lee of The Leawood Group, LTD., at the 1986 National Plant Engineering & Maintenance Conference. The title of Mr. Lee's talk was "Layout for the Just-in-Time Plant."

Techniques Involved in the Toyota System

The Toyota System is a manufacturing procedure with an objective of constantly reducing inventory until it ultimately reaches zero. It includes a group of tools, techniques, and practices for accomplishing this objective. According to the Toyota philosophy, zero inventory will result in delivery of the products wanted by customers at precisely the right time, with perfect quality, and without any waste.

While there are many techniques involved in just-in-time (JIT) operations, all are applicable to U.S. manufacturers and workers although some specific practices must be altered. Two of the most critical techniques are:

1. *Group technology procedures.* They include classifying parts and assemblies, identifying similarities, and using these similarities to improve design, manufacturing, and purchasing operations. The classification and resultant grouping of parts into families streamline many activities and allow some to be done for entire groups of parts rather than for each part individually.

    Most manufacturing today requires production in small lots. Moreover, the increased use of numerical control, flexible manufacturing systems, and JIT manufacturing will increase rather than decrease batch production. Although a line layout is the simplest and most efficient production arrangement, it can only be used when volume is high and the entire line is dedicated to one or a few nearly identical items.

    The alternative to the line layout is the job shop or functional layout. As shop size increases, however, complexity increases at an accelerated rate. Parts with similar shape, material, and manufacturing characteristics may often be made together on the same equipment. If these machines can be grouped, scheduling, routing, tooling, transporting and setting up are greatly simplified.

2. *Kanban.* This system tells each department and worker what to make and when. It serves as the production control for JIT operations, but it differs from most conventional scheduling systems in that it is a *pull* as opposed to a *push* force. Parts and assemblies are made as a response to the demands of the operation immediately following rather than to a schedule.

    With the Kanban system, each workplace or production area has an immediately adjacent stock point where a small predetermined quantity of each part made in the department is maintained. This point serves as a small stores area for the subsequent operation. When the downstream operation requires a particular part, a worker is sent to the area to withdraw a small predetermined number of the items. The worker is authorized to do this by a withdrawal Kanban, which is simply a card with the part number, description, quantity, and other appropriate information.

When the worker takes the needed parts, he or she removes a production-ordering Kanban from the parts container and places it at a specified location, usually at the supervisor's desk. This Kanban authorizes the supervisor to produce more parts, but only in the quantity of those just removed.

Withdrawal and production ordering Kanbans authorize only very small quantities, usually no more than what is needed for 8 hours of production and sometimes less. The procedure enables the plant to come very close to the ideal of JIT production by making and delivering parts only in very small quantities. Ideally, it would make and deliver only one part at a time. The Kanban system accommodates changes in production requirements but only within a limited range. It can compensate for shifts in product mix or quantities of about 10 to 20 percent on a daily basis.

How Layouts in Just-in-Time Plants Differ from Conventional Layouts

Arrangements and positioning of machines and equipment in JIT plants are different from conventional manufacturing layout in several key respects. Here are six of those ways:

1. *Less space required*. A JIT plant can operate with 40 to 60 percent less space than conventional plants because far less space is required for inventories and material handling. In most of today's plants, production equipment occupies only a small portion of the total space. The largest space user is that required to receive and store materials, hold work-in-process between operations, allow queues in front of machines, and aisles for transporting materials.

2. *Flow lines and cells*. JIT is characterized by flow lines and cellular processes patterned from Henry Ford's original assembly line. The workpiece moves from one operation to the next with little or no inventory between operations. Operations are balanced and synchronized along the line.

3. *Kanban areas*. Ultimately, the entire manufacturing process should be a continuous flow line, but that is seldom possible; in practice, there will be cells, isolated flow lines, and individual processes. Kanban, the link between them, requires a small stock area at each cell or flow line, which is replenished by the cells as required.

4. *Material handling*. While JIT plants require a constant flow of materials, the flow is steady in small units, and the intensity at any given time is low. This requires a different material-handling system than that of

conventional plants. The JIT layout accommodates this with short travel distances and manual handling. When mechanized handling is required, it consists of fork trucks or trailers, which pick up and deliver small quantities on regular routes.

5. *Focused production.* A single JIT manufacturing plant cannot effectively make a wide variety of products in different quantities using many fundamentally different technologies. It is necessary for a plant to focus on a limited set of markets, products, and technologies when it operates on JIT procedures.

6. *Point-of-use delivery.* As a plant adopts more and more JIT principles, conventional receiving docks, inspection areas, and storerooms disappear. Deliveries are made where the material is needed, such as at assembly and fabrication areas throughout the plant. This means easy access at many points for small delivery trucks, and reduction in size with eventual elimination of the central storeroom.

How to Ensure that Plant Workers Avoid the Pitfalls of Kanban

While the Kanban technique has received much favorable publicity in recent years, little has been said about the pitfalls inherent with it. Here are some of the pitfalls that can prevent successful use of the technique if they are not side-stepped:

- Unless implemented under the right environment, little can be gained from Kanban. For example, if the plant's production schedule is unrealistic, or if you have poor inventory data, you could make the mistake of producing the wrong parts or stopping production because you don't have the right parts.

- If all members of production control are not fully aware of the principles of Kanban, its practice could be wasteful. For example, if making parts prematurely is more costly than having idle workers, production should stop.

- You should have other productive activities to start if you stop normal production. Possibilities are practicing setups, doing maintenance work, and starting other projects. Not only must you be prepared to accept idle workers, you must be assured that management supports this untraditional way of running the plant.

- Practicing Kanban does not guarantee that queues will be reduced, lead times cut, quality improved, or setups made faster. Instead, the technique goes along with current conditions, such as the number of Kanban cards in use.

- If the total number of Kanban cards in use remains the same, no improvement is occurring in expanding JIT. While it is up to the users to reduce their numbers, the wrong way to do it is by arbitrarily decreasing them. This may only create new problems.

How Just-in-Time and Quality Control Go Together

Many progressive and technologically advanced plants feel that just-in-time (JIT) and quality control are closely related to each other. They see JIT procedures exposing problems and quality control solving them. The way to exploit this relationship is to make a few small, controlled steps. While a big change in procedures may greatly cut costs, it risks a lowering of productivity and workmanship. Here's how to proceed:

Step 1. Gradually reduce your inventory, observing the result of each reduction. As soon as a problem is encountered, stop lowering inventory and determine the reasons for the problem. Check for problems of setup time, accessibility of tooling, or shortages of material.

Step 2. Apply the techniques of quality control to resolve the problems. When you make the correction, lower the inventory again. Look for improved performance or another problem.

Step 3. Continue to make small changes in JIT procedures, applying quality control as necessary.

HOW TO SET UP AN EFFECTIVE HI-USE STORES SYSTEM

Efficient handling of materials is essential to increasing the productivity of plant workers, cutting material handling costs, and controlling inventories. One way you can improve efficiency is by creating one or more stores areas separate and distinct from the main storeroom. It's appropriate to refer to these "branches" as *hi-use stores (HUS) areas.* They pay off particularly with items that are used by maintenance workers in relatively large quantities. By making such items handy to them in their work area, you can save them the time of going to the main storeroom.

Although elimination of such unproductive work time is the most important benefit you can derive from creating HUS areas separate from the main storeroom, there are other benefits to be realized. You create more space in the storeroom for handling and stocking items that do not have a high usage, and you reduce storeroom attendants' work in handing out items. The following procedural steps for setting up and controlling a

HUS system have been proven to be successful in limiting costs and assuring availability of material:

Step 1. Determine what to put in the HUS areas by reviewing several month's engineering stores withdrawals. Select items preferably that are used frequently by the craftspersons and that can be manually handled rather than requiring chain hoists or rigging. Do not include items that have a high theft potential, such as operating supplies or insurance items that are important enough to keep under control in the main storeroom.

Critical equipment parts should also be stored in the main storeroom rather than in a particular zone. Note that if you want a historical record of an item's usage, you must keep the item in the main storeroom rather than in a HUS area.

Step 2. Locate a HUS area in each zone and also outside, but near, the main storeroom. Back up some but not all items with additional supplies in the storeroom itself. Long delivery items plus items not limited to a particular zone are good backup choices, as are large bulky items that will not fit in bins, nor are they available in large quantities. Any item that isn't in a bin must have a backup supply in the storeroom to trigger its reorder.

Step 3. Store HUS items on racks or shelves using a double bin for each item whenever possible. Put large or awkward items on lower shelves. Place the second bin of an item behind the first bin and level with it. Shelf heights should be such that you can't reach into the second bin.

Step 4. Determine the size of the bins for an item from the order quantity. If you don't have a backup supply of the item in the storeroom, you must be sure that when the first bin goes empty, there is enough time to get in a new supply before the second bin runs out. The quantity contained in the bin is your order size. If you have a backup supply in the main storeroom, you can use smaller bins because you will reorder when the storeroom inventory reaches the reorder point.

Step 5. Provide a *HUS item locator list* in each area. It should be arranged in sections. Key words, such as "switch" and "fuse," should be used to make item location easy for craftspersons and stores personnel. Explain in the HUS list the bin tag that is being used on each bin.

Step 6. Inform craftspersons, stores personnel, and supervisors how the double bin system works, that when one bin becomes empty, it should be removed from the shelf and the bin behind it pulled up to the front of the shelf. The empty bin should be placed in an area designated for it so that steps can be taken to have it refilled.

Step 7. Ask the craftspersons to fill out a HUS requisition card for an item that is too large or awkward for the bins. This requisition card should be unique in color or size so that it isn't confused with other storeroom cards. The card should be placed with the empty bins when that item is removed from the HUS area.

Step 8. Use storeroom personnel to deliver all HUS material to each HUS area once a day. Have them put refilled bins on the shelves using the locator number and pick up empty bins. Have them also pick up the HUS requisition cards so that these items can be replaced in the area from which they were removed.

Step 9. Charge materials out when they leave the main storeroom in the refilled bins. If you have no backup supply in the storeroom, you must have a purchase order issued every time a bin is emptied. The number of items that should be put in an empty bin is shown on the front of the bin.

Step 10. Adopt a way of identifying HUS items that you stock in the main storeroom. It will prompt storeroom attendants to mention to craftspersons who ask for such items that the item is in their HUS area.

Giving Workers Instructions on the Use of Double Bin Systems

Following is an explanation of the double bin system and bin tags. Posting it in each HUS area is recommended because it can thus serve as a reminder to all workers who use the system.

The parts and material stored in the HUS are shown on the HUS item locator list next to this posting. Section numbers are:

1. Electrical.
2. Pipefitting.
3. Mechanical.
4. Bolts, Nuts, Screws.
5. Clamps, Fasteners.

After locating the item you need on the list, go to the bin number for it. Each bin carries a bin tag, which looks like this:

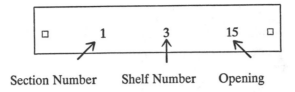

Section Number   Shelf Number   Opening

This is a double bin system. When one bin becomes empty, remove it from the shelf and pull the bin behind it up to the front of the shelf. Place the empty bin on the empty bin shelf.

Several items in the HUS stores are too large for the bins. To replace these items after you use them, fill out a HUS requisition card for the item and put it on the empty bin shelf.

The bin number of the item must be put on the top of the card. You do not have to fill out a HUS requisition card for items in bins, just place the empty bin on the empty bin shelf.

HOW TO CONTEND WITH EQUIPMENT SHORTAGES

If plant management is more concerned with short-term cash flow than with long-term expense reduction, you may have a problem of low inventory of equipment in your department. At the least, you may have to provide considerable justification to acquire new or additional equipment. Even in less cost-conscious plants, however, few supervisors can spend much money on equipment. But there are several answers to this problem. Here are four you may consider:

1. Many machines and other equipment can be rented, including lift trucks, maintenance tools, and even computer terminals. Although renting is in the long term more expensive than buying, in the short term it reduces the immediate outlay of cash. Looking at the problem another way, you may choose to write off a lease as an expense rather than make a capital investment.

2. Occasionally an equipment manufacturer may finance your acquisition. The usual arrangement is that you pay the manufacturer a monthly rent for a fixed period of time. Since the manufacturer has no further use for the equipment at the end of the lease, a clause is put in the contract that transfers ownership to you for a nominal amount at the end of the lease.

3. Dealers in used equipment may also be a source for a particular type of equipment you want to acquire. They buy up equipment at auctions or from firms that have surpluses and sell it at much lower prices than similar new equipment. Although used equipment is going to need more maintenance, with proper care it can be as useful as any new equipment.

4. You can ask new equipment vendors if they have any returned equipment or demonstrators available for sale. While you can expect the vendor's prices to be higher than those of used equipment dealers, the chances are good that this equipment will require less maintenance and may have a better warranty.

Tip: When taking inventory of all the plant's equipment, don't underestimate the value of a machine or piece of equipment that has been removed from service for any of a number of reasons. What might appear to be scrap metal could be used to knock down the price on a new similar machine. Or it could be sold to a used equipment dealer.

HOW TO GET PLANT WORKERS' INPUT ON JUST-IN-TIME OPERATIONS AND INVENTORY CONTROL

If your plant is implementing JIT operations or plans to do so, involving plant workers in the procedures will increase the likelihood that these operations will work out well. Employees can also make contributions to minimize inventories in other ways. Here are some suggestions on how to encourage workers' participation in these efforts to both their and the company's benefit:

- Promote quality control and good workmanship as ways the plant can reduce defects and scrap. Such activities cut the need to stock materials and products beyond those required to meet customer's orders.
- Ask them for ideas on ways to come closer to the goals of group technology and gearing production toward product families.
- Request their help in eliminating bottlenecks and delays in the process. Point out that JIT presents problems that the company would like to solve.
- Provide them with training in materials and inventory control procedures. Talk about how the Japanese manage these activities.
- Keep them up to date on how the plant is progressing on reducing inventories. Report management's plans for the future.
- Give workers recognition for their suggestions and efforts to smooth out flow of parts and products through the plant. Recognition usually leads to additional suggestions and enthusiasm for the work.

13

Getting Plant Workers to Adopt Japanese Management Techniques

UNDERSTANDING THE TOYOTA MANUFACTURING SYSTEM

Japanese management and manufacturing techniques have been highly publicized ever since the 1970s when Japanese manufacturers outperformed their competition with carefully chosen products of exceptional quality and value. While most of the attention has been directed to the automobile industry, what has been accomplished with automobiles has also been matched with television, computers, cameras, sound equipment, and other electronic devices.

Perhaps the most important of the Japanese manufacturing techniques is the system that has variously been called *Toyota* or *Just-in-time/total quality control*. It is defined as a manufacturing production system based on constant inventory reduction towards an ultimate goal of zero inventory. It includes a group of tools, techniques, and practices for accomplishing this objective.

The Toyota system, however, is not one peculiar to Japan. Kawasaki and Matusushita Electric have used it successfully in American plants with American workers and managers. Moreover, American companies such as John Deere, Chrysler, General Motors, and Ford have used these manufacturing methods with impressive results.

Since inventory carrying costs in many manufacturing plants range from 30 to 40 percent, most managements agree that inventory reduction within reasonable limits is desirable. Reducing inventory results in greater return on capital and frees funds for more productive use. In the metalworking industry, the average plant turns over its inventory 4 to 5 times a year, and well managed plants may make 8 to 10 turns. But there doesn't seem to be much to gain beyond that point because the effort and investment necessary to decrease inventory become greater and the returns less. Yet Toyota system plants often achieve turns of 60 to 100. The Toyota system justifies this because it forces excellent performance.

When the Toyota plant was just getting started, it, like most small companies, operated with low levels of inventory out of necessity. As the company and its inventories grew, however, management saw that the employees worked less efficiently. There apparently was a connection between the effectiveness of the employees and the level of the plant's inventory.

Management deduced that inventory compensates for problems or weaknesses in the production process; eliminate the problems and inventory would no longer be necessary. This led to the conclusion that if inventories are low and the production is still maintained, the entire operation must be very effective. Thus, inventory levels were a guide to the efficiency of the plant operation.

Worker Involvement: Key to the Toyota System

While American management recognizes the need to eliminate waste and maintain high quality, respecting the capabilities and qualities of production workers is a different matter. But personnel factors must be considered with the Toyota system for two reasons:

1. A great deal of teamwork and coordination is required for just-in-time operations.
2. It is the workers who must eliminate the waste and maintain quality.

Because the Toyota system requires well coordinated teamwork, any employee who doesn't carry out his or her job function may disrupt the entire plant. At the same time, the system actively encourages and rewards teamwork. The incentives of team performance help to make employees perform to their best abilities.

Most large American plants employ staff personnel, highly trained individuals who solve problems and provide service for the workers and supervisors in the process areas. These individuals are usually engineers, technicians, and electronic specialists who hold positions in the maintenance and engineering, production control, planning, and quality control departments.

Staff functions, however, are often contrary or antagonistic to the feelings and wishes of plant workers and supervisors who are close to their work and justifiably think they know more about it than anybody. They may resent staff persons telling them how to do their work, and they have few, if any, reasons to go out of their way to help staff personnel.

The Toyota philosophy, in contrast, focuses on workers' and supervisors' responsibilities. It is each worker's responsibility to maintain quality, prevent equipment breakdowns, work efficiently, and produce in the quantities required by fellow team members. With the Toyota system, staff personnel are advisors and trainers.

Because of the high degree of motivation and competence required on the part of workers and supervisors under the Toyota system, both are undoubtedly better qualified for their jobs than their American counterparts. It is commonly believed that the average worker in Japan knows more about statistical quality control than the average supervisor in America, and the average Japanese supervisor knows more about planning and time study than the average industrial engineer in America.

Techniques Involved with the Toyota System

Inventory reduction is just one of the management techniques the Japanese have employed in developing one of the more efficient and envied production systems in the world. Here are the specific techniques of the Toyota system:

- *Focused plants.* Instead of constructing large plants where many operations are performed, Japanese manufacturers prefer to build small plants that carry out a minimum of operations but do them very efficiently. Small plants are easier to manage. They also are more conducive to teamwork.

- *Just-in-time production.* Workers make only the required parts in the needed quantities and deliver them to the right place at precisely the time they are needed.

- *Kanban control.* A system of cards and containers similar to the two bin system is used. It is based on very small amounts of inventory and constantly adjusts itself for changing demand or conditions.

- *Group technology.* This is a manufacturing method whereby similar parts are grouped in the work area to achieve the advantages of mass production in small lot sizes.

- *Worker responsible for quality.* This concept places responsibility for quality with the worker rather than with a quality control or inspection department.

- *Minimization of setup time.* By using conventional method analysis and applying common sense to reduction of setup time on conventional machine tools, reductions of 90 to 95 percent are achieved.

- *Preventive maintenance.* This consists of scheduled inspection, repair, replacement, and adjustment of equipment and machines to avoid major breakdowns.

- *Quality circles.* Small groups of workers meet with a trained leader to work on problems in their areas of responsibility. While originally these meetings tackled quality problems, they now cover safety, production, environmental, and other subjects as well.

- *Subcontractor involvement.* Focused plants require an extensive system of subcontractors to supply parts and meet the demands of just-in-time operations.

- *Uniform plant output.* Homogeneous production involves mixing of various models of a product at final assembly to minimize changes in the demand for components and subassemblies.

- *Bottom round management.* This style of control operates on the principle that problems should be solved and decisions made at the lowest possible level of management.

- *Promotion of automation.* The Toyota system emphasizes use of automation and robotics to free workers from menial or hazardous jobs, enabling them to make better use of their mental and physical skills.

- *Attitude toward workers.* Workers are considered partners in the business organization. They are not looked upon as simply a resource to be obtained and used to satisfy current production requirements.

- *Company unions.* Japanese unions are established along company lines instead of by industry or the skills of members. Combined with the acceptance of workers and management as partners, the unions promote common loyalty to the company and common goals for everyone.

- *Lifetime employment.* Employees join large Japanese companies when their education is complete. In return for being assured a job for their careers, they are expected to be loyal and give their best efforts to the company.

UNDERSTANDING TOTAL PRODUCTIVE MAINTENANCE

Total productive maintenance (TPM) is one of the major reasons that Japanese manufacturing plants are producing better-quality products at substantially lower costs than their U.S. counterparts. Although TPM is primarily concerned with assigning basic maintenance tasks to equipment operators, it also changes corporate culture. In addition, it permanently improves and maintains the overall effectiveness through the active involvement of workers.

While many of the basic objectives of TPM (zero downtime, zero defects, and zero accidents) are well grounded and justifiable, they do not provide answers to all the factors that limit U.S. plants' performance. Manufacturing plants in Japan generally are designed, operated, and maintained with life cycle costs and long-term profit in mind. Reliability, availability, and maintainability are built into their plants. The management philosophy creates an environment dedicated to optimum plant performance, and TPM management concepts are applied to eliminate the remaining inefficiency in a plant. Thus, the focus of TPM is to handle any problems that were created by design mistakes or that may have developed during the operation of the plant.

How to Implement a Total Productive Maintenance Program in the Plant

If management decides to implement a total productive maintenance (TPM) program in the plant, the installation should be conducted in steps to ensure that it is carefully managed and controlled. The following procedure is the 12-step plan developed by Seiichi Nakajima (the "father" of TPM) and the Japan Institute of Plant Maintenance:

Step 1. Announce and explain the TPM program to plant employees. Fully inform and gain the support of all unions involved.

Step 2. Train managers and supervisors in TPM procedures. These individuals must understand and be in agreement with the principles of TPM if it is to be a success.

Step 3. Create line and staff TPM groups. The line personnel must be involved to develop strategy, policies, and goals. The staff personnel will be responsible for planning and executing the installation including the training function.

Step 4. Establish equipment-related goals from an analysis of current equipment losses. Set priorities and target dates, especially for bottleneck equipment.

Step 5. Develop a TPM master plan for the installation. Prepare a Gantt chart to cover the entire process, broken down by department.

Step 6. Start the implementation, formally announcing it to promote enthusiasm. Begin the skills training to enable workers to acquire equipment knowledge and learn the basics in maintenance activities.

Step 7. Improve the effectiveness of each piece of equipment. Form project teams of maintenance and engineering personnel for this activity. They should use Pareto and fishbone analyses and other problem-solving techniques during this phase of the program.

Step 8. Thoroughly clean all equipment and machines using teams of workers and maintenance personnel. During this key step, workers learn much about the equipment and become more involved in the program. After this is done, develop cleaning procedures and time goals for the workers to keep their equipment clean in the future. With additional training, the workers will gradually do more preventive maintenance work on the equipment.

Step 9. Improve the maintenance management process by adopting and expanding planning, scheduling, and control functions. Develop annual schedules for preventive and predictive maintenance, and organize the handling of spare parts, tools, and instruments.

Step 10. Conduct training programs to improve maintenance skills of both workers and maintenance personnel. Ensure that maintenance crafts' needs are satisfied.

Step 11. Develop an equipment management program starting with equipment design. Include a procedure for workers' and maintenance personnels' involvement in the life-cycle cost of equipment.

Step 12. Firmly establish TPM as a way of life in the plant. Consolidate all efforts to make the program an ongoing process.

HOW JAPANESE MANAGEMENT METHODS ARE DIFFERENT FROM AMERICAN METHODS

While they are not doing much to improve the quality of American education, foreign companies operating in the U.S. seem to be doing a better job of training their lower-level workers and helping them to raise their productivity. For example, Japanese companies have been spending about $1000 more each year per employee than their American counterparts in the same industries.

This extra training is paying off in that better products are often produced. Although the *1990 Consumer Reports* ranks most Japanese cars higher in quality than American cars, it finds no difference between the quality of Japanese cars produced by American workers and those made in Japan. In addition, Americans who work in Japanese automotive plants in the U.S. are almost as productive as their coworkers back in Japan, and far more productive than American workers in U.S. auto plants. For example, in 1990, an American worker in a Japanese plant assembled a car in 19.5 hours, compared with the 19.1 hours it took an average Japanese autoworker in Japan and the 26.5 hours it took an average American autoworker in an American auto factory.

Foreign companies in the U.S., including Japanese, also are more concerned about the skills and workmanship of their workers. They screen and test prospective employees more carefully, and they provide more job security and higher wages. Further, they emphasize on-the-job training and the continuous development of new skills to a greater extent than do American companies.

Several explanations have been suggested to account for these differences in Japanese and American management methods:

1. Japanese-owned companies are not pressured as much by the demands of financial markets for immediate earnings, and thus can take a longer-term view of their employees and operations. A large portion of the stock of Japanese companies is permanently held by other companies in the same industrial group. The group is virtually committed to aid any member in trouble, and measures corporate success by long-term market share rather than short-term earnings.

2. Japanese companies are accustomed to stress training and developing of their work forces. In the early postwar era, they were required to do so if they were to compete with American multinationals. That meant, among other endeavors, substantial investments in procuring and training workers to be effective and efficient. American companies did not need to do this. Reliable workers were readily available in the early postwar years, as were technicians trained by the Defense Department.

3. Japanese companies, over the years, have always put greater emphasis on work force participation in managing and operating manufacturing plants. Lifetime employment is common in large companies, and much is done to keep peace and promote cooperation between management and labor. In general, the reciprocal bonds of loyalty and responsibility between the company and its workers have been much stronger in postwar Japan than in the U.S.

HOW THE JAPANESE HANDLE THE MAINTENANCE FUNCTION[1]

In 1987, Du Pont contracted with an American consulting firm to help in developing a method to measure the effectiveness of the maintenance function in Du Pont plants. The benchmarking technique that evolved from

[1]Much of the data and information in this section were reported in Edwin K. Jones, "The Japanese Approach to Facilities Maintenance," *Maintenance Technology*, August 1991, Applied Technology Publications, Inc., Barrington, IL 60010.

that study was then applied to Du Pont's industrial plants and those of other companies worldwide.

The Japanese companies that were studied were selected on the basis of their reputation for performance and excellent results. Here are the results of that study on how the Japanese handle the maintenance function in their plants compared to U.S. plants:

- *Organization.* Maintenance workers in Japan make up a smaller fraction of the work force than in the U.S., and plants in Japan use a higher percentage of contractors for maintenance. The ratio of workers to supervisors/managers is lower than in the U.S.

- *Cost of maintenance.* Japanese companies spend less to maintain their plants than American companies because productivity per maintenance worker is higher. Their productivity is influenced by their contracting levels, a longer work week, and the Japanese culture.

- *Material management.* Japanese companies carry considerably less stores investment and employ fewer stores personnel than their U.S. counterparts. Plants that manage their own inventories have turnover rates higher than 4. Plants that work closely with local just-in-time suppliers maintain slow-turning critical spares at a turnover ratio lower than 0.6.

- *Computer use.* There is substantially less use of computers on maintenance functions in Japan than in the U.S. This is also true, in general, for automation and robotics. While plants in the U.S. have developed high technology and computer applications, the Japanese have focused on increasing the productivity of workers through approaches such as quality circles, minimization of inventory, and continuous improvement.

- *Total productive maintenance use.* Japan is far advanced over the U.S. in the use of TPM. Japanese workers are responsible for normal operation and daily maintenance of equipment. Workers and maintenance personnel share responsibility in other maintenance categories. Maintenance personnel handle periodic and preventive maintenance, and have primary responsibility for repairing breakdowns and improving maintainability.

- *Culture and relationships.* The Japanese place a high value on relationships. There are many more partnerships with suppliers and contractors than exist in the U.S. Trust between workers and management is unquestioning and strong. Trust between plant workers and contractor workers is equally strong.

HOW TO EXPLAIN JAPANESE BUSINESS SUCCESS TO PLANT WORKERS

In the early nineties, many U.S. manufacturers have sent management teams to Japan to tour industrial plants, listen to top Japanese business experts, and experience the Japanese way of life. What these teams see and learn is carefully studied and analyzed to determine if the management methods and procedures can be adopted to advantage in U.S. manufacturing plants.

Much of the information from such visits is published in newsletters, trade magazines, and management journals. In progressive U.S. companies, the information and data are also passed on to employees. The publications provide excellent sources of information you can give to your workers. For example, following are some pertinent observations and comments of an European management group that visited Japan in 1990:[2]

- Employee involvement and communication are among the key reasons for Japanese success. Contrary to Western belief, Japanese employees are not poorly paid, downtrodden, timid, acquiescent individuals who merely do as they are told. Through their quality circle meetings, suggestion programs, and similar activities, employees provide ideas for improving everything from machine operations to customer satisfaction.

- The Japanese have an unrelenting drive to improve on anything they do from service to manufacturing. They pay an almost obsessive amount of attention to small, detailed improvements rather than giant leaps forward. Most important of all, the profits of an organization are the result of satisfied customers.

- Manufacturing in Japan is based on rigid standards. The focus of all plants is on quality improvement and cost reduction. Products are designed to meet customer expectations, and the plant function is to make them with the best possible quality at the lowest possible cost.

- Nearly all the companies in Japan put customer satisfaction, through a total quality approach, at the forefront. They view the customer as a responsibility of the *whole company*, not just the sales and marketing department.

- Japanese commitment to a just-in-time (JIT) philosophy is vital to their success. This comes from attention to detail and an obsession with continual improvement that have allowed the Japanese to lower inventory levels and perfect the use of JIT systems.

- Japanese companies, aided by low interest rates and a strong currency, usually take a longer-term approach to business decisions than is done in the West. They spend money to gain market share, accepting that bottom line profitability will come later.

---

[2]*Goodyear World*, May 1990, Public Affairs Department of The Goodyear Tire & Rubber Company, Akron, Ohio 44316.

PLANNING AND CONSENSUS: JAPANESE STRENGTHS

Visitors to Japan invariably learn how the Japanese approach problems, especially if business relations are involved. As soon as Japanese understand a basic problem, they immediately get together as a group to agree on the plan of action. The Japanese will spend what Americans consider excessive amounts of time negotiating among group members to get everyone to accept a plan. Although groups in Japan are inherently hierarchical, it is very important to the Japanese that everyone sincerely agree with a course of action. Once the consensus is arranged, they can be counted on to execute it with precision and speed.

The Japanese are also noted for expecting exact, detailed instructions for performing a job or carrying out a project. As soon as they are given a method or procedure, they will practice it over and over until they have it perfected. This applies to just about everything they do from assembling something on the factory floor to the simple act of opening a car door just so.

If the Japanese don't have a plan, or if the plan changes suddenly, however, they are uncomfortable or even lost. Because the plan is worked out by consensus, it can take a long time for the Japanese to change course. This characteristic also means that Japanese are somewhat ill at ease in unstructured situations; they tend to implement an artificial arrangement into a situation that doesn't really need it.

One of the notable attitudes the Japanese possess is the value they put on hard work. While they value talent and flashes of inspiration just as Americans do, they regard persistent hard work as more important. If Americans aren't good at something, they are likely to say they lack the skill. If the Japanese aren't good at something, they say they need to work harder.

HOW TO TAP THE CREATIVE CAPABILITIES OF YOUR WORK TEAM

Author Tom Peters recently pointed out a striking contrast between Japanese and American business.[3] In Japan, the average employee submits 24 ideas to management every year. In the United States, the ratio is one new idea for every seven workers. Also, while 77 percent of the Japanese suggestions are put into effect, American companies implement only 26 percent of their employees' ideas.

---

[3]*Successful Supervisor*, January 7, 1991, Dartnell Corporation, Chicago, IL 60640.

To explain this, it has been suggested that U.S. management may not recognize the creative capabilities of work teams. You can turn this around, however. Here's how to go about it:

1. Talk to your team leaders about the problem.
2. Encourage them to develop good, presentable ideas.
3. Tell them that when the team comes up with an idea that can contribute to the plant's profitability, top management will listen.

PROBLEMS WITH ADAPTING EMPLOYEES TO JAPANESE MANUFACTURING METHODS

U.S. manufacturers of autos, electronic components, and many other items are increasingly patterning their production operations along the lines of methods pioneered in Japan. But difficulties are being encountered along the way. It is recognized that because of differences in culture and tradition, there probably will never be complete acceptance of Japanese procedures and manufacturing methods. Following is a list of both management and labor problems that need to be resolved if U.S. manufacturers are to successfully use Japanese manufacturing methods:

1. *Defining goals.* If you visit almost any U.S. manufacturing plant and ask a worker what the company's main goal is, you'll hear that it is to beat last year's plant output, or to reduce labor requirements, or to cut manufacturing costs. In a Japanese plant, the answer will be different. It will consist of one word: *kaizen. Kaizen* is a Japanese term that is translated as continuous improvement. That is the goal of every plant employee including the managers.

2. *Empowering employees.* To keep employees satisfied and to ensure a high level of productivity, Japanese plants don't have any "workers." They have "associates." Every person employed, from the plant manager to a welder, is a member of a team that is composed of associates. Too many U.S. companies do not listen to their employees. Since employees have no part in the decision-making process, they have no say in how to make the plant's products better. Japanese companies, in comparison, highly encourage their employees to participate and contribute to the management of the plant.

3. *Investing in technology.* Some upper-level managers and executives in the U.S. are reluctant to tie their company's future to a technology that they don't understand. For example, many U.S. plants balk at investing in automatic guided vehicle systems for several reasons. Maybe they should consider this: During the past few years, several leading Japanese

corporations have installed Japanese-designed and Japanese-made systems in Japanese-owned plants located in the U.S. Clearly, the Japanese believe that this technology is worth investing in, even in other countries. Part of this problem may be traced to how few engineers hold high-level executive positions in U.S. corporations compared with Japanese companies.

4. *The work ethic.* The Japanese work ethic is extremely strong and culturally bound. Other attributes are a fierce sense of loyalty to one's employer, and a willingness to sacrifice for the good of the whole. In Japan, management is receptive to employees' input in that it is sincerely solicited, appreciated, and very frequently used.

5. *Individualism vs. unanimity.* Although the Japanese have done a truly impressive job in eliminating waste, cutting inventory, flexible scheduling, and increasing their overall productivity, U.S. plants cannot do these things in the same way because of the cultural differences between the U.S. and Japan. The Japanese have a very homogenous society. Everyone knows they are limited in natural resources and must excel in adding value at low cost to produce exports. It is a national priority to which all elements (management, labor, government, finance, and academia) subscribe totally. Contrast this to the U.S. where there is no unanimity of purpose. Americans have been trained to be free and independent thinkers, and dissenters are everywhere.

6. *Emphasis on quality.* Japan's thrust in business and industry has been learning to produce quality products to erase the bad image of prewar Japanese products. The Japanese were helped tremendously by having a uniform structure and composition, characterized by reverence for age, common religion, no ethnic groups, no immigrants, common language, and most important, common understanding of what it took to survive as a nation. While it is probable that U.S. employees can adapt to Japanese manufacturing methods such as JIT, emphasis on customer satisfaction, high quality, high productivity, and continuous improvement, management will need to approach employees in a different way and use different methods to motivate them.

7. *Working with the union.* Getting unionized American workers to accept Japanese cultural attitudes toward the workplace may be a difficult task. Break time in Japanese plants is often used for team meetings to discuss production problems and new techniques. Some American workers feel strongly that break time is *their* time. Management must change these workers' thinking if American plants are to keep up with Japanese ones.

8. *The American educational system.* A major concern for American industry's ability to pull up with and eventually exceed Japan in business

is how the United States' educational system compares to Japan's. The U.S. system has deteriorated significantly in comparison to the rest of the world, and it is not amenable to a quick fix. There is at least one generation of workers coming along who are several grade levels below their Japanese counterparts.

14

Techniques for Supervising Plant Maintenance Workers

MAINTENANCE: A MAJOR FUNCTION IN MANUFACTURING PLANTS

Without an effective maintenance program and a strong commitment to carrying it out constantly, today's manufacturing plants would be unable to operate, much less be profitable. Companies must minimize manufacturing process failures if they are to be competitive and grow. Yet in many plants, the maintenance function doesn't receive proper respect or get the attention it deserves. There is the belief in some plants that, since maintenance doesn't add value to a product, the less spent on it, the better. Because of this false and harmful thinking, nonprogressive plants have:

- Failed to implement basic maintenance practices.
- Neglected to train and develop maintenance personnel.
- Not adopted preventive and predictive maintenance.

Excessive equipment and machine failures have been the result, and the consequent downtime of productive facilities have hurt the plants' output. In addition, maintenance costs have been much higher than they should be. To minimize such malpractices and equipment failures in your plant, you must make maintenance a management priority.

UNDERSTANDING THE TYPES OF MAINTENANCE
USED IN PLANTS

While a few traditional manufacturing plants try to get by with limiting their maintenance practice to equipment failures and breakdowns, most of today's plants have progressed to higher and more effective procedures. Successful plants have recognized that "breakdown" maintenance is extremely costly. Besides, if you adopt and implement the other types, it is usually avoidable. Here are the other types along with a brief description of what each accomplishes:

1. *Preventive maintenance.* An effective preventive maintenance program anticipates the continuous wear and changes that equipment, machines, and systems undergo during operation. It calls for regular and appropriate action to minimize deterioration and breakdown. This involves periodic inspection and replacement of components.

2. *Predictive maintenance.* This practice foretells potential problems by sensing the operating characteristics of a machine or system. The procedure consists of monitoring operations, diagnosing undesirable trends, and pinpointing probable areas of failure.

3. *Corrective maintenance.* By adjusting or calibrating a machine or system, corrective maintenance improves either its quality or performance. The need for corrective maintenance results from preventive or predictive maintenance or from statistical process control.

HELPING PLANT EMPLOYEES UNDERSTAND
PREVENTIVE MAINTENANCE

While most employees know that preventive maintenance involves inspections and replacement of parts on equipment and machines, many may not know about the factors that must be considered in setting up a preventive maintenance program. To help then understand, tell them that plans for inspection and replacements are determined from the following:

- *Age and condition of machines and equipment.* If machines are old and worn, they should be inspected more frequently.

- *Severity of service.* If machines are operated 24 hours/day, or put under heavy load conditions, they need to be checked more frequently.

- *Exposure to the elements and chemicals*. If environmental conditions are poor or extreme, machines should be examined for corrosion and deterioration frequently.
- *Reliability*. If machines must operate without fail for safety or other reasons, inspections and parts replacements should be increased accordingly.

Explain to employees that by considering such factors, maintenance experts can work out a program that maximizes system efficiency and prolongs equipment life while reducing the cost of maintenance itself. Initially preventive maintenance may cost more than breakdown maintenance because of additional time spent in planning, keeping records, and making periodic adjustments. However, in the long term, overall costs will be lower.

If employees ask you how much the company should spend on preventive maintenance to prevent major and costly equipment breakdowns, make a sketch of Figure 14-1 for them. Point out that the lowest point on the total maintenance cost curve corresponds to the optimum cost of preventive maintenance.

GETTING EMPLOYEES INVOLVED IN PREVENTIVE MAINTENANCE

An excellent way to raise the interest and enthusiasm of employees, particularly maintenance workers, in the importance of preventive maintenance is to explain how it comes in play at protecting critical equipment and machines from major breakdowns. You can start by pointing out that planned maintenance programs for plant equipment are a necessity because of the type of machines and equipment being used, their high cost, and the value placed on keeping productive machines operating.

But follow up those words by saying that not every machine should be included in a preventive maintenance program, nor can all breakdowns be eliminated. The variability of breakdowns is a factor as is the time required to make repairs, and the relative costs of each. Excessive repair work and high costs, however, can be minimized by concentrating inspection and repair on machines and equipment considered critical. A machine should be classified as critical if upon abnormal performance or failure it:

- Endangers the health or safety of employees.
- Affects the quality of the product.
- Slows or stops other productive operations.

By analyzing equipment and machines in this way, you can determine where preventive maintenance should be applied—on those machines that

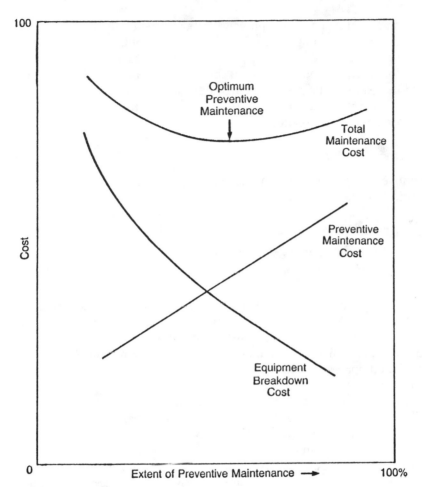

FIGURE 14-1
Relationship of Costs

will give the greatest return in production without sacrifice in product quality or safety of employees and the plant. Other machines may need only periodic or routine maintenance to perform satisfactorily within these critical concept limitations.

You can inform employees about what machines should be included in preventive maintenance programs by telling them that from an economic viewpoint, it might be best to let some noncritical equipment run until breakdown rather than attempt preventive maintenance. For example, in many plants, this policy is followed with fractional horsepower motors by considering their original cost and the cost of preventive maintenance that would be required.

Conclude talking about preventive maintenance by saying that inspecting and maintaining *all* equipment under a rigid schedule to try to eliminate *all* breakdowns is not practical. Labor costs would be excessive and undoubtedly exceed the value of the benefits to be gained. A machine should be included in a preventive maintenance program if the cost of the preventive maintenance is less than the cost of production lost time, repairs, or replacement upon breakdown.

Preventive Maintenance of Critical Machine Parts

Preventive maintenance procedures also play an important role with parts for critical machines. Needed are:

1. Recognition of what specific parts are critical.
2. A record or file system giving pertinent information on the parts.
3. Rapid accessibility to the parts.

Most equipment manufacturers provide a list of recommended spare parts for their machines. You would be wise to follow these recommendations, at least during the beginning period of operation of the machine. With time, this policy may be modified based on the machine's performance. The equipment vendor should be able to furnish information on part lives that will act as a guide for the quantity of parts to be stocked.

The efficiency of a plant's preventive maintenance program can be improved by setting up and using a good record system on equipment and parts. An illustration of the importance of such a system is the planning and scheduling of repairs to a critical machine. The work to be done on the machine should be carefully planned before the machine is shut down for the maintenance workers. If the diagnosis is to replace the machine's bearings, for example, then the correct type and size should be known before the machine is shut down. If they are not in the storeroom, they can be procured and be on hand. Nothing can be more discouraging to an embarrassed maintenance department and an anxious production department than to have production at a standstill waiting for a part that should have been available.

EXPLAINING PREDICTIVE MAINTENANCE

Predictive maintenance is the practice of determining the condition of machinery as it operates enabling maintenance personnel to monitor faults as they develop. This process not only helps you to eliminate the possibility of a catastrophic failure, it also allows you to order parts in advance, plan the repair, and schedule the maintenance workers.

It has been proven that breakdown maintenance is simply too expensive. While preventive maintenance is a cost-effective alternative, its success depends on the senses and judgment of inspectors and other maintenance personnel. Technicians and craftsmen rely on their experience to know when equipment and machines need attention and should be shut down.

On the other hand, the predictive maintenance approach tells you whether there is a problem and when it's appropriate to shut down for maintenance. Predictive maintenance relies on observed physical parameters—vibration readings, temperatures, electrical resistance, and others—measured against known engineering limits to determine the condition of the equipment.

Perhaps the best way to explain predictive maintenance is to say that it is an engineering approach to maintenance inspection that recognizes the importance of maximizing productive equipment uptime. Its purposes are to:

- Identify defective machine components before breakdown.

- Diagnose the problem.

- Give advance warning to permit repair without disrupting production schedules.

HOW TO SELL PREDICTIVE MAINTENANCE TO PLANT EMPLOYEES

An easy way to convince plant employees of the great value of predictive maintenance is to point out the benefits that can be derived from its use. Downtime in manufacturing plants can cost from $100 to $1500 per minute depending on the industry and the productive machines involved. Experience proves that plants using predictive maintenance are able to:

- Increase the availability of equipment and machines by 3 to 5 percent.

- Save $250,000 to $2,000,000 per year in maintenance costs.

- Virtually eliminate plant downtime due to unexpected machine failure.

- Substantially increase product quality.

Most plant programs result in a payback on equipment and training costs within six months. Considering the savings predictive maintenance offers in maintenance costs, downtime, and product quality, it is not surprising that more and more plants are installing these programs.

HOW PREDICTIVE MAINTENANCE TECHNIQUES WORK

Most of the plants using predictive maintenance are in the process industries such as steel, paper, electric power, chemicals, pharmaceuticals, and waste treatment. In process plants, the biggest economic factor is lost production from an unexpected shutdown of the process. But even if you're not employed in a process plant, you can still use predictive maintenance to advantage. Look for machines or equipment that are either production bottlenecks or are critical to your operation. They are good candidates for this maintenance technique.

Be aware, however, that predictive maintenance isn't limited to one way of maintaining machines and equipment. It is a group of different techniques that require various types of test equipment or services. Following are explanations of the most common techniques used in manufacturing plants worldwide.

Vibration Analysis[1]

Predictive maintenance programs involve a basic concept: All rotating machinery has some vibration and noise, and periodic checks for vibration reveal machine operating conditions. Vibration is the motion of a machine, or part of a machine, back and forth from its position of rest. The total distance of movements is the *peak-to-peak displacement* of the vibration. The number of cycles of this movement for a given period of time is the *frequency of the vibration*, and the position of the machine at any given instant with reference to some fixed point is the *phase of the vibration*.

Since the frequency of the vibration indicates its cause, this characteristic is the most important one measured. By comparing frequency of vibration with the rotating speed and multiples of rotating speeds, the point of vibration in a particular part of a machine and the cause of the vibration can be determined. Phase is used in balancing and is also helpful in identifying certain causes of vibration.

Using a vibration analyzer, you can measure and indicate the amount, frequency, and phase of vibration of a rotating machine. When a vibration occurs at several frequencies, the analyzer separates one frequency from another to measure each vibration characteristic. To implement an effective vibration analysis program, you need to take three steps:

1. *Detect and record the vibration.* This is done by placing pads (pickups) at various points on a machine where the most useful vibration information can be obtained; and using hand-held meters, automatic data

---

[1]Parts of the following explanation of vibration analysis came from "Using Vibration Analysis Effectively," *Plant Services*, October 1990, Putman Publishing, Chicago, IL 60611.

collectors, on-line surveillance systems or continuous monitoring instruments to make periodic vibration measurements.

2. *Analyze the data.* Vibration analysis quickly pinpoints a trouble spot. Because imbalance, misalignment, bent shafts, bad gears, defective bearings, and looseness cause vibration, each in a unique way, you can identify the problem without question.

3. *Correct the problem.* By identifying machine problems and impending failures early, you can plan the downtime and schedule the repairs before major breakdowns occur. If a problem is diagnosed as imbalance, it may be possible to correct it without disassembly. See Figure 14-2 for a troubleshooting guide for vibration analysis.

Ultrasonic Monitoring

All machines and their components emit identifiable sounds while operating. Because different components emit sound at different ultrasonic frequencies, specific components can be zeroed in on. For example, you can listen to bearings at 28–32 kilohertz and hear leaks at 40 kilohertz. You can use ultrasonic inspection for mechanical analysis of pumps, motors, compressors, gear boxes, valves, and bearings; it is also commonly used for both liquid and gas leak detection.

A typical acoustic test system includes a sensor, signal conditioning and processing equipment, and data recording or data storage equipment. Most systems are also furnished with headphones and instrumentation to convert ultrasound to something that can be heard, so that users can hear what they are tracking.

To use ultrasound inspection, you hold the sensor against a machine as you would a stethoscope. Some sensors scan a machine or an area for abnormal readings, then tune in to and make contact with a machine or component in question. The procedure may be made easier by putting the machine under a bit of stress, so that a bad bearing or developing leak becomes noisier. Facilitating the inspection, a sound source can often be quickly located because the intensity of the signal falls off rapidly from its source of emission.

Although a trained operator can make assumptions based simply on immediate analog or even aural data, newer and more sophisticated systems store data for trend analysis. Using a computer, you can make a comparison of the latest readings with a "signature" of the ultrasound emitted under normal operating conditions.

Oil Analysis

Two basic items of concern with oil analysis are lubricant condition and machine condition. You want to know if a lubricant is contaminated, but

FIGURE 14-2
Troubleshooting Guide for Vibration Analysis

Machine Parts	Frequency Relative to Machine RPM	Other Symptoms	Probable Causes	Corrective Action
All machinery, foundations and supports	Frequency determined by originating source	Excessive vibration amplitude. Slight changes in speed produce large changes in amplitude and phase angle. Slight corrections give large results	Resonance of machine part, foundation, or support	Raise or lower RPM or vibration frequency of source part, or make resonating part more rigid or less rigid relative to the weight it supports. Change length, position or part, or rigidity of bearings.
All rotating machines with more than one vibrating source	Frequency not related to RPM usually very slow from several minutes apart to over 1000 cycles per minute	Thumping action or pulsating sound superimposed over a higher-frequency vibration	Two vibrations of nearly equal frequency (or multiples of) affecting the same structure, causing beats	Separate either the frequencies by changing RPM on one part or separate rate by keeping vibrations from adding to each other. Dampen. Balance to reduce.
Nonbolted down or nongrouted machinery	2 × RPM	Double image with strobe light	Poor mounting on foundation. Imbalance supplies action as machine base pivots about one line of contact, twice per revolution	Shim, bolt down, and grout in machine's base.
All rotating parts	1 × RPM		Unbalance or off-center rotor	Check centers and/or balance.

Component	Frequency	Symptom	Cause	Correction
Armatures and electric rotors	1 × RPM	Looks like unbalance but immediately disappears when electric power is cut off	Eccentric armature	Correct eccentricities.
	7200 cycles/minute	Buzzing sound; immediately disappears when electric power is cut off	Loose iron affected by + or − of 60-cycle power input	Proper dipping or encapsulation, or otherwise correct looseness.
Couplings, shafts, and bearings	Often 1 or 2 × RPM; rarely 3 or 4 × RPM	High axial vibration, especially when axial vibration reaches half or more of radial vibration. May also not produce high axial vibration.	Misaligned coupling or shaft bearings. Occurs also in flexible couplings. Especially prominent in slender, long shafts to coupling position.	Align to tolerance required for smoothness.
Rotors and shafts	1 × RPM	High axial and radial vibration	Bent shaft	Prove with strobe before straightening.
Gears	1 × RPM	Looks like unbalance but motion is torsional vibration. Could well be resonant torsionally.	Eccentric gear pitch circle due to machining or mounting errors	Correct eccentricity. Try other *line to line* contact points between gear box and shaft.
	Number of teeth × RPM	Usually torsional vibration but not always. Could be in torsional resonance.	Bending due to unbalance causes side thrust between mating teeth. Eccentric gear pitch circle due to machining errors causing pulsating acceleration and deceleration of gear rotation	If resonant, change shaft or bearing stiffness, or RPM, or number of teeth.

TABLE 14-2 Continued

Machine Parts	Frequency Relative to Machine RPM	Other Symptoms	Probable Causes	Corrective Action
Universal joints	1 × RPM	Looks like imbalance.	Too tight universal joint	Relieve tightness.
Universal joints and driveshaft	2 × RPM	Double image strobe picture	Unequal corresponding angles between input and output ends of driveshaft	Equalize corresponding angles through proper alignment.
Sleeve bearings	Slightly less than ½ × RPM	Oil whirl. Very rough amplitude; disappears suddenly with sufficient reduction in speed	Excessive clearance or bearing loads that are too light relative to its rotational speed. Can also be caused by misaligned coupling.	Use pressure pad or pivoted shoe bearing or relieve sides of sleeve to decrease oil wedge pressure.
Anti-friction bearings	Usually relatively high frequency	Usually very low amplitude; noisy. Most often frequency is unsteady and many times rotor RPM	Excessive friction or rumble due to bad balls, rollers, rough races, poor lubrication, or too tight fit	Replace bearing. When applicable, relieve press fit.
V belts	1 × RPM	Very high axial vs. radial vibration	Mismatched multiple belt tensions	Replace with matched belts.
V belts and other drive belts	1 × RPM	High axial vibration (sometimes not too noticeable due to mass of structure but shows up in bearing wear)	Drive and driven sheaves not aligned so as to be in same plane of action	Align sheaves to act in same plane.

Source: Oil, Gas & Petrochem Equipment, June 1984, Penn Well Publishing Co., Tulsa, OK 74101

more important, whether or not avoidable wear is occurring. Selecting the sampling spot is critical because the sample should not only be representative of the lubricant in the machine, but also be from a spot where contaminants are likely to be caught. Samples should be taken when the system is hot, at a point in the main lubricant flow, and at a place where outside contamination cannot occur.

One of the biggest differences between this predictive maintenance technique and others is that oil analysis is almost always performed by a contract laboratory; only the large airlines and power plants do it in-house. As a result, there is a time lag between sampling and receiving analyses reports. Yet it's not hard to cost-justify when an analysis costs only $20 to $25 a sample. Generally, you can recover the cost of a yearly program by catching just one incipient failure.

Trend analysis is a strong, statistics-based technique that works well with oil analysis, but it isn't simply graphing the test results. A comprehensive trend analysis requires use of complex math. Additionally, a basic essential of trend analysis is correcting the data for the time that the oil has been in use. Although interpretation of the data is partly based on calculated trends, many oil analysis laboratories report only raw test data to the customer.

You can benefit the most from an oil analysis program if you ensure that your workers get fully involved. Here is how to proceed:

1. Assign permanent workers to the oil analysis program. Problems will develop if the responsible personnel see the program as a temporary assignment or feel it is an extra duty they must handle. You also want to make it clear to the laboratory who they will be working with.

2. Make sure that workers document completely the samples and sampled components. The laboratory can't draw valid conclusions from the test results and trends without operating data and information on the components and lubricants in service.

3. Ask the laboratory to determine the best sampling points and sampling intervals. Once sampling points and methods are agreed to, review the machine manufacturer's guidelines and maintenance recommendations to establish optimum sampling intervals.

4. Define and respond to critical analyses reports. After critical conditions have been detected and reported, it's up to you to conduct an overall performance assessment, and then place the timing and extent of further action.

5. Provide feedback to the laboratory. Avoid assuming that you bias the lab by giving it information concerning your observations, and consider the human factor in this process. Depriving the person interpreting the

test results of the facts needed to make informed judgments directly limits accuracy.

6. Document the cost savings of the program. A good way to calculate the economic benefits of oil analysis is to compare parts and labor expenses for machine repair and component replacement, plus production loss during downtime before oil analysis, with the same cost factors, plus the analysis expenses, after the program has been established.

Infrared Imaging (Thermography)

This technique entails the study of heat given off by objects, particularly heat that is more radiant then normal in an area. Infrared imagers (instruments) sense very small temperature differences and detect infrared radiation of middle and long wavelengths by converting the invisible radiation into visible light. The representation of infrared (heat) is viewed through an eyepiece that magnifies a tiny television screen or is displayed on a full-size television screen. A typical system consists of a camera, often accompanied by a video recorder, which shows the heat ranges of the items in view. The temperatures can be portrayed in either a gray scale for a black and white system or in colors.

Finding hot spots in electrical wiring systems and detecting building heat losses were two of the early industrial uses of infrared imaging. Thermographers have done the most work and documented substantial savings in checking the integrity of insulation and refractory of furnaces and ovens, and insulation of boilers, ovens, and pipelines; the regularity of process flows; and the proper functioning of bearings in rotating equipment. In addition, infrared imaging has been used to spot scale buildup in heater tubes.

According to the Infraspection Institute, infrared imaging does three operations either exclusively or better than other technologies:

1. Predictive maintenance of electrical systems.
2. Nondestructive testing of insulation.
3. Monitoring of fluid flow, if the fluid is either hotter or colder than the surrounding temperature.

HOW TO HELP WORKERS PREVENT BEARING FAILURES

There is considerable evidence that predictive and preventive maintenance are the keys to minimizing equipment downtime caused by bearing failure. Identifying and replacing bearings in poor operating condition before they fail can cut a plant's equipment downtime and reduce its maintenance costs. But, just as important, bearing failures can be minimized if you properly train maintenance workers on how to handle them. You can help the cause by discussing the subject with them. Here are some points you should make:

- Cleanliness is critical in handling bearings because just a small amount of contamination can lead to premature failure. Consequently, manufacturers use extreme care in packaging bearings to ensure that contaminants do not enter them during storage or shipment.

- Most bearings are coated with a protective slushing compound at the factory. This coating should not be washed off unless the lubricant to be used is a polyurea grease or pure synthetic oil or grease. Prelubricated sealed bearings should never be washed before assembly.

- Never put a bearing on a surface other than the moisture-resistant paper in which it was packaged. Always cover bearings that are not being worked on at the moment with a clean, lint-free cloth.

- Use only tools designed specifically for bearing work. They are safer, do not damage bearings, and save you time. Several tools are available for bearing monitoring, installation, and removal.

- Never use a hot oil bath or a torch to heat a bearing. Both methods are hazardous, time consuming, and inefficient. Induction heaters control bearing temperature precisely, are not hazardous, and constitute the fastest method available to heat a bearing today.

- Oil and grease, the two primary bearing lubricants, have two main functions: separating the components' moving parts, and protecting the bearing from the environment. Lubrication guidelines are usually provided in bearing manufacturers' catalogs.

HOW TO CONTROL THE QUALITY OF PLANT MAINTENANCE

In recent years, maintenance managers and supervisors have become aware that quality control can be applied to plant maintenance to advantage. Through an effective quality control program, you can:

- Upgrade the maintenance function.
- Increase the efficiency of maintenance personnel.
- Serve the production department better.
- Reduce the costs of the maintenance department.

Today, a maintenance department would be hard pressed to operate efficiently and provide the service expected of it if it didn't adopt the tenets of quality control. Because of rapidly increasing costs of maintenance, value analysis has received more attention and quality control has accompanied it. With higher standards of performance now expected of equipment and facilities plus more governmental regulation of design and operation, the quality of maintenance has had to improve.

More, however, remains to be done. There is still a strong need for maintenance workers to do higher quality work as well as more of it. There will always be a need for management to find ways to reduce and eliminate repetitive repairs. Controlling the quality of maintenance may be a big job, but it is not beyond the capability of plant personnel. The job should be approached in several ways because many factors should be considered.

Purchasing

Controlling the quality of maintenance begins with purchasing. If the company buys first-class material, the repairs made to equipment and facilities are more likely to also be first class. You can expect a paint job to look better and to hold up longer if you use good quality industrial paint. You can expect a wooden structure to last longer if your carpenters have high-grade lumber to work with.

The same logic applies to the tools you provide your workers. A worker who has only makeshift tools won't be able to do a high-quality repair job, nor will he or she take pride in the work done. Pride often is behind high-quality work. Special tools, such as ergonomically designed ones, which you purchase or rent for the department will enable workers to handle tough jobs safer and more efficiently, and their workmanship will also be better.

Work Performance

One of the ways to determine the quality of maintenance in the plant is to analyze the performance of the maintenance workers. While the task logically falls on your shoulders, it may be difficult for workers to be efficient and cost effective when they are occupied principally with breakdown work because there is little if any time for planning. Since much of this work consists of troubleshooting, the skill of the worker is critical. But the fact that breakdown work must be performed quickly should not be an excuse for you to accept poor quality workmanship. You can still control the quality of the work with close supervision.

Variances of Quality

Perhaps the most crucial practice from a quality viewpoint is performance of maintenance work in an irresponsible and shoddy manner. The worker who damages equipment and machines when making repairs cannot be tolerated. Nor can the worker who makes improper adjustments, fails to replace lids, caps, bolts, and nuts, and does work that results in stripped threads on connections. Other variances of quality workmanship concern how machines and work areas are left after the maintenance work is performed. Spills should be cleaned up, and worn-out parts as well as waste material should be properly disposed of.

Failure to do a thorough and complete job on a repair or inspection assignment is another example of poor-quality maintenance. If an order calls for several operations to be performed such as determining motor load, testing for vibration, and making drive adjustments, then the work should not be considered complete or acceptable until all of these operations are handled.

You can control the quality of maintenance only if you set standards of performance and make workers aware of them. Establishing standards is especially appropriate when formulating a plant's preventive maintenance program. Standard procedures must be followed with inspections, oiling and lubrication, painting, winterizing, putting machines and equipment in standby condition, and other preventive procedures.

Motivation of Maintenance Workers

There are several ways you can motivate plant workers:

1. Give them the opportunity to troubleshoot equipment malfunctions and to decide how repairs should be made. Pride and motivation go together and both will be greater than if you use only their hands and not their minds.
2. Train workers who are not technically qualified to do the work. When they develop a high level of skill, they will know they are good on the job. And when they realize others recognize they are good, they are motivated.
3. Post work schedules and jobs completed as a way of pointing out the skills and accomplishments of individuals. In addition to informing peers of special achievements, this may also induce a competitive spirit in the group.

Planning and Scheduling

Controlling the quality of maintenance requires planning and scheduling of the functions and operations that affect it. This is particularly true with preventive and predictive maintenance. Planning pays off in setting up inspection and testing procedures. For example, persons assigned inspection work must be thoroughly instructed in what to look for when inspecting machines and equipment. Preferably, they should have had several years of maintenance experience so that they are familiar with the operation and control of the machines and equipment they are inspecting.

Planning affects the quality of maintenance in the degree to which it is applied to the specific task to be performed. You can't expect workers to do a high-quality maintenance job unless you:

1. Study the job before you assign it.
2. Anticipate difficulties and provide for them.
3. See that the workers have the right tools and material.

Reliability and Verification

Reliability, as it affects the quality of maintenance, is ascertained by a study of the life characteristic of a machine or piece of equipment. Most machines provide useful service through three periods of their life:

1. A start-up period of likely failure immediately after being put in operation.
2. A normal operating period of unlikely failure.
3. A wear-out period just before complete failure or obsolescence.

Quality control of maintenance is most critical in the first and third periods. Inspection frequency should be high in the beginning until the machine enters the normal operating period. When wear appears in the third period, quality control should be stepped up—parts may need to be renewed. Soon thereafter the entire machine replacement can be anticipated because maintenance costs become excessive and performance characteristics decline.

Maintenance work should be considered satisfactory only if you can verify the adequacy, timeliness, and completeness of the work performed. The operating and production departments of a plant are probably the best judges of this. Verification should consist of checking each completed work order to see that the job was done properly and according to instructions. In some plants, the production supervisor is called to a machine or system by the maintenance workers after they have completed repairs; the machine is operated in the supervisor's presence to confirm that the work is finished and satisfactory. With planned work, the preventive maintenance specialist, planner, or maintenance supervisor may check out a completed work order.

Timeliness is important in controlling the quality of maintenance. Although a reasonable backlog of work for the department is desirable for planning, scheduling, and efficient use of labor, breakdown work must, of course, be handled as quickly as possible. Proper timing of inspections is essential if preventive maintenance costs are to be kept in line and justified. The quality of the maintenance work a department performs may be affected by how successful it is in timing inspections to reveal the need for adjustments and repairs before major breakdowns occur.

SELLING PLANNING AND SCHEDULING TO MAINTENANCE WORKERS

It is essential that the plant maintenance department have a system of planning and scheduling for the maintenance work load. Just as the production department cannot effectively operate without scheduling and control, maintenance personnel must also have planning and scheduling to control their operations. This should be your theme in selling planning and scheduling to maintenance workers.

Proper planning and scheduling are the keys to how any maintenance operation can effectively meet changing priorities. Planning determines the work that needs to be done, when it should be done (based on a priority system) and what resources will be needed to complete the job.

Scheduling involves coordinating workers, material, equipment parts, tools, and equipment shutdown to assure that all are available at the prescribed time. A scheduled program of preventive and predictive maintenance is required to keep production equipment downtime to an absolute minimum. Advance planning and scheduling of work before jobs are assigned enables personnel to be used as efficiently as possible.

Planning and scheduling maintenance work in the plant should be directed toward aiding, complementing, and strengthening maintenance supervision. It should not, however, encroach upon the authority or responsibility of supervisors. Unless a maintenance department is very small and has a strong supervisor, a planner position should be included in the maintenance organization.

THE ROLE OF THE MAINTENANCE PLANNER

The primary function of a maintenance planner is to handle all the administrative duties required in the preparation of major repair jobs so that they can be carried out more effectively. This function consists of checking out the work site, determining job details and materials needed, estimating labor requirements, confirming availability of tools, and coordinating equipment shutdown. Effective planners benefit the company because planned major maintenance jobs will be completed with less labor and less productive equipment downtime.

There is generally a short period of time between the initial planning and the scheduling of maintenance jobs. During this period, the planner establishes the best tentative timing of the shutdown of the equipment with the production scheduler. He or she then coordinates arrival of materials, equipment, tools, and other items to coincide with the shutdown. In some plants, a schedule meeting is arranged and attended by key maintenance and production supervisors to discuss next week's maintenance jobs. With the concurrence of production personnel of the best timing for the various shutdowns, the planner allocates labor to approved jobs by priority, obtains approval of the schedule for execution of the work, and publishes the schedule.

Although small maintenance departments may need only a single planner, plants that do not agree on the importance of the planner's job try to combine it with a supervisor's job. This practice is not recommended because the two jobs are different. A small maintenance department should use the planner to help the largest number of supervisors. With such an arrangement, the planner reports to the manager of maintenance and provides direct support to the supervisors as needed to help them carry out major jobs.

The number of planners needed in a plant should be based on the amount of planned work the maintenance department handles. Planning and scheduling 70 to 80 percent of the total workorders ensures that maintenance operations are controlled. In most industrial plants, there should be one planner for about every 15 to 20 workers who maintain productive equipment. If each supervisor has a crew of 10 to 12 persons, about 8 crew members should do planned and scheduled work.

However, shop work (machining, fabricating, rebuilding, and refurbishing) is handled differently. In a shop environment, you can supervise more persons because work is concentrated in a smaller area. Although the managerial job may be more detailed, it is somewhat easier. Shop supervisors can manage more workers; 18 to 20 is not an unusual number. Shops lend themselves more readily to the use of standards, and more work (85 to 90 percent) should be planned and scheduled. Operating under these conditions, a shop planner might support about 30 maintenance personnel, managed by two supervisors.

HOW COMPUTERIZED CONTROL IMPROVES MAINTENANCE OPERATIONS

Plants that have computerized their maintenance operations have gained many benefits. Computerized maintenance increases the efficiency of personnel, improves the service to the production department, and most important, reduces maintenance costs. The direct benefits to you and other supervisors are also noteworthy:

1. You are aware of machine breakdowns almost immediately after they occur. You can establish a priority for the repair job, know what craft is required, and even get repairs started within a few minutes.

2. You can collect history on machine and equipment performance so that studies can be made to identify problem areas in order to further reduce maintenance costs. When you have good records of the plant's equipment, machines and facilities in the computer, you can do a better job of keeping those things up and running.

How a Computerized System Works

The dual function of a computerized maintenance system is defined with a real-time operation in control in the plant through a minicomputer, while equipment performance data and history are accumulated and stored in a mainframe computer. Industrial plants can gain much from this computerized operation. Maintenance and engineering personnel can better control work orders, both verbal and written. They can plan and schedule work, increase the productivity of maintenance workers, and provide for spare equipment and parts. But because many plants must contend with a large number of worker orders, the system must be designed to be flexible, versatile, and wide in its coverage.

Work Orders

The work order is the basic instrument of a computerized maintenance system. Job origination, identification, and authorization materialize with the work order. You make job assignments with work orders, and you get information feedback for job costs, equipment history, and worker performance through the work order. Maintenance work orders are of two types:

1. Those suited for planning involve work that requires scheduled equipment downtime. They must represent enough expenditure of manhours or dollars to justify estimating and scheduling the job. Another requirement of a planned work order is that the lead time must be sufficient to permit the time it takes to process an order.

2. Those not suited for planning involve jobs that are of such high priority that work must begin too soon for planning to be effective, or those that are of short duration and do not require scheduling of equipment downtime. Unplanned work orders are referred to in the computerized system as verbal work orders, or as breakdown work orders.

An efficient system uses the computer to issue work orders to the maintenance workers, a work order being required and created for each maintenance job. Whenever a worker starts or completes a job, the order is updated in the computer data base. This enables you and others to make inquiries through the computer to get information. The most common requests are questions such as:

- Which machines are awaiting maintenance?
- Which machines are currently being worked on?
- What are the top-priority jobs in the department?
- How many work orders are backlogged for electricians?

Thus, you can determine the status of maintenance work in the plant at any time by making a few simple inquiries on the computer.

With this system, you store the work orders on a disc that is attached to the minicomputer in the plant. When the work orders are completed, they can be sent to a mainframe computer where they may be stored indefinitely. Usually, only one month or two of data is stored in the mini-computer because it doesn't have sufficient capacity to analyze the large amount that would accumulate over a longer period of time.

Analyzing by the Computer

Work orders stored in the mainframe can be analyzed using a software system programmed specifically for that purpose. One such package that is finding a lot of use today is called the *Statistical Analysis System* (SAS). In order to use SAS, you must know what information is available in the data base. Also, when requesting information, you must be very specific and inclusive to avoid receiving a large amount of data, much of which may not be of value to you.

Requesting a report on equipment failure, for example, requires that you make the following inquiry: the time frame (beginning and ending date and time) of the activity you want analyzed, the equipment number, and the type of failure you want to analyze. With information on the type and number of failures occurring with the plant's lift trucks, for example, you can decide which type should be addressed in a training program. If, for instance, you learn that steering box failures are frequently occurring, you may be able to remedy this by giving maintenance workers appropriate instructions.

The type of reports that you can generate by the mainframe computer using SAS software is almost endless. You can obtain reports that give such information as:

- The average time it takes for a worker to begin repairs on a machine after it breaks down.
- The average length of time it takes to fix a particular failure.

- Which machines require the most repair labor or parts.
- Which machines are the most costly to repair.
- Which repair items have been withdrawn most frequently from the store-room.
- What repair material is costing the company the most money.

But that isn't all that a SAS report can do for you. You can also request data and information on the computerized procedures of purchasing, receiving, shipping, and stores operations. Thus, you can have access to much information to help you in reaching your objectives of lower maintenance costs and better performance of employees.

PROVIDING WORKERS WITH KNOWLEDGE OF MAINTENANCE COMPUTER SYSTEMS

You can supply information of the maintenance computer system most easily to workers by explaining its benefits. Here are the major items you can talk about:

- Less planning time per job is needed. This results in more job plans produced, fewer backlogged jobs, and fewer breakdowns requiring emergency repairs.
- Job planning is improved because of more and better information in the computer data base. A planner has backlog and status reports available, and can quickly retrieve repetitious job plans and historical job analyses.
- Job scheduling is more efficient because only jobs with materials available are scheduled. This results in fewer schedule changes and faster delivery of materials to workers.
- More productive time of machines and equipment is assured because less outage of parts occurs. When parts are not available, maintenance workers must either be given new assignments or spend time trying to locate or fabricate substitutions.
- Running time of productive machines and equipment is increased because of more effective preventive and predictive maintenance programs in effect. The ability of the computer system to automatically schedule these programs puts them up front and thereby increases the likelihood of their being carried out.
- Lower inventories results from computerizing stores materials. The computer automatically counts, updates, and orders parts to minimize inventories yet prevent outages.

PITFALLS TO AVOID WHEN INSTALLING A
COMPUTERIZED MAINTENANCE SYSTEM

Although the benefits and advantages of computerizing your plant maintenance system justify its installation, you must be cautious when adopting and implementing it. To assure that you aren't plagued with continuing problems, take the following steps:

1. Be wary of an incorrect assessment of the plant's needs on what functions are to be computerized.
2. Plan for the long rather than the short term.
3. See that someone in the maintenance department is assigned full time to implementing the system.
4. Number and put into the data base all machines and equipment.
5. Avoid improper estimates of the time or cost to load data into the computer.
6. Recognize that an in-house software system may not be as cost effective or as permanent as a purchased system.
7. Assure that a work order system is in active use before implementing the computer.
8. See that employees are given the necessary orientation and training in system use and goals.
9. Include support for job estimating, planning, and scheduling in the system.
10. Link the maintenance system to other systems already operating in areas such as process control, purchasing, receiving, stores, and accounting.
11. Assure employees that the computer is not being installed to monitor the performance of individual workers but to help improve the overall maintenance function.

TIPS ON CUTTING MAINTENANCE DOWNTIME OF
MACHINES AND EQUIPMENT

You've probably noticed that the productive equipment in your plant is arranged and installed to reduce wasted motion and to aid material flow. With good layouts, quick changes in setups and process equipment can be made when necessary as can other steps to assure continuity of manufacturing and just-in-time inventories.

Since maintenance operations are an integral part of manufacturing, you should see that provisions are made to carry them out similarly to production operations. When productive equipment breaks down, it must be brought back on line as soon as possible. Yet many plants are not prepared to do that. Here are some suggestions on how you can cut maintenance downtime of machines and equipment in your plant:

1. Place cabinets for storage of maintenance parts and supplies near major concentrations of production machinery. Too much time is lost when maintenance workers must retrieve material to repair a machine from a distant part of the plant.

2. Treat special tooling and supplies required to maintain a specific machine in a similar manner. Store wrenches, clamps, setup and adjustment tools, shims, and other support supplies nearby. Include with the tools the operating and maintenance manuals for the machines.

3. See that parts stored in the cabinets are exact replacements for those in use. Also, attach all necessary fittings and hardware to parts so that they are ready to install.

4. Label and organize parts so they can be retrieved quickly. Replace parts as you use them to assure the cabinet's usefulness.

5. Install electrical and pneumatic outlets on major pieces of production equipment. They will eliminate the need to run long power lines and hoses to operate repair tools needed to make repairs to that equipment.

6. Use quick-disconnect fittings on hydraulic, pneumatic, and electrical lines that feed wear-sensitive parts such as cylinders, strainers, filters, solenoids, and similar items. Such fittings can cut part replacement times significantly.

COORDINATING MAINTENANCE WORKERS' JOB ASSIGNMENTS WITH PRODUCTION OPERATIONS

The procedures that you, as a maintenance supervisor, must follow in order to operate at maximum efficiency on work that has been planned and scheduled deserve your close attention. To minimize downtime of equipment and maintenance costs, you must handle several matters before and after you assign workers to a job:

- Learn from the production department the time at which the work can start.

- Assure that your workers are available at that time. This is particularly important if special skills are required.

- Determine what tools, materials, and parts will be needed and assure that they are available.

- Be very familiar with the job scope and details so that if problems come up during the work, you can handle them immediately.
- Check the workers frequently after the work starts so the job does not lag and is done as originally planned.
- Have workers report as soon as the job is finished so that the production department may resume operations.

COORDINATING PRODUCTION OPERATIONS WITH MAINTENANCE ACTIVITIES

While some production supervisors would prefer to operate equipment for the longest possible time until a breakdown seems imminent or occurs, and then make quick repairs to get back into production, maintenance supervisors do not agree with such thinking. Maintenance personnel, in general, prefer to make repairs and adjustments on a planned and scheduled basis, thereby eliminating as much as possible the emergency situations that arise with breakdowns. They feel that planning and scheduling their maintenance work results in better efficiency of labor and machines as well as prolonging equipment life. They also want an inspection program that will enable them to catch malfunctioning machines before major breakdowns occur.

If you are a production supervisor, you should be aware of what you can do to coordinate production operations with maintenance activities. Here are some simple, and perhaps obvious, ways you can do that:

1. Run only part of the process line when maintenance personnel want to do preventive maintenance, repair work, or cleaning. There are several advantages to getting maintenance handled this way:
   - You don't entirely interrupt the plant output or upset operations in other process steps.
   - You eliminate the need for a large number of maintenance and cleaning personnel at one time.
   - You avoid labor overtime, which is costly in money and efficiency.
2. Provide spare equipment in standby condition ready for immediate service. When this is not practical because of cost or space reasons, have maintenance workers replace the machine with a spare unit, repairing the faulty component in the maintenance shop later. The advantages of this procedure are:
   - Equipment downtimes are shorter.
   - Repairs or component replacements are made under better conditions—on a work bench or in the maintenance shop.

- Workers have the opportunity to inspect and do other work on the machine (such as seal and bearing replacements, lubrication, general cleaning, and painting) while it is in the shop.

3. Include as much information as possible about an equipment problem when submitting a maintenance work order. The maintenance supervisor may be able to expedite repairs if the problem is clearly defined. For example, the supervisor could be looking for a replacement motor if the order said the one in use was smoking, rather than learn that after an electrician made tests.

4. Be alert to plan and schedule maintenance work into the time period prior to a plant shutdown. Many industrial processes, particularly in the chemical and oil industries, must complete the product finishing instead of leaving it in-process. Thus machines and equipment are shut down in steps. The equipment that is shut down first can be turned over to the maintenance department.

HOW TO USE CHECKLISTS TO REDUCE EQUIPMENT DOWNTIME

The use of checklists in both the maintenance and production departments helps greatly in coordinating repairs, preventive maintenance, and cleaning operations. Whenever a process line or a major piece of equipment is shut down for one or more of these operations, make a list of the work to be done and the jobs to be handled. Provide space on the sheet for initialing each item when it has been completed. Here is what you gain by using checklists:

- You can readily see at any time during the shutdown period what still needs to be done. Depending on the resources available, you can do what is necessary to satisfy those needs.

- Use of the list aids in coordinating cleaning and maintenance activities because labor can be assigned to different areas so that workers do not interfere with each other. Safety and worker efficiency are better with such arrangements.

- The list is a boon to multishift plant operations because status of the downtime work can be kept current from shift to shift. Whenever a job is completed, it is initialed by the supervisor whose workers accomplished it.

- No job or activity is overlooked; every job and procedure should be initialed before plans are made to resume production.

HOW TO TRAIN MAINTENANCE WORKERS

Whether your maintenance workers are classified as technicians or craftsmen, they need training to perform maintenance jobs safely, effectively, and efficiently. The general objective for a worker training course is: to be able to analyze machine malfunctions and isolate malfunctioning components; to quickly repair or replace faulty components to minimize machine downtime.

Experience has shown that a logically organized technical course for plant maintenance personnel includes:

1. *Basic principles and theory*. Regardless of the level of the course, basic principles are critical to the training program. They are not only essential for the beginner, they serve as a valuable review for the older service employee.

2. *Equipment, machines, and components*. Knowing the operation, construction, and function of individual machines and their components are necessities for each worker. The worker cannot make an intelligent decision to adjust, repair, or replace a component without knowledge of how that component works and what it is supposed to do.

3. *Systems and circuits*. This portion of the course should relate directly to the particular systems and circuits in use in the plant. Specific drawings and blueprints should be selected for classroom training. The symbols used on the drawings must be studied first to enable the workers to read the drawings.

4. *Troubleshooting*. Learning to troubleshoot is the most difficult job for the worker. Training on troubleshooting is most easily carried out on the job rather than in the classroom. The more knowledgeable workers are in basic principles, machines, and systems, the more competent they will be in troubleshooting.

Elements of Typical Courses

A maintenance course usually proceeds from principles to machines and equipment, to systems, to troubleshooting, with each course based on the specific machines, equipment, and systems in the plant. For example, a hydraulics course would cover pumps, valves, cylinders, and other equipment that are hydraulically operated. Figure 14-3 lists the elements of typical maintenance courses in manufacturing plants.

Most vendors, whether representatives of machine and equipment manufacturers or component suppliers, can furnish detailed information on their products. This material, distributed through their sales, service, or training departments, is invaluable for training maintenance workers.

FIGURE 14-3
Elements of Typical Maintenance Courses

	Electric Course	Hydraulic Course	Pneumatic Course	Instrumentation Course
Theory	Ohm's law Voltage Current Resistance	Pascal's law	Pascal's law	Theory of process control
Components	Motors Timers Relays Transformers Switches Solenoid valves	Pumps Valves Reservoirs Cylinders	Compressors Valves Cylinders	Temperature controllers Pressure controllers Level controllers Timers
Systems	DC drives AC motor controls SCR drives Adjustable speed AC drives	Machines operated entirely or partially by hydraulic systems	Machines operated entirely or partially by pneumatic systems	Systems controlled by instruments

It includes catalogs and bulletins containing parts and service information, application data, and operating instructions.

Providing a Qualified Trainer

You have a choice of three alternatives in selecting a trainer or instructor for maintenance workers:

1. If the training sessions are to be short and one time only, the most practical approach is to hire an instructor from outside the plant. Component suppliers (vendors) usually conduct training courses. The suppliers use members of their sales or service force to conduct classes at customer facilities. Sometimes this training is free.

2. If your maintenance requirements call for the course to be set up on a permanent basis, it would probably be more practical to use someone from within your plant. He or she would then be responsible for organizing and conducting the training sessions. In selecting this individual, job competency and a willingness to teach are more important than previous teaching experience. Also, an ability to get along with people is an important qualification.

3. If it is not appropriate to conduct sessions, consider having the workers attend classes held at local technical or vocational schools. If none are offered, local educators might be persuaded to come into your plant to teach a course.

TRAINING MAINTENANCE WORKERS FOR PLANT AUTOMATION

More and more plants today are looking at ways to automate their production processes as a way of increasing workers' productivity and cutting labor costs. Accompanying this movement, there is a need to train maintenance workers to upgrade their skills to meet the plant automation requirements. Since more than one work or process area in the plant may be automated, workers need to be trained on systems with machinery from several different manufacturers.

Vendors and manufacturer's representatives supplying the equipment are usually the best source for training. They have the best subject matter expertise, engineering resources, and knowledge of the functions performed by the equipment. However, unless they understand training as well, and have the personnel and facilities for teaching, you may have to go elsewhere for that expertise. Consultants can also provide training, although their resource materials may be limited. Their fees are usually higher than those of equipment vendors. Basically, you have a choice of three methods to use for training maintenance workers:

1. *On-the-job training with someone who knows the equipment.* The advantages with this method are that the trainee receives one-on-one instruction, and that it is given in a real environment. The disadvantages are that the procedure is time consuming, and the equipment is not appropriate because it is too expensive.

2. *Classroom training by vendors or consultants.* The advantages with this method are the instructor is likely to be an expert who will use simulators and models of the equipment, and the procedure will be time efficient. The disadvantages are that it will consist of group, instead of one-on-one, instruction, it will not be in a real environment, and it will probably be expensive.

3. *Computer-based training on the job site.* This method simulates the best of the on-the-job and the classroom methods by combining the communicating of information with the giving of individualized attention to the trainee. Adding an administrative feature and a friendly computer program with quality audio and visual aids ensures that each trainee will get the appropriate information as quickly as possible. With these

advantages, this method is the best of the three from both the trainee's viewpoint and management's.

How to Ensure That Maintenance Employees Work Safely

One of the most effective ways of protecting maintenance workers and other plant employees from a serious injury or death is to enforce the use of lockout/tagout procedures. The OSHA lockout/tagout regulation lets you decide to use lockout, tagout, or both, depending on whichever system you deem is best for your plant. To explain this safety system to maintenance employees, tell them that three steps are required to use the lockout method:

1. Put a circuit breaker, disconnect switch, valve, or other energy isolating mechanism that supplies energy to machinery or equipment in the safe or off position.
2. Place a device over the mechanism to hold it in the safe position.
3. Attach a lock so that the machine or equipment can't be energized or turned on.

With the tagout method, the energy-isolating mechanism is put in the safe or off position, and a warning tag is attached to it.

To make sure employees understand the lockout or tagout procedure, explain that they should use it whenever they are servicing, maintaining, or repairing a machine where they could be injured by the unexpected startup of the machine or by the release of stored energy. Tell them that they are most likely to need lockout or tagout in two situations in the plant:

1. When they must remove a guard or other safety device.
2. When they must place any part of their body where it could be caught by moving machinery.

Add that they should use the procedure when:

- Repairing electrical circuits or equipment.
- Clearing and releasing jammed mechanisms.
- Cleaning or oiling machinery with moving parts.

15

Guaranteed Methods for Dealing with Union Matters

HOW TO PREVENT UNIONIZATION OF THE PLANT

The same law that gives workers in a plant the right to decide whether they want to be represented by a union also gives management the right to try to convince the workers that they would be better off by not having a union. If your plant is not unionized, you should want to keep it that way. No union will, nor should it be expected to, handle any portion of your management's responsibilities. It has responsibilities of its own which it frequently considers as opposing those of management.

Keeping your plant nonunion should not be left to chance. You and other members of management must make a conscious sustained effort to prove to the plant employees that their needs and expectations can best be met by plant management. Here are the ways you and management can put that across:

- *Pay suitable wages and fringe benefits.* Keep them at least equal to, and preferably above, those of the surrounding plants in the area. If the workers believe that they are getting more than unionized plants can provide, you are ahead of the game.

- *Recognize the importance of job security.* Workers want continuous employment and fair treatment if layoff becomes necessary. If you see that you might not be able to avoid a layoff, issue a detailed procedure long before the need to use it arises.

- *Handle complaints promptly and fairly.* This is best done by establishing a formal, legal, and workable grievance procedure. Publish it, give a copy to every employee, and train all members of management how to use it.

- *Treat employees courteously and with respect.* Workers want to feel that their jobs are important and their efforts are appreciated. Most of them also want challenging work and opportunities for advancement.

- *Keep communications open.* Nothing can hurt plant management more than to be unaware of the problems and wants on the minds of its employees. You must know exactly where the sensitive and rough spots are in your worker relationships, what employees like and what they dislike. The best way to learn that is to visit the plant's work areas frequently and talk with the workers.

DISADVANTAGES OF HAVING THE PLANT UNIONIZED

Not only are there few if any benefits of having a union in the plant, there are three major disadvantages:

1. *Waste of managerial effort.* Large amounts of managerial time at all levels of the company are spent in preparing for and handling union negotiations, grievances, and demands. Such time could be better spent in improving operations and conditions in the plant and managing processes for more profits and growth. The security of the plant's employees rests not with the union, but with the efforts of both management and employees to improve the factors that make the plant's products competitive: quality and cost.

2. *Interference with managerial decisions.* The one-on-one relationship between a company and its employees ends when a union exists in the plant. The union may have no interest in the profitability or growth of the company, yet it must be consulted on every major matter affecting employees. Union headquarters may order that decisions at your plant must conform to some regional or national pattern that has no relation to your company's particular situation. In addition, the union may promise benefits to employees that the company has no ability or intention to grant.

3. *Possibility of slowdowns and strikes.* If the union decides to make these economic moves, the plant's output may be cut or it may be shut down.

While many of the plant's costs continue, customers are lost and employees become bitter toward the company. Worse, even though such events and incidents are settled eventually, they may have long-lasting effects.

Answers to Why Employees Join a Union

It's essential that you know why plant employees may want to belong to a union. Such knowledge provides insight to getting along with it. You also learn what workers expect of the company. Of the several reasons why employees join unions, four are more common than others:

1. Management typically believes that money and benefits lie behind most dissatisfactions, but these things are often not the real problem. Money becomes the big issue when employees feel they are ignored; this is the major reason why employees join unions.

2. Some employees believe that membership in a union gives them an opportunity to develop more self-respect. They occasionally would like to "tell the boss off," and they might do so if they had a group such as a union behind them.

3. Other employees feel that unions satisfy their emotional needs so that they no longer need a paternalistic employer. In other words, unions tend to take the place of the disinterested employer who serves as the economic father of the employees.

4. Many workers decide they want a union to represent them when they see that management doesn't listen to them and when they learn that management is indifferent to their needs. Plant workers show these feelings in many ways. Turnover and absenteeism increase, productivity is erratic and usually declines, scrap and waste are high, and safety records are poor.

UNDERSTANDING THE UNION/MANAGEMENT CONTRACT

Workers in industrial plants have the right under law to decide whether or not they want to be represented by a union. If they so decide, they meet with management to draw up a contract or agreement that covers such subjects as wages, fringe benefits, working conditions, seniority, grievance procedures, and other industrial relations subjects. The contract usually contains a "management rights" clause as well as a statement recognizing the duty of both parties to establish and maintain peaceful labor relations and to operate the plant safely and efficiently.

Relations between management and employees do not suddenly change when the plant becomes unionized. Employees continue to want to be treated similarly to nonunion workers, and they expect good leadership from management of the plant. What is different is the existence of a written contract, the intervention of a third party, and the threat of strikes to enforce employee demands.

How Management Prepares for Contract Negotiations

Although plant supervisors seldom become involved in contract negotiations with the union, you should be aware of the procedures followed by your company's collective bargaining team in negotiating contracts. Besides, there is a good likelihood that the team may call upon you for information on past grievances and to get your input on possible contract changes. Here are the specific actions and steps the team should take to ensure they are adequately prepared for the negotiations. Members should:

1. Study the current contract to determine whether there are areas that require modification or change. Members should also review any arbitration decisions made since the current contract went into effect since such rulings may suggest other contract changes.

2. Analyze past grievances to learn of conditions and situations where the union will likely make demands. Decide what stand the company will take if any of these become reality.

3. Survey the plant supervisors on what changes they feel should be made in the contract. You and other supervisors are generally a good source of information on employees' opinions, likes, and dislikes of the current contract.

4. Meet with plant union leaders to discuss the current contract, its coverage, its effectiveness, and potential contract issues that will be brought up at the next negotiation meeting. Get together with the union leaders at least six months in advance of actual negotiations.

5. Keep up to date with developments on collective bargaining, labor legislation, and industrial relations by reading appropriate labor and management journals. Look particularly for statistics on such matters as employment, payrolls, and cost of living.

6. Obtain financial information from upper management on the company's status on profits, costs of doing business, industry conditions, tax laws and their impact on the company, and market forecasts. This information will be needed during negotiations when replying to the union's wage demands.

7. Anticipate and plan how negotiation meetings will be conducted. Plan to:
   - Negotiate in private and away from company headquarters.

- Start with easy issues.
- Agree on the procedure for communicating progress.
- Work at bringing about a "win-win" situation.

How to Help the Company During Contract Negotiations

If you have the opportunity to participate in a bargaining session, by all means join the team. You can be very helpful in preventing the union's representation of what goes on in a particular department from becoming too one-sided. You will also develop a greater appreciation of the problems faced by the company bargaining team, as well as learn more about management's position on various issues. In addition, you will be less subject to distorted rumors about the course of the bargaining when you get back in the plant.

You can contribute much more to the company's cause, however, when you are not at the sessions. Here are a few such ways:

- The rumor mill is most active during contract negotiations. Wild versions of what the company wants and is doing in the negotiations circulate among both the plant workers and the lower salaried personnel. With your knowledge, you can stop a wild story before it gets started and kill the rumors as well.
- There will be a lot of discussion, disagreement, and arguments in the plant among the workers and between them and their union leadership during the negotiations. If this activity is allowed to get out of hand, production output may suffer. It's up to you to maintain a calm, businesslike atmosphere in the plant, which includes a minimum of idle time in all departments.
- Closeness to the union workers puts you in a good position to pick up bits of information that may be of value to the company bargaining team providing, of course, you pass it on. While the law forbids you to engage in spylike activities designed to intimidate plant workers, in the normal course of carrying out your responsibilities, you will see and learn much about union politics, the relative importance of union demands, and the mood of the union members. Relaying this information along to management will undoubtedly help the company during contract negotiations.

COLLECTIVE BARGAINING: WHAT IT IS AND HOW IT WORKS

When representatives of management and the union work together to establish wages, hours, working conditions in the plant, and fringe benefits for union employees, the procedure is called *collective bargaining*. Various labor laws cover what subjects can be included in collective bargaining and what can not. Generally, however, the term *working conditions* is so broad that just about anything that affects employees on the job or the way they work can be included.

Collective bargaining normally takes place in the 60 to 90 days prior to the termination of the current union contract, but some companies make arrangements to continue the bargaining process throughout the life of the contract. State and federal laws require that unionized plants participate in the collective bargaining procedure. Management or unions that refuse to meet and consider proposals and make counterproposals are liable to charges of unfair labor practice.

Whether or not an issue is an appropriate subject for collective bargaining has no bearing on which party controls the way it is handled. The union can bargain for what it wants, and management has to bargain in good faith on the issues. Both sides have offensive tactics they can use to force the other side into agreement. The union's strength lies in the threat of a strike, and eventually the strike itself. The company can use the lockout, but seldom does so because it wants to keep the plant running. The company's best means of contending are its ability to withstand a strike longer than the union can, and its rights to hire permanent replacements for economic (as opposed to unfair labor practice) strikers.

Applying the contract and interpreting its meaning day after day are what makes collective bargaining work. The contract is rarely changed during its life. But there are many situations and occurrences between you and employees that must be carefully studied to determine how they should be handled in order to carry out the meaning of the contract. It is such interpretation and difference of viewpoint between management and unions that make labor relations a key supervisory responsibility.

Contending with Claims of Unfair Labor Practices

While either the union or management can commit unfair labor practices at any time, most charges are made during organizing campaigns. Whenever either party claims that the other party is guilty of unfair practices, the National Labor Relations Board should be contacted. Representatives of this organization will investigate and rule on the claim. As for what constitutes unfair labor practices, here's how the National Labor Relations Act identifies them:[1]

---

[1] A copy of the latest revision of *A Guide to Basic Law and Procedure Under the National Labor Relations Act* (Washington, D.C.: Office of the General Counsel, National Labor Relations Board) is available from the superintendent of Documents, U.S. Government Printing Office, Washington, D.C. 20402.

Unfair Management Practices:

1. To interfere with, restrain, or coerce employees in the exercise of their rights to self-organization; to form, join or assist labor organizations; to bargain collectively through representatives of their own choosing; or to refrain from such activities.

2. To dominate or interfere with any labor organization, or contribute financial or other support to it.

3. To discriminate in regard to hire or tenure or employment, or any condition of employment, in order to encourage or discourage membership in any labor organization (the law specifically exempts a union shop agreement, however).

4. To discharge or otherwise discriminate against an employee because he or she has filed charges or given testimony under the Act.

5. To refuse to bargain collectively with representatives of employees.

Unfair Union Practices:

1. To restrain or coerce (a) employees in the exercise of their rights (listed in 1. above) (b) an employer in the selection of his or her representatives for collective bargaining or the adjustment of grievances.

2. To cause, or attempt to cause an employer to discriminate against an employee, or to discriminate itself against an employee whose union membership has been denied or terminated on some ground other than failure to pay regular initiation fees and dues.

3. To refuse to bargain collectively with an employer.

4. To engage in a strike or refusal to handle goods or perform services, or encourage other employed individuals to do so, or to coerce or threaten any person engaged in commerce (including employers) where the object is to (a) force an employer or self-employed person to join any labor or employer organization, or to enter into a "hot cargo" agreement,[2] (b) force anyone to boycott the goods or business of another, or forcing another employer to recognize or bargain with a union which is not certified to represent his employees, (c) force an employer to recognize or bargain with a union when a different union has been certified as the representative of his employees, (d) force an employer to assign work to employees in a particular union, trade, or class rather than those in another union, trade, or class.

5. To charge an excessive or discriminatory initiation fee.

---

[2]A *hot cargo agreement* is one in which a union and employer agree to refrain from handling the goods of another employer and from doing business with him. Hot cargo agreements are forbidden by the Act (with certain exceptions in the construction and apparel industries), whether or not they were entered into voluntarily.

6. To cause or attempt to cause an employer to pay for services which are not performed.

7. To picket an employer to force him to recognize or bargain with a union, or force his employees to select that union (unless the union is currently certified as the representative of his employees) if the employer has lawfully recognized another union, a valid election has been held within the past 12 months, or the picketing has continued for 30 days without the union filing a petition for an election. (However, the law exempts truthful informational picketing which does not induce a boycott or a strike).

Understanding Bargaining in Good Faith

Section 8(d) of the National Labor Relations Act defines *bargain collectively* as "the performance of the mutual obligation of the employer and the representative of the employees to meet at reasonable times and confer in *good faith* with respect to wages, hours, and other terms and conditions of employment, or the negotiation of an agreement."

The application of good faith always has been debatable because it tries to answer the question of whether the parties have negotiated with a sincere desire to reach an agreement. However, since evidence of a resolve not to enter into any agreement is seldom available, the state of mind of the parties generally has to be inferred from their conduct. One of the most troubling problems is determining the kinds of such conduct that warrant the inference of lack of good faith. As for certain conduct, here are some examples of a desire not to reach an agreement and thus bad faith:

- Stalling the negotiations by unexplained delays in replying to correspondence.
- Entrusting the negotiations to representatives without sufficient authority to bind the employer contractually.
- Refusing to reduce terms otherwise approved to writing.

The difficulty occurs with using evidence concerning the positions taken by the parties during negotiations.

How to Lawfully Restrict Union Activity

While union organizational activities occur in many areas and places, one of the most important is the workplace, where both members and prospective members spend most of their time and where they are most frequently found in groups. But workplaces are usually the private property of the employer, who ordinarily considers them as a place where employees have a right only to work or to perform operations incidental to work.

Since the National Labor Relations Act guarantees employees the right of self-organization, and since the exercise of this right would be considerably hampered if all organizational activities in the workplace were completely prohibited, a major conflict exists. If the employer issues rules prohibiting solicitation on company property, this conflict is brought to a head.

In general, the rule that has been developed by the Board and the courts is that an employer may lawfully prohibit solicitation or distribution of union literature during working hours since such activity would obviously interfere with production. But the employer may not lawfully prohibit such activity on company property during nonworking time, including lunch and rest periods.

TIPS ON PROMOTING GOOD UNION/MANAGEMENT RELATIONS

You are the management person who feels the impact of a union in the plant most consistently. But you should expect this because you associate directly with the workers. It is you who occasionally must make quick decisions, only to have them result in union grievances and possibly second-guessing from upper management. Every move you make is closely watched by union stewards who may only be waiting for you to make a mistake. It's no wonder that you want management and the union to be on good terms, get along well with each other, and work together for the common cause. Good union/management relations can make your job easier and less stressful.

However, don't overlook the fact that you are in a position to contribute much toward achieving and maintaining good union/management relations. Here are some of the things you can do:

- Create and foster confidence and trust among employees. Encourage a team spirit by letting each worker know how valuable his or her contribution is to the company and how employees working together in team efforts can improve productivity.

- Be a good listener when employees indicate they are dissatisfied with their work, want something, or have problems they would like to talk about. This is not to say that you should give employees whatever they ask for, but that you should try to understand them. You should also make a point to explain why not all of their requests can be granted.

- Do what you can to bring about a pleasant and comfortable work environment. The company says more about what it thinks of its employees by the way it maintains the plant than in almost any other form of communication. Good industrial relations are established when work areas and personnel facilities are clean, attractively painted, kept up, and properly lighted and ventilated.

- Adopt and implement a comprehensive safety program. Employees are favorably impressed when the company is willing to spend time and money to protect them from injury. Despite some occasional grumbling, they will respect the company for enforcing safety rules.

- Keep the disciplinary system as simple as possible. A four-step progression of disciplinary action for a repeatedly offending employee is recommended. It consists of a verbal warning, a disciplinary letter, a suspension period, and finally discharge. Such a progression is clear to everyone involved, and it will meet with the approval of an arbitrator.

- Treat all employees with respect. Being compatible with employees is a positive step toward maintaining harmony because small differences of opinion can easily be handled when they arise. If you can resolve problems before they become grievances, you serve to cement the union-management relationship.

WHY KNOWING THE CONTRACT IS A "MUST"

Employees expect their union to protect their economic interests, health, and safety, and to make their jobs more secure. You cannot fault workers for wanting this. An employee who works for a considerate supervisor, one who recognizes this relationshp of the employee to the union, usually will be cooperative and will try to do a good job for the company.

It follows that you must be informed on the contract. Without this knowledge, you cannot fully carry out your responsibility as a member of management, nor can you always be right in how you handle and treat employees. Rest assured that your counterpart, the union steward, knows the contract well. To be his or her equal in the eyes of your workers on matters covered in the contract, and to get along with the union, you must be just as well informed.

Most plants today assure that supervisors receive training on the contract. The training and instruction is usually given by persons from the industrial relations or personnel departments of the company who know the contract provisions well. The training should include briefing on past practices and the unwritten understandings that the union and management have reached over the years.

The grievance procedure in the contract is very likely the most important part of the document to you. As for other matters contained in it, you'll never regret taking time to study and discuss them with your peers and your superiors. As a result, you'll have an easier time on the job whenever a situation covered by the contract arises.

Tip: Before you answer a grievance or make a decision on a matter covered by the contract that could have plantwide implications, review the facts and circumstances with your boss. Not only can this save you embarrassment if you have overlooked something, it serves to keep your boss informed if the subject and your decision comes up in management meetings.

HOW TO GET ALONG WITH UNION STEWARDS

Some plant workers identify their union officials as stewards while others call them "reps." Regardless, since they are the first level in the union hierarchy, and usually elected by the workers, you should try to be on good terms with them. You must recognize, however, that your relationship with stewards may be complicated by the fact that they are also employees. They report to you and other supervisors, are members of the work force, and at the same time serve as liaisons between employees and the union.

The best way to establish good working relationships with stewards is by taking the following steps:

1. Get to know them as well as any other employee. The better you do, the easier it will be to understand how they think and what motivates them to represent the union. You and the steward in your department will have many mutual problems in your daily work. Just as the steward will frequently come to you to straighten out matters, so should you periodically ask for his or her help on your problems.
2. Be empathetic and sympathetic to stewards. They are individuals in the middle in human relations' situations. Stewards must be good employees and also good union officials. Understand the difficulties of their positions and show consideration for them.
3. Always let stewards know about changes in the workplace and other potential problems that may lead to grievances. Do your best to answer their questions. Often, they can help work out little problems before they develop into major ones.

DEALING WITH EMPLOYEES' RIGHT TO UNION REPRESENTATION

More than a decade ago, the U.S. Supreme Court ruled that an employee had the right to have a union representative present when management was conducting an investigatory interview which the employee reasonably believed might result in disciplinary action. More recently, the National Labor Relations Board took two further steps:

1. It ruled that an employee has the right to consult a union representative *prior* to an investigatory interview, which the employee reasonably be-

lieves might result in disciplinary action. In doing so, the board recognized the possibility that an employee called to a meeting with management might be too fearful or inarticulate to relate accurately the incident being investigated. In such situations, the employee might receive assistance from a knowledgeable union representative.

2. It agreed that management doesn't have to postpone the interview because a particular union representative is unavailable for reasons for which management is not responsible, where the employee could have requested the presence of another union representative who is available.

ARBITRATORS: HOW THEY ARE SELECTED AND THEIR RESPONSIBILITIES

Most union/management contracts state how the parties have agreed to select arbitrators and how the person(s) will function. The services of the American Arbitration Association or the Federal Mediation and Conciliation Service are frequently used in making these decisions. The three common methods are:

1. An individual is selected, hears the evidence, and renders an award or decision for one particular case or set of cases.

2. An individual (or group) is selected and serves as arbitrator as long as both parties are satisfied.

3. A board consisting of a company and union representative and an impartial chairman serves as long as both sides are satisfied.

The parties usually select arbitrators from either attorneys who practice labor arbitration or university professors who teach economics, industrial relations, and labor law. Arbitrators' responsibilities are to make decisions and rulings based on the evidence and facts presented by both parties. In making decisions, arbitrators cannot add to, subtract from, or modify the labor contract; the contract language must be applied as written. But they can interpret, apply, or rule on compliance with the contract provisions.

However, the parties should recognize that since contract language may be subject to different shades of meaning, past practice (the way the contract language has been applied in the past) serves as a guide to ambigious contract language. Arbitrators typically take past practice into consideration. They also consider consistency or the lack of it in past company action as important.

Dealing with Employees' Claims of Past Practices (Precedents)

If both management and the union have permitted a particular practice to prevail in the plant for some time, that practice may become the rule. It doesn't make any difference if the contract forbids the practice or is silent on it. For example, if an employee has prepared coffee at least once a day on company time for several years, you can not order the employee to stop making coffee on company time. In the opinion of the arbitrators, any change in the coffee-making procedure must come through negotiations, not through unilateral action.

Although such an example of establishing a precedent may seem to be a matter of minor importance, you should look beyond it to reach another conclusion: Be sure that you enforce the plant rules and contract provisions that are important to management. If you don't, they may turn out to be ineffective when you do decide to enforce them.

HOW TO HANDLE SENIORITY/ABILITY PROBLEMS WHEN PROMOTING

Almost invariably when negotiating a contract, a union demands promotion by seniority, while management wants the right to promote the most qualified person regardless of length of service. A compromise is sometimes reached that gives some, but not equal, weight to both seniority and ability. For example, the parties could agree that the three most senior bidders for any promotion would be the only official candidates, one of which management would choose.

However, when it comes to judging the relative ability of employees, your opinion is entitled to great weight, at least in the eyes of most arbitrators. This is illustrated by the following ruling of one such arbitrator:

> The union complains that, besides seniority, there is no objective yardstick which can be applied to measure relative ability and aptitude. The company agrees that these matters cannot be measured with perfect objectivity, but insists that experienced supervisors can reliably judge men. . . . To accept the union's thesis here would amount to saying . . . that when the union disagrees with the company's judgment, it may have the decision reviewed by a third party. This way lies general confusion. Aside from its internal contradiction, the proposition is defective in its faulty assumption that outside parties, unfamiliar with the employees involved could make better

judgments as to their relative abilities and aptitudes than could the supervisors.[3]

DISCIPLINING EMPLOYEES FOR CAUSE OR JUST CAUSE

Most union/management contracts contain statements on the discipline or discharge of employees for cause or just cause. Just cause is contingent on three conditions being met:

1. An improper act was committed.
2. The offense was serious enough to warrant discipline.
3. The penalty imposed was appropriate to the offense.

Before disciplining or discharging a union worker, you must be able to justify or provide proof that each condition existed because the union can protest and appeal any condition. If the case goes to arbitration, you can expect the arbitrator to review all three conditions. For the discipline you impose to be upheld, a series of questions must be answered yes. If there is one or more no answers in the opinion of the arbitrator, your discipline will probably be voided or amended. The questions are:

- Was the employee adequately warned that his or her conduct could be subject to discipline, including possible discharge?
- Was the violated rule reasonably related to the safe, efficient, and orderly operation of the plant?
- Did you investigate before imposing discipline?
- Was the investigation fair and objective?
- Did your investigation result in substantial evidence or proof of guilt?
- Were the penalties applied uniformly and without discrimination?
- Was the penalty appropriate to the seriousness of the offense?
- Did the penalty take into account both other employees' and this employee's record with the company?

3 REQUISITES FOR IMPOSING DISCIPLINE IN A UNIONIZED PLANT

It is axiomatic in today's industrial environment that employees found in violation of work rules or lacking certain performance standards be spe-

[3](Hercules Powder Co. Award, 10 LA 624)

cifically counseled and officially notified of such performance shortcomings. This is the reason why most union/management contracts contain provisions for application of progressive discipline, i.e., written warning and/or suspension for offenses not serious enough to warrant discharge for a first occurrence.

The purpose of discipline is to correct, not punish. If discipline doesn't succeed in reforming an employee, it fails in its objective. With this in mind, you should try to tailor discipline to the individual or specific situation. A discipline program is effective only if it is characterized in three ways:

1. *Uniform.* A uniform program prevents the imposition of different discipline for the same offense. Without a guideline, you might issue a written warning for fighting in the plant while another supervisor might suspend the guilty individual for two or three days. A spelled-out, understood penalty for fighting prevents such inequities.

2. *Corrective.* This discipline defines proper conduct thus giving an employee the opportunity to correct his or her improper conduct. Corrective discipline also warns other employees that improper conduct or the breaking of plant rules will not be tolerated and will subject guilty individuals to disciplinary action.

3. *Progressive.* When a discipline procedure is progressive, it provides for increasing the severity of the discipline with repeated offenses. A typical procedure in a unionized plant might be oral warning for the first offense, written warning for the second, a one-day suspension for the third, a five-day suspension for the fourth, and discharge for the fifth.

GUIDELINES ON WORKING WITH THE GRIEVANCE PROCEDURE

Effective grievance handling requires a positive attitude toward workers. You also need to develop the ability to accept and handle complaints promptly in a nonthreatening manner. Another requisite is to make the employee with the grievance feel that he or she has your full attention. If you happen to be tied up at the time, it's essential to explain the reason why handling the grievance must wait. In such a case, set a later time to meet with the employee. Following is a procedure that will get you good results with plant workers:

1. When a worker verbally complains, repeat the person's main points in your own words to make sure you completely understand the problem. You may have to probe a bit to get at the real issue if your summary doesn't accurately reflect the worker's concern.

2. If you see that the grievant is upset or angry, take him or her aside so you can talk in private. This move allows the worker to blow off steam without embarrassment. It also tells the worker that you are concerned.

3. Listen carefully and keep your cool. Always assume that the complaint is real. But be alert because a grievance may be concealing some other problem that has gone unnoticed.

4. After a worker has finished telling you his or her complaint, assure the person that you will act promptly. Then review all the information you have and investigate to confirm what you have been told.

5. Decide where you can find the answer to the complaint. If it involves a company policy, for example, the employee handbook may contain the information you need. If the complaint concerns interpretation of the contract, study the wording in the applicable section.

6. Be ready to accept the logical conclusion that comes from the facts you uncover. If you find that you have made a mistake, admit it.

7. Give the worker a definite answer. State your decision in such a way that there is no mistake about what you mean.

8. Make it clear to the worker that your verbal answer is the *company's answer* as well. If the company is in the wrong, then tell the worker that corrective action will be taken. If the complaint is based on misinterpretation, clarify the matter for the worker. By explaining your decision, you will seem to be less of a dictator and more of a communicator.

9. Make a record of the grievance and your answer. If your company has a procedure on grievance handling, follow it to the letter.

10. Pass how you handled the grievance to your boss. Give him or her the complete story with emphasis on the part that was critical to the final action or decision. The information will be valuable to management in future dealings with employees and/or the union.

EMPLOYEE OFFENSES THAT ARE RESOLVED BY THE GRIEVANCE PROCEDURE

Violations of plant rules and regulations that are resolved by the grievance procedure generally fall into five different types:

1. Contract violations:
   - Refusal to accept a work assignment or job transfer.
   - Refusal to work overtime if required by the contract.
   - Participation in a work slowdown or stoppage.

2. Rule and regulation violations:
   - Safety.
   - Smoking in restricted areas.
   - Poor attendance and lateness.
   - Sleeping on the job.
   - Use of alcohol or drugs.
   - Possession of weapons.
3. Misconduct on plant property that affects plant operation:
   - Horseplay.
   - Gambling.
   - Neglect or abuse of tools and equipment.
   - Littering.
4. Misconduct on plant property that is illegal in the community.
   - Stealing.
   - Rape.
   - Fighting.
   - Molesting others.
5. Misconduct off plant property that affects other employees or the company:
   - Selling/giving company trade secrets.
   - Confronting/attacking another employee or supervision.

Determining When a Grievance Goes to Arbitration

In most plants, the majority of grievances resulting from offenses are resolved at the lower levels of union/management relationships. However, in some cases each party honestly believes his or her interpretation of the contract is correct, even when relations are friendly and amenable. In such cases, a neutral third party decides.

Arbitration is defined as the settlement of a dispute by a person or persons chosen to hear both sides of a disagreement and come to a decision. Thus, it is usually the final step of the process to resolve grievance disputes by submitting them to a third party who renders a final and binding decision.

Many different grievances can go to arbitration. The most common include:

- Discharge and disciplinary disputes.
- Contract interpretation or application.

- Seniority, promotion, demotion, and layoffs.
- Wage rates and pay issues.
- Job classification and work assignment disagreements.

HOW TO CONTEND WITH A STRIKE

Plant employees may decide to strike (refuse to work) for any of several reasons. Depending on the union's objectives during negotiations, strikes are of several types:

1. An *economic strike* occurs when there is a disagreement on wages, hours, or working conditions. Most industrial strikes are economic.
2. A *contract strike* occurs when the parties can't agree on the contract language. But words and wages are usually closely related.
3. A *grievance strike* occurs when the union disagrees with how management interprets the contract.
4. A *jurisdictional* strike occurs when two or more unions disagree on what jobs should be organized by each union.

As soon as management sees that a strike is inevitable, you and other salaried employees will probably be assigned to special duties. Typical ones are likely to be operating the productive equipment, maintaining and repairing it, and attending to plant security. Management may want to keep the plant operating at least at some level, using supervisors and other salaried employees.

When the strike begins, the union will place pickets at the plant gates. Since large numbers of pickets may tend to become unruly or disturb the neighborhood, the company responds by obtaining a court order to prevent mass picketing. As the strike continues, legal advice becomes important. Letters to employees, newspaper ads, and other forms of communicating may be used to tell the facts.

After a period of time, if no progress is made, the company may begin looking for replacement labor. Hiring, however, will cause more friction and even violence on and off the picket line. Meanwhile, salaried employees will work long, hard hours to get through this difficult period. Managers will expect complete loyalty as they try to keep the plant in readiness to resume full production at the end of the strike. The strike will end when both parties make concessions or the weaker party gives in.

What to Do When the Strike Is Over

You are in a key position when the strike ends because you are the first contact for employees returning to their jobs. It's up to you to quickly establish cooperation and harmony as you try to get the plant up and running again. Depending on the length and bitterness of the strike, this may seem like a difficult if not impossible job. Here are some suggestions on what you should do and not do during the first few days when the workers return to the plant:

1. Before you do anything else, get up to date on the new contract, what it contains, and how it reads. You want to be in a position to answer any worker inquiries in a sure and positive manner.

2. Make a work schedule with definite assignments for each of your workers. Plan and schedule operations so that there will be no delays in getting jobs started; busy workers will bring about the right atmosphere and minimize the likelihood of bull sessions getting started.

3. Greet *each* returning worker by name and in a friendly manner. Say, "Hi, John. Good to see you again," or "Glad to have you back, Tom."

4. Do not talk at length with any worker. Be careful to not show special attention or partiality to either a striker or a nonstriker.

5. Do not discuss the strike or its history. A strike is costly and emotional. Any words from you will long be remembered and may negatively affect your supervisory ability.

6. Watch for possible conflicts. Stop unfriendly remarks between strikers and nonstrikers since tempers may be lost quickly. Do not permit groups to form to discuss emotional issues.

7. Try to stay in the work area constantly during the first several days. Look for opportunities to encourage workers and remind them to work safely. Be friendly and refrain from criticizing.

8. Follow up on jobs and progress of work projects, but don't get so close that you are breathing down a person's neck. Keep production and maintenance operations going so that workers get accustomed to the work routine.

DEALING WITH COMPLAINTS OF SUPERVISORS DOING UNION EMPLOYEES' WORK

A major stumbling block that you must overcome in the plant is to resist the urge to do work that you should not do, work that belongs to union employees. Union/management contracts usually cover this matter clearly with such words as: "Except in cases of emergency or for purposes of instruction or training, supervisors and company personnel excluded from the provisions of this agreement shall not perform work assigned to employees covered by this agreement."

Many contracts also contain statements covering *de minimis* situations. This refers to a Latin phrase, *de minimis non curat lex*, which translates to "the law is not concerned with trifles." You can interpret it to mean that the union may overlook the work performed by a supervisor if it is trivial, insignificant, or inconsequential. But be careful. What you might think is insignificant, a union official may feel is considerable.

The Extent of *De Minimis*

An arbitrator recently ruled on this subject by saying:

> There are no hard-and-fast rules on *de minimis*. One can easily say that the law does not observe small or trifling matters. I would rule that a supervisor's work of 10 minutes is not trifling if the supervisor readily and frequently "jumped in" to expedite bargaining unit work.
>
> A company may not say that any minimal work is *de minimis* when the contract has reserved certain tools or production work to the assigned employee. To illustrate this, if a supervisor relieves an air hammer operator one day in order to continue a rush job and give an employee a needed rest, I would consider the operation trifling, if not frivolous. If not the first day, by the second day appropriate arrangements could be made. However, over a four-day period, the *de minimis* rule cannot be applied.

How to Handle Training Situations

Although you may be frequently called upon to train workers in how to do their jobs, there will be occasions when they will receive training from other individuals. Fire control training, for example, may be given to employees by the company's Fire Department personnel. In such situations, you are not permitted to do bargaining unit work in your workers' absence from their jobs. The exception applies to your training of bargaining unit employees on their functions and duties and does not refer to the training of employees by others.

You are also not permitted to do bargaining unit work to train yourself. To explain this ruling, consider the following case history. A plant manufactured a variety of steel products including a bar straightener, a machine that was used to straighten steel rods and bars that had been bent in the production process. For each use, the machine had to be adjusted or "set up" to accommodate the size of the steel part to be straightened. The setup was normally performed by a mechanic and an oiler, with the actual operation of the machine performed by production workers.

One day, two supervisors set up the machine for a new job, a task that took them several hours. The union filed a grievance, claiming a violation of the plant's union/management contract which states: "Supervisors shall not do production or maintenance work normally performed by employees except in connection with training or in emergency situations."

The company told the union that the contract had not been violated. The two supervisors were training themselves so they, in turn, could train the mechanics and the oilers who didn't know how to set up the machine. The work they performed came within the scope of the contract's wording "in connection with training."

The union disagreed. It maintained that the contract did not allow supervisors to perform bargaining unit work solely in order to train themselves. If it did, supervisors could perform many other bargaining unit jobs under the guise of training themselves. The union conceded that a supervisor may have to become familiar with the operation of a machine in order to train others, but on those occasions, he or she must do this in concert with the training of other workers.

An arbitrator upheld the union's grievance. He said, "The problem reduces to the question of whether the wording 'in connection with training' covers the work performed by the supervisors. I conclude that it does not. In my judgment, this 'connection' standing alone is too tenuous and too remote to gain sanction under the contract."

All-out efforts to meet a schedule, another aribitrator ruled, are also not permitted. This arbitrator said:

> A rush job does not in itself create an emergency. A supervisor's statement that he wished to help out and that his actions were not calculated or preconceived is not questioned. If a qualified employee who was at work had refused the operation, a non-unit employee could be used to complete the operation.

The Effect of Supervisors Doing Nonsupervisory Work

Supervisors who work rather than supervise others cost their companies a great amount of money because what they do lowers the productivity of other employees. Their working lowers productivity in two ways:

1. By taking the work away from the employees who should be doing it thus increasing the employees' idle time.
2. By making other employees less productive because these employees are then not being properly supervised.

If you are singlehandedly trying to conquer every challenge thrown your way, you're overlooking a major responsibility of your job as a supervisor: You are expected to get work done through others. Although you may have good intentions, you should realize that you have limitations, and the company doesn't expect you to handle all matters by yourself. Worse, you compound the problem when you try to circumvent the union/management agreement by doing work that is strictly forbidden to you.

16

Working with Contractors and Service Organizations

DECIDING WHEN TO USE CONTRACTORS IN THE PLANT

Part of every manager's and supervisor's jobs is knowing how and deciding when to use contractors in the plant. Because there are advantages and disadvantages to both in-house and contract work, the choice is usually not one of either/or, but rather one of making an optimum division of the two. Experience indicates there's no one right answer. You have to decide what is best for your plant.

The problem is not a minor one when you consider the number of factors involved. It is a kind of "make or buy" decision with a few more considerations thrown in. But the economics of most contract versus in-house decisions are largely determined by three factors:

1. *The type of work to be done.* This determines the skills required. When the skills are highly technical, and especially when they are needed only infrequently, contracting may be the only rational option. Economics favors contracting also when lack of demand does not warrant having such skills available continually.

2. *The amount of work to be done.* If it is beyond the ability of the existing work force to accomplish in a reasonable time (or in the time required), then contracting is an attractive option. An example is a turnaround project or a major process equipment overhaul.

3. *The amount of time available to do the work.* When the work peaks, adding to the in-house work force by contracting is an economic way to meet schedules, commitments, and production quotas without incurring the penalty of having an oversized and underutilized permanent work force on hand at off-peak times.

HOW TO SELECT CONTRACTORS

When you or some other member of management select a contractor, the firm is either a:

- New contractor not having done any previous work for the company, or a
- Previously used contractor familiar with the plant, or a
- Presently approved and possibly certified contractor.

New contractors must first be identified and approved. This is usually the function of the plant's purchasing department, particularly when the company operates only one plant. The purchasing department develops approved vendors, qualifies them, negotiates and places contracts, and administers contracts after they are placed.

Establishing relations with new sources is also the responsibility of the purchasing department, but it is frequently aided by in-house technical personnel and sometimes by supervisors. New sources are always investigated before they are approved. This is done by use of a qualification form, a standard form that is filled out by contractors before they are permitted to bid on a job. The contractor is asked to supply general information about the firm and its management, financial data, experience, and references. All this information should be reviewed and verified before placing the firm on the approved contractor list.

Certified contractors have a good record of performance for the company. Since they usually offer cost reduction and savings ideas as well as promote new technology between themselves and the company, they should rank high on the company's approved contractor list.

Contractors who are qualified for a particular job should be selected from the list of approved contractors when there are enough available for the particular job. If there are not, purchasing should look for additional firms. Usually, the minimum number of bidders should be at least three.

The Selection Procedure

Before selecting a contractor for the job you want performed, formulate a bid package to be given to the firms you want to submit proposals or bids. The package outlines the specific work you want the prospective contractors to address in their bids. Include drawings, material specifications, and conditions of work procedures. Request a contractor to send the firm's cost quotation and the estimated time to complete the work to the plant's purchasing department. Then take the following steps:

1. Finalize the list of contractors you will ask to bid, and send them the bid package.
2. Invite all the contractors to visit you to answer any questions about the bid package. All should visit at the same time and tour the job site as part of the visit.
3. Contact other local manufacturing plants that have used the services of the contractors you are considering. Ask them about the firms' performance on the type of work you are planning to do.
4. Review and rate the bids with the purchasing department. Make your recommendations for awarding the contract.

MAINTAINING GOOD PLANT EMPLOYEE RELATIONS WHEN CONTRACTING

Like the majority of industrial employees, your workers likely will hate the thought of outsiders coming into the plant to do their work. As a result, they dislike contractors and will do their utmost to keep the work for themselves. Their solution to the problem of peak workloads is to delay some of the jobs or work unlimited overtime.

Your solution to the problem, however, should be the development of criteria for contracting that is acceptable to the employees. If your plant is unionized, a provision in the union/management agreement covering contract work could typically read as follows:

> It is agreed that the use of outside contractors in the plant will not be restricted as long as the employees affected are working at least 40 hours per week. In the event work for these employees has dropped below 40 hours per week, or some of these employees are laid off because of a lack of work, such outside contracting will be restricted to the jobs employees are unable to do.
>
> In determining what work will be done by outside contractors, the parties recognize that the following are among factors that must be considered:

1. Need for special skills, staff, or equipment to assure a satisfactory job
2. Where the work involved would interfere with normal maintenance requirements
3. Where outside contracting would be less expensive to the company
4. Where a warranty or guarantee would normally be inoperative unless the contractor's workers handled the job.

The company will discuss the situation with the union prior to letting an outside contract where a reasonable doubt exists on any of the above points. Any disputes arising out of this provision will be subject to the grievance procedure.

Additional steps you can take to keep peace between employees and contractors are as follows:

- Go all out to keep workers informed about jobs that are being given to contractors. If there is any doubt, discuss the matter with the union so that feedback to the workers is prompt. Where no doubt seems to exist, inform the union of a contract job by memo. Arrange for a discussion if the union requests one.

- Where it is impractical to have a contractor correct a fault or mistake of the contractor's doing, have your workers make the correction. But be sure the contractor is billed for the work and that your workers know it.

- Keep a close check on contractor personnel because they can create some real problems. Brush up on how to handle contractors before you hire them.

HOW TO ASSURE SUCCESSFUL USE OF CONTRACTORS

Using contractors for construction, installation, service, or maintenance can result in many benefits for the plant. For it to be a success, however, a partnership must exist between the contractor and the plant. The process will fail if you don't handle it with integrity, honesty, and fairness. If you treat contractors as second class citizens, you're going to get second class performance.

Skeptics to the use of contractors in the plant feel that you take on a high risk when you make such arrangements. Advocates defend such ventures by noting that high risk can mean high return. Both sides can point out advantages and disadvantages. You should be aware, however, that much of the risk can be reduced. To do so, you must adopt and maintain control over four steps that are critical to working successfully with contractors:[1]

1. *Selection.* It's axiomatic that managers must select a contractor that is fully qualified to do the required work. Unfortunately, some managers handle this first step poorly. They end up with a contractor that, through no fault of its own, is not adept or experienced enough to perform the given work. Among the causes is that some managers don't anticipate far enough in advance that they will be needing a contractor. When it becomes necessary, they rush the procedure, not taking enough time to investigate and choose a reputable one. Other times, a manager may not fully understand the company's needs.

2. *Commitment.* Full management commitment is an essential component to the successful use of contractors; weak commitment will neutralize many of the potential benefits. Several reasons can explain less than total commitment. Some managers view contracting as intruding on their authority or responsibility. Thus, the prospect of "outsiders" taking over is perceived as a threat. In other situations, managers feel pressure from workers who fear for their own job security. Faced with cost-based arguments in favor of contracting jobs and the sentiments of workers they've supervised for years, some managers may side with employees. In still other cases, managerial commitment is weak because certain managers believe contract arrangements are not the best way to get the job done.

3. *Organization.* If management decides to contract part of the maintenance function, the plant maintenance organization must be properly structured. It must accommodate and cooperate with the contractor staff rather than hinder it. The organization chart should be examined to determine where the contractor employees fit in. When maintenance managers are obsessed with preserving the status quo, contract arrangements are usually hampered. Since these managers see change as unnecessary, they would rather have the department inefficient than alter the organization structure. Other times, they avoid modifying the organization because they believe doing so would create unnecessary work.

4. *Communication.* One of the major problems managers encounter in working with contractors concerns the contractor's authority; the full extent of authority should be defined when organization is discussed. Whatever a manager decides, he or she needs to ensure that the contractor knows precisely where the firm's authority begins and ends. In

---

[1]Portions of this section contain information and data that appear in "How Contract Maintenance Can Work; Why It Can Fail," *Plant Services*, Jan. 1990, Putman Publishing Co., Chicago, IL 60611.

addition, during the period the contractor is working for the company, the issue of authority periodically should be brought up. Successful use of contractors depend on communicating this information in as clear a way as possible.

GUIDELINES ON HANDLING CONTRACTOR PROBLEMS

If you decide to use contractors in your plant, it's helpful to be able to anticipate the various problems that might arise.[2] This may enable you to prevent them before they occur, or at least to know how to handle them afterwards. With contract maintenance, in particular, it's worthwhile also to summarize the requirements for effective contractor use. Here are what they should include:

1. A frequency schedule specifying how often each job is to be performed on each piece of equipment.
2. A list of supervisors, workers, equipment, and materials with which to accomplish the stated frequencies.
3. A contract inspector or liaison person who verifies the frequencies and inputs.
4. A deduction program to reduce monthly payments to the contractor for failure to provide proper frequencies and/or inputs.
5. A cancellation clause in the contract.
6. A performance bond in the contract.
7. A statement on insurance and legal requirements.
8. A cost schedule for extras and/or unanticipated activities based on the cost/hour for each type of worker.

These requirements should forestall or at least provide guidelines on handling typical contractor problems as follows:

- If you do not like the manager or other persons that the contractor is using, make sure the contract gives you the right to remove such person(s). You should not have to name the cause or reason.
- If damage is being done to the plant's equipment or facilities by contractor's workers who are not doing a careful job, require, within the contract, that the workers be given orientation, on-the-job, and/or class-

---

[2]Parts of this section include ideas and information given in "Contract Maintenance: Problems/Solutions," *Plant Services*, Mar. 1991, Putman Publishing Co., Chicago, IL 60611.

room training. In addition, make claims against the contractor or the contractor's insurer for damage done in the plant.

- If security is a concern, both with respect to theft of personal employee property and company property, have the plant's security department or retained security agency make periodic checks. Further, contract in the future with a firm that uses an advance investigation system.

- If the contractor is not responsive to your needs and/or is not knowledgeable about some of the work the firm is doing, obtain proposals for future work from contractors who have been in business at least 10 years. Be sure to also check their references, including former customers for whom they are not now working.

- If you are concerned that the contractor may go out of business in the middle of a project, contract with a firm that has been in business for a long time, and check the firm's financial status in advance. Also, confirm that your contract furnishes the firm a reasonable profit and overhead.

- If the quality of service begins to diminish when the contract is within a few months of expiring, specify that jobs that are to be handled annually are completed by midyear of the contract; and quarterly jobs are completed by the middle of each quarter. A longer (3- or 5-year) contract helps to avoid this problem, especially when it may be renewed for more years.

- If the contract looked advantageous at first, but you are now having to pay additional costs for unanticipated items, come up with a good controlled input specification, based on your measurement of needs in advance. Then, see that the contract contains a schedule of rates to carry out specific activities, including labor-hour rates for various types of workers. Examples of such activities are waste recycling and hazardous waste removal.

HOW TO ENSURE THAT CONTRACTORS WORK SAFELY

While many of today's industrial plants effectively manage their own safety programs, some have difficulty ensuring that contractor personnel working in the plant adhere to established safety rules and regulations. Success in this endeavor depends on good company/contractor communications and relations accompanied by enforceable and compulsory procedures including follow-up by management. You can ensure that contractors work safely in your plant by implementing the following five-step program:

Step 1. As stated earlier, set up a bidders list for work that is to be contracted. The list should include all contractors who are qualified to perform work in the plant. To be put on this list, contractors must provide proof of their technical and financial competence.

They must also supply information on their accident history and the effectiveness of their safety programs. This information is critical because contractors with good safety records and good safety programs are more likely to work safely than contractors with poor records and programs.

Step 2. When requesting bids from qualified contractors, furnish them a list of the plant's safety rules and regulations plus safety requirements along with your tender documents. Provide the safety information in concise and easily understood form such as in a booklet or manual. Be sure to tell the contractors exactly what you expect of them on safety matters. Stress that you expect compliance and that deviations from your safety standards will result in cancellation of a contract.

Step 3. Hold a meeting with the contractor you select before permitting the firm to start the job. Have the contractor's supervisors and the plant's supervisors review the work to be done and the safety precautions that must be taken. Put the procedures and scope of the job in writing and have the contractor's in-charge supervisor sign the paper to acknowledge understanding of all the job's requirements. Follow this meeting by safety-orienting every member of the contractor's work force, including supervisors, in the plant's safety program and site procedures.

Step 4. Once the job is started, conduct regular detailed site inspections to monitor the contractor's compliance with your safety rules and regulations. Don't tolerate any deviations or omissions. Document all observed noncompliance and discuss the problem with the contractor's in-charge supervisor. Identify the basic cause of any noncompliance and do what is necessary to correct it. Periodically visit and tour the job site. Such tours give company management high visibility and demonstrate your commitment to the safety of both company and contractor employees.

Step 5. Provide the contractor with feedback on the safety performance of the firm's employees. Request the contractor hold regular meetings, at least biweekly, with the site crew to discuss hazards of the job and work site, and what is being done to combat them. Attend these meetings to answer any questions and to reiterate the plant's safety rules and regulations. You can't overdo communicating about safety.

COMPARING IN-PLANT WITH CONTRACT MAINTENANCE COSTS

To decide whether to use contractors or in-house labor for maintenance, you should review each type on performance and cost. This procedure requires you to keep good records covering the functions both groups perform and to periodically compare them. The cost factors that should be used in comparing are as follows:

Cost of contract services. In addition to the estimated or actual contractor's bid that includes the firm's labor, materials, profit, and overhead, you must determine the cost of:

- Writing specifications and preparing drawings, preparing bid documents, soliciting and evaluating bids, negotiating and awarding the contract, and managing the contract.
- Equipment, utilities, and material you will supply the contractor.
- Incentive or premium provisions in the contract.
- Maintaining facilities or equipment that will be used by the contractor or that will become inactive because of the contract, unless they will be used for some other function or eliminated.
- Overhead other than that for contract management.
- Other events or transactions including terminating of employees, security checks and additional security measures, and losses incurred in the sale of organization-owned equipment.

Cost of in-house services. In addition to the costs of labor and fringe benefits, you must determine the costs of:

- Materials and supplies.
- Storage, handling, and custody of materials and supplies.
- Equipment and facilities maintenance.
- Utilities and the protection of property.
- Direct and indirect overhead.
- Depreciation of facilities and equipment.

HOW SERVICE CONTRACTS HELP PROTECT PLANT EQUIPMENT

Whether your plant is small or large, it simply cannot run profitably and competitively today without sophisticated equipment. Just as important, it takes more than average technical knowledge today to repair the electronic programmers and controllers on the production line, not to overlook the fax machine, the copiers, the computers, and their peripherals. In addition to well trained repairmen, it takes service or protection plans, say the companies that supply them. Without such plans, even the most carefully prepared plant budgets can easily be overrun.

Since idle productive and nonproductive equipment threatens profits, it's easy to understand why service plans, extended warranty plans, or protection plans, as they are called, are becoming more and more popular. Not only do they make it easier for you to see that repairs are completed or equipment replaced if necessary, they also help you plan your budgets accurately. As companies begin to see that keeping track of repairs for each piece of equipment in the plant and office is time consuming, they will find service plans convenient and cost effective.

Because it became too costly to make repairs, manufacturers of electronic equipment, who traditionally serviced the products they sold, have withdrawn from the repair business. Instead, they offer customers extended service warranty contracts supplied to them by protection plan companies. Protection plan companies have the financial resources to repair or replace equipment themselves; they also have backup insurance in case funds are extended.

Extended contracts provide you peace of mind. Today's plant and office equipment is simply too sophisticated and too valuable to be left to just anyone for repairs. By contracting for service, you will get guaranteed repairs, whether they are done in the plant or taken to service areas.

UNDERSTANDING TYPES OF AGREEMENTS AVAILABLE FROM SERVICE COMPANIES

Because labor makes up the greatest portion of a plant's operating expense, machines and processes are becoming more and more automated in today's manufacturing plants. The automation is primarily accomplished by installing sophisticated electric, hydraulic, and pneumatic driven data processing systems that control the plant's product output.

But only a few large plants can afford the large number of skilled maintenance personnel that are required to keep such equipment operating efficiently and productively. It is very difficult to hire qualified persons or train present employees to service that equipment with a prescheduled, step-by-step inspection/preventive maintenance program. The only alternative is contracting the service from a special equipment supplier, an area service dealer, or a contract maintenance service firm.

Following are the different types of service agreements available from service companies:

- *Inspection only.* With this type, the service technician inspects the equipment using a printed inspection guide and check sheets. If there are any necessary adjustments, fine tuning, cleaning, repairs, or parts/materials replaced, an extra purchase order is obtained to cover these costs.

- *Inspection with labor coverage.* With this type, the technician performs all of the required inspections, preventive maintenance, and repairs for all equipment malfunctions covered by the service agreement. The service company must determine the necessary number of inspections because it absorbs all emergency service labor hours. Parts and materials are not covered by this type of agreement. These items generally are invoiced to the customer on an extended discounted invoice.

- *Complete parts coverage with reduced labor coverage.* This type automatically reduces and sometimes eliminates customer nuisance calls. The service company forecasts the minimum number of service calls to be scheduled during the contract coverage period. The agreement is attractive also to customers who only want protection from purchasing parts during the agreement coverage period, yet still be assured of priority service response time.

- *Time and material.* This type is different from the others because it is only a written agreement with no exchange of funds when it is signed by both parties. The agreement compels the customer to pay for all labor, parts, and material used by the service firm to restore and/or maintain the customer's equipment to efficient operation to meet production requirements.

- *Complete parts coverage only, no labor included.* With this type, the service firm assumes all cost of parts for the equipment during the agreement period while the customer pays all labor costs. The agreement appeals to customers who are willing to gamble on future labor costs but not on the cost of parts.

- *Complete labor coverage only, no parts included.* With this type, the service firm assumes all labor costs during the agreement period while the customer pays all parts costs. Some customers would rather gamble on future parts costs, but are afraid to gamble with future labor costs.

- *Full coverage.* This type of service agreement includes necessary labor, parts, and materials for all prescheduled inspections and preventive maintenance periods, together with cleaning, checking, testing, adjusting, and tuning for the agreement time coverage. This is the ultimate of service agreements in that the customer pays the service firm for all service including labor, parts, and materials used to maintain the equipment.

Guidelines on Evaluating the Options in Service Contracts

Too many managers buy service contracts offering maximum coverage on every purchase or lease, without giving any thought to cost effectiveness, or to whether they are obtaining the most efficient service. Others take chances and sometimes end up big losers. You should take the same care when you buy repair and maintenance contracts as you take in selecting the equipment to be covered. Considerable time and money are at stake. While several factors are applicable to all decisions involving service contracts, others are peculiar to the equipment itself.

For example, service contracts on computers and peripherals are offered by small, locally owned repair shops, including area chains, authorized dealers, and so-called third-party national maintenance organizations. The levels of service provided by contract, however, vary from mail-in, carry-in, 48-hour on-site response, and the services of one or more resident technicians.

You must determine the best service firm, as well as the level of service, by assessing your needs. Tradeoffs may be involved. Needed parts and current maintenance manuals for your particular brand or model may not be readily available, and service from some firms may not be as fast as you'd like. Authorized dealers, on the other hand, are likely to employ factory-trained technicians, use the latest fault analyzers and maintenance guides, have direct contact with the factory, be well stocked with parts, and offer quick, efficient service. But a particular dealer may not offer on-site service, pick-up or delivery, and the dealer's expertise may be limited to the brand or brands sold.

The large, third-party maintenance organizations probably provide the best service when a wide array of equipment is involved and many brands are represented. These firms hire the best trained personnel, maintain large inventories of both new and reconditioned parts, pretest parts prior to installation, and supply fast on-site response.

DEALING WITH SERVICE ORGANIZATIONS WORKING IN THE PLANT

Undoubtedly, employees of outside service organizations periodically will be working in the plant. Sales and delivery persons, truck drivers, utility company workers, and various contractors are commonly found in most manufacturing plants. While such persons rarely cause trouble with company employees or are guilty of theft, they do present a problem in that they usually are not aware of plant hazards, safety rules, and regulations. To control such persons, you should take the following steps to prevent accidents and injuries:

1. See that all visitors are clearly identified. This is best done by issuing them badges that must be worn in conspicuous places.
2. Give all outside personnel written instructions. Include where they can and cannot go in the plant, and what facilities (rest room, lunchroom, canteen, smoking area) they may use.

3. Instruct key company employees on their responsibilities concerning outside personnel including the issuance of safety glasses and hard hats when appropriate. These employees should know when outside personnel enter the plant, what they do while in it, and when they leave.

GUIDELINES ON USING A REPAIR SERVICE VS BUYING NEW EQUIPMENT

Many factors are involved when you must decide whether to use a repair service to rebuild/repair equipment or buy new. While immediate costs are important, they should be considered only after you study and analyze the following factors:

1. Learn the time constraints:
   - The lead time required to obtain and install new equipment.
   - The time required to rebuild the equipment on-site.
   - The time required to remove, rebuild, and reinstall the equipment. Remember, idle equipment means lost production. In addition to lost profits, customers may also be lost if the equipment is down for a long time.
2. Decide if the equipment is wholly or in part obsolete, causing parts and/or service to be very expensive and difficult or impossible to obtain.
3. Find out if the plant has similar equipment in service where commonality of spare parts or maintenance techniques are interchangeable.
4. Check to see if improvements could be made in rebuilding the equipment.
5. Determine if modernization of the equipment would be very beneficial.
6. Look into differences in maintaining the rebuilt equipment and new equipment.
7. Investigate if additional training or higher skill levels would be required to operate or maintain new equipment.

The knowledge and information you acquire from analyzing these factors will help you to decide between rebuilding or replacing plant equipment. However, if a significant capital expenditure seems inevitable, get the assistance of the accounting or financial department in making a cost justification study of the project. Simple payback time is often used, but other methods may be more cost effective, especially for large expenditures. These include depreciation, income taxes, and/or the present value of money.

HOW TO SET UP IN-HOUSE REPAIR OF MACHINE AND EQUIPMENT COMPONENTS

Despite the benefits and advantages of using contractors and service organizations to handle various jobs, a company can sometimes achieve significant savings by performing operations that manufacturing plants normally don't handle. In-house repair of machine and equipment components is an example of such an undertaking. Three requisites for success with such efforts are:

1. The program or operation must have the backing and support of management.
2. The employees involved should be highly skilled in this type of work.
3. There must be strong interest and desire on the part of the employees to do high quality work.

If you want to set up an in-house repair program in your plant, here are step-by-step guidelines to follow.

Step 1. Determine if the item can be repaired. The program begins when a maintenance worker withdraws from the storeroom an item that will replace a similar item that has failed in service. If the stores records identify the item as one that is repairable, the clerk or storeroom attendant asks for the defective item so that it may be considered for repair.

Step 2. Tag the item for repair. The defective item should be tagged by the maintenance worker with the item's plant code number. The tag should also say what is wrong with the item.

Step 3. Issue a work order. The storeroom attendant lists the item on a form with other repairable parts and equipment, and makes out a work order for its repair. The item is placed on a pallet with other items needing repair, and the work order is given to the supervisor of the repair crew.

Step 4. Log the work order. To assure that the repair procedure is organized, that no items are lost, and that costs are properly allocated, all work orders are logged in a book by the code number of the item. In addition, a folder with that number is created for the files. The folder will contain a copy of the work order, copies of requisitions and purchase orders for repair material, and repair procedures if they are complex.

Step 5. Obtain necessary parts for repairs. Since many items need new parts, the first task of the repair crew is to determine if such parts are available in stores. If they are not on hand, a requisition is immediately issued for what is needed. The defective item is put on a shelf until the material is received.

Repair job priorities are established by the storeroom attendant. Priorities are dictated by both the inventory levels in the storeroom and demand for an item in the plant. When parts are available, a crew member completes a repair, tests the item's performance, and returns the rebuilt item to the storeroom. Labor and repair material used are charged against the code number of the item in determining the cost or value of the returned item.

Benefits and Advantages of the Program

Several benefits result from a well conducted, in-house repair program:

1. Repairing storeroom items is more economical than purchasing new ones. Making in-house repairs is a more economical procedure than contracting such work.
2. Attention is called to equipment malfunctions quicker when defective or inoperative items are turned into the storeroom for repair rather than set aside or scrapped.
3. Better design and longer life of machine parts are an outgrowth of the repair function provided the repair crew are highly skilled.
4. The program results in a parts quality improvement because obsolete, high-maintenance models, and weak designs are scrapped rather than repaired.
5. The program promotes standardization. This results in lower inventory of spare parts.
6. The company can assign a lower cost to the repaired items in stores, thus reducing taxes on inventory.

Index

A

Absenteeism, 33
Accidents: 173–178 (*see also* Safety)
  frequency and severity, 178
  investigations, 175–182
  reports, 177–178, 180, 181
Action:
  orders and instructions, 9
  plan, 15, 297
  time, 24
Activity:
  maintenance, 382
  routine jobs, 293
  union, 395
  with PERT, 293
Acts, unsafe, 152–153
Advancement opportunity, 2
Air:
  pollution, 230–236
  quality standards, 230–231
Alternative solution, 16

Analysis:
  oil, 365
  trend, 369
  vibration, 364
Appraisal interview:
  benefits, 25
  means of motivation, 26
Arbitration, 404
Arbitrators, 399
Arguing, 22
Asbestos, 264–267
Assignments, 71, 285, 288
Attitude, worker, 117
Authority:
  lines of, 2
  supervisory, 5
Automated storage, 321
Automatic guided vehicles, 315–316
Automation, 386, 419
Awareness of hazards, 146

B

Bar coding, 322–324
Bargaining, collective, 392, 395
Barriers:
  better productivity, 79
  communication, 60
  machine hazards, 148
Bearing failures, 370
Bin systems, 340–342
Brakes, machine, 150
Breakdown cost, 361
Brigade, fire, 273–275
Budget, computer, 128

C

Carrying cost, 327
Carrying loads, 157–158
Cause, just, 401
Change:
  explaining, 49
  making efficiently, 50
  selling, 49
Charges, discrimination, 42
Checklists, 383
Circles, quality, 119–120
Cliques, 36
Clothing, protective, 161–169
Coaching, 70
Coding, bar, 322–324
Collective bargaining, 392, 395
Color-coding equipment, 155
Combustible materials, 271
Communication:
  admit a mistake, 403
  affect on productivity, 80
  barriers, 60
  company policy, 46
  downward, 61
  giving orders, 58
  improving, 52
  making changes, 50
  making sure you're understood, 55
  memos, 56
  negotiating, 23, 391
  nonverbal, 58
  plant information, 61
  portable terminals, 132
  requirements for efficiency, 52–53
  selling suggestions, 54
  staff, 57
  upward, 53
  with plant workers, 58, 85
Company policy, 46–49
Complacency, 22
Complaints:
  plant, 32
  union, 389
Compliance:
  with EPA regulations, 236–237
  with hazardous material regulations, 270
  with OSHA regulations, 216
  with right-to-know laws, 261
Components, computer, 126
Computers, 125–140
  advantages in project management, 295
  analyzing by, 378
  anxiety over, 132
  benefits, 128–134
  capabilities, 125–126
  control of maintenance, 376
  ensuring documentation, 127
  ergonomics applications, 161
  getting budget approval, 128
  how they improve productivity, 134
  implementation plan, 129
  instructing employees, 131
  making employees literate, 139
  management systems, 133–134
  networks, 295
  overcoming fears, 132, 138
  payback on investment, 129
  pitfalls to implementing, 130
  plant use, 125
  portability, 132
  reports, 129
  role in material handling, 135
  selling workers on use, 133, 134, 139
  software, 129, 134, 136, 138
  systems, 91, 377, 379, 380
  training workers to use, 140
  used for process control, 137
Confined spaces, 192
Conservation of energy, 104, 106, 108, 219
Contract:
  service, 418
  union, 397
Contractors: 410–424
  commitment, 414
  communication, 414
  costs, 417
  organization, 414
  problems, 415

selecting, 411, 414
using successfully, 413
when to use, 410
working safely, 416
Control:
air pollution, 230–236
computerized, 376
process, 109, 111
production, 297–299
quality of maintenance, 371
Cooperation:
between shifts, 123
promoting, 13, 86
supervisory, 11
Coordination:
job assignments, 381
maintenance activities, 281
production control, 297–299
production operations, 382
Corrective maintenance, 359
Costs:
breakdown, 361
equipment, 102
labor, 101
machine, 102
material, 101
operating, 99, 103
preventing increase, 103
untrained workers, 64
utility, 102
Creative capabilities, 354
Critical machine parts, 362
Critical path method, 293, 296

D

Dangerous work, 173
Decisions:
made under pressure, 18
snap judgment, 19
steps to making, 15–17
Defects, 116
Defensively, working, 146
Delegating, 14, 84
Descriptions, job, 4
Design, plant, 107, 160, 302–318
Devices:
protective, 151
respiratory, 255
safety, 150
Discharge permits, 224

Discipline:
corrective, 402
for just cause, 401
how to, 37
in unionized plants, 401
positive, 38
progressive, 402
uniform, 402
when to, 401
Discretion, 19
Discrimination, 42
Disruptions, production, 95
Dock safety, 195–196
Documentation, 127
Double bin systems, 340–342
Downtime:
equipment, 93, 380, 383
machines, 113, 380

E

Economic order quantity, 328, 330–332
Efficiency, affect of ergonomics, 308
Effluents, control, 222–223, 227–230
Electrical:
hazards, 186
safety, 182
shock, 182–183
systems, 187
Employees (*see also* Workers)
complaints, 32, 389
idle time, 90, 408
loners, 45
part-time, 40
temporary, 40
training needs, 63
unproductive, 90
wasting time, 98
young, 44, 45
Energy conservation, 104, 106, 108, 219
Environmental laws, 238–242
EPA, 199–237
compliance, 236–237
organization, 221
protecting the environment, 238–240
Equipment:
breakdown cost, 361
downtime, 93, 383
protection, 360
repair, 423
sampling, 236
shortages, 343

to control pollution, 234–235
Ergonomics:
applying to jobs, 309
improving efficiency, 308–309
improving safety, 159–161
Evaluation:
company policy, 48
performance, 25–26
training programs, 67
Event, PERT, 293
Expedite point, 328
Explosion hazards, 252
Extinguishers, fire, 275–276
Eye protection, 163

F

Face injuries, 163
Failures, bearings, 370
Faith, good, 395
Fears:
computer, 132
hazardous materials, 243
Fire:
extinguishers, 275–276
prevention, 271
protection, 273
First aid, 156
Floor space, 303, 305

G

Gantt chart, 291–292
Gases, hazardous, 250–251
Gloves, protective, 162
Good faith, 395
Grievance:
leading to arbitration, 404
procedure, 402–403

H

Hand protection, 162
Hazardous:
gases, 250–251
materials, 238–278
waste, 241
Hazards:
electrical, 186
explosion, 252
machine, 148
plant, 146

respiratory, 253
working in confined spaces, 192–195
Health:
hazards, 244, 251, 254, 257, 261
of employees, 1
right-to-know laws, 259–261
safeguard, 244, 254, 267
Hi-use stores, 340–343
Housekeeping:
affect on productivity, 92
affect on safety, 154
how OSHA promotes, 214
Human relations, 7

I

Idle time, 90, 408
Inexperienced workers, 70
Information:
how to handle it, 52, 60, 61
management systems, 133–134, 295
material safety data sheets, 258
on safety devices, 150
Infrared imaging, 370
Inspections:
OSHA, 201–202, 204
procedures, 122
safety, 171
Insurance item, 335
Inventory, 319–344
accuracy, 320
bar coding, 322–324
control, 319, 325, 329–333
management, 322
relation to just-in-time production, 336
stores materials, 326–333
tools, 325
worker's input on control, 335, 344
Item:
adding to stores, 334
insurance, 335

J

Japanese, 345–357
attributes, 353, 354, 356
business success, 352
maintenance function, 351
management methods, 350
manufacturing methods, 345
planning and consensus, 354
problems with adapting to manufacturing
methods, 355

Job:
   assignments, 71, 285, 288
   descriptions, 4
   sharing, 42
Judgment, 19
Just cause, 401
Just-in-time:
   affect on plant layout, 338
   operations, 321
   production, 336–340
   relationship of inventory, 336
   relationship to quality control, 340
   Toyota system techniques, 336–337
   worker's input, 337–339

K

Kanban, 337–339

L

Labels, safety, 257
Labor:
   cutting costs, 101
   unfair practices, 393
Laws:
   environmental, 219–220
   right-to-know, 259–261
Layout, plant, 160, 302–304, 338
Leader:
   effective, 1
   rather than driver, 8
Lead time, 327, 333
Lift trucks:
   handling, 312
   selecting, 311
   training of operators, 313
Lifting loads, 157
Log, OSHA, 208–211
Loyalty, 23

M

Machine:
   costs, 102
   downtime, 93, 113
   hazards, 148
   operators, 72
   parts, 362
Maintenance:
   activities, 382
   contract, 417
   computerized system, 380

   corrective, 359
   costs, 417
   courses, 384–385
   operations, 376
   planner, 279, 282, 283, 375
   planning and scheduling, 373
   predictive, 362, 363–370
   preventive, 359–362
   quality, 371
   safety, 387
   total productive, 287
   types, 359
   variances of quality, 372
   workers, 73, 74, 96, 373
Management systems, 133–134, 295
Material:
   costs, 101
   flow, 302–318
   handling, 304, 306, 310, 315, 317, 321
   hazardous, 238–278
   how planning cuts costs, 282
   resource planning, 135
   safety data sheets, 257
   spills, 243–248
   stores, 326–335
Meetings, productive, 28
Memos, 56
Mistakes, employees, 97
Monitoring:
   air pollutants, 235
   systems, 252
   workers, 248
Motivating:
   ways, 84
   workers, 65, 82, 262, 373

N

Near miss reports, 179
Needs, training, 63
Negotiating, 23, 391–392
Network:
   management systems, 295
   plan, 293
NIOSH, 200–201
Numerical control, 136

O

Objectives:
   managing by, 30
   training workers, 66
Obsolescence, maintenance workers, 74

Operating:
  costs, 99
  specifications, 60
Operations, production, 381, 382
Operators, machine, 72
Order cost, 327
Orders, work, 377
Organization:
  chart, 3
  objective, 1
  personal, 9
  structure, 1
Organizations:
  plant, 1
  service, 421
OSHA, 199–237
  achievements, 200
  affect on housekeeping, 214
  employees:
    adherence, 199
    responsibilities, 213
    rights, 205
  functions, 200
  incentives for compliance, 216
  inspections, 201, 202, 204
  keeping up with changes, 219
  method of reporting statistics, 214
  penalties, 203
  posting requirements, 206
  record-keeping, 206
  violations, 203
  ways to enforce compliance, 216
Oversupervising, 9

P

Parts, machine, 362
Part-time employees, 40
PCB:
  spills, 269
  waste, 268
Penalties:
  EPA, 225
  OSHA, 203
Performance:
  appraisals, 25
  work, 109, 122
Permits, discharge, 224
PERT (Program Evaluation and Review
    Technique), 293–296
  analysis by computer, 295
  network, 293

Plan:
  of action, 15, 297
  spill prevention (SPCC), 244–246
  steps in formulating, 280
Planner, 279, 282, 283, 375
Planning:
  benefits, 279, 282, 284, 286
  maintenance, 373
  payoff, 280–282
  selling employees, 375
  techniques, 289
Plant:
  design, 107, 160, 302–318
  effluents, 227–230
  equipment, 358–370
  layout, 338
  organizational structure, 1
Policy:
  company, 47, 48
  explaining to workers, 49
  understanding, 46
Pollutants, types, 222
Pollution:
  air, 230–236
  regulations, 222
  water, 221, 225–227
Portable terminals, 132
Positive discipline, 38
Poster, OSHA, 207
Practices:
  labor, 393
  union, 394
Predictive maintenance, 362–370
Presence sensors, 149
Preventive maintenance, 359–362
Priorities, 281
Probationary employees, 34
Problems:
  alternative solutions, 16
  contractor, 415
  diagnosing, 16
  lead time, 333
  preventing from becoming big, 29
  quality, 118
  shift operations, 300
  seniority/ability, 400
  socializing, 35
  training employees, 70, 76
Procedures:
  grievance, 402–403
  inspection, 122
  introducing, 51

Process control, 109, 111
Production:
  control, 297–299
  disruptions, 95
  just-in-time, 336–340
  standards, 287
  workers, 75
Productivity:
  effect of good housekeeping, 92
  how communication increases, 80
  how technology raises, 82
  how to improve, 79, 81
  improving with the computer, 91, 134
  improving with work sampling, 86
  improvement barriers, 79
  maintaining, 83
  optimizing, 96
Products, poor quality, 121
Program Evaluation and Review Technique
    (PERT), 293–294
Programmer, 296
Programs:
  energy conservation, 104, 106, 108, 219
  evaluating training, 67
  first aid, 156
  hand protection, 161–162
  in-house repair, 423
  quality circle, 119
  total productive maintenance, 348
  training, 66
  wellness, 215
Project:
  management, 289, 296
  organization, 290
  scheduling, 373–375
Promoting:
  company policy, 48
  cooperation, 13, 86
  handling seniority/ability problems,
    400
  team effort, 86
Protection:
  from electrical shock, 182
  from machine hazards, 253
  from respiratory hazards, 253
  of plant equipment, 360
Protective:
  clothing, 161–169
  devices, 151
  equipment, 161
Pull-backs, 149
Purchasing, 372, 411

Q

Quality:
  effect of maintenance, 113
  effect of worker attitude, 117
  effect of worker stress, 116
  effect on costs, 115
  problems, 118
  rework of products, 121
Quality circles:
  benefits and advantages, 121
  commitment to, 120
  functions of meetings, 120
  participating in, 119
  setting up, 119
Quality control:
  defects, 116
  inspection procedures, 122
Quality standards, how to set, 114

R

Radon, 277–278
Recall, rapid, 19
Records, OSHA, 206, 212
Regulations:
  enforcing, 10
  on pollutants, 222
Relations, employee, 412
Reliability, maintenance, 374
Reorder:
  level, 328, 329
  point, 328, 329
Repair, in-house, 423
Reports:
  computer, 129
  safety, near-miss, 179
Representation, union, 398
Respiratory:
  devices, 255
  hazards, 253
Responsibilities:
  employee, 5
  OSHA, 213
  safety, 172
  training, 63
Retraining:
  production workers, 75
  selling, 75
Rework products, 121
Right-to-know laws, 259–261

Robots, 197, 314
Rules, enforcing, 10

S

Safety, 141–198
   accidents:
      frequency and severity, 178
      investigations, 175–178
      which keep repeating, 173
   clothing, 161, 162, 168–169
   communicating, 142
   creating employee interest, 141
   data sheets, 257, 258
   devices, 150, 151
   dock, 195–196
   electrical, 182–187
   glasses, 163, 164
   identifying hazards, 155
   indoctrinating workers, 143
   information, 169
   inspections, 171
   lifting and carrying, 157
   loading docks, 195
   machine hazards, 148
   material handlers, 310
   personalizing training, 144
   preventing slips, trips and falls, 153
   promoting with housekeeping, 154
   protection against injuries, 163–165
   reports, 177–178
   responsibility, 172
   shoes, 165–166
   statistics, 214
   stock level, 328
   training employees, 142
   unsafe acts, 152–153
   use of ergonomics, 159
   warehouse, 196
   welders, 189
   working on vertical structures, 188
Sampling:
   effluents, 227–230
   instrumentation, 235–236
   methods, 228
   programs, 227–229
   reasons for, 227
Scheduling, selling employees, 375
Services, 678–682
   companies, 418–422
   contracts, 418, 420
   repair, 422
   types of agreements, 419

Shift:
   cooperation, 123
   operations, 289, 301
   problems, 123, 300
Shortages, equipment, 343
Simulation, 295
Skin disease, 267
Socializing, 35
Software:
   selecting, 129, 134, 136, 138
   user friendly, 138
   vendor packages, 129
Space utilization, 305
Span of control, 4
Specifications, operating, 60
Spills:
   avoiding, 248
   control, 244
   hazardous material, 243–248
   plan, 244–246
   PCB material, 269
   training employees on prevention, 247
Staff, 43, 53
Standards:
   air quality, 230–234
   bar code label, 324
   production, 287
   quality control, 114
Statistical:
   process control, 110
   techniques, 112
Steward, union, 397, 398
Storage, automated, 321
Stores:
   adding an item, 334
   hi-use, 340
Stress, worker, 116
Strike, union, 405
Structure:
   managerial, 2, 3
   organizational, 1
Style, communication, 57
Suggestion systems, 54
Supervisors:
   communications, 57
   doing employees' work, 406, 408
   getting along with others, 11, 124
Support, plant workers', 26
Systems:
   computerized, 91
   double bin, 340–342
   management, 295
   material handling, 321

monitoring, 252
water treatment, 225–227
work order, 282

T

Team effort, 86
Teamwork, 21
Techniques, statistical, 112
Temporary employees, 40
Terminals, portable, 132
Thermography, 370
Thinking, quick, 19
Tolerances, 287
Tools, 160
Total Productive Maintenance, 287
Toxic substances, 242
Toyota manufacturing system, 345–348
Trainers, 385
Training, 63–77
  coaching, 70
  employees, 66, 73, 140, 384, 407
  evaluating programs, 67
  for plant automation, 386
  how much at one time, 69
  machine operators, 72
  maintenance workers, 73, 384
  methods, 67
  needs, 63
  objectives, 66
  on inventory management, 324, 335
  on quality control, 112
  programs, 66
  responsibilities, 63
  selling workers on, 65
  truck operators, 313
  using hazardous materials, 262–263
  using respiratory devices, 255
  with videos, 69
Troubleshooting guide, 366–368

U

Ultrasonic monitoring, 365
Union, 388–409
  arbitrator, 399
  collective bargaining, 392
  complaints, 32, 389
  contending with strikes, 405
  contracts, 390
  disadvantages of unionization, 389
  grievances, 402–404
  knowing the contract, 397

management relations, 396
negotiations, 391
past practice claims, 400
preventing unionization, 388
restricting activity, 395
rights to representation, 398
seniority problems, 400
Unit cost, 327
Universal Product Code, 322
Unsafe:
  acts, 152
  conditions, 53, 217–219
Untrained workers, 64

V

Vehicles, automatic guided, 315–316
Verification, maintenance, 374
Vibration analyzers, 364
Videos, training with, 69
Violations:
  EPA, 237
  OSHA, 203

W

Waste:
  disposal, 40
  how to avoid, 283
  liquid, 239
  of time by employees, 98
  PCB, 268
  solid, 239
  treatment, 242
Warehouse safety, 196
Water:
  pollution, 221, 225–227
  treatment, 225–227
Welders, 189–192
Wellness program, 215
Work:
  assignments, 71, 285
  dangerous, 173
  defensively, 146
  improving employees' performance, 109,
    122, 372
  orders, 282, 377
  sampling, 86–89
Workers (*see also* Employees):
  attitude, 117
  explaining company policy to, 49
  gaining their support, 26
  idle time, 90, 408

inexperienced, 70
jobs, 84
maintenance, 73, 74, 384
monitoring, 248
motivating, 65, 82, 262, 373
performance, 174
productivity, 78–79, 80–81, 82, 83, 86, 91, 96
retraining, 75
selling change, 49

selling energy conservation, 108
selling retraining, 75
selling training, 65
slow learners, 70
training:
  on computers, 127, 379
  on maintenance, 384, 386
  to avoid disruptions, 95
  with videos, 69
untrained, 64
young, 44